German Home Towns

Community, State, and General Estate
1648–1871

GERMAN HOME TOWNS

Community, State, and General Estate

1648-1871

MACK WALKER

Cornell University Press

ITHACA AND LONDON

HT
137
.W33
1971

First published 1971 by Cornell University Press.
Published in the United Kingdom by Cornell University Press Ltd., 2–4 Brook Street, London W1Y 1AA.

THIS BOOK HAS BEEN PUBLISHED WITH THE AID OF A GRANT FROM THE HULL MEMORIAL PUBLICATION FUND OF CORNELL UNIVERSITY.

International Standard Book Number 0-8014-0670-6
Library of Congress Catalog Card Number 76-162540

Printed in the United States of America by Vail-Ballou Press, Inc.

73-4827

This is Irma's book

Acknowledgments

My aims, methods, and themes are set forth in the Introduction. A key to abbreviations and citations is at the end of the book. Here I must try to sort out and remember my many debts.

Formal work began in 1964–1965 with a grant from the Social Sciences Research Council, and was concluded with the help of the American Philosophical Society, the Cornell Center for International Studies, and the Cornell Humanities Faculty Research Grants Committee. The departments of history at Harvard and Cornell universities have allowed me to take time from my institutional duties; and I have learned much more from students at both places than I have been able to show in the scholarly apparatus here, for they above all have helped me to think. Brun Appel, now diocesan archivist at Eichstätt, provided working space and counsel at critical times. Helmut Koenigsberger read part of the manuscript, and Walter Pintner and Edward Shorter all of it, with critical care; to them, to the publisher's referee, and to the staff of Cornell University Press I tender the special thanks due those who assume a thankless task.

A true list of debts to acquaintances and colleagues would be limitless. I am sure many could find here ideas of theirs whose source I have forgotten, and many others have contributed who will never hear of the book at all. But I must especially mention Franklin Ford, Andrew Milnor, and Fritz Ringer, some of whose passing remarks to me over a decade and more have emerged here after long incubation and elaboration. My wife's role in making this book is something that only those who have known us for a long time can guess at.

MACK WALKER

Contents

MAPS

German Home Towns

Community, State, and General Estate
1648–1871

Introduction

THIS will be the story of thousands of towns. But each lived apart from the others. And none was just like any other. What was common to all of them derived from the individuality of each of them. This is the first step in defining the home town.

The next step is to find common terms to identify the communities that are compatible with their individual disjunction. Two observers of their own times and society tried, at critical points, to do this: Justus Möser, writing in the period of eighteenth-century administrative ambition that has the name enlightened despotism, and Wilhelm Heinrich Riehl, writing in the aftermath of the Revolution of 1848.

From the social geographer Riehl, I take his map of the "individualized country [*individualisiertes Land*]." Riehl divided German "social ethnography" into three parts: North, South, and Middle. The North and Northeast, and the far South, he called "centralized country"; here the governments of Prussia, Austria, and Electoral Bavaria had found, or had been able to establish, uniform social landscapes. Over against the "centralized country" of North and South, Riehl located the "individualized country" of Middle Germany, from Westphalia in the north to the Danube in the south, and from the Rhine on the west to Upper Saxony in the east. Here was what he called "the motley encyclopedia of our society," with its rolling landscape dotted with middle-sized communities, in contrast with the characteristic open landscape and

1

great towns of the centralized country.[1] There is no need to take issue with his geography; no doubt parts of Prussia and Bavaria, for example, were more like his individualized country at times, and parts of the Rhineland more like his centralized country. What helps define the home towns is the way Riehl thought out his geography in terms of their experience. The individualized communities, he thought, had been the distinctive society of the old Holy Roman Empire; modern law and administration, modern learning, skills, and industry, modern population movement and growth, all were alien to it. These alien things had caused and now revealed a breach between community and society at large, between *Gemeinde,* he said, and *Gesellschaft;* these alien things had transformed the internal integrity of communal groups into fearful particularism; these alien things had made the solid citizen, the *Bürger,* into a philistine and a bigot.[2]

From Justus Möser I take the quality he called *Eigentum.* In the opening parts of his "History of Osnabrück," Möser described a primeval German communal society, and what had happened to it. Here it is best to think of his description as we think of other arguments from a state of nature one really knows little about: take it as a more or less conscious allegorical device for speaking of his own times. In Möser's description of the Germanic communities, Eigentum has a central place. Interpretations of what he was thinking about differ and even contradict, for Möser himself was never systematic, and was at the same time quite aware of the fluid meanings of words.[3] Eigentum means property, of course, and so when Möser spoke of it as something held in common within the native German community he seemed to be describing a kind of primitive communism; and so, sometimes, he was. Eigentum means property; and so, when Möser spoke of it as prerequisite for full membership in a community he seemed to be describing a personal property qualification for citizenship, and sometimes he meant that too.[4]

[1] *Land und Leute* (2d ed.; Stuttgart, 1855), pp. 132–135, 139–141, 159–217.
[2] Ibid., pp. 99–118, 181; *Die bürgerliche Gesellschaft* (3d ed.; Stuttgart, 1855), pp. 218–225.
[3] Cf. *Osnabrückische Geschichte,* in *Sämtliche Werke,* XII, I (Oldenburg, 1964), 33–34.
[4] For an introduction to the Markgenossenschaft theory as it developed from Möser, see Otto von Gierke, *Das deutsche Genossenschaftsrecht* (3 vols.; Berlin,

But in the allegory and in Möser's real concern there is no conflict, because Eigentum is a social quality and only derivatively an economic one; in the end he meant social self and dignity, which come from membership in a community and in turn constitute it; neither identity nor community precedes the other, they stand together. Even when he used the term conventionally to mean economic goods and facilities, what interested him was what conferred property and what property conferred. This propriety means self, individuality within a community, which is the only real kind: Möser calls its possessors *die Echten*. Eigentum—literally own-ness —gave identity as a silhouette projected on community, but it could be rendered and reflected only by community. In Möser's context its enemies were above all the state and its agents—Roman emissaries, Carolingian counts and missi dominici in the allegory— whose nature it was to strive for uniform territorial states, and to destroy what Möser called "honorable and communal identity"— *edles und gemeines Eigentum*.[5] Strangers and outsiders by definition cannot have this propriety and identity. Nobody can who is free of communal bonds and perquisites; nobody can whose identity rests on recognition from the state, for such a man has no home, no *Heimat*. The "free" who belong nowhere cannot know what will happen next, a condition akin to servitude.[6] Eigentum was the word Martin Luther had used for the verse "He came unto his own, and his own received him not." [7]

Möser's "artistry," wrote Riehl in the 1850's, had made him "the great forefather of our sociopolitical literature." His great contribution had been to show the principle, Riehl claimed, that any valid German social politics had to rest on the intimate study of separate localities.[8] Much the same principle may apply to any social politics, and the characteristics I shall discern in the German home

---

1868–1881); for a Möser whose views "anticipated latter-day Marxist historians" (p. 317), see Klaus Epstein, *The Genesis of German Conservatism* (Princeton, 1966), pp. 297–338, and the citations there and in the Bibliographical Essay, pp. 684–685.

[5] *Osnabrückische Geschichte*, pp. 38, 91, 101, 243–254, 274–282.

[6] Thus such a "freeman" sought bondage: ibid., pp. 74, 121, 151, 279; on servitude as a condition of not knowing what will happen next, David B. Davis, *The Problem of Slavery in Western Culture* (Ithaca, 1966), pp. 97, 107.

[7] John 1:11. "Er kam in sein Eigentum [ἴδια], und die seinen [ἴδιοι] nahmen ihn nicht auf."

[8] *Land und Leute*, p. 12.

towns of early modern times are not uniquely theirs. It is partly a question of degree, and of the relation between typology and history. In similar circumstances but at other times and in other places (if it comes to types) similar communities have surely existed. Yet the German home towns between the Thirty Years' War and the Second Empire represent a certain social style and character in the purest historical form I can think of, and one especially amenable to historical examination; and if there is any place to explore the meaning of social community it is in modern German history, in many ways a caricature of all our histories. There is no need to pursue conjecture of that kind here, beyond this point: that although the community described here is located in Germany between 1648 and 1871, to think of it as a transitory stage between model medieval towns and industrial cities would be to mistake its substance. I shall treat it neither as a "medieval remnant" nor as "preindustrial society." Elements of both will occasionally appear, but the home town ought to be understood as it lived, in its own terms.

A commonplace of German history is to say that "Germany lacked a strong liberal bourgeoisie," one of those negative comparisons that plague the interpretation of German affairs. This book, though, is not about the liberal bourgeoisie that Germany did not get, but about the hometown *Bürgerschaft* that Germany preeminently did get. Another commonplace of German historical pathology is that liberal ideas emanated from authoritarian sources and not from popular ones. Explanations are sought in philosophical traditions, in the structure of political thought, and in that same missing bourgeoisie. To represent bureaucracy as a "substitute middle class" is sometimes a useful notion, but a misleading one too. There is much to be said for these explanations, but it seems to me they suffer from coming at the problem backwards, so that they stand history on its head.[9] They assume a proper historical pattern and then punish the phenomena for their unwillingness to

---

[9] That is why Leonard Krieger's *The German Idea of Freedom* (Boston, 1957) is so difficult a book, and an early impulse to this study was to stand Krieger's argument back on its feet. The formulation "bureaucracy as a substitute middle class" I have from my former colleague Fritz F. K. Ringer; similar notions cropped up often in early-nineteenth-century German political analysis.

conform. For here again it is important to see that the German hometown *Bürger* was not a pale, underdeveloped imitation of the *bourgeois* who figures so prominently in modern European history; he was something quite different and even antithetical in principle, a distinction badly garbled by the term "petty bourgeois."

We seek out the histories of important states, of social classes, and of economic concentration because they are points of human collectivity. They are places where experience is shared and generalized, where interest is focused and compromised, and where group action takes place—and where evidence of a collective kind is accumulated for historians to find. But the community this book is about did not share the life of any such collectivity. Historians also seek out motion and change, not only to make a story but also to expose the nature of the thing they are studying. But the home town could not live with motion and change; stability, like separateness, was a condition of its existence and part of its definition. The dispersed and static nature of German civic life, though, offers an unexpected opportunity: the quiet localism common to the communities makes it possible to generalize about them. What seems a paradox can make a virtue out of a necessity, and consistency out of incoherence. Where separateness and stability were the basic facts of community life, most habits and procedures grouped around those features, thus creating a basic similarity among the localities, so that the histories of German localities are in many ways more coherent and enlightening than the histories of more clearly organized or more restless places.

That does not mean they are easy to find out about, nor that they fall readily into uniform patterns. To an unusual degree, this book runs the well-known risk of generalizing from the particular. A less commonly recognized peril is that of particularizing from the general, which has condemned very many local studies to redundancy and robbed them of any chance of discovery: the forcing of specific histories into preestablished patterns because "this was the age of absolutism," or of "revolution," or of "industrialization." My procedures reflect a conscious effort to navigate between the twin perils. The investigation began from observing a rhythm in the legislation of certain German nineteenth-century states, a bunching together of laws on local government, economic regulation, and social and moral legislation particularly concerning marriage. From there the trail led to some intensive local studies undertaken to discover if and how these various laws held together, and what they actually meant: things not at all clear from the letter of them. The context that gave them meaning, and the focal point of their coherence, turned out to be that entity I am calling the hometown community. When the general hypotheses thus formed respecting the communities were brought back to broad political and legal history, they explained much there that had seemed obscure or eccentric before. From there I turned to the countless local histories prepared by others to see whether the hypotheses would hold there, and began writing this book when I seemed to learn nothing new from them, when the form of any given community was familiar and its behavior unsurprising, so that I thought I understood how all of them worked. This is then an effort to state in a general way and bring to a general arena what has heretofore been the effective realm of case study. But it cannot be done by "synthesis" in the usual cumulative sense of adding up and weighing particulars, because the home towns' faces were intensely individual, and their essential qualities circumscribed within each of them. The important condition for reading or writing about the home towns collectively is always to remember that they lived individually. When they ceased to do so they stopped being home towns.

The study's goals have, of course, changed shape during the pursuit of them. Still at the end I find that their essentials persist. The main plot of the story is built around the tension between familiar communal society and the requirements of change, magnitude, and power. Through this theme I have tried to do several things harmoniously. In terms of scholarly discipline, I have tried to work toward a sociopolitical typology to replace traditional ones clearly inadequate for present purposes, especially for modern Germany and its history. The strategy is historical and sequential: first, an analysis of social community, its form and sense, in the most specific historical embodiment known to me, what I have called the home town of seventeenth- and eighteenth-century Germany; second, the meeting of the community with the state, meaning with the imperatives of systematic law and administration and with those who exercise them, around the turn of the eighteenth century, in which encounter subplots appear, around the bases of political liberalism and the origins of modern historiography and sociology; third, the meeting of the community with demographic and economic changes, and from that nineteenth-century encounter the elevation of its characteristics to a sociopolitical ideology applied to other forms and scales of organization.

I have tried to inform these abstract problems with the historical substance of the German experience, where I think they are historically telling. I have been quite conscious of their relation with contemporary themes like community, reform, and alienation. I have tried to make that relation clear to those who may bring such concerns to the reading—balancing that aim against a historian's fastidiousness about the particularity of his instance and the limitations of his professional right to speak.

The heart of the story remains the collective history of Germany's home town, the kind of place where nearly every modern German has felt, somehow, that his origins as a German lay.

Part One

THE HOME TOWNS

CHAPTER I

The Incubator

THE German hometownsman's sense of politics and society came from the nature of his community; the nature of the community was set by its autonomy and stable integrity over a long period of time (as men's memories go); and these it maintained because nobody was able to get hold of it, break it open, or change it. That was the constitutional principle of the Holy Roman Empire itself, by which I mean the political organization of Central Europe for more than two centuries after the Treaty of Westphalia. Its stability and strength too came from the phenomenon that nobody could get hold of it, break it open, or change it, so that the elastic strength of the German hometown community was of a piece with the resiliency of the Empire, its constitutional incubator.

The constitutional strength of the Holy Roman Empire is easy to mistake for weakness because it protected weak polities and even insisted on their weakness; it has regularly confounded analysts because of the close working relation of this kind of strength with the absence of power. It was built not on internally developed force but on a remarkable mechanism for the restraint and limitation of force; its stability came from the perpetual frustration of disruptive energy and aggressive power. The principle permeated the Empire. It was supported by the great powers of Europe and acted as a check upon them too. It was applied by the emperor himself, and against him; by the component states, and against them; and in that environment the hometown communities assumed a character that seemed perpetual and in the nature of things. In Europe's hollow center, from the end of the Thirty Years' War until the events that made the Second Empire, states were able to exist without developing the power and freedom of action that would, among other things, have swallowed up the hometown communities and made their members something different from hometownsmen.

European politics and the Holy Roman Empire

Nobody won the Thirty Years' War, at least nobody before Bismarck, and there is room for doubt whether Bismarck did. The Treaty of Westphalia, an international agreement that became the main statement of the German constitution, proclaimed not a decision but an impasse among competing powers. It acknowledged and codified a situation that had become apparent over three decades of almost constant, seesaw (but never too seesaw) warfare that always seemed to return to the same place. New initiatives or added force by any one of the participating powers had always been met by countervailing force or new initiatives by the others.[1] German soldiers and princes moved from the camp of one great power to the camp of another in defense of their liberties—making sure nobody could get hold of them. By this process the German principalities had been able to avoid being swallowed up by greater powers or by one another, and so survived in a condition of individual weakness. The Treaty of Westphalia, by providing that the states of the Empire might freely make and change independent alliances in defense of their liberties, and by including the European great powers as guarantors, afforded a mechanism for defending the status quo that had already been tested in a war of stalemate.

The mechanism was not systematically described in the treaty, for the powers did not plan it just that way; nor would there have been much difference if it had: great powers are not bound by contracts. And it was promptly and vigorously challenged in conflicts between Louis XIV of France and the imperial house of Habsburg,

[1] Compare Helmut G. Koenigsberger on "escalation" in "The Thirty Years' War," *The Age of Expansion*, ed. Hugh Trevor-Roper (London, 1968), pp. 143–174.

with the other European powers putting in their hands to serve their ends. But still it held. By the end of Louis XIV's reign and the War of the Spanish Succession, that classic exercise in the balance of power, it was clear that the situation codified at Westphalia was not just an agreement, it was a fact of European political life, in which two basic principles bearing on Germany intertwined. First, the emperor could exert power and influence enough to protect the status quo from upset generated within or without, but not enough to achieve full sovereignty within Germany for himself; and second, this apparently delicate balance would be kept in constant adjustment by the working of the principle of the balance of power, on a European scale, with a German fulcrum. Such was the history of the first Confederation of the Rhine in the 1660's, German client states of France against the Emperor until France came to seem the greater threat; such was the amazingly flexible foreign policy of the Electors of Brandenburg.

The interstate structure of Europe and the internal constitution of Germany interlocked to sustain this arrangement; the powers of Europe and the German principalities shifted political stance with a kind of unconscious precision as threats developed now from one quarter, now from another. The regularity with which the mechanism worked in one circumstance after another made it seem almost a mystically self-governing, perpetual motion of politics. The resiliency of the system lay in its capacity to hold state power below the threshold where the system might be overturned. It brought individual wills into its service, into the service of restraining one another. Its logic was circular.

European and German politics for nearly a century after the Spanish Succession War reaffirmed, over and over, what had become apparent then. Toward mid-century the War of the Austrian Succession was for Germany an action to prevent the uniting of the imperial crown with a permanent territorial Habsburg state contemplated by the Pragmatic Sanction, a conjunction whereby the Habsburg house threatened to exceed the limits traditionally set upon its power in Germany. In response the German principalities led by Prussia and France delivered the imperial crown for a time over to the weaker and thus ostensibly safer house of Wittelsbach.

But when it appeared that so weak an emperor could not withstand the threats to the status quo offered by France and now by Prussia, the German princes who had voted to a man for the Wittelsbach emperor shifted their allegiance to Maria Theresa of Habsburg, to an Austria which had the organized political resources to balance off the threats coming from the north and the west, but an Austria whose power was developed outside the Empire and not within—to an Austria, again, that could and would protect the Germanies without seizing and changing them. The mechanism absorbed the rise of Prussian power under Frederick the Great into itself, so that the main effect was to transpose the more fragmentary constitutional balance checking imperial authority to a balance between territorial states: the Austro-Prussian dualism that lasted for a century, until Austria's defeat at Königgrätz in 1866. French entry into the Seven Years' War on the side of its old enemy Austria amounted to recognition, shared with the German principalities, that Austria at that time seriously threatened neither. The initiatives Emperor Joseph II undertook in Germany in the last quarter of the century, notably on the Bavarian Succession question, were similarly frustrated; there the German liberties were defended by a coalition of German states led by the sometime robber king of Prussia, supported now by the Russian Empress Catherine. Catherine said that Joseph's efforts to extend and consolidate the imperial power in Germany were "repugnant . . . to the Treaty of Westphalia, which is the very basis and bulwark of the constitution of the Empire . . . a violent shock to all the bordering states, a subversion of order, and the destruction of the balance of all Europe." [2]

The outburst of French power under Napoleon Bonaparte, by temporarily upsetting the balance of power in Europe, temporarily upset the German status quo as well—and the crisis this brought to the hometown communities is a reminder that their stability and autonomy relied directly on the balanced European and German status quo. But Napoleon's France too was thrown back in the end, and the old system was reasserted at the Congress of Vienna, where, said an experienced contemporary observer, the "wisdom of

[2] Quoted by Johann S. Pütter, *An Historical Developement of the Present Political Constitution of the Germanic Empire*, tr. Josiah Dornford, III (London, 1790), 202–204.

the allied powers" simply confirmed the Treaty of Westphalia by creating a German Bund which acknowledged the necessary close interrelation of European politics with the internal constitution of Germany—a Germany that would be the "peace state of Europe." [3]

Even revolutionary imperialism had been absorbed and contained. The repressions of Metternich's Europe were themselves an exercise based on the familiar pattern of the German politics of the status quo; and in purely political terms (though by then subversion from other sources was well under way), the system prevailed even when Metternich and repression fell away in 1848: it defeated revolution then. "The Treaty of Westphalia," said the socialist revolutionary Proudhon, "preeminently identifies justice with the force of things, and will last forever." [4] The rules of Central European politics seemed hardly different in 1850 from what they had been in 1648. Adolphe Thiers really addressed critical issues of contemporary politics when he brandished the Treaty of Westphalia before the Corps Législatif, Napoleon III, the German states, and Bismarck on the third of May, 1866: "I beg the Germans to reflect that the highest principle of European politics is that Germany shall be composed of independent states connected only by a slender federative thread. That was the principle proclaimed by all Europe at the Congress of Westphalia; it was the principle adopted when the great Frederick signed the Peace of Teschen on the Bavarian Succession matter." Thiers did not mention the Congress of Vienna, which had signalized French defeat half a century before. But he pointed to the conjunction between the constitution of Germany and the European balance: "the constant aim of all the nations in modern times, each with its eye upon the other to see that no one of them reaches proportions threatening to the others . . . what has taken on the name of equilibrium." [5]

Thiers made of the European political structure after Westphalia a more deliberately willed and a more peaceable thing than it really

[3] Arnold H. L. Heeren, "Der Deutsche Bund in seinen Verhältnissen zu dem Europäischen Staatensystem," *Vermischte historische Schriften*, II (Göttingen, 1821), 431–433.

[4] "Le traité de Westphalie, expression supérieure de la justice identifiée avec la force des choses, existe à jamais." Quoted by Fritz Dickmann, *Der Westfälische Frieden* (Münster, 1959), p. 7.

[5] *Le Moniteur Universel* (Paris), May 4, 1866.

had been; and again it is by no means certain how fully it was overcome in his time, or how. But this much can be said about the timing and nature of these events: that during the ten years before Thiers spoke and before Prussia defeated Austria at Königgrätz and broke the German balance, the German home towns had been stripped of the defenses they had built and relied upon since the seventeenth century.

Protection of the powerless

The "force of things" was the resistance by diversity to power and change in Germany. In 1648 the Emperor was obliged to recognize the political independence and internal supremacy [*Landeshoheit*] of those principalities and estates that had been strong enough to achieve it in fact and had been able to sustain it through the preceding tumultuous years. But codifying that independence in constitutional and international law had a curious effect: recognition of the independent strength of the states became then a protection of their weakness, and also of the weak elements within their borders. For one thing, the security the Empire provided reduced the stimulus to aggression without and reform within that a more precarious situation, or more inviting opportunities, might have afforded. Thus there were few changes, and internal situations were let alone to jell; society could stabilize because there was no compelling reason to change anything. But a second more active force for stability and the protection of weakness developed out of the constitutional situation. Inasmuch as it was impossible and illegal for the Emperor to seize control of the states, he used the legal and political powers he had to prevent them from mobilizing power within their territories or at the expense of one another; and similarly every German polity and estate found it easier to seek security in weakening its rivals than in dominating them.

The distinctive genius of the Holy Roman Empire was that, in practice as well as in law, to preserve the powerless was to defend one's interests and to uphold the imperial constitution. Where one's own appetite for political power was frustrated and smothered, the obvious policy was to help smother and frustrate the aspirations of others; and this applied not only to a rival's efforts at territorial expansion but also to any effort a ruler or estate might make to impose full control over his individual or corporate subjects. The imperial patriot Johann S. Pütter spoke thus of Germany's West-phalia constitution: "that when every thing is in its proper order, each territorial Lord has sufficient opportunities for doing good; but that if, on the contrary, he is inclined to injure his country, either the Provincial States may interfere to prevent him, or else his subjects in general, or any individual among them, may seek redress from one of the supreme tribunals of the Empire." [6] This was a judicial (and idealized) statement of the political fact that almost anybody could invoke outside help against an energetic and overbearing ruler; and, as a matter of law and politics, those threatened could as readily call upon neighboring states as upon the Empire to defend their rights and privileges. Even imperial judgments and executions against any state were in practice en-trusted to other states; and even more commonly, an ambitious prince was checked by his neighbors without any reference to imperial institutions at all. Legal grounds for calling in outside help to restrain a ruler could almost always be found if he posed a serious threat, and if, as was likely to be the case, neighboring potentates shared with the threatened nobles or corporations an interest in restraining him. The muddy complexity of jurisdictions and of political and familial relations rarely confronted any or-ganized element of German society, or any organized community within it, with a clear choice between the violent alternatives of submission or rebellion, either of which would have meant dislo-cation and exposure to the leveling effects of power. Rather they found a peaceful in-between where little changed, save the firmer development of their distinctiveness.

The claim that variety and stability were specifically German constitutional qualities was widespread when these principles were being articulated and the Treaty of Westphalia being composed. Hippolithus à Lapide's (Bogislav P. Chemnitz) *De Ratione Status in Imperio nostro Romano-Germanico* was an anti-Habsburg tract published first in Stettin, Swedish Pomerania, in 1640; and it was republished on several appropriate later occasions—1647, 1712, 1761—to arouse German fears of the imperial ambitions of the

[6] *Constitution of the Germanic Empire*, II, 194–195.

Austrian house.[7] The agents of oppressive power and imposed unity, Chemnitz argued, were the systematic Roman law and its practitioners: "such corrupters of the law as know nothing but the Roman civil codes." Hence the defense of freedom lay in political variety and autonomy based upon German customs and German history. Roman-trained *Doktorchen,* he wrote, petty pedants, sought to infiltrate German society with oppressive formal rules in the service of autocracy.[8] This was wrong, both politically and legally. Regular state administrative powers—*Verwaltung*—properly came into play only to deal with matters outside the familiar and the traditional, with "alien goods and situations": just the opposite, that is, of Möser's *Eigentum.*[9]

The German constitution and the home towns

The constitution Pütter and Chemnitz defended was the one in which the German home towns flourished. They developed their bewildering structural variety precisely because they had so little to do with "alien goods and situations" that would invite the attention of administrators, tax collectors, and Roman lawyers. They were subject to no common rhythm of economics or politics. Consequently their formal institutions precipitated out at different times, under different circumstances, and there they stabilized. Their idiosyncrasy resulted from the unchanging character of political and economic life: nothing happened to bring them into step. But that circumstance they had in common, and it gave the variety of institutional forms their common content; thus the same static conditions that allowed the dissimilarity of forms filled the forms with very similar patterns of communal life. That is why a basic definition of the home towns is that there was almost no penetration into their internal affairs from the outside. Few governments were

[7] I have used the German translation edited and extended by J. P. Carrach, published under the title *Abriss der Staats-Verfassung, Staats-Verhältniss, und Bedürfniss des Römischen Reichs Deutscher Nation* (Mainz, 1761).

[8] Here he cites, in addition to the eternal Tacitus, the first-century rustic writer Columella: "dass Städte und Länder zu der Zeit weit glücklicher gewesen, als man noch nichts von Rechtsgelehrten and Advocaten gewusst, und dass sich der alte Blühende Zustand wieder hoffen lassen, wann diese Arten von Leuten aufhören würden." Ibid., I, 4–10, 36 for the quotation, 72–76, and passim.

[9] "Fremde Güter oder Angelegenheiten." Ibid., I, 115.

equipped to intervene systematically, nor was there any compelling reason why governments should wish to do so. Intervention ordinarily came only to clear up some specific controversy or to take advantage of it. Constitutional statutes of the communities usually came out of that kind of irregular intervention *ad hoc,* and reflected the particular situations that had brought the intervention about; and intervention usually served, as subsequent chapters will show, to reinforce the communities' existing character against those who sought to change or violate it.

The frame of the German towns' external relations was quite different from the pattern discerned in most of Europe, because of the division of juridical and political power between the constitutional sovereignty of the Empire and the territorial sovereignty—*Landeshoheit*—of the territorial rulers, the *Landesherren,* large and small: a vague and flexible division of authority that reflected the vague and flexible political balance. Most European towns, traditionally, were likely to support strong monarchs over against local landed nobility, and thus came to be incorporated into monarchic states as the price of local security. That had been the pattern of German medieval politics too. But the Holy Roman Empire of early modern times offered the German towns the chance to have their cake and eat it too. "Sovereign" imperial authority was able to defend them against the territorial princes, and did so as a means of keeping its hand in and maintaining political leverage, but it was unable to dominate them.

Imperial protection most obviously benefitted the *Reichsstädte,* the free imperial towns recognized in the Treaty of Westphalia as territorially independent estates, as *Reichsstände,* directly subject to the empire and not to other territorial states. But in practice and even in law it was also applied to *Landstädte,* towns within the jurisdiction of territorial princes.[10] Imperial and territorial towns

[10] See the imperial defense of the Saar towns against their *Landesherr* and his officials described by Edith Ennen, "Die Organisation der Selbstverwaltung in den Saarstädten vom ausgehenden Mittelalter bis zur französischen Revolution," *RA,* XXV (1933), 139–153, 195–196, and passim; cases and statements of the constitutional principle in Johann Jakob Moser, *Teutsches Staats-Recht,* V (Frankfurt/Main, 1752), 506–517, and in his *Von der Landeshoheit im Weltlichen,* I (Frankfurt/Main, 1772), 187–188; and also the cases scattered through Johann C. Lünig, *Das Teutsche Reichs-Archiv . . . ein vollkommenes*

cannot be distinguished absolutely as falling into two contrary conditions of sovereignty, one free and the other subject; rather there
was a long gradation of imperial protection. Imperial towns fell
generally on the freer end, but not invariably; they had to pay
close attention to the politics and power of their territorial neighbors, and sometimes this was recognized in law: the free imperial
town of Esslingen, for example, stood under the special influence
and protection of the Duke of Württemberg.[11]

Constitutional lawyers, to be sure, tried to draw a clear distinction. The Treaty of Westphalia had listed 51 towns as imperial
towns, juridically "immediate" to imperial authority. But Johann
Jakob Moser in the 1740's listed 139 other towns as "fallen away
from the Reich, or exempted by others, or which affect immediacy
or erroneously claim imperial status, or sought to become imperial
towns." [12] Most of these held some specific immunity or privilege,
granted by the empire, judged to fall short of full exemption from
territorial state authority. The ingenuity with which communities
expanded almost any right or immunity in the direction of effective
autonomy was boundless, and they were engaged in endless—albeit
usually desultory—litigation over them with the territorial governments. Moser's 139 were only a small fraction of the very many
towns that held privileges and immunities against their territorial
rulers that might be enforced by the empire; he could have extended his list almost indefinitely by broadening his definition only
slightly, but it took him more than three hundred quarto pages to
get through the ones he did list.

The imperial rights of the communities, though, like most rights
of German princes, estates, and corporations, actually were en-

---

Corpus Juris Publici des Heiligen Römischen Reichs Teutscher Nation (24
vols.; Leipzig, 1713–1722), for example, the imperial guarantee in 1659 to the
"Bürgermeister, Rath, und Bürger" of the territorial town of Braunschweig of
their "Freiheit, Brieff, Recht, gut Gewohnheit, und alt Herkommen." Lünig,
Pars IV, II. Theil, pp. 228–229.

11 Otto Borst, "Esslinger Bürgertum in der Spätzeit der Reichsstadt," *ES*,
IV (1958), 62 and passim; Karl S. Bader, "Johann Jakob Moser und die
Reichsstädte," *ES*, IV (1958), 53–54; for the powers of ordinary *Landesherren*
in a number of *Reichsstädte*, Georg L. von Maurer, *Geschichte der Städteverfassung in Deutschland*, IV (Erlangen, 1871), 189.

12 *Teutsches Staats-Recht*, XXXIX (Leipzig, 1749), 77–399. Many of the
towns listed were by then in French, Dutch, or Swiss territory.

forced not by the emperor's own officers but rather by jealous neighbors acting in the name of imperial law. The constant game of beggar-my-neighbor that the German princes played against one another sustained the autonomy of one another's subject communities. Because legal pretexts for invoking protection could almost always be found in the form of some judicial or fiscal right, invocation was politically and not constitutionally determined. But for the communities the legal and constitutional side was vitally important, because it meant that the outside rival protected the community rather than seizing it. It meant that the intervening outsider blocked the development of the threatening prince's power rather than seizing and replacing it; he restored the community's rights and then withdrew lest he summon retaliation against himself. The German constitution translated the political rivalry between state and empire and between state and state into a force for communal defense far beyond anything the communities could ever have mustered on their own. Along with the autonomy of the states, the autonomy of the communities within the states survived in a condition of powerlessness and internal quiescence.

Self-governing rights were not only imperial in origin; in fact, only a small portion of them were. Many towns held rights guaranteed by other territorial princes than their own. More important, territorial towns held rights and immunities of their princes much as imperial towns held of the empire. In the mid-eighteenth century, 176 Bavarian communities were legally identified as "bearers of sovereign rights and special jurisdictions"—*Träger von Hoheitsrechten und besondere Gerichtsrechten*—and these were not administrative functions delegated unilaterally by the Elector at his pleasure and convenience, but established local rights very difficult to modify or reduce. The constitutional powers and immunities of these and other Bavarian territorial towns and markets in 1748 fill fifty volumes in the Munich archives. Such communities were not much more subject to Electoral domination than the imperial towns were subject to the Emperor's.[13]

The sharpest contrast along the shaded column that runs from communal freedom to subjection falls not on a constitutional line

[13] Hans Rall, *Kurbayern in der letzten Epoche der alten Reichsverfassung, 1745–1801* (Munich, 1952), pp. 484–490.

between imperial towns and territorial towns but on a regional line between the towns in individualized country and the towns subject to Brandenburg-Prussia. The Prussian state stands as a main foil to the story of the German hometown community, at least until the nineteenth century, when patterns of community life in Prussia and in other parts of Germany began to move closer to one another. There is little doubt that Prussian towns in the seventeenth and eighteenth centuries—certainly at the end of Frederick William I's reign in 1740—presented a quite different picture from places of comparable size elsewhere in Germany.[14] This has to do with the well-known centralizing and leveling activities of the great Hohenzollerns. But it can be misleading to think of this in terms of the challenge-response theme so often applied to the history of Prussian state power. It was not quite a matter of terrific obstacles heroically overcome. The success of the Prussian government in dominating Prussian towns was more directly related to the internal looseness and the paucity of towns in the lands it ruled. The towns it faced in the seventeenth and early eighteenth centuries were small, semi-agricultural, and new: less fully developed, less balanced internally, less stable than comparable groups to the south and west; and the Prussian administrative juggernaut creaked and faltered when it met the stronger towns of Silesia after 1740, and then the Westphalian, Rhenish, and Franconian towns at the end of the century.[15] Guild structures—always an integrating component of the hometown community—were very weak in the older Prussian territories, and disassociated from town life. Relations within the trades were regional rather than locally imbedded within the social and political communities.[16] The economy of the region was proportionally more devoted to export goods like woolens and linens, and that encouraged economic organization different from what was natural

14 For the classic and perhaps overdrawn exposition relying on central state materials (which almost always exaggerate state efficacy), Gustav Schmoller, "Das Städtewesen unter Friedrich Wilhelm I," ZPGL, X (1873), 589 and passim.

15 Johannes Ziekursch, Das Ergebnis der friderizianischen Städteverwaltung und die Städteordnung Steins: Am Beispiel der schlesischen Städte dargestellt (Jena, 1908); and below, pp. 198–199.

16 Gustav Schmoller, "Das brandenburgisch-preussische Innungswesen von 1640–1806, hauptsächlich die Reform unter Friedrich Wilhelm I," FBPG, I (1888), 63–75.

Location of towns mentioned in the text

in an economy based almost entirely on local consumption of local production. Textiles were virtually the only German manufacture for which there was a mass market, and German textile guilds everywhere were likely to be looser in structure and more state-dominated than trades whose markets and whose competition were nearer by.[17] And whereas communities that lived unto themselves and were part of no larger economy were relatively invulnerable to market crises which might prevent them from developing the characteristic social immunity and stability of the home town, communities engaged in export were subject to disruptions resulting not only from changes in outside markets but also from the efforts of governments to control and increase their productivity for the sake of what it would bring to state revenues. That meant a state administrative and social policy inimical to hometown balance and stability.[18] A main motive for the Prussian state's systematic control over local government was to facilitate population growth and to develop foreign commerce: tens of thousands of artisans, notably weavers, were encouraged to immigrate into Prussian towns, and were offered full local citizenship rights and economic rights: a process which no community willingly accepted, for it tended to its destruction.[19] Consequently the Prussian government was obliged to seize local controls, and generally succeeded in doing so. Prussian guild laws often tried to distinguish between the hometown trades and the outside-market trades in which the state was really interested, but that economic distinction did not shelter the civic and social communities from the movement of population nor from the consequences of attachment to an export economy.

Freedom from economic penetration from a larger outside world was as important for the preservation of the home town's autonomy and integrity as freedom from political penetration was, and the two usually went together. It would be wrong to suppose home-

[17] Cf. Karl Spannagel, "Die Gründung der Leinweberzunft in Elberfeld und Barmen im Oktober, 1738," *ZBG*, XXX (1894), 181–199.

[18] For the ways in which weaving attracted state intervention and controls over local government, see, e.g., Siegfried Pohl, "Studien zur soziologischen, sozialen und wirtschaftlichen Struktur Bielefelds im 18. Jahrhundert," *JHVR*, LIX (1956/57), 1–68.

[19] Moritz Meyer, *Geschichte der preussischen Handwerkerpolitik* (2 vols.; Minden, 1884–1888), I, 1–71, 109–132, and II, 1–98.

town economic organization to have been primitive; economically the communities were primitive only from the perspective of specialized large-scale manufacture and commerce—economic forms called advanced because of their larger scale and later development, but in many ways far simpler. The home towns produced no surplus for export, to be sure; but within the walls the hometown economy was elaborately articulated and complex for the very reason that everything had to be provided there without the exchange of some specialized native product for goods and services from the outside. The economic organization that the individualized country bore into the nineteenth century had best not be called a crude one; it was rather a high development of small-scale commerce and manufacture in a time and place where great commerce and manufacture were all but impossible, or at least were economically inappropriate. Territorial fragmentation had a good deal to do with this: the tariff policies of territorial princes who wanted to raise revenues where hands could be laid on them, on goods crossing borders. That was an element of the economic incubator that derived from the political; but it was probably not the most important one. The main export items of the time produced on a large scale were, besides weaving, extensive agriculture and mining; and none of these was prevalent in regions where the home towns were. Prussia, that had them all, is the main contrast to the hometown country; Hanover, with its heavy agricultural predominance and its cottage weaving, and Saxony, with its weaving and mining and the industry that developed out of them, fall uneasily in between, and neither was an altogether congenial habitat for the hometown community. Hanoverian states attempted policies toward communities and guilds very like Prussia's in the seventeenth and eighteenth centuries; [20] but although the Hanoverians tried

[20] Braunschweig-Lüneburg was Prussia's main ally in the campaign for an imperial law on guilds which would facilitate their control and reform by state administrators, culminating in the Imperial Trades Edict of 1731 (see below, pp. 93–98 and Appendix); in 1675 Braunschweig-Lüneburg issued a general Landesgesetz based on Roman law and explicitly abrogating Sachsenrecht, dissolving and abrogating local statutes and practices: Christian G. Riccius, Entwurf von Stadt-Gesetzen oder Statutis vornehmlich der Land-Städte (Frankfurt/Main, 1740), pp. 631–635. See also Jacob G. Sieber, Abhandlung von den Schwierigkeiten in den Reichstädten das Reichsgesetz vom 16. Aug. 1731 wegen der Missbräuche bey den Zünften zu vollziehen (Goslar, 1771),

they did not succeed: a friction that may be a reason why so many of the sharpest critics of the kind of bureaucratic centralism associated with Prussia were Hanoverians like Möser, Stein, Stüve, and their successors. In Hanover the conflict between community and state was frequently exposed, but in eighteenth-century Prussia, with the partial exception of annexed Silesia, the conflict hardly appears. The apparent crushing of the Prussian communities by Frederick William I which Gustav Schmoller elaborately described in the nineteenth century [21] seems rather, from local perspectives, to have been a transfer of control over flaccid communities from noble domination to the state's own officials without the towns' showing much substance anywhere in the process.[22]

Thus Prussian communities seem already to have been structurally weaker than the home towns of the individualized country at the middle of the seventeenth century; and in the years that followed, movements of population and exposure to a larger economy and polity outside kept them from jelling as the home towns did; and the civil service party in Prussia both benefitted from the situation and pressed it further. In this respect at least the Prussian civil service interest did not conflict seriously with the other major political interests in Prussia, with the landed nobility engaged in food production for outside markets, nor with the crown.

The conditions of community

If home towns did not develop in Prussia because of the importance of extralocal commerce and of the agrarian countryside (here considering administrative factors to be derivative), then, by the same token, the home towns of the individualized country were communities free of outside commerce and distinct from the rural countryside. They were neither city nor village, but a kind of polity quite different from both; and city and countryside, from the communal perspective, had far more in common with each other than either had with the home town. Unlike either city or

---

setting aside Hanover and Prussia as *Landen mächtiger Reichsstände,* administratively equipped to enforce such a decree.

[21] Principally in the articles cited in notes 14 and 16, above.

[22] E.g., Hannelore Juhr, *Die Verwaltung des Hauptamtes Brandenburg/ Ostpreussen von 1713 bis 1751* (Berlin, 1967), pp. 118–134.

countryside, the home towns lived unto themselves, so that each could develop its self-sufficiency, whereas city and countryside both attracted and were subject to outside influences and controls. The kind of state interference that characterizes Prussia taken as a whole characterizes city and countryside elsewhere, leaving the home towns as a separate category; they should not be pictured as lying somewhere in a continuous spectrum that runs from rural to urban. That would—and at the time it often did—disguise their real character and their place in German society, politics, and history. Only in size—simple numbers—can they be defined as falling between village and city; and that intermediate size gave them a distinctive civic character of remarkable internal strength and resiliency.

Political scientists at least since Aristotle have said that the sheer size of a polity, the number of its members, circumscribes the ways in which its affairs can be effectively conducted. There is a limit in size above which a political unit cannot operate as does one whose members know each other, one another's backgrounds, one another's circumstances and interests. Above that critical size, familiarity is lost, and a more formal and anonymous pattern of law and politics is necessary. Of course there can be no precise statistical boundary; it must vary with the individual conditions of each community; rapid internal change or outside pressure, for example, would presumably lower the threshold by eroding familiarity.

For the German hometown community of early modern times, the upper limit appears to lie at about ten thousand population, perhaps fifteen. That would mean a maximum of about two thousand Bürger or communal citizens—not a remarkable number for one to come to know in the course of a lifetime living, trading, and worshipping together with the rest, but close to the limit of familiarity—it would be hard to encompass more than that into a single view in which each still kept his own face and individuality. In towns above that size one is apt to find two social and political elements not characteristic of the hometown community, where both are present in tendency but too rudimentary and too vaguely defined seriously to affect social organization.

First, in a great town there is likely to be a distinct and permanent ruling caste of families, a patriciate. It might or might not be constitutionally recognized under some such title as *Patriziat* or *Geschlechter*, or by the name of some local governing institution it had succeeded in monopolizing. Except for its hereditary character (though that was far from pure) and contemporary usage, it might almost as readily be called oligarchy, and on appropriate occasions I shall use the latter term. Such a group really was to be identified by its ability to live mainly from government functions or in some other way free from dependence on the local citizens' economy, and to rule rather independently of the political influence of the common Bürgerschaft. And it had to be large enough, or possessed of extensive enough connections with the outside, so that it did not have to intermarry with the common Bürger or replenish its numbers from among them.[23] This is a functional description and not a legal one; it relies more upon the observation of home-town politics and society than on formal recognition of status. A direct comparison between population size and formal constitution is possible only for imperial towns: in the later eighteenth century about three-quarters of the imperial towns with populations over fifteen thousand had legally recognized governing patriciates, while three-quarters of those under fifteen thousand did not; the median patrician town had a population of about twelve thousand, the median nonpatrician town, under six thousand.[24] In a patrician town, governed by a relatively fixed and independent elite, the citizenry, the common Bürgerschaft, was not integrated into nor familiar with local political processes in the way characteristic of

[23] See below, pp. 59–61. For an excellent description of the tripartite patriciate of Frankfurt am Main as it took form in the seventeenth century see Gerald L. Soliday, "The Social Structure of Frankfurt am Main in the Seventeenth and Early Eighteenth Century" (unpubl. diss., Harvard, 1968), pp. 97–166; it was composed of 1) urban-noble governors with income from public funds and from rents, 2) wealthy merchants, and 3) academically trained professional jurists and physicians.

[24] Moser, *Teutsches Staats-Recht*, XLII (Hanau, 1750), 435; Pütter, *Constitution of the Germanic Empire*, III, appendix, pp. 67–71; Wilhelm Franke, "Die Volkszahl deutscher Städte am Ende des 18. und Anfang des 19. Jahrhunderts," ZPSL, LXII (1922), 112–120. Note also the provisions in the Bavarian edicts of 22 V 1668 and 9 VII 1718 that *Bürgermeister* in capital towns were to be juridically treated as *Geschlechter*, whereas those of secondary towns came before regular courts: Georg K. Meyr, ed. *Sammlung der Kurpfalz-Baierischen allgemeinen und besonderen Landesverordnungen*, III (Munich, 1788), pp. 42, 50.

the hometown community, and the interests and aims of governors prevailed over the interests and aims of Bürger. There will be more detail on the organization of leadership and the relation of citizenry to governance in Chapter II and elsewhere.

Secondly, below the Bürger class in a large town there was likely to be a large body of noncitizens, or partial citizens. Their legal status and names were various; they might be called *Beisitzer* or *Beisass,* or in some instances *Untertanen,* or bear some local name; several such categories commonly appeared in a single place, holding distinctive legal status but alike in their exclusion from full communal membership. They are the hardest part of the population to identify or count because they appear only erratically in a town's records; for they were not citizens, nor masters, nor participants in community property, and they might come to a town or leave it without attracting much attention. Call them "tolerated residents": scarcest in the home town because the middle-sized community was least tolerant of their presence. The home town needed no class of mobile, dismissable, unskilled labor of the kind that found place in city and countryside. But although their relation with the civic community was precarious, they were by no means always poor; among tolerated residents were quite wealthy and powerful people who lived from independent or outside resources and who thus did not seek citizenship in order to enter the hometown trades. More of them, though, were persons who could not afford to buy their ways into the community or who were excluded for some other reason denoting inferiority: the illegitimately born for example, or Jews, or indigent aunts, or menial servants, or immigrants from the country who settled in the suburbs. Tolerated residents were likely to include the rich and the poor of a town; the hometown Bürger was neither.[25] Both rich and poor were attracted to large towns and were less likely to be excluded from them than from the home towns where the communal citizen's standards ruled. And in the patrician towns where the common Bürger exercised no important political powers, the difference be-

---

[25] Ludwig Klein, *Die geschichtliche Entwicklung des Gemeindebürgerrechts in Württemberg* (Tübingen, 1933), pp. 17–18; Soliday, "Frankfurt am Main," pp. 82–83; Georg Fischer, *Fränkisches Handwerk: Beiträge zu seiner Geschichte, Kultur und Wirtschaft* (Bayreuth, 1958), p. 23.

tween ordinary citizen and tolerated resident was slight and the two classes tended to merge, in effect if not in legal status, so that citizenship was of small value there. The hometown community was one that escaped patrician rule and leveling as it escaped state rule and leveling.[26]

The lower population limit of the hometown community comes with the undifferentiated peasant village. There one does not find the intertwining diversification of civic and economic functions that appear in a self-sufficient and balanced community. Put this lower level at 750 people, or about 150 families, although any figure must be so imprecise as to be all but arbitrary. Contemporary administrators and commentators often tried to draw some such rough numerical boundary. Or sometimes at their wits' end they tried to distinguish a town from a village by its possession of a wall, which makes sense insofar as a wall implies a market the community seeks to protect against outside intruders—something the farm village had no interest in doing. Village society was called *das platte Land,* the flat country, the simple country; and the phrase has more to do with the social terrain than with the physical.[27] There the craft guilds did not exist, for example, and the town crafts were usually forbidden. Moreover, in the countryside political authority was usually exercised by an officer of the state or of a noble, who was no part of the community he governed but rather an outside professional full-time governor, in that sense comparable to the patrician rulers of the cities, but unlike the civic leadership of the hometown communities. The difference this made for the stability and integrity of community life appears in a juridical distinction drawn by Johann Pütter respecting the admission of new members: "Citizens of towns are normally to be received by the councils, but countrymen by whoever holds patrimonial jurisdiction, always in-

[26] Hugo Preuss, arguing that an older German local self-government was destroyed by the absolutism of the seventeenth and eighteenth centuries, equates the effects of bureaucratic despotism (he means Prussia) with local oligarchic despotism (he means the large towns I have called patrician). See Chapter II below, n. 48.

[27] Thus Georg L. von Maurer, *Geschichte der Dorfverfassung in Deutschland,* I (Erlangen, 1865), 99: "Die Dorfgenossenschaft war . . . keine juristische Person, also keine Korporation oder Gemeinheit im Sinne des Römischen Rechts. Sie war und hiess vielmehr nur darum eine Gemeine oder Gemeinde, weil die ungetheilte Mark selbst noch gemein . . . war."

cluding homage." [28] The hometownsman drew the line in his own terms: "No shit-hens fly over the town wall." [29]

The hometownsman was more likely than either peasant or city dweller to live in the place where he had been born. Both city and countryside experienced greater mobility of population than the small town; at any rate that was the case when figures permitting this kind of analysis were developed in the mid-nineteenth century, and it fits the social state of affairs for two centuries before that. Here again, posing the small town conventionally as something between village and city turns up an oddity: if one were to prepare a graph of which one axis represented the size of towns and the other axis the proportion of the population locally born, it would show a bulge in the area of middle size, with the cities on one end and the countryside on the other both tapering off into greater fluidity. Statisticians who made the discovery drew a line between town and country down the middle of the bulge and concluded that in towns, the proportion of the population locally born varied inversely with the size of the place, whereas in rural communities on the contrary it rose with the size of the place. [30] The home town lies at the intersection. That is to say, in its social demography (as in the location of authority) it did not fall along a symmetrical "folk-urban continuum," to cite the phrase of modern sociology. Rather, the larger a city became, the more its mobility of population was like that of the village; and the smaller the village, the more like the city, with the middle-sized town showing maximum stability of membership. City and country had lesser stability; and their politics and administration, also in many ways resembling one another more than either resembled the home town, reflected the difference.

Using these population boundaries, a conservative estimate is

[28] "Municiporum Cives à Magistratu, Rustici à quolibet Jurisdictione patrimoniali praedito, modo haud neglecto homagio, recte recipiuntur." Quoted by Moser, *Landeshoheit im Weltlichen*, III (Frankfurt/Main, 1773), "Unterthanen," p. 35.

[29] "Keine Misthenne fliegt über die Stadtmauer." Joseph V. Lomberg, *Historisch-politische Staatsrechtsabhandlung von Abstellung der Missbräuche bey den Zünften und Handwerkern in den Landen teutscher Reichsfürsten* (Bonn, 1779), p. 13.

[30] Karl Bücher, *Die Entstehung der Volkswirtschaft*, I (16th ed.; Tübingen, 1922), pp. 443–444.

that some four thousand German towns, with a population of about seven million, fit into the statistical picture of the hometown community in about 1800. That meant about a quarter of the total German population, including German-speaking Austria and all of Prussia, not just Riehl's "individualized country": in the latter, the hometown proportion of the population was much greater. The three dozen or so great towns made up another 7 per cent, and the agricultural population was the other two-thirds.[31] Some nineteenth-century figures on the frequency of towns in the several German landscapes show roughly but unmistakably where the communities were; they were in the individualized country, beginning with one town for every square German mile in Württemberg and then along the scale of lesser frequency and so greater distances between towns.[32]

Württemberg	1
Nassau	1.25
Hessen-Darmstadt	1.3
Thuringia	1.5
Baden	1.7
Saxony (Kingdom)	1.7
Hessen-Kassel	1.8
Bavaria	2.35
Prussia (entire)	3.7
Hanover	3.9

A stroller through Württemberg could (and can) expect to strike a recognizable and incorporated town every seven kilometers, or every four English miles, without even staying on the main roads. In the Württemberg of 1821, with a population of a million and a

[31] The estimate is computed mainly from the figures in Franke, "Volkszahl deutscher Städte," p. 118. In Franke's tables the number of towns increases by a factor of about two and a half as the population halves; I project that pattern below his lower limit of five thousand to reach an approximation with which other evidence generally agrees, though most of the latter suggests that the hometown share of the population was actually greater than the projection from Franke allows. Note Johann Justi's estimate of about 40% below, Chapter V, n. 44. See also [Friedrich] Zahn, "Die Bevölkerung des deutschen Reichs im 19. Jahrhundert," VSDR, XI (1902), pp. I.167 to I.190; and Bevölkerungs-Ploetz: Raum und Bevölkerung in der Weltgeschichte, II (Würzburg, 1956), 60–76, 156–166.

[32] Otto Hausner, Vergleichende Statistik von Europa (Lemberg, 1865), I, 190.

half, almost exactly half the population lived in communities of hometown size; just under half lived on the land; and in the capital twenty-three thousand Stuttgart citizens lived alongside some five thousand tolerated residents and an unenumerated court and military establishment.[33]

The hometownsman was far more intimately involved with the total life of his community than either the city dweller or the peasant because all the spheres of his activities fell within the same boundary walls, and so did the activities of all his neighbors. The peasant lived close to his neighbors, but economically he was on his own and political power he had none; the city dweller lived by exchange, but among people who were not his neighbors and cousins and whose polity he did not actively share; the hometownsman lived by exchange among people he intimately knew and whose polity he fully shared. Peasants knew one another but did not need one another, and their politics were passive and rudimentary; city men needed one another but did not truly know one another, and politics were remote, formal, and abstract. The hometownsman both needed his neighbors and he knew them, and his politics incorporated what he needed and what he knew into a stable and circumscribed world. It will often be necessary to separate out the spheres of community life—political, economic, and social—in order to describe them, just as the states developed a kind of legal cloverleaf when they came to judge and legislate the community. But the hometownsman hardly distinguished the spheres, and the community in turn regarded him as one personality: citizen, workman, and neighbor.

[33] Computed from "Bevölkerung des Königreichs am 1 ᵗᵉⁿ November, 1821," *WJ*, 1822, pp. 89–176. Probably the true proportion for Germany in the period with which this study deals falls somewhere between the estimate of one-fourth based on Franke and the 1821 Württemberg case of one-half. The conditions of statistical knowledge allow no greater precision.

CHAPTER II

The Civic Community

No hometown constitution was quite like any other, but the communities behaved very much alike.[1] One handy theoretical way of saying just this would distinguish between structure and function: hometown institutions were structurally different but functionally similar. Explore this for a moment. Their structural diversity was a safeguard of their autonomy inasmuch as formal law and central administration must work with structures, not functions.[2] Consequently each community had a real interest in its own formal uniqueness; the more eccentric its institutions, the greater the advantage of those familiar with it. That was an important factor for the preservation of structural diversity.

The theoretical distinction, put together with the home town's middle size, leads to a further point, this one regarding functional similarity. Administrative practice itself tended to support the particular way in which the communities were like one another and unlike other administrative entities. In middle-sized communities, administrative and juridical powers legally deriving from state authority were organized into units coterminous with the social and political community, and in such places it was natural to ac-

[1] For a seventeenth-century general statement of the nature of towns, their weal and woe, Philipp Knipschildt, *Tractatus politico-historico-juridicus, de juribus et privilegiis civitatum Imperialum* . . . (Ulm, 1687), Book I, "Generalia continens circa Civitates municipales, quàm Imperiales," pp. 1–152.

[2] Cf. Cyril E. Black, *Of Modernization: A Study of Comparative History* (New York, 1966), p. 44.

cord those powers to the community's own leaders. Jurisdictions over sections of large cities, or over specialized activities within them, did not match up with social community, and neither did jurisdictions over aggregates of rural settlements; consequently in those places the organization of state authority conflicted with the boundaries of social community and tended to dissolve them, rather than coinciding with them (as in the home town) and thus tending to preserve the community's wholeness and individuality.[3]

Why the civic leadership of the communities should have wished to stay independent of the outside needs no explanation; conversely it relied entirely on its local position, on local resources and support. A town whose governing elements could operate independently of the internal social community lost its identity as home town. Consequently the civic leadership needed not only legal familiarity with peculiar local institutions, it also required social familiarity and close mutual ties with the community at large. There had to be regular reciprocal relations between leadership and citizenry; from that political fact resulted the extraordinary integrity and coherence of the community. Institutional eccentricity and close social integrity were two sides of the same familiarity that governed the life of the home town, upon which its stability and its independence depended, and to which it clung as the condition of its survival. The preceding chapter sketched the political incubator of the German hometown community from the outside; this one describes civic constitutions and leadership within; then the description will turn to the integrating functions of economic guilds; then the first section of the book will conclude with the community's defenses of familiarity, and its place within the German society that confronted the changes that began at the end of the eighteenth century.

Constitutions: Their sources and forms

By constitution I mean here those documents and accepted practices that described a town's rights of self-government and its particular internal institutions and procedures. Three main constitutional bases were Customs, Privileges, and Statutes. These were

[3] Karl Brater, "Gemeinde," *Deutsches Staats-Wörterbuch,* IV (Stuttgart, 1859), 113–114, n. 12.

names for technical legal categories, not definitions of substance. A Privilege usually was sovereign acknowledgment of a Custom, and a Statute was a written compilation of Customs and Privileges. The categorical name only identifies the law's immediate and formal source of authority. Custom was the name and justification for laws and procedures for which no written basis could be found, and a town's own constitutional basis normally resided in its Customs: *Stadt-Gewohnheiten* or *traditione*.[4] They became explicit only when they were adduced to support some legal decision or legislation. "Time out of mind" was their ultimate documentation, which is to say that they were practices for which nobody could find any obvious legal reason or any previous documented foundation. In legal analysis, Customs were any rules that had neither been provided nor annihilated by sovereign authority. The assumption that a Custom was ancient was a legal fiction or at best expressed the faulty memory of a generation. The assumption might or might not reflect historical reality; there was no way to tell, because by definition there was no documentary evidence of such a practice's antiquity or it would not have been called a Custom.

Laws based on medieval documents had no reason to carry the customary tag; neither did laws based on Roman or canon codes. Accordingly there is just as much reason to believe in the relative novelty of a Custom as in its antiquity, although of course much local law and constitutional autonomy did adduce very old legislation or litigation for its authority. Even Otto von Gierke, who as a convinced historical corporatist liked to assign a dimension of antiquity to customary law, could in honesty state only two criteria to validate it: *Ueberzeugung* and *Uebung*. That is, for a Custom to have the force of law it had to exist as a conviction of right and it had to be expressed in practice. Moreover, that conviction of right and that practice could not come from an individual or a transient aggregate of individuals; Custom had to be a communal understanding—*Gemeinüberzeugung*—of how the community did and properly ought to run. According to Gierke any corporate community, but only a corporate community (*organische Gemeinschaft*), might bear a body of customary law.[5]

---

[4] Riccius, *Stadt-Gesetzen*, p. 317.
[5] *Deutsches Privatrecht*, I (Leipzig, 1895), 164–166.

Consequently to pursue the moot antiquity of Custom here would be to sniff after red herrings. The important feature of Customs as hometown constitutional bases was not their unspecified age but their very specific localism and communalism. Inasmuch as they relied neither on principles of Roman law nor on general legislation by a sovereign (nor on any serious notion of natural law), they were almost by definition idiosyncratic; they drew their force from the community's individuality and gave force to the defense of its autonomy. Hometown leaders therefore emphasized Custom as the constitutional core of the community whenever they could; another good reason for doing so was that most of the vital life of most communities did in fact follow patterns that were unwritten, informal, and unsystematic. And finally, the contrast with written and codified Roman law and statute law meant that local law could be identified as German: it made "ius commune" an implicit equivalent for "praxi Germaniae", and "Gemeinderecht" an equivalent for "deutsche Gewohnheiten".

Because Custom, as Gierke said, had to be embodied and accepted by the whole community, the resort to it had the effect of integrating town government with the community as a whole. The communal base of customary law that Gierke saw was not his sentimental fancy, for Custom's strength rested politically on the need, by a magistracy subject to a nearby sovereign, to accommodate itself to the will and beliefs of the community it governed, so as to attract community support against that rival authority. Custom, consequently, was more important in territorial towns than in free imperial towns, so that in this respect territorial towns conform more nearly to the model of the hometown community than imperial towns do. Territorial town constitutions especially recognized that the source of constitutional Custom was the whole community, not its officers or rulers. Custom sought formal confirmation by "the town in common, the Bürgerschaft." [6] The authorities of an imperial town rarely could act against the will and conviction of the community they governed, to be sure, but they had less need to reflect the community's sense and will in order to govern it. They derived sovereign rights to legislate, judge, and administer from their status as imperial estates, and they had clear imperial protection against

[6] Riccius, *Stadt-Gesetzen,* pp. 354, 406.

neighboring territorial princes.[7] Imperial town constitutions depended more on Privilege and Statute, in writing, emanating from sovereign authority; their political and juridical situations favored that kind of derivation. Customs by contrast did not descend from sovereignty but arose from community, and so did the authority they rendered.

The name *Willkür* was often used to distinguish an individual local constitution, reliant upon Custom, from Privileges or Statutes coming from territorial or imperial authority; but a Willkür, though it emanated from the town, might be recognized by the sovereign too, if only to assert his right of recognition. *Willkür bricht Landrecht* was a slogan that helped the communities to assert their constitutional priority to state law; this was a variant of the more common and general legal tag, *Stadtrecht bricht Landrecht*—town law breaks state law. The rights embodied in a town's Willkür applied only to full community members, the Bürgerschaft, distinguishing them from the others who simply lived in the town space as direct subjects to territorial authority. The term Willkür itself has an instructive history. It had been used in medieval times to describe the statutes medieval corporations issued for themselves; in the course of the eighteenth century, according to Grimm, its legal meaning evolved from the original "free choice or self-determination" through "autonomy" to the "lawlessly individualistic, unprincipled, unmethodical choice and action" of an early nineteenth-century dictionary and its present meaning.[8]

Hometown constitutions could be made from scratch, brand new:

[7] But it was not clear in constitutional law whether *Landeshoheit* in an imperial town resided with the magistracy or the whole community; see Moser, *Teutsches Staats-Recht*, XLIII (n.p., 1751), 67–70. His reasonable conclusion: "Es kommt also auf die Verfassung einer jeden Statt insbesondere an: Wie vil Antheil an der Administration derer Reichs-Standischen Gerechtsamen der Magistrat, oder die Burgerschaft habe? [*sic*]" See also note 57 below.

[8] From "freie Wahl oder Selbstbestimmung" through "Eigenmächtigkeit" to "gesetzlos-individuelle, principienlos, unmethodische wollen und handeln"; the word and its variants occupy columns 204–217 of Vol. XIV, Abt. II, of the 1960 Leipzig edition of Jakob Grimm's *Deutsches Wörterbuch*. For a general treatment of the concept (mainly in the Middle Ages), Wilhelm Ebel, *Die Willkür: Eine Studie zu den Denkformen des älteren deutschen Rechts* (Göttingen, 1953); also Gierke, *Deutsches Privatrecht*, I, 183–184.

Willkür, Customs, and all. Christian G. Riccius, born son of a Lusatian master cloth worker and town councilman, himself a practicing lawyer and ultimately professor of law at Göttingen, described the procedure. In 1740 he published a book, "The Drafting of Town-Laws or *Statutis,* Especially for Territorial Towns." [9] After going through hundreds of territorial town privileges, statutes, and Willküre, he wrote a general guide for preparing communal constitutions. It was an almost impossible undertaking, for his task as lawyer and scholar was one of analysis and distinctions, whereas the essence of hometown law, eccentricities apart, was synthesis and blur. The legitimate sources of a town's constitution, he said, were Customs and Statutes, the two overlapping in fact when, as was commonplace, Statutes were confirmations of Customs. The Customs upon which town Statutes were based might be established in either of two ways. The first was in the case of a town with *ius statuendi,* an autonomous right somehow established in the past "to introduce good and useful Customs"; in such instances there was no need for state authorities to confirm or even know about them. Statutes of these towns did not need to conform to state codes or Roman law.[10] A town without *ius statuendi,* the second case, had to have state confirmation or at least "silent assent" for a new Custom to be valid. Either explicit recognition or a judicial decision based on a Custom had the force of positive confirmation; but a ruler's plain lack of interest was confirmation too as long as the new Custom did not conflict with state laws already existing. It was not necessary for the new Custom to be put in written form as long as it was publicly known—*ausdrücklich publiciret.*[11]

[9] *Entwurf von Stadt-Gesetzen oder Statutis vornehmlich der Land-Städte* (Frankfurt/Main, 1740). This is the best source of its kind: certainly the most sympathetic one, amidst the general and increasing hostility of lawyers and scholars.

[10] Ibid., pp. 318, 352–353. Very small towns rarely possessed the formal *ius statuendi;* apparently no Württemberg towns did; but that only meant that they might not introduce new statutes that directly contradicted state legal codes. Ferdinand C. Harpprecht, *Consiliorum Tubigensium . . . volumen,* II (Tübingen, 1696), 506–507.

[11] Of course there was uncertainty and controversy over what that meant: Riccius, *Stadt-Gesetzen,* pp. 314–324.

To lay out a town's constitution or to adjudicate by it, there had to be a system of ranking the different kinds of law that might come to bear and that were almost sure to conflict if they did. Riccius ranked them as follows:

1. the Customs of each place
2. its Statutory laws
3. the Customs preserved and practiced in the territory or state
4. state ordinances
5. imperial traditions and edicts
6. Roman and canon law.[12]

He described the Willkür as an arrangement between citizens and magistracy; it was a kind of constitutional law that did not require state confirmation because, he said, it was in the nature of private contract, not public law—here resorting to a distinction with no meaning whatever for the internal lives of the communities but which constantly plagued those who tried to analyze them. To modify such a pact, all Bürger or their representatives had to be summoned and to assent, whatever the state might say or do.[13] If a ruler, for example at the time of his accession, undertook to uphold the laws and customs of the corporate communities in his territory—*Städte und andere Universitäten* was the conventional formula—that had the effect of confirming existing institutions whatever their source. But since the ruler had a sovereign right to act in the interest of the common weal, he could correct Statutes whenever they began in the course of time to do injury to the town itself or to the "movement of trade." [14] The prince's advantage therefore lay (Riccius did not remark on this) in showing that times were changing or that the citizens' welfare was being neglected, in showing progress and disaffection. The magistracies' advantage lay in showing that all was well, and just as it always had been.

Riccius really meant to say that local affairs should be left to local people and state affairs to the state, but the effort to sort them out in terms of constitutional authority, and of private and public law, created contradictions, confusion, and even legal absurdities of a kind not apparent if a town was left to itself and its consti-

---

[12] Ibid., pp. 324–327.   [13] Ibid., pp. 403–407.   [14] Ibid., pp. 356, 376.

tution left unformulated. Drafters of constitutional documents tried to include the elements of authority Riccius identified, but could only jumble them together. In 1698 the little Lusatian town of Seidenberg promulgated a constitutional document with a title that got most of them in: [15]

STATUTE
and
WILLKÜR
of the
TOWN OF SEIDENBERG
in Upper Lusatia
as it has been
renewed by sovereign consent
amplified by the will of the whole citizenry
and graciously confirmed
also made public and read out
for the regular observance of the inhabitants
with ratification by the Town Council in the month of
February, 1698.

The declared aim of most written town Statutes was to bring peace and composure within; they were efforts to create conditions of assurance, or familiarity. The Seidenberg preamble said that next to divine guidance, what a community needed most was "the maintenance of good governance, and together with that, confident neighborly life within, so that each will understand where his living comes from and his rights, as well as his obligations, and have them before his eyes." Frequently they appeared after a time of flux or dissension. Territorial Bautzen's constitutional draft of 1687, composed of earlier Statutes combined with Customs "from ancient

---

[15] "*Statuta* und Willkühr des Städtchens Seidenberg, in der Ober-Lausitz, wie solche auf Herrschaftlichen *Consens* erneuert, mit Bewilligung der gesammten Bürgerschaft vermehret, und gnädig *confirmiret*, und zu der Einwohner beständigen *Observanz* bey der Raths-Bestätigung *mens. Febr.* 1698 *publiciret* und abgelesen worden." D. August Schott, ed., *Sammlungen zu den Deutschen Land- und Stadtrechten*, II (Leipzig, 1773), 171–190. The first part of the document was a promise by Hans Hanbold von Einsiedel, Lord of the territory of Seidenberg, etc., etc., to uphold the statute, and an order to all his officials and subjects to recognize it and observe it. The official signature was the Bürgermeister's.

times," undocumented before and now stated for the first time, alluded repeatedly to recent turmoil and change that had made it necessary to clarify the town's rights, especially against outsiders.[16] The imperial town Nördlingen's constitution of 1650 opened by speaking of "the unsettled course of many years past, with its resulting disorders, dissensions, errors, and abuses," which the Council hoped publication of the Law and Custom of the town would overcome, by assuring to government and citizenry "peaceful conditions, propriety, and respectability."

The Nördlingen Statute had five main parts. It began with religious and moral questions: such things got close attention in seventeenth-century constitutions but less later on, when guilds assumed a more important role in such matters.[17] It listed the curses and blasphemies that were forbidden, on pain of a transgressor's "body, life, honor, and goods"; it ordered church attendance, especially on Easter, and promised to punish fornication with a jail term on bread and water followed by a public shotgun wedding; it denounced excessive drinking ("such drunkards as pour anything they have down their gullets") and gambling ("regardless of class —*ohne Standts Unterschied*"). It forbade nocturnal street disturbances by apprentices and journeymen "when they have a snootful (*wenn sie die Nase begossen*)"; they were to be put in jail and kept there until they were "good and cooled off (*abgekühlt*)." A second part described the conditions under which citizenship might be acquired, including a continuous five-year period of observation by the Council, and it regulated business relations among citizens, including a prohibition of the sale of real estate to outsiders without special dispensation from the Council. Part three governed marriage and family relations: laws on the degree of permissible kinship, on parental consent, on inheritance, and so on; loss of citizenship was to follow any marriage with an outsider not sanctioned by the Council. Part four organized the care of orphans, overseen by a commission of three: two Councilors and a member elected by the community; and part five laid out certain police jurisdictions: a court to handle brawls, assault, and libel, another to issue building permits, fire regulations, and the like. In the concluding clause, citizens were forbidden to appeal decisions of town

[16] Ibid., II, 1–35.   [17] See below, pp. 105–106.

courts to imperial courts; the Town Council was last resort. Then in boldface underneath: "NOW EVERYONE KNOWS HOW HE SHALL ACT—*Darnach weiss sich jeder zu richten.*" [18]

"One cannot give," wrote Johann Jakob Moser, "any description of what a town is, or of what town law is, that would be applicable everywhere in Germany or at all times; this is my view, and I shall now proceed amply to prove it." He did, amply. The best generalizations he could manage were that a town community included both civic authorities and subordinates within it, it was rather a nicer place than a village, and there was some organization of the trades; but none of these particulars was invariably present. It depended on local circumstances and usage.[19] Territorial community ordinances of the eighteenth century made little effort to impose uniformity. Moser himself wrote one for Württemberg, promulgated in 1758; and what it said for example about the election of town officers was that "communities shall keep their traditional rights of choosing and electing their leaders, officials, and common servants, unimpaired and henceforth," though they were urged not to have too many officers, and on the other hand not to yield political authority into too few hands.[20] The Bavarian Town and Market Instruction of 1748, though full of sage political advice, stipulated no forms for local elections and made no definitions of the electoral body, nor any outlines of administrative procedures; it simply assumed that town officers would be chosen somehow, and the town would run somehow, and declared that the state would use its confirmation power as a veto right in obvious cases of miscarriage.[21] The Baden Community Ordinance of 1760 was a purely fiscal document, autocratic enough in tone but not political at all; it ordered clear financial accounts, to follow elaborate tables supplied in the ordinance; there was nothing whatever about how Baden towns worked or ought to work politically.[22] State ordinances were really

[18] Schott, *Sammlungen*, I (Leipzig, 1772), 201–240.
[19] *Teutsches Staats-Recht*, V (2d ed.; Frankfurt/Main, 1752), 325–328.
[20] Quoted in Moser, *Landeshoheit im Weltlichen*, III, 157.
[21] Wiguläus X. A. Kreittmayr, ed., *Sammlung der neuest- und merkwürdigsten Churbaierischen Generalien und Landesverordnungen . . .* (Munich, 1771), pp. 558–574.
[22] Carl F. Gerstlacher, ed., *Sammlung aller Baden-Durlachischen . . . Anstalten und Verordnungen*, III (Frankfurt/Main, 1774), 1–34.

directed not to the communities themselves but to the states' own civil servants, instructing them on how they should deal with the communities and the posture they should take toward them if there was trouble, not on how the communities' own affairs should normally be conducted. No pattern of the life inside the home town can be found in them.

Constitutions: Internal structure

A pattern of hometown political institutions consistent enough to be useful does emerge, though, from inspecting a great many of them, if one may blur or ignore the formal differences in a way no jurist or civil servant could. To think of institutions as patterns of civic behavior, and to discern them in events and social relations rather than in legal diagrams, is to approach the kind of understanding of the community that the hometownsman had, even though doing this can produce no clearer general evidence of it than the jurist could: indeed, probably less. That is the price of it. The jurist's own problem was not so much that he did not understand what went on in a home town if he went into one. He understood all too well; but his discipline, the tools of his trade, did not allow him to seize or manipulate it. Behind the screen of idiosyncratic labels and procedures there was a regularity in the organization of status and authority, a regularity a hometownsman might have recognized if he had traveled from place to place, and if in each place he had taken the time and trouble to work out which people were in which political body, and what they could do: something he knew in his own community without troubling much about labels.

The most important political body was the Inner Council, usually with from six to a dozen members. It might be called the Smaller Council, or the Magistracy, or the Court, or the *Schöffenstuhl* or the *Vogtei*, or bear some other name, depending on the occasion when an institution so named jelled as a hometown Inner Council; it might simply be called the Six or the Nine. The Inner Council were the main formulators and executors of community policies and affairs; they held most judicial authority; we should have to use a great many words to describe the things which they did without, again, needing to think much about what kind of authority they were exercising. Membership was ordinarily for life, either stipulated so in law, or in fact by customary reelection, or by effective control of the elective process by the Inner Council.

Major decisions were joint, and were issued collegially. But each member had a particular sphere of authority, responsibility, and patronage. One member might administer town properties outside the walls, attributes of the community rather than of individual citizens: forests, fishponds, inns, even villages. That would include the power to lease such facilities, and authority over the people who lived in them or used them.

A second Councilor might administer community rights or properties held as trusts or endowments. Many of these had once been church, imperial, territorial, or personal attributes that had come into the sphere of town authority for charitable and social purposes: schools, churches, hospitals and poorhouses, loans and donations to the needy. They were very important resources, providing important patronage powers, and commonly they were entrusted to a special committee composed of councilmen and one or two other citizens: *Pflegamt* or *Pflegerat* was the commonest name for it. Its powers might include the appointment of pastors, though pastoral appointments usually followed a procedure of their own, with joint participation of the town with ecclesiastical and state authorities.

A third Councilor might have special responsibility for taxes and fees: those levied on full citizens, and the special ones levied on such civic categories as tolerated residents and Jews. That authority would include, especially in the case of noncitizens, important powers over the people taxed. But in many towns there were large bodies of people who escaped the system altogether, or nearly so: a monastery, with its own population and its own civic scheme, or a university, or a state court or administrative center which, although it resided within the town, had a quite separate political life.

Another Councilor might bear special responsibility for police, meaning not just public discipline and security—the American blue-uniformed arm—but sanitation, foodstuffs, public amusements, economic regulations, information media, perhaps the maintenance of roads. Police authority touched so many matters that the Council was especially likely to exercise it collegially; trades guilds too were apt to become involved in preparing and enforcing police decisions; moreover, in towns of any importance, the state government was likely to keep an eye on police affairs insofar as they affected interests outside the town.

Also collegial was an equally important power: the acceptance of new citizens into the community, the extension of the *Bürgerrecht*. Here again the guilds had important rights, to be examined later. Reciprocally each Councilor had special authority over certain of the community's guilds, and got special perquisites from them.

Chief of the Inner Council was the Bürgermeister. He too might bear any of a great many names, and often there was more than one office with Bürgermeister in its title, but, if so, one man usually acted as governing or first Bürgermeister, and here I shall identify him alone with the title. He usually held office for life or for a very long time, by law, by seniority on the Council, or by election; or else the office circulated among a very small handful of men. Changes rarely reflected a conflict of political factions or of interests within the town; that would be a sign of serious trouble for the hometown community, a situation for which it was not equipped.[23] Rather it was a polite succession or rotation. Often, where the rules prohibited self-succession but where there was no internal party division (as in parts of the American South of modern times), alternate Bürgermeister served as front men for those temporarily out of office but still in effective authority. The Bürgermeister directed day-to-day business of the town, although the actual administrative labor, especially in larger places, was carried out by appointed officers.

Bürgermeister and Inner Council (or a committee they dominated) appointed lesser town officials and servants, from treasurer to organist to midwife to goosegirl—a civil patronage list of several dozens even in very small communities. Appointive office might include the headship of guilds, but guild offices usually were filled through some joint procedure involving guild membership or its

[23] See the case of Aachen, Ch. IV below.

elected representatives. The appointive power, like leasing and police powers, was an important connection among Bürgermeister, Inner Council, and citizenry.

There were more formal connections too, working in both directions. Inner Council membership was reached by way of an Outer Council (or Greater Council, or Citizens' Council; here the variety of forms and names was infinite). Not only was the Outer Council the main recruiting ground for new Inner Councilors, it itself sometimes elected them, or else Inner Council joined Outer as an electoral college, or the heads of certain guilds were added for electoral purposes; or there might be a special electoral committee appointed *ad hoc* for any election, assuring a degree of cooptive renewal consistent with political circumstances. The Outer Council itself was chosen by similar procedures, but with greater participation from lower political levels and a wider choice of candidates: usually the whole citizenry was eligible in the home towns, though there might be a distinction between those who were eligible for Council membership and those who were not. The Outer Council was much larger than the Inner, with twenty-five to fifty members, or even a hundred or more. In addition to its electoral functions and its place as a stage along the road to higher office (and as a place to give civic recognition to those who sought it), it traditionally had a right to oversee town finances—insofar as they were intelligible, and insofar as it could get at them.

The Outer Council therefore represented the citizenry in some degree and served as a check upon the magistracy. Often it had been established originally with that mandate, and legal analysts sometimes tried to describe it so: the Inner Council as an executive body, and the Outer Council as a representative one. But to distinguish executive from representative processes, like so many other distinctions, not only misses the quality of hometown political life but obscures it. Executive authority did not act on its own and then citizenry respond, nor did citizenry determine that authority should take a given action. Magistrates knew pretty well how any executive action would be received, by whom; and citizens could make their views known before a decision was reached, or even when it was announced to them; for the issues did not change, and the process of decision was continuous. Authority met citizen constantly in a simultaneous and reciprocal encounter, grounded in familiarity and in the absence of outside sanctions. The guilds were another channel through which authority communicated with citizen and citizen with authority. Yet another channel (especially where guilds had not assumed explicitly political powers) were leaders associated with the several districts of a community, or with some other appropriate breakdown of the citizenry—*Viertelmeister*. Community officials called upon the Viertelmeister to ascertain the community's views, and to communicate their own decisions to the community. A town's Viertelmeister were precinct captains in an emphatically one-party polity.

Turn now from an imprecise institutional model that never really existed to a precise constitution that did exist but was unique: there is no middle ground, as the jurists learned. The town of Rottweil is a practical choice because there are detailed studies both by an eighteenth-century native and by an able modern historian.[24]

The political institutions of Rottweil were so smoothly tucked back into one another that it is hard to know where to take hold and where description should begin. Probably the best place is with its council of twenty-six magistrates (plus a Town Clerk [*Syndicus*] with no vote) which I shall call a Greater Council; there, if anywhere, lay the center of constitutional authority in Rottweil, and the leading members of the smaller working organs of the town were drawn from it. Two elements composed this Greater Council: Members or Assessors of the Imperial Court, eight in number, and eighteen Guildmasters. There were two Guildmasters from each of the town's nine guilds, elected, when vacancies occurred, by the guilds, and then appointed by the continuing Council after its own investigation. For political purposes the guild Eighteen was divided into an Old and a New Bench.

The Court was in form a vestigial remnant of an actual imperial court that had once had jurisdiction in that neighborhood, but in the seventeenth and eighteenth centuries it had lost any real im-

---

[24] Johann B. Hofer, *Kurzer Unterricht über die äussere und innere Verfassung der Reichsstadt Rotweil, zum Gebrauche ihrer obern Schule* (Ulm, 1796); Adolf Laufs, *Die Verfassung und Verwaltung der Stadt Rottweil, 1650–1806* (Stuttgart, 1963).

perial judicial functions and the town had gained control of it—
whether it had lost its outside powers because the town had got
control, or the town had been able to get control because it had
lost its outside powers, is not the kind of question to ask. As a
town organ, besides combining with the Guildmasters into the
Greater Council, it provided the community's most active execu-
tives.

Election to the Court was lifelong except for cause, and was
semicooptive: each year a committee made up of the Bürgermeister,
the *Schultheiss* or chief officer of the Court, two specified Guildmasters, and another Guildmaster chosen by these four met to appoint
an electoral college for the coming year; it had to be composed of
one Assessor and six Guildmasters. Whenever a place on the Court
became vacant, these seven elected a replacement, but their choice
was normally determined by seniority on the Greater Council of
twenty-six, of whom all but the existing Court itself were the heads
of guilds. Thus political advance in Rottweil came from Guildmas-
tership to member of the Greater Council to Assessor of the Court
and thus to executive office. If in the course of a year the office of
Bürgermeister or of Schultheiss became vacant, the electoral seven
proposed three names from the Court, and the citizenry chose
one.[25]

The magistracy was distributed into a number of administrative
bodies:

1. The main executive organ of the town was the Narrower
Council (*Engere Rat*), composed of the Bürgermeister, the Schultheiss of the Court, three other Assessors, and the Speakers of the
two guild Benches, plus the Clerk.

2. The Town Court, with the Schultheiss presiding, included the
Assessors of the Imperial Court (but excluding the Bürgermeister)
and the Guildmasters of the New Bench (but excluding the
Speaker of that Bench). It dealt with debts and with adjudication
that required written procedures and legal knowledge.

3. The Bürgermeister's Office was presided over by the Bürgermeister as chief executive and responsible officer for the town, but
the Office included Schultheiss, Town Clerk, and a rotating Guildmaster. It served also as a judicial court of first instance, with

25 Hofer, *Rotweil*, pp. 99–104.

summary procedures; it could refer cases to the Town Court.

4. The Schultheiss' Office—Schultheiss and one other Assessor from the Court, and the Speaker of one of the guild Benches—exercised police powers and oversaw the town budget.

5. The Chief Steward's Office (*Obervogteyamt*) supervised the government of several villages subject to Rottweil's jurisdiction as successors to the Empire: one Assessor as Chief Steward and one Guildmaster from the New Bench as Controller.

6. The Hunt Steward's Office (*Pürschenvogteyamt*), with its one Court Assessor as Steward and another Guildmaster of the New Bench as Controller, governed another rural area with its villages and their inhabitants.

7. The Fraternal Office (*Bruderschaftsamt*) controlled a number of charitable endowments and governed the town's four Fraternal Villages, revenues from which were ostensibly directed to social services: again one Assessor as Chief Caretaker (*Oberpfleger*), a Guildmaster of the New Bench as Controller, and a regular administrative officer called the *Bruderschaftshauspfleger*.

8. The last of this category was the Hospital Trust—the *Spitaloberpflegamt,* with the same organization as the Fraternal Office, charged with administering the public hospital, and with civil jurisdiction over the one village of which the hospital was landlord.[26]

Each of these offices had therefore one of the eight Assessors of the Imperial Court at its head, in the pattern of the distribution of functions among Inner Councilors described in the general model of a hometown constitution. An elected guild officer sat on each too; here as in many other places, administrative offices had to include a representative of the Outer Council or of the guilds. In Rottweil the constitutional role of the Inner Council in the model was divided between Court and Narrower Council. But the personnel of the two largely overlapped, and the pattern of authority was the same. An unusual feature of Rottweil was the large territory and many villages outside its walls, governed by virtue of its territorial sovereignty as an imperial town—a difference of degree, and not a clear distinction, but one which gave extensive

26 Ibid., pp. 105–109.

powers to the offices that controlled such places. The town itself had about four thousand inhabitants, almost all citizen families; but it governed twenty-five villages with almost nine thousand inhabitants, and these were not citizens but subjects, with no constitutional role in town government. Their interests against the townsmen were defended neither through Rottweil constitutional channels nor by means of corporate institutions of their own, but by outside professional officials—in 1783 for example by a Privy Councilor from the principality of Fürstenberg, one of Rottweil's largest territorial neighbors, with its seat at Donaueschingen.[27]

Beside the eight main political offices was a handful of fiscal departments: the Treasury, whose director, an Assessor, received as the town's chief fiscal officer the income from its properties and leases; the Department of Public Buildings and Forests, with a mixture of political leaders and technical specialists; a Buildings Inspector to oversee private construction. There was a Town Bursar's Office, with a Cashier who accounted for all direct cash incomes: citizens' taxes, permanent fees levied on business locations within the town, tolls, beer and wine excises, emigration tax, fines, fees for entry into the trades, for liquor licenses, for rural distilling, and leases of legal monopolies including the sale of salt, and the collection of ashes, rags, edible greens, and gravel. And there was a similar Land Bursar's Office to collect rural taxes due the town.[28]

Finally came a long list of standing government committees. First in protocol and probably in importance was the Accounts Committee, composed of Bürgermeister, Schultheiss, Speakers of the two Benches, and Speaker of the Eighteen: they undertook to inspect the town's books and report on them publicly. By dropping the last member this became the Economy Committee, which had to approve large expenditures by any of the agencies. The Highway Committee was the Economy Committee, plus the Clerk, plus the Assessor with special responsibility for roads, plus the Land Bursar. The Crafts Committee—Schultheiss, speaker of the Old Bench, and a secretary—administered certain economic regulations. The School Committee included the town pastor along with

[27] Laufs, *Rottweil, 1650–1806*, pp. 112–115.
[28] Hofer, *Rotweil*, pp. 109–112.

the usual contingent from the Greater Council. There was a Committee on Orphans to administer wardships, and a Boundary Court, and a Committee on Cattle and Meadows, and so on.[29]

The paid civil list of Rottweil included 132 offices in 1783. About a third of them were held by the political officials already described, the 26 Court Assessors and Guildmasters who dominated the departments, agencies, and committees; and the rest were a long list of civic employees: chief physician at 231 gulden, mole catcher at 60 gulden, gatekeepers at 22 gulden, a trumpeter at 12 gulden. A hundred and thirty-two public appointments in a town with surely no more than eight hundred citizen households, probably under five hundred: no wonder it worked as a Bürger regime and not one of civil administration. Regular representative bodies would have been pointless and redundant. Administration was intermeshed with social life and circumstances; appeals from executive decision could be formal but more probably were informal, taking place before or after a decision—if that is the word—had been made.

Constitutions: Government and citizenry

The great complexity of Rottweil's legal institutions when converted into written form (I have simplified them drastically here) and the small size and social intimacy of the living community are incongruous to one another; and the incongruence shows the impossibility of reducing the interwoven skein of civic relations into a scheme based on hierarchy of authority, on a principle of whose right to tell whom what he shall do. The incredibly involved and top-heavy organization of government cannot possibly have determined how the town ran, and its very symmetry is implausible; but if it did not control still it reflected political interplay within the community, especially in the way every civic position was elaborately related with every other. The tangled elaboration of Rottweil's constitution results from an effort to reflect formally a kind of relation and influence that was essentially informal. These were laws and constitutions that tried to do work we might now assign to sociology. Personal and group relations were the important thing, and constitutional office followed from them. But there were also direct constitutional channels for the reciprocal relations

[29] Ibid., pp. 112–114.

among citizens with high office, citizens with lesser office, and citizens without office; in Rottweil these were organized through the groups into which the citizenry was divided: the nine guilds and the *Herrenstube*.

The Herrenstube, though its name means something like gentlemen's chamber, was in no sense noble, nor was the term "patriciate" ever applied to it. Membership was accessible; it depended on profession or office, not on birth. It included town officers, and those citizens who "earned by the pen" or who lived from independent incomes: thus generally those who were not members of any of the craft guilds; but craftsmen and their sons could and did enter it by way of town office. Many communities had some local corporation like the Rottweil Herrenstube as one of the divisions of their citizenry, comparable to the guilds but not made up of ordinary craftsmen. The Herrenstube was perhaps a first among equals, alongside the guilds properly called. It included (among others) the most prominent people in town. But it was not a party to political contention with guild citizenry along class lines: that is one mark of the hometown community. Its chief, the *Oberstubenherr*, was elected by the whole chamber from among three candidates nominated by a special committee of the Court (its three senior members after the Bürgermeister and Schultheiss), and its internal constitution was very like those of the guilds.[30] It differed from the guilds mainly in its semiofficial composition, a presumptive prestige that went with membership, and a ceremonial precedence over the craft guilds. It does not seem to have had any special constitutional powers of its own.

The nine constitutional guilds (*Zünfte*) of Rottweil were the main link between citizenry and administration; for every citizen belonged to a guild (or the Herrenstube), and guild representatives, the Eighteen, sat in the politically central Greater Council and on the administrative organs. Thus in Rottweil the guilds themselves were recognized as important political bodies, and assumed there a character as appropriate to their political functions as to their economic ones, or more so. They followed occupational lines

[30] Hofer describes the Herrenstube constitutionally in *Rotweil*, pp. 119–120; Laufs gives a more functional and social description in *Rottweil, 1650–1806*, pp. 42–46.

but were not occupationally pure, for to assign a separate constitutional role to each of the dozens of organized occupations in the town would have produced chaos. The occupations had their own economic corporations (called *Innungen*), and these were grouped into the nine constitutional guilds. Some small unorganized trades were not specifically assigned to guilds; and their practitioners, called *Gespielten,* were assigned by lot to those guilds which included such occupational odds and ends. There was some occupational logic to the groupings, and some hometown social logic: it is hard to tell where logic leaves off and the distribution of trades among the constitutional guilds was accidental or governed by factors we cannot perceive. Some seem determined by status, some by materials used, some by the kind of relation with customers, some arbitrary.

1. The Smiths' Guild included all the metal-working trades.

2. The Bakers' and Millers' Guild included only those two trades.

3. The Clothiers included some of the textile trades, wagoners, some specified but miscellaneous minor trades, and Gespielten. The logic may be that textiles and wagon-making were trades with a rural cast to them.

4. The Butchers included butchers and Gespielten.

5. The Retailers included small sellers of ready-made goods, surgeons and bathers, certain decorative trades, druggists, bookbinders, wigmakers, and Gespielten. These were all trades with inferior or suspect status in the hometown view of things.

6. Tailors included most of the clothing trades, cabinetmakers, and Gespielten.

7. The Shoemakers' and Saddlers' Guild included those trades and Gespielten.

8. Tanners included certain miscellaneous trades and Gespielten besides the tanners themselves.

9. The Weavers' and Ropemakers' Guild included those two relatively unskilled trades, and Gespielten.

Each guild was organized in a pattern analogous to the constitution of the town itself, but with more emphasis on economic matters and a stage closer to the citizenry. In each there was a Guild Court of thirteen, which indirectly produced a nominating committee (the Five) for internal guild offices and for the two representatives on the Eighteen; when an office was open the whole guild chose one from among three candidates proposed by the nominating committee. Should there be conflict between the town executive magistracy and the Eighteen, immobilizing town government, the nine electoral Fives were supposed to mediate, a procedure approaching intervention by the citizenry to resolve conflict; should that fail the citizens were to be assembled by guilds, to vote by majority within each guild on the issue at stake. Should this last expedient fail, the town faced open conflict between government and citizenry; hometown institutions had broken down, and there had to be recourse to outside arbitration or the imperial courts.

The purpose of this staged apparatus for resolving disputes was, candidly, "to smother conflicting emotions"; at no point did anyone in the town have the power to overrule one side and enforce a decision.[31] "Smothering" is a good word for the way the home town coped with internal differences. Rottweil possessed a detailed legal description of the process because of imperial intervention to meet conflicts that arose in 1579, 1688, 1713, 1752, and 1782, and the outlined procedure comes from an imperial recess of 1782. Rottweil's free imperial status encouraged full constitutional description of its internal procedures. A territorial town, with its more subtle and precarious relation to sovereignty, was unlikely to find it feasible or wise to work things out in such detail, though sometimes they did. But the process there was very similar: differences within the leadership were resolved by gradual appeals down through the levels of influence, expanding progressively toward involving all the citizenry if need be. The smothering of friction was all the more effective when done socially without resort to formal procedures; it was very effective indeed, and the internal key to the preservation of the community's individuality and autonomy. The virtue—if it is a virtue—of smothering conflict rather than adjudicating it is that friction is overcome before it takes explicit form. Put in political terms, that is the advantage of a one-party system

[31] Hofer, *Rotweil*, p. 137; his discussion of the guild structure, pp. 120–137; that of Laufs in *Rottweil, 1650–1806*, pp. 46–50.

over organized partisan debate and over systematic adjudication: the suppression or evasion of conflict.[32] Evidence of partisan or constitutional conflict in the communities is rare, and that is not only because few people cared to write about it; more significantly, conflict rarely crystallized into a sorting out of sides.

Like any other polity, the home town at any given time had an indistinctly defined group of influential insiders that might be called an elite. But they were located within irregularly concentric circles, or an uneven shading from great local influence to little, rather than clearly set apart: perhaps that is always so. Certain families tended to persist in community leadership over the generations, and older families had an advantage over newer ones. But their positions were not prescriptive, or only vaguely or partially so; they could be lost in a generation. Ruling circles were not closed, although a new family might take a generation or two to develop an accepted position. The achievement of influence was probably slower in a community based on familiarity than in a place that must turn instead to special skills, money, or support from outside to identify its leaders—qualities easier to acquire quickly. The base of a hometown leader's influence was with the community, and depended in the end on the possession of qualities —family tradition included—that his fellow townsmen respected and needed more than they envied or mistrusted them, and that is a long way from hereditary right. Established political families came persistently to lead hometown regimes because they chose to and because they operated that kind of regime well, and if they ceased to do either they disappeared from high office. Family tree was probably more important for becoming a Bürger in the first place than it was for a Bürger to become a Councilor.

It was a regime not of oligarchs but of communarchs, a regime of uncles. For the hometown leader was a Bürger, and could not think of his place in terms other than those of his own town and its Bürgerschaft. The Bürgerschaft were his acquaintances or his relatives; a great many of his acquaintances *were* his relatives, and almost every Bürger had a relative or a close acquaintance in a

---

[32] Ralf Dahrendorf's discussion of this issue in contemporary German society could be addressed directly to the home town of the eighteenth century: *Society and Democracy in Germany* (New York, 1967), pp. 135–148.

position of political influence. Social, political, and economic relations intertwined, giving the community great strength even as it gave great local power to the uncles. That was the situation that written constitutions and electoral schemes sought to embody and assure. What one thinks of the community depends on whether one chooses to emphasize its integrity and stability, or the power of the regime. In ordinary circumstances the citizenry had no formal participatory power to legislate, directly and freely to elect, or demand an accounting. As for informal ways: what the citizens had to say about politics to their joint uncles that governed the community was rarely severe, though there was grumbling sometimes, and occasionally a crisis. They had to get along at birthday parties, weddings, and funerals, and then there was the disposition of the family bakery to think of, and the master's certificate that went with it. Similarly the uncles were bound to observe the ties of family, trade, and friendship. And so there was no serious dissent, and the community worked very smoothly on the whole. A difference in political status and in legal authority between citizen and councilman caused little trouble while the other lines of relation held—but remember that the principles of all this coziness were diffusion and suppression. The community could and did absorb fiscal disorders and domestic grumbling, and even outside pressure, unless the difference between leaders and citizenry became not only political but social and economic as well, creating lines of internal division that were clear and rigid.

The citizenry without office was not politically helpless. Ordinarily it did not influence government by regularly electing new leadership, throwing out the old, or even threatening to do so. There might, though, be procedures for just that. An apparently common procedure for electing town councils in the non-Prussian parts of eighteenth-century Westphalia was for the citizenry annually to assemble and for an electoral committee to be chosen from among them by lot. The electoral committee chose the Inner Council, in some instances voting in conjunction with the old Council or a comparable body. It tended to choose members of prominently established families, but not because citizenry had been excluded from the election. In the town of Warendorf, which followed a procedure like this, seventy-eight family names appeared on the Inner Council between 1749 and 1802, thirty of them only briefly. For fifty family names to recur in the course of fifty years in the Council of a town with thirty-five hundred inhabitants—meaning probably no more than two hundred surnames in all the town—hardly constitutes oligarchic rule.[33] In the Lower Bavarian town of Plattling the citizenry (about 170 families) came annually to the town hall, where the Outer Council and the Inner Council joined to elect the Bürgermeister; Inner Council vacancies were filled from the Outer, and Outer Council vacancies were filled by election by the whole citizenry.[34] These were territorial towns. In Reutlingen, commonly held to be the most democratic of the imperial towns, all officers left office several days before each annual election, in which then all citizens participated on a formally equal basis. That refreshed the relation between citizenship and leadership periodically. But mainly it served to remind officers that they as hometown leaders were Bürger like the rest; the patterns of Reutlingen politics, whatever the election procedures, were not very different from those of other towns.[35]

The influence of citizens lay less in procedures like these than in the fact that the leader could not get away from them any more than they could get away from him. A position of influence in an enclosed familiar community required at least the toleration of the citizenry. In such circumstances there were far more effective ways to influence leadership than elective machinery could have offered. They were different ways. Anybody might have a pretty daughter or an energetic son to bargain with, for example. A leader's business could drop off; he could be slandered and ignored; his children could be ridiculed and bullied by their fellows in the

[33] This despite the efforts of Alfred Hartlieb von Wallthor to make it seem so, in conformity with received historical generalizations: *Die landschaftliche Selbstverwaltung Westfalens in ihrer Entwicklung seit dem 18. Jahrhundert,* I. Teil (Münster, 1965), pp. 25, 29–31. He also notes a sharp contrast between the territorial towns of Prussian Westphalia and non-Prussian territorial towns in a natively identical region: evidence of the effects of Prussian local administration in the early eighteenth century.

[34] Franz Zacher, "Plattlings Kampf um Selbstverwaltung (16.–18. Jahrhundert)," *VHVN,* LXXI (1938), 51.

[35] For the constitution of Reutlingen see D. Fetzger, "Ueber die Regierungsverfassung der Reichstadt Reutlingen," *JM,* V (1795), 254–292; and Laufs, *Rottweil, 1650–1806,* pp. 54–56, and the sources cited thereto.

street, at the well, and in the schoolyard. For one Bürger to say to another, "We do not go to the Stag any more," or "I think I shall start buying my meat from Kräutlein"—these are serious statements in a small German town nowadays, seriously received and silently digested as the wary hearers think out what postures they will adopt to this phenomenon; and I am confident that they were even more serious in the circumscribed world of the home town of two centuries ago. To be sure the speaker risked (and risks) retaliation. But where leaders were men whose family made shoes, who gossiped and drank at a regular tavern, and whose children grew up with the children of the rest of the citizenry, that kind of influence from the citizenry penetrated the leadership even as patronage and administrative power from the leadership penetrated the citizenry. It was a little like two folded hands that met and interlocked, except that the two did not have to be equal and balanced to unite, and anyway the relation was more complex than a bilateral one. It was more like a round net, its cords and threads of many different gauges, but each tied somewhere to every other, and tied everywhere to all the rest. That gave the community its form and its strength.

Infirmities and remedies

Such a community could keep the close texture and tough circumference upon which its strength depended only for so long— using the same examples—as the leadership was vulnerable to the community's esteem and economic choice, and its children vulnerable to the community's cruelty. That is why the emergence of a freed and self-contained leadership, summarily described before as a patriciate, almost surely meant trouble for the home town. This kind of oligarchy differed in several rather clear ways from normal hometown leadership, and a hometown constitution ceased to work effectively if its leadership assumed patrician characteristics.[36]

The most obvious patrician characteristic was its exclusive or at least highly privileged position in the government of a town. That is the burden of Moser's definition: "certain old indigenous families

[36] The first four patrician characteristics are listed neatly in Alfred O. Stolze, *Der Sünfzen zu Lindau* (Konstanz, 1956), p. 13.

which by virtue of the town's constitution [*Regiment*] or their personal rank [*Würde*] enjoy, either by law or customary observance, privileges over the rest of the citizens or inhabitants of such towns." Patrician status was a caste, an estate or *Stand*, recognizable in places away from home (hometown leadership was not). It was not the same thing as nobility, and it might appear either in a territorial or an imperial town.[37] Hometown leadership tended to fall into family patterns too, and recognized patriciates, on the other hand, were by no means impregnable. Formal reinforcements undoubtedly made the patriciate more exclusive, less mobile, and genealogically more static. But legal definition was not the most important difference between patrician oligarchy and hometown communarchy.

A second mark of a patriciate is social distinctiveness from the Bürgerschaft, and stubborn resistance by the patrician estate against penetration by the commonality, on principle: something beyond the usual prejudice against marrying below oneself. Patrician families married among themselves, or with other patrician families from other places, and rarely with the lower elements of their own cities (although this happened). By contrast, hometown leadership, however stabilized and influential at home, rarely intermarried with similar leading elements from other towns. Sometimes a hometown leader had married outside, but apparently no more often than other citizens had, and I suspect in fact less often; commonly his children married members of other Bürger families of the community.

A third criterion was the economic or occupational one: wealth or at least a secure economic position deriving from land ownership, investments, state salaries, or wholesale commerce: all these being lines of connection with the outside, and sources of immunity from local pressures. Permanent ruling castes of German towns, with minor exceptions, excluded persons from the local trades and crafts on principle, so that one mark of a hometown polity is the presence of artisans in political office.

A fourth quality, an educational one, followed from these three. If a town's leading families began to educate their sons at the university, especially in law or administration, that was a symptom of

[37] *Teutsches Staats-Recht*, XLII (Hanau, 1750), 434, 454–461.

an emerging patriciate (such as existed embryonically in the Rott-weil Herrenstube). It meant an element of professional govern-ment in the town when the son returned to take advantage of his position there, and it removed leading families from the occupa-tional guild system that encompassed the regular Bürgerschaft. They were entering what some have called the *Bildungsbürgertum,* which did not really belong in the hometown scheme nor rely upon it. High education among families in leading political positions (here ignoring inferior and transitory figures like parsons, clerks, and schoolmasters) may be the clearest sign of the absence or breakdown of community integrity. It is a useful perspective from which to view hometown complaints about "learned doctors," and Roman law, and government by scribblers—and from which to view the attitudes of the learned toward the home town.[38]

In all four ways, finally, the patriciate of any town that had one was the only element that regularly faced and dealt with the out-side. Any and all relations with the outside were implicit threats to communal mutuality; and if they were monopolized by a special group independent of the commonality, they underlined an actual break in its integrity.[39]

A separate ruling caste converted the normal working principles of the home town into a disease. It may be true of any civic body that the main implements of political coherence and elasticity are at the same time the main opportunities for favoritism and corrup-tion. In unicellular hometown politics, coherence and corruption were not just two aspects of the same thing, they are hardly worth distinguishing objectively. What marks the abnormality is not gov-erning processes themselves, but dissension over them; and talk of

[38] An intermediate variety of leadership was fairly common but harder to discern: the *Honoratiorentum* described fuzzily by Johann H. Mitgau, *Alt-Quedlinburger Honoratiorentum: Genealogisch-soziologische Studie über den Gesellschaftsaufbau des 17. und 18. Jahrhunderts* (Leipzig, 1934). It was a kind of educated equivalent of a political-commercial patriciate, distinguished from it by its accessibility to persons of all qualities of birth: in that respect comparable to state civil service, but entirely locally oriented. This *Honor-atiorentum,* incidentally, was quite different and almost the reverse of what Max Weber and those following him meant by the term, which no doubt has inhibited useful study of it.

[39] Cf. Ronald A. Warren's theory of vertical integration in *The Community in America* (Chicago, 1963).

corruption and nepotism—*Vetternwirtschaft* was the blunt German word—came with the appearance of what I have called a patriciate in the home town. It meant a breakdown of the web of familiar relations that held town government and citizenry together. Nobody with an uncle on the Council accuses him of nepotism. Nor is anybody likely to accuse a friend and customer of corruption and fiscal favoritism. Such accusations show that the links of patronage, familiarity, and informal influences were breaking; a gap was developing between governors and governed; a ruling group was developing political independence of the rest and simultaneously was ceasing to hold the rest together in hand as one community. A patriciate found cousins enough within its own number, and so indeed might be presumed likely to operate in its own interests. Patronage and familiar favoritism were being kept within a governing caste, or else (very much the same thing) they no longer reached far enough into the community to prevent the formation of an anti-administration party among the citizenry that was strong enough to speak. Hometown moral indignation at "corruption" arose at a point where communal methods of government were transferred to prescriptive dynastic government, another scheme of authority, so that the community at large was cut out; and, in a larger frame of ideas, it is easier to identify "bourgeois" political and social morality with hometownsmen than with business entrepreneurs.

Open conflict came when an alienated element of the town got control or strong footing in important guilds, or perhaps even the Outer Council, and issued its charges of nepotism and corruption against the ruling group. If matters had reached such a state as that, the dissident group could fairly be called the citizenry, and so often it was called, although such a group did not of course include all citizens and was likely to have some influential local persons, estranged from the inner magistracy, among its leaders. There might well be violence, for if the situation had not been an extreme one, it would not have come to the surface at all. Internal partisan conflict gave the territorial states an opportunity and even a duty to intervene with force; it offered a handle on town politics where no handle had protruded before, when the system had been intact and enclosed.

The nature of historical records sufficiently explains a partial inconsistency in what historians have said about early modern German towns: on the one hand that they were leveled out and subjected to absolutist state autocracy and on the other that they were ruled by petty local oligarchies.[40] For state intervention in local affairs, which produced most of the accessible political records, came ordinarily in places and at times where oligarchic and "corrupt" rule marked a discomposition of normal civic mechanisms: thus records of the same events support both the notion of absolutism and that of local oligarchy. And because most broad evidence of hometown political life comes from such instances of breakdown, much of their normal functioning must in truth be inferred from the causes of the trouble and the correctives proposed. It is also generally supposed that internal corruption, oligarchy, and state subjection all increased with time toward the end of the eighteenth century: a belief supported by a growing body of formal litigation (though even this cannot be certainly shown) and by a growth of systematic literature defending both state power and the rights of individuals.[41] There are logical reasons, too, why they should have increased. Population was generally growing, albeit slowly by modern standards; population movement and especially growth threatened hometown institutions.[42] The presence of commercial elements with interests and resources outside the town was another threat, and instances of this seem to have increased toward the end of the eighteenth century, but not at all clearly or uniformly, and surely at nothing like the rate of the century that followed.[43] And there are in fact some signs that home-

[40] E.g., Pütter, *Constitution of the Germanic Empire,* II, 209–217; and Maurer, *Städteverfassung,* IV, 114–296; also below, pp. 66–67 and the citations there.

[41] See Chapter V below.   [42] *Bevölkerungs-Ploetz,* II, 60–70, 156–158.

[43] For examples of the political disruption of hometown institutions by extralocal economic interests within the town see the case of Aachen, Ch. IV below; and Roland Schönfeld, "Studien zur Wirtschaftsgeschichte der Reichsstadt Regensburg im achtzehnten Jahrhundert," *VHVO,* C (1959), 5–147. For a fascinating speed-up history of a home town, created whole—guilds, customs, and all, with no "medieval remnants" in sight—at the beginning of the eighteenth century, and then deliberately reconstituted in 1785 to suit commerce and industry, see Franz T. Cramer, "Gewerbe, Handel und Verkehrswesen der Freiheit Mülheim a. Rh. im 18. Jahrhundert," *DJ,* XXII (1908/09), 1–100.

town governing groups tended to settle out as hereditary oligarchies in the century and a half of incubation that followed the Thirty
Years' War. Dortmund's experience of some such process can be
tabulated.[44] Fewer family names appeared among Dortmund town
councilors in the eighteenth century than at any time since at least
the fifteenth; but more striking, the proportion that came from old
established families increased markedly with time.

1500–1600	49 names, of which	18	had appeared	1400–1500
1600–1700	51	23		1500–1600
1700–1800	39	22		1600–1700

That is to say: in the sixteenth century, 37 per cent of the Dortmund councilmen were of old political family; in the seventeenth,
45 per cent; and in the eighteenth, 54 per cent. But there are instances where a contrary case can be made; no general tendencies
appear from among discordant particularities. Contemporaries
noted none, except insofar as their attention was drawn to "oligarchy" for reasons other than its over-all objective increase; that
they could only guess at anyway, and we cannot do much better.
Whatever the actuality may have been, the main reason for the picture of growing communal decadence and subjection is that contemporaries who wrote about such matters at the beginning of the
eighteenth century, and before, had tended to like communities at
least in theory, whereas those who wrote about them at the end
of the century tended not to like them in any way at all. Political
thought changed faster than hometownsmen.

The particular circumstances of state intervention, though, had
a curious and important consequence: the state almost always
favored the party of the citizenry against the emerging oligarchy.
This can partly be explained on the merits. A citizenry bestirred to
the rare stance of political dissent had on the face of things come
to feel deprived of rights and a place in the community they
thought properly theirs, so that the way to restore peace and order
and even justice was to give back those rights and place by reducing the independence from them that the patriciate had attained.
But more important: state officials shared with citizenry a jealousy

[44] From G. Mallinckrodt, "Die Dortmunder Rathslinie seit dem Jahre 1500,"
BGD, VI (1895), xxi–xxii. The figures probably reflect in large part a growing
stability of population.

of an independent governing caste in the community. That attitude was an important condition for the preservation of the home towns, and when it began to change toward the middle of the nineteenth century the home towns were failing. State officials had good fiscal reasons too, for the undercover juggling of funds and neglect of accounts ("corruption and fiscal mismanagement") that was possible within a small and close-knit governing group ("favoritism and nepotism") was likely to deprive the state of the share it claimed of local revenues. A common Bürger demand was that the books should be opened and explained, and the states were all in favor of that; the more money they could locate, the more they could get their hands on.[45] Budgetary malfeasance was an accusation that could on the merits be leveled at almost any town at almost any time, and officials without and alienated citizenry within were ready to seize upon it.[46]

[45] Rall, *Kurbayern*, pp. 491–492, describes Bavarian state intervention in the finances of territorial towns as motivated purely by fiscal interests, not by political *Machthunger;* but surely that was not invariably so, and the distinction is hard to make.

[46] A related problem is the one of "fiscal decline" or growing indebtedness of towns, especially imperial towns, in the eighteenth century; citizen discontent is associated with that. But again and again it appears that debt rose even in times of high prosperity, increasing revenues, and budget surpluses: a process that indeed has a corrupt smell about it. See, e.g., Erwin Schell, *Die Reichsstädte beim Übergang an Baden* (Heidelberg, 1929), pp. 1–14; Borst, "Esslinger Bürgertum," pp. 64–66; Andreas Schlittmeier, "Die Entwicklung der kommunalen Finanzen der Stadt Landshut von der Mitte des 18. bis zur Mitte des 19. Jahrhunderts," *VHVN*, LXXXV, Heft 2 (1959), 45–48, 70–76; Johann J. Moser, *Von der Reichs-Stättischen Regiments-Verfassung* (Frankfurt/Main, 1772), p. 293. One answer lies in opaque town accounting methods, designed to record transactions, not to reveal financial condition (how much cash there was on hand, for example): thus the towns seem to have been selling more securities or *rentes* than they were buying, which raises interesting speculations about the preindustrial, prebanking German capital market, with a higher demand for secure private investment than for credit. Such town securities appeared as debt, but loans out of town accounts that had a surplus do not seem to have been listed as assets: cf. Timothy Wright, "Weissenburg from the Pflegamt" (MS, 1966 Harvard seminar paper). Ernst von Meier, *Hannoversche Verfassungs- und Verwaltungsgeschichte, 1680–1866, II* (Leipzig, 1899), 424, notes a community practice of borrowing from Bürger (selling securities) at high interest rates and lending to them at low; the Bavarian government in 1748 forbade Bürgermeister and administrators of local endowments *Geld auf Interesse aufzunehmen* without the approval of state or ecclesiastical authorities: Kreittmayr, *Sammlung* (1771), p. 568.

Another problem is the contradiction between the commonplace historical theme of absolutist state subjugation in Germany in the seventeenth and eighteenth centuries on the one hand, and the manifest survival of the home towns into the nineteenth century on the other. Local historians have always been troubled by the need to explain why the town they have studied was an exception to the general rule of absolutism, which generality, however, they cannot venture to challenge on the basis of their single instance.[47] One explanation already touched upon is that state and imperial records are condensed accumulations of crises; local historians by contrast know the long periods of stability in between, and know the places where no serious trouble occurred and where the state hardly was evident. But there are substantial explanations that go beyond the nature of records and historians' use of them. Hugo Preuss got partly around the problem by arguing that local authority was absolutist too in the seventeenth and eighteenth centuries, so that independent local rule amounted to the same thing as state absolutism as far as any real communal life was concerned; either way, German town life was leveled and destroyed.[48] Georg Ludwig von Maurer, who was better informed, knew he had a puzzle; but even with the right pieces in his hands he seemed unable to put

[47] E.g., from among endless examples the contrary descriptions of town politics (especially of Osnabrück) in Wilhelm Havemann, *Geschichte der Lande Braunschweig und Lüneburg*, III (Göttingen, 1857); or on the effective participation of guilds, Laufs, *Rottweil, 1650–1806*, pp. 46–47. For a rejection of the decline thesis, Wolfgang Zorn, "Die Reichsstädte Bayerisch-Schwabens, 1648–1806," *SBHV*, X (1959), 113–122.

[48] *Die Entwicklung des deutschen Städtewesens*, I (Leipzig, 1906), especially pp. 143–154. The democrat Preuss wished to show not only that autocracy and oligarchy were evil but also that Stein's communal reforms were not built out of old traditions, that rather they were a new departure: thus democratic institutions could be created fresh by rational will and intelligence, with no medieval mortgage on them (note his role in preparing the Weimar constitution). That purpose may explain why he unexpectedly broke off his history of German towns when he got to the early nineteenth century. On the clash of views between Preuss and Erich Becker and his school, who with incidental National Socialist sympathies wished to show a continuity of German corporate life throughout the centuries, see Heinrich Heffter, *Die deutsche Selbstverwaltung im 19. Jahrhundert* (Stuttgart, 1950), p. 180. n. 1. Becker's case is put most thoroughly in Franz Steinbach and Erich Becker, "Geschichtliche Grundlagen der kommunalen Selbstverwaltung in Deutschland," *RA*, XX (1932), 1–205.

them together: "Constant struggles between the citizenry and their town councils made possible the subjection of all the towns within a territory to territorial rule, or at least facilitated the victory of the territorial princes over the towns. . . . Yet it is a peculiar phenomenon that despite this territorial absolutism, the constitutional reforms in the territorial towns was always in a *bürgerlich* direction, indeed in most towns even a democratic direction." [49] Maurer went on to speculate darkly about the equation of absolutism and democracy. But surely what he had in mind was that in the instances he knew of state intervention into town affairs—something that happened at times of division between community and council within the towns—the usual outcome was the reentry of citizenry into leadership and the pressing of emerging oligarchies back into the community.

In the town of Erfurt, territorially subject to the Archbishop-Elector of Mainz, trouble developed in the first decade after the Thirty Years' War between the governing council and a citizens' committee made up of Viertelmeister, guild representatives, and other "leading citizens." As a result the fiscal and elective systems broke down, and the Archbishop sent in a commission with imperial sanction (the Archbishop of Mainz was Archchancellor of the Empire), which found for the citizenry. It ordered in 1655 that elections should be dominated three to one by guilds and quarters over councilors, and forbade the council's practice of requiring any artisan to give up his trade in order to take a council seat. The Archepiscopal government imposed a condition of "imperial attention [*kaiserliche Acht*]" upon the town and undertook to enforce the commission's decision upon the council. As a result the council and the representatives of the citizenry reached formal agreement in 1662: the council agreed to accept the election reform; the citizenry promised thenceforward to bring any complaints to the council sitting as a whole rather than to individuals or to the Mainz government; and both agreed on the importance of keeping alive certain protective treaties between the town and the nearby government of Electoral Saxony. In 1664, after the council by dismissing an unruly Viertelmeister had brought renewed intervention from the government at Mainz, the townsmen made another agree-

[49] *Städteverfassung*, IV, p. 235.

ment, mutually promising to suppress all internal friction, so as to put an end to outside "attention" and intervention at the cost of the town's rights and autonomies. "Mistrust, disorder, and violent activity [*Thätigkeit*]" must be replaced by "confidence, order . . . love, and peace" if troublesome outsiders were to be kept away.[50]

In Lüneburg in the seventeenth century the territorial duke intervened in a crisis between the town council and a dissident citizenry that demanded more information and representation on fiscal decisions: he sent troops and officials, and a new constitution was prepared that guaranteed more influence to citizenry and guilds, with a right to appeal a council decision to the ducal government, in order to establish "better confidence among the civic elements [*Ständen*] . . . a healing conjunction between the families and the rest of the citizenry." Officers were to be more widely distributed, and the duke promised in return not to interfere in local justice. A very similar sequence occured in Braunschweig a few years later.[51] Or to come at it from another direction: the Saar towns grew more independent of the states from the seventeenth into the eighteenth centuries; and as they did so the leadership located in Inner Councils, Guildmasters, and Outer Councils began locally to separate away from the Bürgerschaft and to exclude them, interlocking both socially and politically within themselves. About 1750 a crisis developed in Saarburg over favoritism and nepotism—*Freund- und Vetternwirtschaft*. A patriciate was taking form, according to the alienated citizenry. The citizens demanded periodic election of the Inner Council from among representatives of the guilds, which encompassed all the citizenry, and the right to oversee the management of town finances. The territorial prince, Archbishop-Elector of Trier, refused to reform election rules, but he ordered an administrative reorganization to provide more voice to the Bürger and more power to the guilds.[52]

In stories like these a pattern appears, a cyclical pattern that shows why intervention by the territorial state and the persistence of the hometown community were not only compatible in this

[50] Lünig, *Reichs-Archiv*, Partis specialis IV, II. Theil, ii, pp. 362–478.
[51] Havemann, *Braunschweig und Lüneburg*, III, 77–80, 181–187.
[52] Ennen, "Organisation der Selbstverwaltung in den Saarstädten," pp. 112, 125–137 and passim.

political incubator, they were part of the same process. Maurer did not remark that after state intervention on the side of a disgruntled citizenry and reform "in a *bürgerlich* direction" the community recovered its autonomy, precisely because it dropped out of his view then: the home towns were not places where eighteenth-century states could afford to use up their limited administrative resources in constant detailed supervision. After its spasm of dissension, intervention from outside and reform within, the community recovered its undivided self-containment. The cycle can be put logically as follows:

1. Begin with a period of external exposure and confusion within: political insecurity and social uncertainty resulting from war, financial strains, civil dissension, radical changes in population, or religious or territorial changes.

2. To bring internal order and assert control over its affairs the town develops or is obliged to develop a mutually reliant and integrated political community.

3. In the condition of stability and autonomy thus achieved, a governing caste gradually takes form; the result, a weakening of community integrity, is called nepotism and corruption.

4. Organized hostility from an alienated citizenry against the governing group invites outside interference, a threat to the community's autonomy and self-protection.

5. The isolated leadership opens its ranks more widely to the community (through guild leaders, Viertelmeister, perhaps Outer Council), under state pressure or to regain civic support within; the political alliance between citizenry and state authority lasts until confidence and integrity are restored, and then lapses, and the community falls silent again.

It is often possible to see stages of the logical sequence in time.[53] One might even descry a grand cycle in time running from the Thirty Years' War, the many constitutional statements that came

---

[53] For variations on the theme: Klaus Flink, *Geschichte der Burg und des Amtes Rheinbach* (Bonn, 1965), pp. 254–256 and passim; Erich Becker, "Verfassung und Verwaltung der Gemeinden des Rheingaus vom 16. bis zum 18. Jahrhundert," *RA*, XIV (1930), 71–78; Josef Niessen, "Landesherr und bürgerliche Selbstverwaltung in Bonn von 1244–1794," *RA*, V (1924), 32–119; Heinz Mohnhaupt, *Die Göttinger Ratsverfassung vom 16. bis 19. Jahrhundert* (Göttingen, 1965), pp. 60–108.

in its aftermath, growing stability in the eighteenth century, a separation of elites toward its end (if that happened), vigorous state intervention in Napoleonic times, and the constitutional restoration of the communities that followed in the early nineteenth century. But it is probably safer and more accurate to think of the cycle not as a sequence in time but rather as an equilibrium in which the three main elements—citizenry, leadership, and state—balanced together to keep the community as it was. Individual crises show sequence, quiet normality shows equilibrium.

The Bavarian ordinance of 1748 described equilibrium. It accepted the individuality of each community's constitution and privileges, and stipulated almost no specific political forms or procedures. It urged the communities to spread civic duties wide among the citizenry, rotating and dividing up offices as far as possible, lest the burden of office reach the point where no one would undertake it save for private advantage. Towns ought to elect their officers every year, not just when vacancies occurred, and to elect them in constitutional (but undescribed) form; the state's confirmation power would be exercised as a veto when cases of malfeasance or breakdown of mutual confidence in the town came to the attention of the state's inspector on circuit (*Rentmeister im Umritt*) during his visit. To assure community respect for the magistracy it was important that only able men, devoted to the communal good, and insofar as possible only prosperous men, be elected to office, avoiding weak-minded persons of small means likely to become plain yes men to the strong and the rich. "Should it appear to the Electoral [Bavarian] officials upon further investigation of a report of council elections that the elections did not take place in the proper manner, but that rather only a few men were quietly invited, and that only friends or worthless *Ja-Männer* were nominated; or should it appear that a dominant councilor controlled the election by bribery, threats, or other means: then let every magistrate know that in such a case, not only will confirmation be denied, but also the names of persons thus chosen shall be stricken from the report, and those responsible removed from office despite their present possession of the powers they have abused, and a new ballot shall be held, man by man, in the presence of a Commissioner . . . until it is clear that an end has been put to the corruption." [54]

[54] Kreittmayr, *Sammlung*, pp. 558–574.

Imperial town leadership was less subject to the cyclical or balancing suppression of oligarchy than territorial town leadership was. Here imperial intervention in local crises tended to uphold the magistracy.[55] The Empire's direct link with the town was the magistracy, and its relation with citizens passed through the magistracy, which held direct full authority as an imperial estate; and the Empire was more concerned to keep the magistracy in power than to ensure confidence of the citizenry in it. Imperial power was more remote from imperial towns than state power was from territorial towns, so that local leadership had less fear of their sovereign and consequently less need for support from the citizenry. Empire and imperial town leadership were both mainly concerned to preserve the town's independence against neighbor territorial princes, so that the natural pattern of political alliance was different from that within the territorial states: Empire and town leadership against disgruntled citizenry and nearby territorial rulers. Moser spoke of the right and obligation of the Emperor to protect Imperial Estates and other "immediate" inferiors, meaning in imperial towns the councils; and he gave as examples the support of the council of Schwäbisch Gmünd against a citizenry "in a condition of tumult threatening the lives of the councilors" in 1701, and the protection of patrician Nürnberg against the pressure of "certain powerful neighbors" in 1717.[56] In Goslar disputes of the late eighteenth century, the Outer Council claimed that it as representative of the whole citizenry, not the executive magistracy, was immediate to the Emperor and thus the source of local authority; but the Imperial Privy Council flatly backed the magistracy and enjoined obedience on the Outer Council.[57]

[55] That may be one reason why historians, perforce relying mainly on imperial town constitutions and records, have spotted growing town oligarchy in the eighteenth century: the cycle in imperial towns halted short of the suppression of oligarchy, and most important imperial towns were patrician anyway.

[56] ". . . in puncto tumultus et intentatae necis Consulis." *Teutsches Staats-Recht,* IV (2d ed.; Frankfurt/Main, 1748), 424–427, 440–442.

[57] August L. Schlözer, "Disputen in Goslar 1779, über das StaatsRecht [sic] dieser freien ReichsStadt [sic]," *Briefwechsel, meist historischen und politischen Inhalts,* VI (Göttingen, 1780), 217–247. There were legal grounds for the Outer Council in Moser, *Von der Reichs-Stättischen Regiments-Verfassung,* p. 523: "Wann schon der Magistrat Superioritätem territorialem administrirt; so constituiret doch die Bürgerschaft das eigentliche Corpus der Reichsstadt, um dessentwillen der Magistrat da ist und es gubenirt." But cf. n. 7 above.

All the same, the rule of cycle withstands the partial exception of imperial towns, for even when the Empire firmly backed the authority of inner councils and told the citizenry to keep its nose out of government, it was likely to enjoin reforms "in a *bürgerlich* direction" upon the councils.[58] Whatever troubles the free imperial towns may have suffered in the late eighteenth century were of a kind they had got past, perhaps more quietly, many times before; and they had survived their powerlessness for a very long time. Free and territorial towns alike were shielded from autocracy and subversion, from suppression and revolt; and the communities developed rules of membership and social conformity to keep it that way. Equilibrium and incubator seriously depended on hometownsmen's wanting to keep it that way, and on how they went about it. Begin with the story of the tinsmith Flegel of Hildesheim.

[58] As in the case of Wimpfen in the 1770's and 1780's: see *JM*, II (1791), 141–184; for imperial intervention in a city on the side of the Bürgerschaft, Soliday, "Frankfurt am Main," passim.

CHAPTER III

Guilds

THE tinsmith Flegel, citizen of Hildesheim, was in love, and he wished to marry. That he should marry was in itself seemly, for the proper pursuit of his trade required a solid domestic establishment supporting and surrounding the workshop: a wife to help out and meet customers, and to provide relatives; a decent home for apprentices and a gentling influence on journeymen; an assurance of Flegel's own diligence and reliability as a valuable member of the community. The trouble was that Flegel had set his heart, not wisely but too well, on the daughter of a fellow citizen named Helmsen; and when he went to register his intention to marry with the tinsmith's guild he was barred from doing so on grounds of indecency. The prospective bride's father—not she herself—had been born out of wedlock and then subsequently legitimized, whether by the belated marriage of his parents or by special government decree does not appear. At any rate Helmsen's legitimacy was recognized by the territorial law of the Bishopric of Hildesheim, in which the community was located, but that did not make him legitimate in the eyes of the Hildesheim guildsmen. Indeed the citizen status of the sometime bastard Helmsen suggests that outside influence had forced him on the community, ensuring the unending rancor of the real Hildesheimer. The guild constitution, to which Flegel had subscribed, provided that wife as well as master must show proof of four irreproachable grandparents; and inasmuch as a master's children were automatically eligible for

73

guild acceptance and support, Flegel's determination to marry the Helmsen girl demanded of the tinsmiths that they sponsor the grandchildren of a bastard before the community.

Flegel had become engaged in 1742. Eleven years before, in 1731, an imperial edict had appeared which provided, among other things, that legitimacy established by "the authorities" should be recognized as valid by the guilds. Accordingly Flegel appealed to the Hildesheim Town Council against the guild decision, citing the imperial decree. But who were the authorities in Hildesheim? The important guilds of the town were directly and constitutionally involved in town government, ostensibly as representative of the citizenry: the *Ämter* of the butchers, the bakers, the shoemakers, the tanners, and the *Gilden* of the tailors, the smiths, the wool weavers, the retailers, and the furriers. Moreover the first four, the *Ämter,* had a special relation with the bishop which they used as leverage against the Council when they felt need of it. The Council therefore (it seems to have been an unusually flabby body to boot) turned the case over to its committee for artisans' affairs; and there nothing was decided. After a year, Flegel took the extraordinary step of marrying Fräulein Helmsen anyway, in a ceremony held somewhere outside Hildesheim. When the guildsmen heard of it they were enraged: never before, they said, had a Hildesheim master artisan thus defied his guild's jurisdiction in marital matters. For Flegel to get away with it would violate one of the most important sanctions the guild had for controlling the composition and the behavior of its membership. And it would make the Hildesheim tinsmiths look bad, and with them all the other Hildesheimer. The guild excluded Flegel from its meetings and functions, and it goes without saying that it imposed economic and social boycott against him, master tinsmith though he was.

For three years, Flegel appeared repeatedly before the Town Council asking that the imperial decree be enforced in his favor; repeatedly he was turned away. In 1745 he appealed to the episcopal government, declaring that the guilds in their defiance of the law sought only after their own "gloire". Also, inasmuch as they were represented in the town government and thus in the highest town court, they were acting in their own case against him. Here he was entering on dangerous ground, for if the guild-influenced town government indeed constituted "the authorities" with the right to establish legitimacy, then his case was lost. But locally it was lost anyway, and his appeal to the bishop invited the episcopal government to assert that they, not the Town Council, were "the authorities" in Hildesheim. The bishopric demanded that the Council issue formal judgment; but the Council, caught between state on one side and guilds on the other, found a temporary way out in a request for an opinion from the faculty of law at the University of Halle: [1] Was the requirement of four legitimate grandparents legal? Was Helmsen legitimate (as book law said) or not (as the Hildesheimer said)? The Halle professors decided for Flegel and against the guilds, and the Council announced that decision. The smiths thereupon countered with the argument that the Halle faculty was not learned in Hildesheim local law and circumstance: community law breaks book law. Flegel was not reinstated nor his wife recognized. In 1747, five years after his marriage, he asked the Council to enforce the Halle decision; the Council issued the order, but nothing else happened. The Council then urged all concerned to try "good will" as a means to solution, and still nothing happened; but finally the bishopric ordered enforcement within two weeks. The Council summoned a meeting of the guild to admit Flegel, fearing military intervention by the bishop, but the hall remained empty; not a single master tinsmith appeared. Finally the Council ordered the guild to readmit Flegel and acknowledge the validity of his marriage lest episcopal soldiers and bureaucrats put an end to the privileges and autonomies of Hildesheim. The guild officers all resigned, and then there was nobody for the law to talk to.[2]

Probably that is enough about the tinsmith Flegel. Eventually he was formally readmitted and his marriage registered, but that did not settle the case; after dragging on for several more years it disappeared into the episcopal courts. It is safe to say that Flegel

[1] Such a request was common procedure in cases of this kind, and the reply approached the force of law.

[2] The outline of the Flegel story is in Johannes H. Gebauer, "Das Hildesheimer Handwerkswesen im 18. Jahrhundert und das Reichsgesetz von 1731 gegen die Handwerksmissbräuche," *HGB*, XXIII (1917), 161–173. A general description of Hildesheim politics at the time is Gebauer, *Geschichte der Stadt Hildesheim*, II (Hildesheim, 1924), 171–254.

never found a peaceable life in Hildesheim, for he had defied the procedures upon which community peace was founded. I cannot tell how he supported himself and his wife during the years of litigation and after, but it would fit the shape of the story if the answer has to do with the prospective father-in-law, with his belatedly acquired legitimacy, and his tainted daughter in need of a husband: money and political connections through Helmsen with the state may have helped evoke Flegel's tender emotions and his fellow guildsmen's righteousness. Defense of their honor against incursions like Flegel's was nothing new to the citizen-guildsmen of Hildesheim: they had defended it before against a master shoemaker who wanted to marry a piper's daughter, against a tailor who turned out to have a wet nurse for a mother, and against a smith who tried to register a miller's daughter as his wife. The social prudery and political stubbornness of the Hildesheim guilds were part of the character of every hometown community, and a role of guild organization was to lock those characteristics institutionally into the community as a whole. "For their functions," wrote Wolfram Fischer, "extended far beyond the economic, and their legal status placed them as integrating constituents of the political and social order of the old Empire. Only when we start with the social location of the guild and bring all its functions into consideration do we see the true role of the economic in the guild system." [3] That "social location" was the home town; only there—not in the city and surely not the countryside—could the guilds assume so broad a role and still remain basically economic institutions. Only in the context of the home town is it comprehensible how the time of the notorious "decay" of the early modern German trades guilds should have been the period probably of their greatest power to impress their values and goals upon the society of which they were components.

To begin to describe them it is useful to separate out the several ways in which the hometown guilds entered into community life: economic regulation, political organization and representation, and guardianship of social or domestic standards.[4] Each of these was

[3] *Handwerksrecht und Handwerkswirtschaft um 1800* (Berlin, 1955), p. 15.

[4] That is, roughly the legal areas of *Gewerberecht*, *Bürgerrecht*, and *Ansässigmachung und Verehelichung*. These categorical terms became far commoner in the nineteenth century than in the seventeenth and eighteenth, and I shall use them in that latter context.

a leg of the tripod upon which the influence of the guild relied. It is never easy to say in the event which aspect of guild life is at issue, for the guild readily introduced them all, and interchangeably to suit the case. Did the tinsmiths seize upon the chance to expel Flegel for economic reasons, because they feared competition from him? It is easy to suspect so, but the record does not show it. On the other hand there are instances enough where economic arguments—the overfilling of a trade, or the inability of a prospective master to support himself, for example—were used to exclude a candidate or prevent a marriage distasteful for quite other reasons. Or was Flegel's exclusion a political exercise? Almost surely it was in part, and if so then the nature of the case caused a political issue to be argued on grounds of domestic morality. The nineteenth century will be a better context for trying to distinguish motives. Here the linking of functions is the important thing to see. As occupational groupings within the community—of butchers, shoemakers, carpenters, and the rest—guilds supervised the recruitment, training, and allocation of individual citizens into the community's economy, and their economic character placed its stamp upon hometown morality and the nature of citizenship itself. As primary political organizers of the citizenry (in Rottweil the *Zünfte* with their component economic *Innungen*), they bore political and civic factors into economic practice and moral standards. And finally as moral and social watchdogs they saw to the quality of the citizenry—the *Ehre*, the honor, of the hometown workman and Bürger.

Still in the exercise of all these linked functions they worked as economic media; their special influence on the community and its membership rested ultimately on that role. That set the forms and the procedures whereby they carried out the rest, and shaped the mirror they held up to the whole community.

The guild economy

The hometown guild artisan ordinarily sold his own products, on the same premises where he produced them; or he performed skilled services within the specifically defined limits of the community. The customs and statutes that governed his training and regulated his activities were quite similar from one place to another, and based roughly on the same principles for each of the hometown trades, although there was wide variety in incidental customs and terminology.[5] Craft guild rules which assumed a local but diversified economy set him apart from the merchant guildsmen of the cities (although some small towns had retailers' [*Krämer*] guilds entitled to sell certain imported goods locally), and set him apart also from the state-licensed or unorganized rural artisan. The rules were usually set down in written articles, statutes or charters prepared by each guild and confirmed or tolerated by some authority, much as the statutes of the towns themselves; and here too official confirmation had that troublesome effect of giving public force to private agreement, and custom had a local validity that was legally indistinct.[6] The territorial government might itself confirm the statute, or even issue one on a conventional pattern; but usually confirmation came at the instance of the guild from the local magistracy or a local court.[7] The guild's formal authority rested on that confirmed or acknowledged statute, which outlined its training program, the regulations governing the exercise of the trade, its powers to elect and to limit membership, the specific economic activity over which guild members held local monopoly (the *Zunftzwang*), and the geographical area (the *Bannmeile*) within which the monopoly prevailed. Sometimes an analytical distinction can be made between the guild's function as a training apparatus

[5] Some of the names a hometown guild might bear, in rough order of their frequency: *Zunft, Innung, Amt, Handwerk, Gilde, Gewerk, Gaffel, Bruderschaft, Zeche, Einung, Mittel.* For general descriptions of guild structures and powers see Johann A. Ortloff, *Das Recht der Handwerker, nach den allgemeinen in den deutschen Staaten geltenden Gesetzen und Zunft- und Innungsverordnungen* (I have used the 2d ed., Erlangen, 1818; 1st ed. was 1803); Ortloff, ed., *Corpus juris Opificiarii* (2d ed., Erlangen, 1820; 1st ed. was 1803); and Joh. F. C. Weisser, *Das Recht der Handwerker nach allgemeinen Grundsätzen und insbesondere nach den Herzogl. Wirtembergischen Gesetzen entworfen* (Stuttgart, 1780). For a body of legal definitions of artisan terminology, Wiguläus X. A. Kreittmayr, *Abhandlung vom Handwerksrecht, worin der Unterschied des bayrischen Rechts mit den gemeinen Rechte gezeigt und beyde unter einander verglichen werden* (Munich, 1768).

[6] Weisser, *Handwerker*, pp. 17–21.

[7] Even where the state undertook to issue large numbers of specific guild statutes, it did so usually at the instance and initiative of the artisan corporations: see, e.g., Leo B. Hoffmann, *Das württembergische Zunftwesen und die Politik der herzoglichen Regierung gegenüber den Zünften im 18. Jahrhundert* (Tübingen, 1906), passim. The drastic exception is Prussia, especially in the 1730's: see below, this chapter.

and as a corporate representative of an economic interest.[8] But the distinction is formal only; within the community, rules to implement training programs were used to serve the economic and familial interests of the guildsmen, by holding down membership and excluding outsiders; conversely the economic interests of the trade were subject to pressure upon the guildsmen as members of the community to see to the useful education and social incorporation of the citizenry. Training and economic interest united in the critical decision of whether or not to admit a new master, and both were absorbed into the broader role of the guild within hometown society.

Guild statutes often set forth rules of guild life in remarkable detail, although of course much guild activity took place informally and unrecorded—which is not the same as to say quietly, by any means—and in conjunction with the cousins and brothers on the town councils and in the other trades. The best place to learn about those less formal practices is in the repeated legislation, state and imperial, forbidding guilds to behave in certain ways: evidence enough that the guilds persistently did so behave. That is the main reason for including the imperial edict of 1731 as an appendix to this volume. In the countryside, in professionally governed or mercantile cities like Hamburg and Nürnberg, and in the Prussian centralized country, incorporated craft guilds either did not exist or their structure was used as the channel for government regulation of the economy. But craft guilds within the hometown communities could not be reached by that kind of legislation or control because the civic community of uncles and brothers lay between, and because the guilds themselves were part of the communal system of authority.[9]

A guild's affairs were administered by a collegial body of from

8 E.g., Johann J. Becher, *Politischer discurs, von den eigentlichen ursachen des auff- und abnehmens der städt, länder und republicken* (Frankfurt/Main, 1759 ed.; 1st ed. was Frankfurt/Main, 1668), p. 18; among modern analysts Fischer, *Handwerksrecht und Handwerkswirtschaft*, pp. 17–18.

9 Johann Jakob Moser, despite a strong belief in state authority over economic matters, conceded that it was not really effective at a local level; and he noted that the state's legal authority over guilds was usually delegated to town magistracies, lower-level officials, or to the guild officers themselves: *Landeshoheit im Weltlichen*, III, 190–197.

two to four Overmasters (I called them Guildmasters in the case
of the Rottweil political guilds), chosen by a process incorporating
both the will of the membership and the choice of the civic authorities: some procedure along the whole spectrum running from
direct appointment by the authorities to free election by a majority
of guild masters. Where guild members elected their members
independently, a member of the civic government (ordinarily a
town councilor) was given the responsibility of overseeing a certain number of guilds and representing them to the government;
and this overseer-patron, like the officers elected by the guildsmen
themselves, was regularly paid by the guild and received certain
irregular perquisites as well.[10] The Overmasters decided internal
conflicts, spelled out rules, levied fines and imposed minor punishments, administered guild finances and properties, saw to the in-
spection of masterworks prepared by candidates for mastership
(though this might be done by a specially appointed inspector),
and generally represented the interests of the trade, within the
community and to the outside if need be. A guild court composed
or dominated by these officials could expel any member who did
not accept its decisions, and thus foreclose his practice of the trade;
and frequently such a court punished members for civil or criminal
misdeeds like theft or adultery, on the grounds (if anybody asked)
that the transgression had brought the trade into disrepute, so that
the trade must punish the offender to clear its name: that brought
the case properly within guild jurisdiction.[11]

The Overmasters were custodians of the Guild Chest, the *Lade*,
a kind of ark of the guild covenant symbolizing the guild's corporate authority and autonomy, repository of its official documents
and secrets, ceremonially opened on the occasion of meetings of
the membership. Plenary meetings (*Morgensprachen*) were sup-

[10] Guild officials on the elective side of the spectrum tended to bear titles
like *Zunftvorsteher, Obermeister, Altmeister, Gildemeister, Geschworne,* or
Altermänner; on the appointive side they tended to be called *Handwerksbeisit-
zer, Handwerksrichter, Obmänner, Obherrn, Wetteherrn,* or *Morgensprach-
herrn:* Ortloff, *Recht der Handwerker,* p. 62. Weisser, *Handwerker,* pp. 26–29,
calls the officer for official oversight an *Obmann,* the elected guild leaders
Geschwornen.

[11] This doctrine of *infamia* or *levis notae macula* was taken seriously: see
Weisser, *Handwerker,* pp. 88–94 and passim.

posed to be held regularly—quarterly as a rule—but extraordinary meetings might be called to consider special problems, like a serious infraction of the rules by one of the members or some action by the authorities or by another trade that threatened the interests of the guild. A list of characteristic sources of guild income shows some of their activities:

1) periodic small fees paid like taxes by every master or widow actively in business;
2) interest on guild funds invested;
3) *Meistergeld,* the regular entry fees levied on new masters;
4) registration fees from apprentices;
5) buying-in fees (*Einkaufgeld*), either from accepted immigrating masters, or else in lieu of the masterwork or some other formal evidence of training; similarly
6) payments in lieu of the wanderyears;
7) fines levied on members for minor infractions.

Important guild expenditures included:
1) interest on loans taken out in the name of the guild;
2) salaries of guild officials and patrons;
3) food and drink for meetings;
4) subsistence money or "gifts" rendered to journeymen passing through town in search of work;
5) legal expenses;
6) relief to poor members for illness or burial, including the burial of poor or foreign journeymen;
7) relief to the bereaved families of members.[12]

The several aspects of guild life converged on the master's estate, as citizen, head of household, and independent craftsman. The process of selection and induction began with apprenticeship. Active masters were expected to undertake the training of the sons of fellow townsmen as apprentices; apprentices were required to be Christians of honorable estate and parentage. After a trial period of a few weeks in a master's shop, petition was made to the Overmasters for formal registration of the apprentice with the guild;

[12] The lists are based on Ortloff, *Recht der Handwerker,* pp. 86–97, and Weisser, *Handwerker,* pp. 51–54. I have added some items they did not mention.

if his birth was properly certified and his other credentials met conditions set by the guild, he was admitted upon payment of a registration fee (*Einschreibegeld*) to the guild and a training fee (*Lehrgeld*) to the master. The registration fee was set by guild custom or statute; the training fee might be set by the statute or negotiated between the master and the parents of the apprentice. The apprentice was bound to serve the master loyally for a stated period, some three or four years, during which time the master for his part was obliged to give the apprentice real training and practice in the trade—not just use him as an errand boy—and a decent place in his domestic establishment. Now: often the sons of masters within the guild were forgiven the fees, or paid reduced fees, or were excused from apprenticeship altogether, or signed in and out on the same day without the regular period of training. The grounds were (again if anybody inquired) that a boy already knew what went on in his father's trade as well as an ordinary apprentice from another trade was expected to learn it; but it amounted to group favoritism and encouraged inbreeding within the trades. State laws frequently denounced the practice; so did the imperial edict of 1731; but enforcement necessarily was in the hands of local magistracies and guilds.

When the apprenticeship was done the young man paid another round of fees, usually underwent some convivial hazing, and thus was promoted to journeyman. The journeyman was presumed to have learned the basic skills of his trade, but he was not yet ready to carry it on independently. First he was to go on a round of travels, working at a wage for other masters in other places, and getting the behavior of late adolescence out of his system, away from home but still free of the responsibilities and encumbrances of a domestic establishment of his own. His training and good reputation were certified by the guild in which he had served his apprenticeship, so that the guild, its reputation at stake, was careful with the certification; similarly the journeyman relied on the good name of his home guild (or absence of a bad name) for his acceptance abroad. His written certification for public display might, especially if his home guild claimed special virtues, be supplemented by some special, secret, visual or oral sign, to commend him to those guilds abroad that would recognize the sign.

When a journeyman arrived at a new town he went to the journeymen's hostel sponsored by his trade there, and applied to the host, the *Herbergsvater* appointed by the guild, for work. The host directed him to a local master looking for help if there was one; if no work could be found within a stipulated short period, probably no more than a day and a night, the journeyman was sent on his way with the help of a small grant from the guild treasury, the gift or *Zehrpfennig*. If he stayed in town without work he was treated as a vagrant, for that is what he was; strange unemployed journeymen meant beggars and thieves to the home town.

There at the hostel he ordinarily lived, while he was locally employed; and his papers were deposited in the guild chest controlled by the Overmasters. Only a master or a master's widow in his learned trade could legitimately employ him: if he valued his prospects as master and Bürger he would not enter the service of a noble, nor of the state, nor work at a factory, nor go as a soldier or a servant. After a given minimum term of employment in one place the journeyman might leave to resume his wandering, or be dismissed by his employer, when proper notice was given and the piece he was working on was finished; sometimes there were customary appointed calender times: for example quarterly for the tailors, after Easter, Midsummer, Michaelmas in September, and Christmas; and for shoemakers, Midsummer and Christmas. His papers were endorsed by the local guild to show that he had worked there, and how he had behaved. If a journeyman ran off he left his credentials behind him in the guild chest, and he needed them, with endorsements, for acceptance into a respectable trade in any respectable place.

Life at the hostel was often organized on the pattern of the masters' guild, with overjourneymen, meetings, and a chest; there were fines, and mutual assistance in case of misfortune. But the journeymen's organizations, with their transient membership of dependent labor, never attained the local influence nor the local interest of the guild of the masters; their interests and influence were rather related to their transience, and differences that arose between them and the masters resulted from their transient status —the fact that they would soon be moving on and would need acceptance elsewhere—far more commonly than from conflicts over wages or working conditions.[13] They were moreover unmarried, and were not made citizens.

The term of travel varied in length from place to place and from trade to trade, and the rules were shot through besides with dispensations for fees, or for familial reasons, or both together: favoritism for sons, or special arrangements for journeymen who married the widows or orphan daughters of local masters. But two or more years of attested wandering was a customary condition for application for mastership.[14] Far and away the best place for a journeyman to apply for mastership—barring a palatable widow or orphan —was in his home town, so there he usually returned when his wanderyears were done. His application was filed with the Overmasters of the guild to which he sought entry, and after their evaluation it was laid before the assembled masters and usually before the civil authorities as well. He had to provide certification of apprentice training that the local masters would accept, proof of his travels to proper places and of proper behavior when he was there, and of course above all he had again to prove legitimate ancestry. All of these conditions were more easily met by a local boy, unless there was something wrong with him, than by an outsider.

The examination of all these qualifications offered plenty of opportunities to exclude the candidate if the masters so chose, and if they could exclude him without offending colleagues, relatives, neighbors, and customers. Yet another hurdle was the masterwork, an exhibition of the candidate's skill prepared in the place where he applied. What the masterwork should be was assigned by local guild statute, by custom, or by the guild *ad hoc* when it authorized the candidate to make and submit it. It was easy to assign a difficult piece of work or an expensive one, and then if need be still to reject it in the name of the guild's high standards: where, young man, did you learn to make things *that* way? If the trade was overfilled—limits on membership might be set by guild statute, by town or even state ordinance, or by the judgment of the guildsmen —then the candidate might be rejected on that ground, or told to

13 See the history of the 1731 Imperial Trades Edict, this chapter below.
14 A 1785 Wanderordnung for the County Oettingen is printed in Ortloff, ed., *Corpus juris,* pp. 419–433.

wait; and there was no guarantee that he might not later be by-passed for a more recent candidate who found greater favor. Another economic condition was that the candidate must prove he had the resources to establish his shop and assume the burdens of citizen and family head, some combination of tools and cash, perhaps; and often he was obliged to commit himself to the community by building or buying a house. Guilds commonly denied mastership to any bachelor, a practice that not only enjoined domestic commitment but helped the marital prospects of guild widow and orphan,[15] not to mention unplaced daughters of the community as a whole: thus marriage ordinarily coincided with admission to mastership. The property requirement was applied most stringently upon outsiders; citizens' sons with presumptive claim on citizenship and a local economic base in the family trade had a far easier time of it. The same was true of the waiting period, the *Muthjahren* or *Sitzjahren*, that lay between the fully trained journeyman's application for mastership and the decision whether or not to accept him. Its main purpose was to give guildsmen and citizens a chance to look him over, and it was mainly strangers that were subjected to the waiting period, not those whose backgrounds and prospects were known.[16]

The stranger upon whom these conditions were imposed was a stranger no more by the time he had fulfilled them all: proof of family background and domestic intent, locally produced masterwork, material resources in the town and a place in its economy, and time to learn about the community and for the community to learn about him. Familiarity and community acceptance was the real purpose of it all. That is why waiving the rules for local boys of respectable family made perfect sense to the hometownsmen, though to anyone from outside the home town, to anyone who

---

[15] Weisser, *Handwerker*, pp. 262–263, emphasizes the latter. Thus either Flegel had been married before, or was somehow forced on the tinsmiths, or else they did not regularly require marriage for membership and that caused the trouble.

[16] A good outline of the qualifications for mastership and its privileges is Hoffmann, *Das württembergische Zunftwesen*, pp. 18–25. Ortloff, *Recht der Handwerker*, passim, gives more detail but with a legalistic official's bias and selectivity; Weisser, *Handwerker*, pp. 142–192, tries to describe "wie es wirklich ist, nicht wie es seyn sollte."

thought of guilds purely as economic instruments, the communal working of the system smelled—and still does—of corruption, decadence, and economic malfunction.

The new master now shared in the local guild monopoly and agreed to abide by its rules. The guild monopoly made good economic sense within the community insofar as it maintained an appropriate balance and relation in and among the trades without exposing any citizen to ruinous competition, and assured that only skilled and responsible practitioners would pursue each of them. It was, to be sure, a system of mutual defense by guildsmen-citizens. But any guild that showed itself so restrictive as seriously to undersupply the local economy (and the local economy is in question here, no more), or to exclude citizens' sons without economic justification, incurred community pressure to ease entries into the trade, and it invited breaches of its monopoly which the community and its authorities would consider justified. If a trade grew very rich, it would attract sons of influential families who could not easily be excluded by numerical limitations. The hometown guild monopolies were enforcements of the rules whereby the community kept its soundness and autonomy, directed first of all against outsiders but also against any citizen who failed to go along with the rules.

Outside trespassers were mainly non-masters who produced or sold articles within the area where the guild claimed monopoly. They were commonly and colorfully called *Böhnhasen,* ground-rabbits; the word *Boden,* of which the first syllable is a contraction, has a fortunate double meaning that encompasses the idea of an unlicensed tailor, say, secretly making clothes in a garret, and the idea of hunting him to earth like a rabbit.[17] Within the community and even within the guild the same epithet and sanctions applied. A glover who made a wallet might have his windows knocked out by the bag-makers, and then a carpenter be hazed by the glaziers for repairing them. The boundaries between respective trade monopolies made for endless controversy when they were not clearly understood in local custom and abided by. Within the trade, a master was punished by his guild or suspended if he stole customers from his colleagues, sold from door to door instead of working

---

[17] Ground and garret are the two meanings of *Boden.* See the article on *Böhnhasen* in any edition of Grimm's *Wörterbuch.*

and waiting in his shop, cut prices or departed from standard materials and method, hired too many journeymen, or otherwise introduced disturbing elements of competition and conflict within the trade. The aforesaid tailor even if he was licensed might be using an improper stitch or improper cloth in his attic; or worse yet, he might try to sell clothes ready-made for pay by somebody outside the town. Peddlers of ready-made goods (*Hausierer*) who ventured from their normal rural circuits into the town sphere were treated as groundrabbits if they trespassed on any local trade, which they were almost certain to do.

When they could get away with it (usually they could), the guildsmen treated freemasters as groundrabbits: *Freimeister* were artisans licensed by state authorities, free of guild membership. In community eyes they were outside invaders and disturbers of the peace, *Pfuscher, Störer,* in direct proportion to the economic productivity the state presumably expected of them. The same was true of artisans supported by nobles to work on their estates: anathema to the hometown guildsmen.[18] And to a lesser degree it was true of *Landmeister* or *Dorfmeister,* village artisans licensed by state officials or tolerated in distinctly local trades, but who might expand their activities into the town trades.[19] Hunting down transgressors and outsiders made for joyous and righteous excitement: compensatory outlets no doubt for pent-up hostility and violence that hometownsmen necessarily had to suppress in their relations with each other in the enclosed community. The master guildsmen unleashed their journeymen to help, and the journeymen were willing.

Only a master might take on apprentices and journeymen, and even he only so many, and only so often, as the guild allowed: the rules differing among trades and places but usually on the order of one apprentice at a time and no more than two journeymen. Masters' widows had important status and rights within the guild (recall the insistence on respectable backgrounds for wives), and the

[18] For an effort to regulate the relation between town trades and *Adelhandwerk,* the 1750 Allgemeine Zunftordung of the Reichs-Ritter-Ort an der Baunach, printed in Ortloff, ed., *Corpus juris,* pp. 331–342.

[19] On *Landhandwerk,* the Braunschweig edicts of 1765, 1776, and 1778, ibid., pp. 189–222; also Moser, *Landeshoheit im Weltlichen,* III, 179–189.

guild had a responsibility for their welfare. A widow could continue the operation of her husband's shop; if she had no journeyman she could demand one from one of the masters; if she married a journeyman of the same trade he was made master promptly, cheaply, and free of limitations on membership because she was already one of the admitted number. She did not attend meetings or vote, for there was no place for women there, nor could she take on an apprentice; but she was freed of most guild obligations and fees. A master's blood son usually enjoyed, along with the special dispensations of fees and training, a presumptive right by birth to enter his father's guild. A master's daughter possessed in a latent way much the same rights, transferring them with marriage to a journeyman of the same trade as her father and working in his shop, so that the journeyman became in effect a son; if she was orphaned those guild rights were her main inheritance.[20] The social and familial appurtenances of mastership were very important, where there was no life insurance and no state social security system; but they pertained only within the familiar home community; nobody recognized them anywhere else.

Mastership could be lost voluntarily or semivoluntarily by ceasing to practice the trade; or a master might be suspended for serious infractions or disreputability, in which case he was likely to be publicly denounced (*gescholten*). News of his disgrace might be circulated through out the surrounding country (*Auftreibung*). That carried the threat of holding any community or guild that received him in similar disgrace, meaning the rejection of any journeyman native to that place or who had worked there, and a bad name for its daughters.

The structure and working sphere of the guilds show the place of economic institutions in hometown life. There is no doubt that the guild system was unsuited to economic growth and social mobility, nor that, if growth and mobility are taken to be the norm, it inhibited them. But that was the obverse of the guilds' vital function in communal society and politics. Their close oversight of membership and their social and moral restrictiveness, their preservation of economic security for citizen-members: the very practices that made

[20] Ortloff, *Recht der Handwerker*, pp. 291–299, for a neat list of a dead master's family's rights.

them such valuable and effective components of the community are what historians and others have meant by the decay or the decline of the early modern German guild. What appears as decadence by general economic standards was really the absorption, into these economic structures, of the important social and political functions they had in the stable communities of postmedieval and preindustrial Germany. No fully reliable comparison of medieval with eighteenth-century guild is possible now nor probably ever will be, but it is generally accepted that the guild assumed the character described in this chapter sometime around the seventeenth century. That was "a decisive turning point," according to the nineteenth-century Württemberg social economist Albert Schäffle, of the "differentiation and isolation of the guilds. Only then did the exclusive working license, the privileged demarcation of the guilds over against one another, and the control of each over its membership become the substantive meaning of the guild." Schäffle ticked off guild iniquities. "Property rights in a trade and its territorial monopoly; subjection of the countryside to the town market; marriage obligations in the interests of masters' daughters and widows; fixing and limiting the number of masters, and of the apprentices and journeymen allowed them; brutality against real and imagined intruders (groundrabbit hunts); overburdening of new masters with extravagant masterworks and all kinds of fees; silly journeyman and masterwork rites; price-fixing and the elaborate regulation of work." [21] The guilds of the economically livelier medieval towns apparently did not behave that way, if we take the word of believing medievalists. There the guild seems to have functioned as

[21] The article "Gewerbe," in *Deutsches Staats-Wörterbuch*, IV (Stuttgart, 1859), 322. Also Wilhelm Roscher, *Geschichte der National-Oekonomik in Deutschland* (Munich, 1874), p. 246, comments that most restrictive guild measures were introduced not at the time of medieval *Blüthe* but in the early modern era of *Verfall*. An interesting example of increasing guild exclusiveness in the seventeenth and eighteenth centuries is Joseph Koch, "Geschichte der Aachener Nähnadelzunft und Nähnadelindustrie bis zur Aufhebung der Zünfte in der französischen Zeit (1798)," *ZAGV*, XLI (1920), 16–122. With the circularity characteristic of studies that try to make early modern guild and communal practices medieval, even as Koch chronicles successive tightening from the eighteenth-century sources that are the earliest evidence he has, he says their behavior "must have been true of older times, because guilds tried to maintain old practices" (p. 62).

a system of economic regulation and training, and indeed as a frame for political action, but without the character of social exclusiveness, communal integration, and the enforcement of morals that it has in this story. It may be that the isolation and stability (stagnancy) of the later hometown economies is what made the difference, compared with the flourishing medieval towns that had guilds and that get studied. If so, that would be to say that the guild system, like any other economic system, worked more freely and more flexibly at times of economic vigor and expansion than at times of weakness and contraction. Yet it may remain a distinctive charactistic of the communal guild system that it responded to the pressure of bad times or of change by shrinking into conservative exclusiveness, rather than by the adaptation or renovation that might be expected of freely individualistic or of state-controlled economic systems. That characteristic came to matter a great deal.

In histories of the early modern German trade guild an inconsistency crops up that is very like the one that appears in the histories of the towns themselves. "Decadence," though agreed upon, takes two contrary forms. On the one hand guild decline appears as degeneration at the hands of the absolutist state which, by converting guilds into its own economic instruments or undercutting their powers, robbed them of their truer older functions; on the other hand guild decline is shown in stubborn, selfish behavior *contrary* to the interests of the whole population and the state, defying the common welfare and the public economy the state sought to further.[22] Again one explanation lies in the identity of sources for both views: repeated complaints and legislation ordering hometown guilds to stop behaving, as they persistently did, in ways inimical to state and public interests. Evidence like this, which separates the guild from its hometown context, is what guild history has had to rely on, apart from scattered, fragmentary, and thus inconclusive local studies. Another explanation is the mixing up of history of the strong Prussian state with the history of the strong hometown guild of the individualized country. But the point is not historiographical; it is rather to show how the period of guild de-

[22] Roughly this is Otto von Gierke's description in *Das deutsche Genossenschaftsrecht*, I (Berlin, 1868), 906–949; and it is followed by subsequent writers. Generally economic historians jump from medieval economy to industrial economy, with some discussion of cameralism but little of early modern guilds beyond reference to their decadence and decline.

cline was precisely that at which guilds were best able to defy state or public policy broadly conceived. That made the difference, for example, between the free fellowship or *Genossenschaft* whose contributions to public life Otto von Gierke (in the nineteenth century) saw in medieval town and guild charters, and the selfish privileged corporations he read about in more recent legislation or commentary, and knew something about from even closer at hand.[23]

Whatever a full comparison with medieval guilds might show, it seems clear enough for the present purpose that the hometown guild was formed and stabilized in the quieter times that followed the wars of religion and empire; it was post-Westphalia, whatever may have existed before. The first great outburst of guild charters in Württemberg came after the middle of the seventeenth century; the guilds of Kiel gained their rights and autonomy over against their territorial ruler in the mid-seventeenth century, and thenceforward the number of closed guilds grew.[24] The first Mülheim guilds were established in the late seventeenth century; the Hanover brewers took on increasingly then the character of a close privileged corporation; the first guilds in Sigmaringen were established in 1695.[25] A careful study of the bakers' guild of Grünberg in Hessen shows a pattern I take as typical: a growing insistence on purity of parentage during the seventeenth and eighteenth centuries ("ehrliche Eltern aus reinem Bett erzeuget"), a steady lowering of entry fees paid by sons and simultaneously a rising level of fees for outsiders, and a corresponding decline of the proportion of outsiders among the Grünberg bakers.[26]

A final element in the story of guild decline is the lugubrious testimony from the guild artisans themselves. They complained constantly of incursions from other trades, other towns, or from unguilded artisans set on their economic ruin.[27] Such complaints were after all public justification for their customary behavior;

---

[23] See note 22 above.

[24] Hoffman, *Das württembergische Zunftwesen*, pp. 7ff.; Fritz Hähnsen, "Geschichte der Kieler Handwerksämter," *MGKS*, XXX (1920), 1–467.

[25] Cramer, "Gewerbe der Freiheit Mülheim," pp. 4–5; August Löhdefink, "Die Entwicklung der Brauergilde der Stadt Hannover zur heutigen Erwerbsgesellschaft," *HG*, XXVIII (1925), 35, 75–91; Anton Bumiller, "Zur Geschichte des Handwerks in Stadt und Grafschaft Sigmaringen," *HJH*, XIV (1954), 15.

[26] Ernst Kauss, "Die Grünberger Bäckerzunft vom 16./19. Jahrhundert," *MOGV* XXIX (1930), pp. 42–45.

[27] Cf. W. Fischer, *Handwerksrecht und Handwerkswirtschaft*, p. 11.

from them one can make no judgment of the economic condition even of the complaining guilds or communities, let alone Germany as a whole or the individualized country; but what one assuredly can discern is the perennial posture of a guild-organized hometown economy. What figures there are make no effective evidence of decline and impoverishment in the hometown trades, though export trades like weaving were subject to market fluctuations.[28] That is not to say there was no reason for anxiety reflected in those constant complaints of decline and impoverishment, only that it was a constant anxiety, addressed mainly to the threat of increased competition, whether by state licensing of artisans, the penetration of manufactures from outside the community, or—eventually—pressure of population.

Any of these could indeed be an economic threat; and the extra-communal source of the threat was enough to make the craftsmen devoted adherents of the community and its autonomy against the outside, for direct economic reasons alone. Or, as commonly appears in cases of political controversy within communities, it made them work and even fight for the kind of political community that *would* defend its autonomy against the outside, a fight to blend the political with the economic commune. Guild organizations were hostile to any separate governing or mercantile patriciate; they were Bürger agents of the cycle that tended constantly to restore the home town, and Bürger elements of the equilibrium. They were an integral part of the incubator whose outer form was the Holy Roman Empire itself.[29]

---

[28] Hoffmann, *Das württembergische Zunftwesen*, pp. 32–34, addresses himself to this question and finds no convincing evidence of decline. See also Wilhelm Rust, "Das Tischlerhandwerk der Stadt Flensburg," *SGFS*, V (1940), 44–66, for the reestablishment of guilds after the Thirty Years' War and the grounds of their complaints of impoverishment and decline. Gustav Schmoller, *Zur Geschichte der deutschen Kleingewerbe im 19. Jahrhundert* (Halle, 1870), dismisses notions of decline as an egotistical error; within the communities the trades were static. For the different histories of weaving and the locally oriented guilded trades see Hans Mauersberg, *Die Wirtschaft und Gesellschaft Fuldas in neuerer Zeit* (Göttingen, 1969), pp. 98–101.

[29] See Ch. I above; also Heinrich G. Reichard, *Historisch-politische Ansichten . . . betreffend die Frage von der praktischen Ausbildung der städtischen Verfassungen in Deutschland* (Leipzig, 1830), pp. 159–164. Ortloff, *Recht der Handwerker*, pp. 56–57, explains the development of the early modern German guild thus: simple craftsmen were driven out of eminence, honor, and public

The Imperial Trades Edict of 1731

The most important empire-wide effort to reform guild procedures and make them uniform had the effect, by virtue of the
empire's peculiar unconscious political magic, of reinforcing the
separateness of the hometown economies of the individualized
country—where it had any effect on them at all. The Imperial
Patent of 1731 to Remedy Abuses among the Guilds, apart from its
attention to specific practices it deplored, had two main objects.
The first was to prevent extraterritorial organization of the trades
and communication among them; and the second was to make the
guilds accountable to the civic authorities of each place. Where
the authorities were in political fact the professional officials of the
state—preeminently in Brandenburg-Prussia, rather less so in
Braunschweig, and perhaps in Electoral Saxony—then the edict
served *their* purposes. Where the authorities were in political fact
hometown governments in which the guilds themselves participated,
then the edict served *their* purposes or was not observed at all.
Where—thirdly—guilds existed independently of civic authority,
then to engage town councilmen or deputies in guild affairs, as the
edict enjoined, could only knit the guild more closely into the
community and reduce its connections with outsiders in its own
trade or others. In the edict guild statutes were still assumed to
emanate from the artisans themselves, subject to ratification by
"the authorities." Because that term *Obrigkeit* was as precise as
imperial legislation could be about the assignment of power, the
edict hardly transferred power at all, but only confirmed it.[30]

The edict was brought about by certain state governments that
wanted to encourage controlled development of their territorial

---

councils (1) by manufactures undertaken especially by French religious
immigrants, (2) by their inability to maintain cultural pace with patricians
and academics, and (3) that "die Rechtspflege künstlich erlernt werden
musste." Therefore they developed the guilds as alternative ways of governing
their affairs.

[30] A translation of the edict appears as an appendix to this volume. A standard text is Christian O. Mylius, *Corpus Constitutionum Marchicarum,* I
(Berlin, 1737–1740), Theil 5, pp. 766–782. The Reichs-Gutachten of August
14, 1731 that included virtually all its substance is printed in Hans Proesler,
*Das gesamtdeutsche Handwerk im Spiegel der Reichsgesetzgebung von 1530
bis 1806* (Berlin, 1954), pp. 54*–70*.

economies, and had the administrative resources seriously to under-take it. They wanted imperial legislation to strengthen their hands against outside interference: that customary motive of imperial politics. Two kinds of outside interference were especially trouble-some. First and more important was the guild practice of denuncia-tion and ostracism, to punish practices which the state for its part considered good economic policy. If, for example, a Prussian guild under state pressure accepted "dishonorable" members—the illegiti-mate, the sons of shepherds or of state officials, or French immi-grants—then other guilds in that trade would declare the Prussian guild and town dishonorable, and journeymen could come to work there only at the risk of eternal disgrace, which could exclude them from finding work or achieving mastership in any guild that con-sidered itself honorable. What the state with its aim of economic development conceived to be abuses were precisely the foundations of the guildsmen's honor; and the correction of abuses was for guildsmen the incurrence of dishonor. Consequently the supply of journeymen and hence of potential new masters was reduced in places that had relaxed their standards under official pressure, frustrating the intent of state (or patrician) authorities in forcing the relaxation. More important, existing Prussian masters (in the example) and especially journeymen in fear of disgrace would resist official reform of abuses; journeymen might pack up and go, leaving their masters flat; or their resistance could reach the point of violence. Journeymen's strikes and riots over just this kind of issue in the 1720's, spreading from the individualized country through Germany, precipitated the 1731 law.[31] Eighteenth-century journeymen were often the most vigorous guardians of guildish abuses, not seekers after their abolition, for their careers were more

[31] Schmoller's history of the 1731 edict, "Innungswesen," pp. 325–343, emphasizes the role of the Prussian civil service; so does Meyer, *Handwerker-politik*, II (1888), 1–98. Georg Fischer, *Fränkisches Handwerk*, emphasizes the rôle of the cameralist Imperial Vice-Chancellor Schönborn, and points out that Brandenburg-Prussia long resisted such legislation on the grounds that eco-nomic affairs were a state and not an imperial matter. Wolfram Fischer, *Hand-werksrecht und Handwerkswirtschaft*, pp. 24–31, writes of a "modern, almost liberal spirit" and of "free competition"; but I think that makes too much of provisions designed neither to dissolve guilds nor blur the divisions among the trades but rather to remove uneconomic features and assign certain of their powers to public authorities.

threatened by the taint of dishonor than an established master's was. They struck and rioted against masters and guilds that engaged in dishonorable practices that would endanger their own standing elsewhere. That was the connection between the journeymen's risings and the edict's efforts to reduce by law the incidence of dishonor, and to interrupt the kind of communication from place to place and from state to state that existed in the transient journeyman's world.[32]

A lesser issue of outside communication and interference was the problem of high guilds or *Hauptladen:* the adjudication of questions arising in local trades by guild lodges located in other towns or territories. Guilds in certain places had special prestige within their trades; and their influence, formal or informal, on craft standards and honor did not respect state boundaries.[33] They rivaled local authority over local economies. The Duchy of Württemberg had even named Hauptladen on its authority (significantly in the residence towns of Stuttgart, Tübingen, and Ludwigsburg) to exercise appeal jurisdiction over the Württemberg guilds; but the towns resisted through the diet of the Württemberg estates, citing among other things the imperial law of 1731; the Hauptladen were dropped in 1764, and the Württemberg guilds kept their local orientation.[34]

The 1731 remedies of abuses were promulgated only in Brandenburg-Prussia, and the contribution of the edict there was really only to give Prussian economic policy the force of imperial law.[35] The Prussian government followed up the decree not with a dissolution of the guild economic system but with a flood of officially prepared, elaborately detailed guild statutes. Sixty-one such statutes were issued for the Mark Brandenburg between 1734 and 1736: one for each of the major trades, but the same statutes applied in every

[32] G. Fischer, *Fränkisches Handwerk*, pp. 13–36; Rudolf Stadelmann and Wolfram Fischer, *Die Bildungswelt des deutschen Handwerkers um 1800* (Berlin, 1955), p. 77.

[33] For example, the Strassburg stonemasons, the needlemakers of Breslau and Munich, the smiths of Breslau, the hatters of Munich. G. Fischer, *Fränkisches Handwerk*, p. 26.

[34] Hoffmann, *Das württembergische Zunftwesen*, pp. 38–43; Weisser, *Handwerker*, pp. 37–40.

[35] Pütter, *Constitution of the Germanic Empire*, II, 132 n., puts it that flatly.

Brandenburg town.[36] Guild organization for economic regulation and training was preserved; guild membership was obligatory, was limited, and conferred monopoly rights; but without the hometown features of local autonomy and individuality. Prussian officials turned the negative imperial prohibition of abuses into positive state control; they made "authority's" confirmation right into legislative right. In the Brandenburg towns it was soldiers directed by royal police officials that hunted down the groundrabbits, rather than hilarious drunken crowds of hometown guildsmen.

The weakness of the 1731 decree elsewhere was that it tried to treat the guilds purely as economic instruments and occupational groupings, ignoring their political and social place. In most of Germany the guild problem was in fact fundamentally a political one; but the edict could not treat politics because the institutions of the Empire offered no real political handles, only a scattered and indistinct disposition of *Obrigkeit*. Therefore it fudged the political issue; and guilds were able to evade the edict, according to a contemporary critic, because of its failure to distinguish between their rights "as representative parts of the citizenry" and their rights "as trades and occupations." That is to say, the edict's legal and political failing was that it did not and could not cope with the strength these economic instruments had in the political institutions that governed them. Consequently it did not succeed even economically. For in the home town the two roles, representation of citizenry and organization of economy, were indistinguishable—in contrast, the same critic noted, with the "lands of powerful princes."

The critic was Jacob Sieber, syndic of the imperial town of Goslar; he wrote a long book to explain why the edict still had not been carried out forty years after it appeared.[37] Sieber gave an example of what would come of enforcing this economic law upon guilds that directly participated in local government. The edict's provisions on honor and legitimacy said that even "despised per-

[36] Mylius, *Corpus Constitutionum Marchicarum* I, Theil 5, Cap. X, Anhang, pp. 1–618; Schmoller, "Innungswesen," pp. 338–339; Meyer, *Handwerker-politik*, II, 82–98. East Prussia, which lay outside the Reich, got new general legislation but no *Generalprivilegien* until the 1750's.

[37] *Abhandlung von den Schwierigkeiten in den Reichsstädten das Reichs-gesetz vom 16. Aug. 1731 wegen der Missbräuche bey den Zunften zu vollzie-hen* (Goslar, 1771); the quotations from pp. 3, 118–119.

sons" should be allowed to enter the trades. But once such people got into the guilds, "they may easily rise to the position of Guild- or Overmaster and so achieve great influence in town affairs. It is natural enough that the other representatives of the guilds as well as the citizenry will offer resistance when they see that persons against whom they as well as others have expressed some contempt should then be able to enter the government. The world is like that." [38] Besides, institutional diversity was such that it was not clear exactly what a "guild (*Zunft*)" was to begin with; the edict made no definition; and a great many associations called guilds claimed to be something else when faced by the decree. In many places the view prevailed that guild or town statutes granting economic privileges took precedence over the imperial edict; Sieber was cautious about that as a matter of law, but emphatic about its effect. The edict itself allowed that its provisions should be adapted "to the special circumstances and situation of each place" (if only, probably, because without such an allowance it could never have got through the Reichstag, nor stood any chance of acceptance if it had). Therefore local authorities could carry out the law simply by reaffirming the old rules, especially where the guilds themselves were the legitimate chartered authorities over their trades. Often the edict was simply ignored, never published: "The direct participation of guilds in town affairs," opined Sieber, "may have had no small influence in the publication of this law." [39] Honest efforts by civic authorities to enforce the edict could usually be blocked by plain noncompliance on the part of the citizen-guildsmen; the best way to avoid political trouble and domestic unrest, Sieber concluded, had been to ignore the decree's existence, so that in many places hardly anybody had even heard of it.[40]

[38] Ibid., p. 23.   [39] Ibid., p. 16.

[40] Sieber's argument is summarized in Ortloff, *Recht der Handwerker*, pp. 137–140. He was writing of imperial towns in defense of his own; but he did not restrict his argument to them, and state legislation and public comment show that what he said was true of territorial towns too. See, for example, the Electoral Mainz decree of 1751 in Ortloff, ed., *Corpus juris*, pp. 293–314, and other legislation he prints, passim; also Lomberg, *Historisch-politische Staatsrechtsabhandlung*, passim, on the 1731 edict in territorial towns. Often the tendency of state legislation was to confirm hometown economic defenses in ways contrary to the intent of 1731—Baden and of course Prussia being the main exceptions.

Guild and home town

The history of the imperial patent of 1731 was a demonstration of how the political constitution of the Empire sheltered the home-town economic systems just as it did the civic systems. Where there was no apparatus of simultaneous uniform enforcement, within a realm, then for any given place to observe the provisions against abuses in the edict would have brought dishonor on the tradesmen of that place and imperiled its economy. The means of economic regulation in most of the empire were hometown instruments, ostracism for disrepute against deviants outside and within, there being no more positive regulative means except in large ener-getic states; and almost nobody could be expected to relinquish them while the Empire remained what it was. By their exercise of these instruments of ostracism and dishonor, the guilds, themselves protected by their place in hometown polity, contributed to its distinctive style.

Guilds derived their character and their influence from their roles as organizers of the hometown economy. Occupations incompatible with guild organization were deliberately kept outside the home town: the agriculture, mining, luxury items, weaving for export, and the large-scale manufacture that found their places in the flat country or the flattened cities.[41] The pursuit of such occupations in such places had little or nothing to do with communal member-ship.[42] There economic organization was controlled by the state conformably with its ends, or by a noble master conformably with his, or else individuals went their own economic ways.

The names and sizes of the hometown trades varied locally, especially because the customary scope of any trade's monopoly varied from place to place; the category of things one guild pro-duced in one town might be divided up among two or three guilds in another, or consolidated into a more broadly defined trade in a third. But the guidelines offered in a statute for the small residence

---

[41] See Ch. I above; on "the rusticalization of industry," Werner Sombart, *Der moderne Kapitalismus*, II (4th ed.; Munich, 1922), pp. 803–808, 903–906.

[42] For nonguild trades and the statutes and ordinances governing them see Wilhelm Ebel, ed., *Quellen zur Geschichte des deutschen Arbeitsrechts (bis 1849)* (Göttingen, 1964), pp. 14–15 and passim.

town of Fulda in the 1780's give some idea of what they were in such a place and how they were distributed.[43]

Butchers	40	Master smiths	8	Coopers	10
Bookbinders	4	Locksmiths	8	Glaziers	8
Wigmakers	8	Cutlers	4	Ropemakers	10
Bakers	20	Coppersmiths	4	Saddlers	10
Tailors	36	Gunsmiths	4	Joiners	10
Shoemakers	60	Nailsmiths	4	Potters	8
Furriers	2	Braziers	6	Dyers	4

Only a very few of the town-organized trades were allowed to country artisans outside the guild ban: the rudimentary work of village smiths and carpenters, coarse shoe repair (not manufacture), wagoners, "peasant tailors," and linen weavers. Country artisans ordinarily were not allowed to take on apprentices or journeymen, and they had no corporate organization.[44]

The guild therefore set off the home town economically from the outside, and no attack on abuses could deny them that capacity for so long as their communal positions were secure and their regulatory and training apparatus was indispensable.[45] No pre-Napoleonic

[43] "Polizeiordnung für die Handwerker 27 Hornung 1784," in Ortloff, ed., Corpus juris, pp. 317–318. The statute was supposed to remedy bad economic conditions attributed to unwise choices of occupation, inadequate training, the overstaffing of certain trades, and bad guild administration; it provided for the official appointment of life-long Overmasters from three candidates put forward by each guild, and urged in the interest of flexibility that sons of one guild be treated as sons in another rather than as outsiders. Fulda's residential character appears in the unusual number of wigmakers, bookbinders, and gunsmiths, though these might appear almost anywhere. The absence of tanners suggests that this trade, always one threatened with low prestige, was exercised in and about Fulda by Landhandwerker or other unguilded workmen. The many shoemakers presumably did all the leatherwork, except for harnessing, for Fulda and environs. The large number of butchers is not abnormal: the meat trade benefited most from the subjection of the countryside to the town market.

[44] Moser, Landeshoheit im Weltlichen, III, 179–189; but see the 1771 analysis of town and land trades described by Carl v. Tyszka, Handwerk und Handwerker in Bayern im 18. Jahrhundert (Munich, 1907), pp. 4–8.

[45] The "absolutist" Johann H. G. v. Justi argued that hometown guild privileges and monopolies should be retained as regulatory devices; and that the trades should be kept out of the countryside; but guild organization should not be allowed into the large-scale Manufaktur or Fabrik of the Entrepreneur. Grundsätze der Polizeiwissenschaft (3d rev. ed.; Göttingen, 1782), pp. 159–163, 386.

reform legislation attacked the latter. Neither the "dissolution" rather emptily threatened by the 1731 edict if the guilds did not behave, nor the reorganization undertaken by Frederick William I of Prussia and contemplated by others, had to do with economic freedom in the sense of opening the trades to all comers: they meant at most to deny the guilds their autonomous authority and to reinvest it in the civic authorities as a police power.[46] Economically guild organization was indispensable everywhere, or at least that was the almost universal belief, and a well-founded one while the Empire existed; and in the individualized country their political role made them unassailable in that sphere as well.[47]

The presences of guild members on a town council, lectured the learned Christian Thomasius, was the sign of a "democratic" town government as opposed to an "aristocratic" one,[48] inasmuch as guilds linked citizen into authority. There was an endless variety of constitutional arrangements reflecting that position. Recall the elaborate system of Rottweil. Justus Möser's own Osnabrück, a territorial town, was much the same, and the guild system with all its ways penetrated Osnabrück's political institutions through and through.[49] In Überlingen the craft guilds joined with a hereditary body of "honorables" to elect the magistracy.[50] The guilds of Sieber's Goslar cited their constitutional rights to block the edict of 1731, but he was at pains to say that *de facto* powers, not the legal position, were what mattered, "for even if I were to set out to refute the arguments the guilds and their defenders bring in, and to prove them illogical and weak arguments, still for all of that the thing itself remains, and the obstructions will not go away." [51]

[46] Schmoller, "Innungswesen," p. 80.

[47] See the attack on groundrabbitry in Bavarian legislation of 1749 in Meyr, ed., *Sammlung*, II (1784), 733–736.

[48] "Von denen Lehren so einem Studioso juris in der teutschen Rechts-Gelahrtheit so viel den Wehrstand betrifft zu wissen nöhtig" (bound MS lecture notes in the Olin Library, Cornell University), p. 591. "Aristocratice" and "democratice" are in roman script.

[49] Joachim Runge, *Justus Mösers Gewerbetheorie und Gewerbepolitik im Fürstbistum Osnabrück in der zweiten Hälfte des 18. Jahrhunderts* (Berlin, 1966), pp. 45–53.

[50] "Ueber das Wahlrecht in Ueberlingen," *JM*, V (1795), pp. 432–470.

[51] Sieber, *Schwierigkeiten*, p. 8; for a description of Goslar in Sieber's time, Eberhard Kreutzberger, *Das Gewerberecht der Reichsstadt Goslar im*

The hometownsman's generalized quality of Eigentum came from his entry into political and social identity through these economic media. Thus Eigentum could not be divided into private economic property on the one hand and civic rights on the other for so long as the trade guilds guarded the gates to community membership.[52] They stood guard through their acknowledged custody of the *Bürgerliche Nahrung*, the "citizen's livelihood," a conception that broadened their economic function into a civic one because it meant that their responsibility for the maintenance of a decent living for citizen-masters implied a right and a responsibility to determine who might be citizen and master.

Bürgerliche Nahrung as prerequisite for citizenship was not a static property qualification nor even a requirement of technical skill. These might contribute to it, but they were not its essence. It meant the economic security and stability of the solid citizen, a trustworthy man because he was committed to local society and totally reliant upon it; like Eigentum, it combined economic and civic status into personal quality. The "nourishment" of that kind of quality required a sound economic base, and property and skills were part of that; but it also required assurance of the other attributes needed for hometown acceptance and membership.[53] Hometownsmen would not buy their sausages from an adulterer, a liar, a blasphemer, a cheat, if only for fear of what their neighbors would say if they did; and if a neighborhood butcher was one of those things they would know it and his business would fail. And so the guilds along with their economic and political functions were custodians of morality as well, often to the point of amazing prurience, and joined moralism into the defense of their honor as tradesmen and citizens.

---

18. Jahrhundert und der Reichsschluss von 1731 (Goslar, 1959); also Schlözer, "Disputen in Goslar 1779."

[52] Property became private and unpolitical "erst in einer Welt, in der all Herrschaftsgewalt bei einer einheitlichen Staatsgewalt konzentriert und monopolisiert ist und dieser eine entpolitisierte Gesellschaft privater Untertanen gegenübersteht," writes Ernst-Wolfgang Böckenförde, *Die deutsche verfassungsgeschichtliche Forschung im 19. Jahrhundert* (Berlin, 1961), p. 119, following the historical arguments of Georg Waitz and others.

[53] For the application of the *Bürgerliche Nahrung* see, e.g., Johann Grönhoff, "Kieler Bürgerbuch: Verzeichnis der Neubürger von Anfang des 17. Jahrhunderts bis 1869," MGKS, XLIX (1958), 14–26; see also pp. 126, 296.

Guild moralism and the integrated personality

The extremes and the eccentricities of guild moralism remain puzzling after all reasonable explanations have been used up, and may be, like some kinds of eccentric personal behavior, a signal of the matter's importance. One explanation is that the notion of honorable status, of *Ehrbarkeit*, with which they were intensely concerned, was so broad and vague a slogan that it provided no reasonable or functional limits. *Ehrbarkeit* (often *Redlichkeit* or decency) could not be clearly defined or objectively ascertained, like wealth, skill, or performance; it was something sensed as it was displayed and received within a community of whom all shared the same standards. Outsiders could detect wealth or skill, and there were laws to define civil crime; but neither could tell about moral honor, not all of it. Its imprecise character led the guildsmen into absurdities of prurience and persecution when they tried to judge and act upon it. There was no check on their eagerness to show their own morality by the severity with which they judged others.

The main preoccupation with legitimacy of birth, which extended by easy stages into questions of sexual behavior and social background, had a reasonable foundation in the domestic character of community and economy: the importance of knowing who somebody was, and the soundness of his family circumstances. The guild encompassed the citizen-master's life, not just his occupation. His family was part of his occupation and his guild; his widow and his orphans were cared for by it and his sons were specially privileged within it. But legitimacy was not only nor even mainly a matter of inheritance rights; there were plenty of adequate laws to handle those. *Ehrbarkeit* meant domestic, civic, and economic orderliness and these were undermined by the promiscuity and irresponsibility implied by illegitimate birth. Legitimate childbirth resulted from sober and responsible intention to have a child, whose conception bore the community's sanction; illegitimacy implied the contrary. The trouble with Flegel's father-in-law, according to the Hildesheim tinsmiths, was that he was not *echt und recht erzielt*, not "truly and rightly begot" in the sense of "intended." Not to have been intended was a fact presumed to have effect on Helmsen's attitude and behavior in the world, whatever the bishop said; and that would influence his daughter too. So much seems clear enough in guildsmen's attitude toward legitimacy of birth, and there is a hint besides that along with the danger of irresponsible laxity, illegitimacy might imply an equally unappropriate and distasteful aggressiveness.

It might be argued that moral sanctions were directed less against loose sexual behavior as such than at its social consequences: the foisting upon the community of persons with uncertain origins and uncertain qualifications for membership. The hometownsman's pride was closely involved in the guild's quest for purity. More mobile elements of German society were held by hometownsmen to be sexually and maritally promiscuous, so that sexual and marital purity were a caste mark that guildsmen-citizens employed to set themselves apart. It was important to be different from lower elements especially, from the rooting peasantry with its servile origins and style.[54] Then there were the merchants and peddlers, traveling salesmen of their day, trying like cuckoos to pass off their bastards into the artisanry; and loose-living aristocrats had to be watched for that too.[55] The guilds took special pains to be sure no artisan married a fallen woman for a price, apparently a frequent source of moral infection and hard to distinguish from more normal pre-marital pregnancies: the 1731 edict mentioned the problem of "marriage of a female person made pregnant when unmarried by yet another person." [56]

No doubt the guilds used ostensibly moral grounds to exclude persons held undesirable for reasons not strictly moral—not directly concerned with sex or marriage, that is, but exclusion for economic or civic reasons. In such cases the search for moral grounds, with their special psychological force and appeal, led to some of the oddities and extremes. Put moralism for the sake of exclusion together with sexual purity as the hometownsman's mark of caste, and guild moralism becomes a specific instrument for excluding unwanted social elements from the community, and as such its use was

[54] Cf. Lomberg, *Historisch-politische Staatsrechtsabhandlung*, p. 13.

[55] Ferdinand Frensdorff, "Das Zunftrecht insbesondere Norddeutschlands und die Handwerkerehre," *HGB* XIII (1907), pp. 44–54.

[56] In § 11: see Appendix below.

stretched to the borders of credibility. It helped screen out unwanted outsiders, regardless of social estate, because it was so much
harder for them than for natives to prove honorable family background. In other moral questions too, not only did the outsider have
little evidence to offer for himself, his very arrival at the gates made
him suspect of having become *persona non grata* elsewhere, and
chances are he had. Why hadn't he applied in his own home town,
where people knew him? It was easier for such a man to rove
countryside and city than it was to enter the hometown as a Bürger.

The taint of illegitimacy lasted for generations; the same was true
of other dishonorable estates. The list of dishonorable occupations
coheres only in the moral sense of the hometown guildsmen who
made it; it is almost without limit because each guild and each
place had to show itself more discriminating than the rest, and no
one could dissent from any instance without jeopardizing his own
honor. Hangmen first of all: the usual taboo of the executioner, but
hometown hangmen got a lot of other disgraceful work as well:
clearing carrion, burying rotten fish.[57] Even the 1731 edict did not
dare call the sons of hangmen honorable.[58] Skinners worked with
dead bodies too, and the word *Schinder* was sometimes used to
mean both hangman and skinner. The line between what skinners
did with carcasses and what butchers and tanners did with meat
and hides was elaborately guarded, but not well enough to keep the
tanners free of taint. Barbers and surgeons worked with wounds, a
disgusting and servile business. So did bathers, and doubtless besides there were promiscuous goings-on at the baths. The lofts of
mills were morally suspect too, and millers swindling middlemen
and speculators to boot. Shepherds were contemptible everywhere.
What kind of a man would be a shepherd? They skinned dead
sheep (the flayed Lamb of God prominent in religious symbolism
of the time may have enhanced that feature), and the same stories
about a shepherd's relations with his sheep seem to have been told
that I heard in New England as a boy. The weaving of linen was
another primitive occupation, and like shepherding had suspect
rural overtones and connections. Musicians and players moved

[57] Helmut Schuhmann, *Der Scharfrichter* (Kempten, 1964).
[58] In § 4: see Appendix below.

from place to place, like itinerant peddlers and beggars.[59] And officials of the state: their sons were adjudged dishonorable by the guildsmen, should they ever think of entering a hometown trade. It was a mark of dishonor to have worked as a peasant, or for a noble, or in a factory, a *Fabrik*. It was a sign of failure and dishonor for a master to work in a factory, wrote Sieber; if he took work there it was because, despite his failure, his master's status kept him from being employed like a journeyman by another master.[60] As for journeymen who worked in factories: what kind of training was to be had in a place where things were made in large anonymous numbers and sold to customers the maker did not know? Not the right kind of preparation for the hometown trades.[61]

Guild morality equated the outsider with dishonor; those two factors of repulsion multiplied together to produce guild moralism's intensity and its righteousness. It is important to note here that guilds, economic institutions, bore this spirit in the hometown community. The fervid moral preoccupation of the guilds, like their social and economic restrictiveness, seems mainly to have developed in the seventeenth and eighteenth centuries. There had been dishonorable occupations for long before that (mainly the more reasonable ones), but little sign that moral fervor had been an important part of guild life. It was a part of the multiplication of their role beyond the custody of economic standards and training.

[59] On transients and their dishonor, Theodor Hampe, *Die fahrenden Leute in der deutschen Vergangenheit* (Leipzig, 1902).

[60] Sieber, *Schwierigkeiten*, pp. 111–112.

[61] A general treatment of dishonor in anthropological terms of cult, myth, and taboo is Werner Danckert, *Unehrliche Leute* (Bern, 1963); closer to the points at issue here is Otto Beneke, *Von unehrlichen Leuten* (Hamburg, 1863). But the relation of guild dishonor with the German sense of industrial proletariat and capitalism (to which I shall return in later chapters) has never to my knowledge been thoroughly examined. The best sources for the guilds' application of honor and dishonor are legislation like the 1731 imperial edict, telling them what they should stop doing. In addition to the special cases of hangmen and transients (notes 57 and 59 above), two rather weak discussions mainly from medieval sources are Christian Meyer, "Die unehrlichen Leute in älterer Zeit," *Sammlung gemeinverständlicher Vorträge*, NF, IX (Hamburg, 1895), Heft 193; and Frensdorff, "Zunftrecht und Handwerkerehre," pp. 1–89, which also explains some of the puzzling guild jargon; on the latter see also Johann F. Eisenhart, *Grundsätze der deutschen Sprüchwörtern* (Helmstädt, 1759).

That role was multiplied by the maintenance of social continuity and stability, and that by the guardianship of civic standards, and finally all united into morality in the sense of personal justification, of the kind traditionally in the hands of religious institutions— *moral* morality, the morality of conscience. The curious stock expression, "The guilds must be as pure, as if they had been gathered together by doves," seems to have originated in the seventeenth century.[62] It may be that in the background of the early modern German craft guild's moral guardianship was the weakening and dispersal of religious institutions after the wars of religion: institutions perhaps with more experience and discrimination in moral questions than the home town. Civic authority had taken up moral custody first: not only state laws but seventeenth-century town statutes were full of religious and moral exhortations. But these had nearly disappeared by the mid-eighteenth century. And when the guild assumed the moral role, it adapted moral questions, unsurprisingly, to its economic structure and interests and to its place in the civic community. The guild, first habitat of the hometown Bürger, blended economic and civic and personal standards together into the moral quality of honor, in such a way that a man's personal morals—and his ancestors'—determined his economic competence and his civic rights; at the same time economic competence was prerequisite for civic and moral acceptance; and at the same time responsible civic membership was requisite for economic rights and personal justification. Such a combination might be called bourgeois morality, but like the political standards mentioned before it was the morality of the hometownsman, not the mobile and sophisticated high bourgeois. Hometownsmen did not have the multiple standards and compartmentalized lives that so many modern moral and social critics deplore: one set of standards for church on Sunday, another for relations with friends, another for business relations. They were whole men, integrated personalities, caught like so many flies in a three-dimensional web of community.

The totality of the web made the moralism with which the hometownsman defended his economic interests, and the righteousness he brought to his politics; it provided the aura of depravity and evil

[62] Eisenhart, *Grundsätze der deutschen Sprüchwörtern*, pp. 60–63; Frensdorff, "Zunftrecht und Handwerkerehre," pp. 44–45.

he attributed to rivals and strangers. The guilds in their connective functions—between citizen and community, and among compartments of life we incline to treat separately—were vital institutions of communal defense and also main determiners of what it was that would be defended, and against whom. Guildsmen were the wall and the web incarnate. The hometown community rested on the guild economy, and fell only when the guild economy was overwhelmed.

CHAPTER IV

Walls, Webs, and Citizens

THE ways in which the home towns were like each other and different from the rest were not apparent even to themselves until trouble began for all of them together at the end of the eighteenth century and the beginning of the nineteenth: not until the forced confrontation that broke into the incubator and challenged familiarity with change, and the powerless with power. The communities' survival then brought the kind of recognition—reluctant on the part of some, sentimental on the part of others—that their style of life had in the Biedermeier period; but still that was not a very accurate recognition, which is why I have had to invent a name for them and write a book to explain it. But although the nature and the place of the home town had to await revelation by crisis and confrontation, the meaning of the crisis to them and the response they made to it were set by postures they had already adopted when it came, so that a summary description of those is something more than an exercise in hindsight. The same is true of the other elements of German society: their past political experience made the terms they used to grasp and to meet the political crises that began in the 1790's and lasted until the 1820's. Especially, it determined or at least foreshadowed the stance each element took toward the others when history forced them into a common rhythm and onto a common stage.

The varieties of political experience

It has often been said that the behavior of Germans during that episode—the subject of this book's next section—showed that they were politically inexperienced or naive. To say this is to give a very specialized meaning to the word political, for no person has ever lived with others without political experience, nor has any group ever lived together without accumulating a set of serviceable political rules and expectations. The cliché becomes more useful when it is taken to mean—and critics of German politics have often meant it this way—that the German small-townsman looked upon political problems with the eyes of a small-townsman; the Mecklenburg rural squire tried to treat politics as if they were bounded by the experience and horizons of an East Elbian estate; or the civil servant looked upon politics as a matter of state administration. That in turn would be no more than the redundancy it sounds like, except that it bespeaks a certain kind of political experience. The kind of political experience which Germany has often seemed to lack relates to the scale and scope of politics.

The important thing about scale, though, was not directly the crude size of a polity, its territory or its population, nor its importance. It was rather the question of commonality among political experience and goals; or conversely, delineations among the several spheres within which political processes worked. The German system of petty principalities was not the cause of German political provincialism (or "inexperience"), although sometimes they were allies. Rather, both the petty principalities and the mutual exclusiveness of spheres were products of the same cause. The same balancing pattern in favor of the powerless and of the status quo that preserved the German petty states preserved the isolation and idiosyncrasies of the several elements of German society, even when all those elements lived side by side in the same state. Criticism of German political inexperience has ordinarily taken the politics of France, England, or the United States to be norms; and German patriotic conservatives have countered accurately by calling western political ideas and institutions "alien ideologies." What that means for the present purpose is that Germany, in the time of which I write and for long after, did not have the administrative and judicial system of the French monarchy, nor the parliamentary cabinet system of Great Britain, nor the party system of United States politics. And these seem to have been, in those countries, critical instruments for relating different localities and social elements into state politics, and thus with each other.

The consequence was (looking at it negatively) that the varieties of German political experience remained different and separate, divided not so much as regions or states but more significantly as social and occupational groupings, mutually exclusive and often hostile, and without the need of submerging or compromising their special variants to a common interest or a common master. The overcoming of that problem, conceived in one set of terms or another and attacked by one means or another, has been the main theme of modern German history (and it is a conception underlying this book). In the abstract it is not a uniquely German problem, surely; it is ubiquitous; but it was discerned as a distinctly serious German problem at the end of the eighteenth century and the beginning of the nineteenth. German behavior in the reform period did not result from political inexperience any more than German acceptance of Hitler's Third Reich resulted from political inexperience; both resulted from the kinds of experience that were brought to bear on emerging issues. In his own terms the hometownsman may have been the most politically experienced German of them all in the eighteenth century, for within his community every action and every encounter was implicitly political. But his experience and his posture were quite different from those of agrarian society, and from those of the educated cosmopolitans of cities and of government.

One reason why the hometownsmen of the eighteenth century could not quite see themselves or be seen as a whole, distinctive category in German society was their mutual isolation and the variety of their institutions. Another reason was the formulation by estates conventionally used in German legal and social description, with its main divisions of nobles, Bürger, and peasants.[1] For that classification never worked out successfully even in the political

[1] Or into *Wehr-, Lehr-,* and *Nähr-Stand,* or into any number of other classifications: see Carol R. Loss, "*Status in Statu:* The Concept of Estate in the Organization of German Political Life, 1750–1825" (unpubl. diss., Cornell,

sociology of the eighteenth century. There were some particular
reasons why it did not, defects of a kind that appear in any system
for sorting out a society. Of these probably the most important was
that the estate system of categories left the civil service out of account altogether, though by the end of the eighteenth century it
was a coherent and quite clearly defined political and social entity,
drawing membership from the several estates of birth. Similarly,
estate categories obscure the place of the German nobility, which
might be either administrative or agrarian; and to identify the
peasantry as an estate attributes to them a coherence and a political
importance they did not possess. Also, to place everybody who was
neither noble nor peasant in the Bürger estate can be misleading
indeed.

These are difficulties that arise mainly from identifying estate
with birth. More generally, classification by estate emphasized rank
and hierarchy in such a way as to obscure the actual lateral boundaries that set one social and political world off from another: noble
and peasant, for example, were at opposite ends of the hierarchy,
but they might live in the same world and know each other very
well; civil servant and hometownsman might both fall into the *bürgerlich* estate, but they really represented political and social anti-
theses. And a final general defect or ambiguity was that estate
classification usually tried to show the participation of each category in a harmonious whole, while at the same time emphasizing
the separateness of each. Consequently everybody devised his own
system of estates: because nobody ever found a really satisfactory
one.

That is the reason for the threefold political sociology whose
description began with the population boundaries of the home
town in Chapter I. Germany by the end of the eighteenth century
had settled out into three realms of experience and habit, three
kinds of political environment. And although every state and every
region contained some of each, and often they lived side by side,
they rarely mingled. The hometownsmen were one world; the rural
regime of nobles and peasants was another; and the third world
was a body of people I shall provisionally call movers and doers,

---

1970). The word estate or *Stand* as I use it here, though, should not be confused with specific active political bodies or diets.

for it is too early to use the term "general estate" that Georg Friedrich Hegel coined for them in Napoleonic times.[2]

The categories of German society were separate cultures; they were, in one kind of analytical language, nominal and not ordinal categories. That is, they are not hierarchic groupings along a scale of wealth, power, skill, or numbers. They do not represent different stages of development along a time scale, either, as in the feudal-bourgeois-proletarian historical sociology of the nineteenth century. They are not big apples and little apples. Nor were they apples at different stages of ripeness that could be matured into one another, given time and sunshine, without changing their essential character. That turned out to be the trouble. The separateness of the three worlds became hostility whenever there was change or stress, and so it is important to compare them and consider their habitual relations with one another before leaving the eighteenth century. For the pictures hometownsmen had of the other two and the lines drawn against them were important and established parts of community life by then—the boundaries of the communal webs that sustained the citizens' right, the *Bürgerrecht*.

Countrymen

The hometownsmen drew most of their sustenance, apart from exchange among themselves, from the nearby countryside. They profited from exchange through the local market, from the processing of agricultural produce, and by performing trades and services only permitted to townsmen or possible in towns. But despite their constant proximity with countrymen, townsmen lived every day in a very different set of circumstances. The interlocking corporate shields in which the townsmen participated made for a different kind of experience and a different kind of authority from the real countryside, be it the villages or settlements where everybody was a peasant-farmer doing the same things but alone, or be it the estate whose lord directly supervised and controlled those who worked the land. The peasantry was not really incorporated at all: no matter where a peasant was legally located between servility and independence, his status was individual and his relation with authority direct, whether immediately with the state and its officials,

2 See below, pp. 197–198.

or with single nobles in their own capacities or as agents of the state. Noble corporations or diets were nothing like the home town either; they were provincial or state bodies composed of a ruling class, a minority among the population of the region where they lived and governed, and where the majority had no voice in governance.[3] The hometownsman set himself off from both servility and nobility, and he appears to have regarded both kinds of countrymen with only slightly varied proportions of resentment and contempt—two emotions that were as one in the hometownsman's breast.

Apart from the differences between the hometownsmen's world and the countrymen's, there was regular conflict along the border that separated them, a conflict of interests. For example: how often should local peasantry be allowed to enter a public town market and sell directly there, thus cutting into the turnover of hometown middlemen? Only often enough to bring the peasantry into town to buy, in the hometown view, leaving a margin of profit in the community when they departed. On the other hand townsmen tried to keep local peasants from escaping the town's market monopoly by taking their produce to any other outlet. And just what should the peasant be allowed to sell in the town market? What about brooms? And from whom should he be allowed to buy? What about peddlers? Conflicting interest on market rules often invited state intervention and legislation, sometimes at the instance of nobles whose peasants' economy, and thus indirectly their own, was affected. Townsmen insisted that brewing was a Bürger occupation, and must be carried out within the town by regular brewers; for among the trades based on the processing and resale of what the peasant grew, only butchering was as important and profitable as brewing, and although peasants could not be kept from killing their own meat, brewing almost inevitably involved exchange. The beer tax was an important source of local revenue; and brewers and innkeepers were likely to be influential townsmen who might be undersold by country brewers who did not pay it, not

---

[3] The description of countrymen relies mainly on the following: Theodor von der Goltz, *Geschichte der deutschen Landwirtschaft*, I (Stuttgart, 1902); Friedrich Lütge, *Geschichte der deutschen Agrarverfassung* (Stuttgart, 1963); and Wilhelm Abel, *Geschichte der deutschen Landwirtschaft* (Stuttgart, 1962).

to mention the loss of market that would come of any bypassing of their monopoly.[4]

Peasants had the right to make their own tools, and to make simple repairs of some of the things they had bought in town: but what if they became good at it, and started helping or supplying their neighbors? Hometownsmen had constantly to guard the line dividing accepted rural activities from peasant groundrabbitry, and the countryman was their adversary. The related problem of *Landmeister* was more severe; for they, trained artisans licensed by the state to operate in the countryside, immune to hometown guild monopoly, linked countrymen with the state against the hometownsmen: an important nexus. And although landmaster trades were ordinarily limited to rudimentary blacksmithing, weaving, and the like, and although they were not supposed to encroach on the towns' immediate neighborhoods, the limits were hard to draw and maintain, so that there was always friction. Nobody really doubted that town crafts ought to be forbidden the peasant, given the nature of peasants, "from which it is clear," according to a legal treatise of 1780, "that it would be mischievous for the peasantry to assume artisan ways unto itself." [5] But the number of landmasters tended to grow in the degree that guild exclusiveness, whether or not justified by the overfilling of local trades, forced artisans to settle in the villages and to seek state protection for their activities there; and then their competition depressed the hometown trades and caused them to be more exclusive still.[6] The sons of landmasters had no easier entry into the home town than the sons of peasants. And the townsmen's exclusion of countrymen from his community meant that those who drifted somehow within the walls were—reinforcing the hometown prejudice—stragglers without sustenance or skills who had either to be supported or driven out.

Hometownsmen and nobles found no bond of sympathy in their common disdain for Germany's predominant peasant population.

[4] See for example the articles on brewing and on the export of grain in the Bautzen statute of 1678 and in the Seidenburg statute of 1698, in Schott, *Sammlungen,* II, 28–29, 177–178.

[5] Ludewig F. Gabcke, *Grundsätze des Dorf- und Bauernrechts* (Halle, 1780), p. 44.

[6] Thus the analysis in the Oettingen Wanderordnung of 1785 in Ortloff, ed., *Corpus juris,* pp. 419–426; also the Braunschweig edict of 1776, pp. 212–218.

Hometown relations with rural nobility were less direct than those with the peasantry that regularly provided the town's economic margin over internal exchange. Nobles had little reason to enter the hometown economy, and ordinarily they had little reason to want to live there. Nobles who were not countrymen turned to the capital cities, and rural nobles bought and sold in the cities what they did not produce and consume on their own estates. A noble could install his own artisans, independent of the guild system. These *Adelshandwerker*, like the rural artisans of the villages, were presumed to stay clear of the hometown sphere, working only on and for their master's own estate. But again there was leakage, the rule meant both friction and separation between town and countryside.[7] The hometown artisan encountered the noble artisan as a dishonorable rival, a groundrabbit and a servile one at that: resentment and contempt. Probably the noble artisan posed only a small threat in most of the individualized country, where there were few nobles resident on the land who held judicial powers that affected towns. The tension rose with the power of the employing or licensing authority. High nobles with pretensions of sovereignty employed *Hofhandwerker* to supply their courts and governing establishments. Such court artisans might or might not have connections with a guild, but they came under the jurisdiction of the lord; they worked for members of his establishment and his employees and were supposed to work only for them. They might make up a considerable part of the craft economy in a residence town with a large court. If a noble's legal position actually reached territorial sovereignty, then his noble right to appoint artisans of his own blended over into a state right to license artisans in its jurisdiction, the freemasters, *magistri exemti*, immune to guild controls within the territory.[8] The individualized country knew freemasters very well.

Rural society was organized differently in different parts of Germany; its relations with the state authority differed; and the differences bore on the relation of the home towns with the countryside and even on their ability to exist. The main division by the end

[7] The 1750 General Guild Ordinance of Baunach, later adopted by the Stift Würzburg, was an effort to order the relation between *Adelshandwerk* and guild artisans. Ibid., pp. 331–342.

[8] Ortloff, *Recht der Handwerker*, pp. 308–315.

of the eighteenth century was the familiar one between East Elbian Germany, to the northeast, and the rest, roughly to the south and west of the Elbe River. The East Elbian pattern of agrarian organization prevailed in the provinces of East and West Prussia, in Pomerania, Posen, Brandenburg, Mecklenburg, and Schleswig-Holstein. Some parts of Silesia, Saxony, Hanover, and Thuringia were East Elbian in character. The basic difference was between the estate lordship (*Gutsherrschaft*) of the East and landlordship (*Grundherrschaft*) prevalent in the West and South, and thus in most of the individualized country of the old Empire. This generally meant that the peasantry of the South and West characteristically lived on family-sized holdings that they worked themselves, independently, paying fixed annual fees to an absentee landlord, fees that might be looked upon as a kind of rent, or, if the landlord was a territorial sovereign—prince, free knight, or imperial town—more like a tax; for the peasant could not be expelled (or at least he rarely was), and his tenure was heritable. Such tenure approached what we mean by private property, real estate, despite the name landlordship.

The divorce of the nobility of the South and West from actual conduct of farming operations meant greater participation by them in court life, high administration, and state political life—something nobles did everywhere, but here it was the most rewarding activity open to them, unless they chose to vegetate and live on rents. And so they became there part of the state interest, rather than an independently powerful agrarian economic interest. The landlordship areas, with no powerful noble class directly engaged in the countryside, was the most favorable ground for hometown communities to grow upon. In the estate-lordship regions of the East, by contrast, the nobility was very close to country life; they lived there and directed what went on there, ran their estates and the local economy, and produced for the market. Estates were entailed, passing as blocks from father to eldest son, retaining the economic viability of the noble class. An East Elbian noble who went into state service, or to the court or to the army, could if it suited him better go home to the family homestead and find enough to do. As a working agriculturalist, or as a brother or a nephew of one, he had a greater interest in state policies that would further the agrarian interest (as against townsmen, for example) than did the absentee collector of fixed rents who was more common in West Elbia. And as an independent figure whose power on his holding was practically unchallenged, he exercised administrative and juridical powers over the people who worked his land, so that they were serfs: the East Elbian noble was both governor and employer over the same people. Town society felt his power too; home towns did not develop where noble estate-lordship combined with strong noble influence on state government in the interest of the agrarian economy.

The making of the East Elbian agrarian constitution seems in the main to have been contemporaneous with the suppression of the towns attributed to the Hohenzollerns of Prussia; that helps account for the greater mobility of East Elbian society and for the rarity of home towns there. Earlier, say in the sixteenth century, East Elbia had been rather more like the West and the South; then it began to move away from that in the direction of estate-lordship.[9] Often it has been said that the Hohenzollerns left local governing powers and economic advantages to nobles of the East because they needed money, soldiers, and political support for their high politics. High politics apart, perhaps the weakness of towns to begin with left the crown with no alternative to noble control over local government before the development of a powerful independent bureaucracy. At any rate state and countryman seemed allied in East Elbia, in the light of which the notion of "centralized country" takes on rather a different cast, but no more favorable one for the home-townsman. The nature of the landscape, suitable for extensive agriculture in nonperishable crops, and accessible to foreign markets, encouraged the expansion of farming operations beyond the subsistence level and the collection of peasant rents. Both state and agrarian entrepreneur had an interest in exports. And the thinner, weaker, more mobile population of East Elbia offered little resistance to absorption into great noble estates and thus to the predominance of noble agrarian interest there, a process which picked up speed during the seventeenth and early eighteenth centuries. That led to measures for the protection of the remaining independent peasants under Frederick the Great (along with other German rulers) and from that to the agrarian reforms of the decades after his death. But peasants were countrymen too, and reform no helpful proposition for hometownsmen.

[9] I accept here the description of Lütge, *Agrarverfassung*, pp. 102–134.

The countryside of the South and West generally resisted the tendency toward amalgamation that mobilized East Elbia, and accordingly the rural constitution was more complex, as terms of tenure stabilized at odd times in different places, in the absence of any general economic tendency to keep them in step.[10] Here the states had always strongly opposed peasant incorporation into estate-lordship. They wanted to tax peasants; and they could not have taxed serfs and could hardly tax nobles. Some aggregation took place, but it was hard to do and uncharacteristic; nobles in the individualized country were slipping instead into the many capitals and into the church especially during the early eighteenth-century days when peasant incorporation was in full swing in Prussia. It seems likely that the many towns and possibly the many imperial knights of the individualized country offered to the governments local counterweights against mediate nobility living in their territories; and the states of the South and West, being able to dispense with rural noble interests, could govern the peasants directly. Moreover, the rights and perquisites that the towns themselves had accumulated in the surrounding countryside served as a block to manorial expansion, and town rights outside the wall were likely to be of a ground-rent character, for towns were not agricultural entrepreneurs. Nor had they any real need to govern the population; they defended their interests against the peasantry mainly at the market, the wall, the guild ban mile. They neither did nor could claim the kind of power over the villages that East Elbian nobles exercised over their peasants, except in the instance of some of the imperial towns; town rights, beyond rents, were mainly negative and protective. The far greater number of religious and local charitable establishments in the South and West similarly tended to a landlord system, with civil jurisdiction essentially in state hands. In Bavaria, for example, which in many ways ought to offer the closest analogy to Prussia, the Elector was landlord over 20 per cent of the peasantry, and religious institutions were landlords over another 50 per cent, leaving little room for the development of an estate-lordship system, and a favorable environment for the home towns.[11]

"No shit-hens fly over the wall" was the hometown refrain.[12] The

[10] Ibid., pp. 134–154.   [11] Ibid., p. 145.   [12] Ch. I above, n. 29.

popular philosopher and professor Christian Garve, in his tract "On the Peasant Character" published in 1786, ran through a catalogued description beginning with peasant suspicion of all outsiders and against higher orders; going on to "mental and physical laziness, empty-headedness, stupidity, coarseness, and drunkenness; slavish subservience mixed with malice, spite, hatred, bitterness, hostility toward authority"; and ending with "unthriftiness, no thought for the future, ruled by sensuality." [13] The hometownsman, unimproved by literary rusticalia and unenchanted by shepherds, surely thought no better of the peasant character than the enlightened Garve did, especially if he saw mirrored there qualities he feared to see in himself and that he was required to expunge from his own character. But already through the writings of men like Garve had begun to run the thread: it was the countryman's legal and social circumstances that had made him what he was, and those might be changed.

Movers and doers

The third main element of German society was numerically the smallest: those whose lives involved motion both geographical and social, and a kind of activity and initiative out of keeping with the lives of hometownsmen and countrymen. They were not conceived as a category or estate until, with the French Revolution and its aftermath, motion and activity became political touchstones and the different elements of the group came to recognize the goals they had in common. Recognition then was weak and reluctant because the devisers of categories were themselves members of the group, and too jealous of the difference of status within it to put bureaucrats, peddlers, professors, merchants, wage laborers, and dispossessed peasants into one estate.[14] But the hometownsmen recognized

[13] *Ueber den Charakter der Bauern und ihr Verhältnis gegen die Gutsherren und gegen die Regierung;* I have used the 2d ed. (Breslau, 1796). These are so many chapter titles.

[14] But Christian Garve in 1792 put *Grosshändler* and *Gelehrten* together into a category distinguished from *Adel* on the one hand and *Gewerbetreibenden* on the other: *Versuche über verschiedene Gegenstände aus der Moral, Litteratur und dem gesellschaftlichen Leben,* I (Breslau, 1792), pp. 302ff, cited in Stadelmann and Fischer, *Bildungswelt,* p. 43. Other partial recognitions will be mentioned below.

them all as parts of the alien crowd that threatened to intrude upon them: disturbers, *Störer*, was a name the hometownsman applied to all of them, though he could not quite think of them collectively until a mobilized outside world seemed collectivized against him. The sea of countrymen that surrounded the walls were outsiders too, but they stayed in place; hometownsmen understood them and were used to dominating them; the walls were firm against them. Movers and doers were not rooted in the countryside. They emanated rather from the cities, and they could and did move regularly from one German city to another without serious change of personal habits or environments. The hometownsman's place in the world depended on who he was in the community, and that was pretty much determined by the time he got citizenship rights; the countryman's rested on what he had, meaning the land he had inherited and lived on; the mover and doer was justified by what he did, a continuing process in which he confronted change and often sought it. Itinerant peddler, court lawyer, busy merchant, and the academically trained shared a social psychology hostile to that which underlay hometown life, and when they came into contact with the home town they displayed it, each in his own way; but despite all they showed in common from the hometown vantage, they were no serious threat for so long as they were not working together.

Commerce and industry

Great merchants and small peddlers were easily recognized by hometownsmen as amounting to much the same thing. One stayed in the city most of the time and the other roamed the countryside, but both were purveyors of alien production, both were raiders of the hometown economy. The peddler retailed what the merchant assembled. Both tried to circumvent the guild system. Both were adversaries to the contract that existed between hometown guildsman and his civic community: that the guildsman would provide goods and services of acceptable quality and in acceptable supply in return for the security of his market and his price.[15] For that contract was enforced by the political and social relations between guildsman and civic leaders, and by the neighborhood familiarity

[15] Such a contract is stated explicitly and defended, e.g., in the Seidenburg 1698 statute: Schott, ed., *Sammlungen*, II, 176–177.

of the community; merchant and peddler participated in neither, and were beyond their reach.[16]

What was true of commerce was true of manufacture. In the hometown economy, where guildsmen sold the goods they made or processed, the making and the selling of things were hardly distinguished. The term *Handwerk*, artisanry, did not so much mean particular working processes or particular products or services as it meant a particular milieu for economic activity and a set of norms governing exchange. It had long been understood that *Handwerk* dominated the hometown economic system, whereas a quite different system dominated the cosmopolitan economy.[17] *Manufaktur* was almost never confused with *Handwerk*, even though the literal meanings of the words were the same (but one, be it noted, of Romance and the other of Germanic derivation) and the working processes might be identical. What distinguished "manufacture" in seventeenth- and eighteenth-century Germany was neither technique nor a central source of mechanical power but rather the scale of the enterprise, meaning more workers in a single enterprise than guild ordinances allowed, sometimes a degree of division of labor, and a market that included customers that the producers never saw.[18] Large size meant a different organization of production and market, and with those even a different spirit. Guilds had no place there. The heading *Industrie* appeared in an economic encyclopaedia of the 1780's: "Meant thereby is the active energy

[16] Cf. Schäffle, "Gewerbe," pp. 334–335.

[17] Ferdinand A. Steinhueser, *Johann Joachim Becher und die Einzelwirtschaft* (Nürnberg, 1931), pp. 34–35; Stadelmann and Fischer, *Bildungswelt*, p. 43; Georg W. F. Hegel, *Grundlinien der Philosophie des Rechts*, in *Sämtliche Werke*, VII (Stuttgart, 1952), 323.

[18] The history of *Manufaktur* and its relation to modern industry especially interested Friedrich Lütge in his latter years, and his students have produced several studies on the subject: Lütge, *Deutsche Sozial- und Wirtschaftsgeschichte* (3d ed.; Berlin, 1966), pp. 365–367; Ortulf Reuter, *Die Manufaktur im fränkischen Raum* (Stuttgart, 1961); Gerhard Slawinger, *Die Manufaktur in Kurbayern* (Stuttgart, 1966); Rudolf Forberger, *Die Manufaktur in Sachsen* (Berlin, 1958). Philomene Beckers, "Parteien und Parteikampf in der Reichstadt Aachen im letzten Jahrhundert ihres Bestehens," ZAGV, VI (1935), 105–109, draws the following distinctions out of the history of that town: *Normaler Betrieb:* master with one shop and a prescribed number of helpers; *Manufaktur:* master with as many journeymen as he chooses; *Manufaktur und Verlag:* merchant with master's license and an enterprise with as many journeymen as he chooses; *Verlag:* merchant without productive facilities of his own.

of free workers and of merchants, together with the so-called *savoir faire* or cleverness at extracting all possible gains from favorable opportunities. And in this sense, Industry is set in contrast with stable property and with land." [19]

The important division in the German town economy lay not between master guildsmen and their journeymen (whose goal it was to become respected masters), but rather between small and locally oriented producers on the one hand and on the other those whose ambition and success made them enemies of guild limits on labor force and markets. When a skilled and ambitious master expanded his enterprise he took on the character of a merchant and an employer rather than an artisan; he entered markets—urban, noble establishments, courts, peddlers' packs—beyond the home town, and sought to increase his labor force to match the opportunities these wider markets offered. And so he farmed out work to landmasters and to others outside the ban mile, to local masters who had failed in the local economy for one reason or another, to tolerated residents outside the civic structure, to retired soldiers, to groundrabbits of all description. Ambition in disregard of the rules was more likely to affect a newcomer or somebody outside the restraints and protection of established hometown membership —even bastards maybe—than it was the community familiar. Against such persons and their dishonorable crews masters and journeymen were united, caste against caste.[20] The trouble that arose when a town admitted or generated within itself that kind of mover and doer goes to explain the caution with which communities admitted outsiders and the persistence of guild limitations. It illuminates the political character of the home town, for such persons were an economic analogy to the civic patriciate, and became that too if they succeeded in taking political control for their own purposes. And the people such persons sought and attracted to their employ were the civic outsiders whose number, if the home town was to be healthy, had to be kept small.

The theme of Aachen politics for the whole eighteenth century

---

[19] With *Vermögensbestände und liegengen* [sic] *Grunden*. Johann G. Krünitz, "Industrie," *Ökonomische Enzyklopädie*, XXIX (Berlin, 1783), 708ff., quoted in Focko Eulen, *Vom Gewerbefleiss zur Industrie* (Berlin, 1967), p. 14.

[20] See Georg Fischer, *Fränkisches Handwerk*, pp. 13–36 for this categorization.

was a running conflict between a hometown party and a mercantile party, alternately in control of the town council.[21] Aachener spoke of the Old Party and the New Party, but the two parties alternated in possession of the name: whichever was in power was called the Old Party, and the one trying to oust it was called the New Party. During the last years of the eighteenth century the name Old Party seems to have settled on the hometown element, but that was because they dominated town politics since the end of the Seven Years' War.

Aachen was something between a home town and a movers' and doers' town, so that its troubles lay out the difference between the two. The citizen population was probably twelve to fifteen thousand souls.[22] It was considered an imperial town, but the Elector Palatine as Duke of Jülich retained protective rights over the town's inhabitants and over its affairs, rights which he exercised as powers whenever he could. Its constitution and council were based on guilds, but there was an independent Royal Court (*Königlicher Schöffenstuhl*) with widespread jurisdictions that paralleled and often rivaled the magistracy even within the walls. The Royal Court, and also a kind of guild for educated citizens— lawyers, physicians, and so on—both participated in the councils and in elections along with the regular artisans' guilds, and thus had a voice in the acceptance of citizens and in the police power over economic affairs.

Certain Aachen trades around the end of the seventeenth century had developed export markets, and thus a pressure for large-scale manufacture and an attraction for entrepreneurial investment. The textile and needle-making trades had split into organizations for each of two stages of production: guilds for the rough preparation of needles and cloth, and guilds for finishing and merchandising. The finishers (*Schönwerker*) came with time to be called merchants (*Kaufleute*), and became partisans of free production in enterprises of unlimited size. In 1695, at a time when they con-

[21] The narrative is from Beckers, "Parteien in Aachen" (n. 18 above) except where otherwise noted. For a similar story Schönfeld, "Regensburg im achtzehnten Jahrhundert."

[22] Pütter, *Constitution of the Germanic Empire*, appendix, p. 70, gives 3,000 houses in the town, and a population of 25,000 including eighteen villages within the jurisdiction.

trolled the government, the mercantile party got legislation permitting untrained outsiders to make rough needles for finishing in Aachen, overriding the local guild's monopoly.[23] That was a declaration of war on the hometown economy and on its polity as well.

Thenceforward the Aachen mixture of home town with mover and doer brought open corruption, in the sense of regular hometown practices turned partisan and maybe more than that: constant bribery and intrigue for control of the guilds that elected the magistracy. The hometown party was naturally strong in the artisan guilds, and when it was in office it could use the police and citizens' acceptance powers to pack them securely with its adherents. But that practice ran into backlash when the guildsmen themselves complained that the trades were being overfilled with "political masters." Outbidding the mercantile party with campaign promises was expensive. Besides, a fair proportion of the citizenry became dependent on the entrepreneurs, either as rough producers or as retailers: the merchants could threaten to give all their work to outsiders and so bring even the hometown guildsmen to heel, or at least split the guilds.

From 1725 to 1755, Aachen had a regime based on the trades guilds and small masters. That inhibited mercantile expansion: imports of rough needles from outside were forbidden and merchants found themselves hailed before town courts for breaches of guild regulations. So in 1755 they began a new campaign for control of the magistracy. With bribery and threats they seized control of politically strategic guilds. They got the support of the Electoral government, a natural ally because Jülich's advocate in Aachen was at odds with the hometown regime over jurisdictional and fiscal matters, and because Jülich subjects surrounding the town suffered from the hometown rules against importing rough manufactures from the countryside.[24] Amid the earthquakes of the winter of 1755–1756 street fighting began in Aachen. The "Pöbel" stormed the houses of hometown party leaders and invaded the town hall. Merchants, state, and "mob" among them brought the fall of the hometown magistracy, and a mercantile regime took over again.

But before long the new government was in trouble. It went beyond bribery to the use of armed force in guild elections (as had

[23] Koch, "Aachener Nähnadelzunft," pp. 74–76.   [24] Ibid., pp. 97–98.

the hometown party before it), and guildsmen appealed to the high Imperial Court at Wetzlar: meanwhile, on the other side, Aachen's mercantile mayor was named an Electoral State Councilor.[25] Resentment against the mercantile government grew in the town; and in 1763, by the usual processes, the hometown party recovered control of town hall. Soon it was engaged in a fight with the Royal Court, the professionals' guild, and the retired mercantile mayor and state councilor over appointments to the Court: a contingent of Electoral troops entered Aachen to defend the Elector's interests there. The hometown party turned again to the Empire for help, and the Palatine soldiers retreated before an imperial mandate.

That pattern of forces prevailed until the arrival of the French in 1792: guilds and their town councilors, with imperial support, against merchants, *Pöbel,* professionals' guild, and Royal Court, these supported by the Palatine government: hometownsmen against movers and doers, incubator against change. The hometown party, despite control of the guilds, was driven out of office in 1786 by force; an imperial decree reinstated it, but despite an appeal for troops from Brabant it never fully recovered power. When the French came, Aachen politics became part of the contest between Austria and France; and in 1794 the French municipal system was introduced and the Aachen hometown party's political position was broken up. Its troubles had begun when some of its artisans became ambitious and successful, developed outside markets, and the town was infected with movers and doers; and yet with its guild foundations and imperial support it had survived merchants, officials, and *Pöbel* from time out of mind: Aachen at the end of the eighteenth century, when the French arrived, was what it had been for a century and more.

Civil servants

Large-scale commerce and manufacture were likely to find favor with the second main category of movers and doers, the officials of the states. There were fiscal reasons, in that these enterprises made a traffic easier to tap for the benefit of public treasuries than hometown exchange was; and they provided commodities for the

[25] Ibid., p. 30.

courts, cities, and for export, to all of which the home towns contributed little or nothing. Such factories as there were—very small and scarce by modern standards—ordinarily were licensed by state governments, outside the guild system (in the case of the imperial town of Aachen, the mercantile party itself had to seek control of the town government). But generally that association between official and merchant affected the hometownsman very little, because the state's interests were either urban or rural; rarely did it try to penetrate hometown guild walls, despite friction over freemasters, landmasters, and court artisans. Jülich's officials were interested in the work and revenues Aachen's merchants provided for the surrounding territory, not in hometown Aachen's internal exchange. Even in matters of civil administration, state officials stayed rather clear of the home towns, doing more to sustain their normal workings than to control them, whatever tables of organization they may have deposited in their own archives; and their failure to penetrate hometown government in the eighteenth century preserved the separate political cultures of both. State officials intervened in the home towns, but they did not govern there. The official appeared briefly on circuit to see that all was well,[26] and to make sure the town's regular contribution to the state treasury was paid—or to try to collect it. If he was resident in the town, neither he nor his staff ordinarily were citizens, and they were exempt from the town's statutes and its jurisdictions.[27] He had no bürgerliche Nahrung and so could be no true Bürger, any more than a peasant or a soldier could, and his sons had difficulty entering guilded trades—if, better for nothing more than that, they should try.[28] He was a stranger in somebody else's home town, and most of the time both he and the townsmen were glad of it; by the end of the eighteenth century the civil service as a professional and social body was firmly associated with other movers and doers, and disassociated from the home towns.

The official's status, like that of other movers and doers, was

[26] Recall the state inspector in Heinrich von Kleist's "Der zerbrochene Krug," and the "Rentmeister im Umritt" of the Bavarian 1748 decree: above, pp. 70–71.

[27] Riccius, Stadt-Gesetzen, pp. 468–471.

[28] Becher, Politischer discurs, pp. 604–606; cf. § 4 of the Imperial Trades Edict of 1731, Appendix below.

determined neither by birth nor by his relations with a static local situation. Of course family connections were valuable, especially for entry into the higher levels of government; but in the middle and lower levels where most civil servants moved, their success depended on achievement, or more realistically perhaps, on professional ambition or aggressiveness. They were of mixed noble and non-noble origins: most commonly, probably, the sons of civil servants (including ennobled ones). Not only were state officials by law and by choice outside the social communities where they resided, they were moved from place to place, deliberately by their superiors or spontaneously in pursuit of their careers, often from the service of one state to another, so that a state official found his home in his professional group, his place in its hierarchy, and his standards in its professional skills and aims. Without the security of the hometownsman or even perhaps the countryman, the mobile civil servant, like the entrepreneur, relied upon energy and cleverness and "extracting all possible gains from favorable opportunities." Conversely he might find opportunities in many places and almost without limit, whereas the countryman was anchored to his land, and the hometownsman was confined to his community by his standing there and only there.[29]

The official's skill lay in dealing with people and pursuits at a distance, from one another and from himself, people and pursuits he did not fully know, and which therefore he categorized. He was constantly obliged to sort out his situation and his duties in ways that accorded with general instructions, and which could be reported briefly and systematically to his superiors. His occupation was to reconcile the particularities of his sphere of authority with the laws and the general aims of his employers and of his caste, with the making of order; what could not be ordered had to be ignored; and so the tone of his style and personality was quite out of harmony with the unplanned balance of disorder that was the life of hometownsmen and the Holy Roman Empire itself. Compared with his way of life those polities were bundles of jackstraws somebody had dropped in inseparable tangle and confusion: take hold of one stick and who knew what others would react? Only the citizen-

[29] Hans Gerth, *Die sozialgeschichtliche Lage der bürgerlichen Intelligenz um die Wende des 18. Jahrhunderts* (Frankfurt/Main, 1935), pp. 3, 109–112.

jackstraw in the pile knew, and the official, outside it, was not one of them.

And unlike the hometownsman, the official had been to the university and had learned to sort things out in the ways taught there: into the forms of books, lectures, and outlines, for piles of jackstraws do not accord well with scholarly analysis. At the university he studied system and consequence from men whose task it was to create them; he learned ordered argument, cause and effect: intellectual patterns incompatible with the life of the home town (and maybe with the writing of its history). The intellectual discipline of scholarship and the professional discipline of administration had much in common. The similarity of method and of style was one reason for the importance of university training in the development of bureaucracy. And the civil servant had shared the university environment with a third element of the moving and doing caste: the intellectual who entered scholarly or literary pursuits, or entered the clergy, or the free professions—literally *freie Berufe,* set apart from the occupations incorporated into guilds.

Intellectuals and free professions

While there was very little movement among the three main German social castes of countrymen, hometownsmen, and movers and doers (except insofar as nobles became upper civil servants), within the mover and doer caste there was considerable interchange among merchants, officials, and intellectuals, or more nearly among their sons; and the university, where they met, was the core of their association. There the particular characteristics of the intellectual were absorbed into the mover and doer caste.[30] The universities were the centers, along with the handful of large cities and courts, of the most cosmopolitan and the freest social and intellectual life in Germany; and whatever leakage there was out of the hometownsmen's and countrymen's caste took place there.

Compared with the rest of German society at the end of the

[30] Some good cultural descriptions are the two books by Walter H. Bruford, *Germany in the Eighteenth Century* (Cambridge, Eng., 1935) and *Culture and Society in Classical Weimar, 1775–1806* (Cambridge, Eng., 1962); also Friedrich Paulsen, *Geschichte des gelehrten Unterrichts,* II (3d ed.; Leipzig, 1921); Adolf v. Knigge, *Ueber den Umgang mit Menschen* (Hanover, 1788); and Gerth, *Die sozialgeschichtliche Lage.*

eighteenth century, the social origins of the university world were quite diverse.[31] Social distinctions remained there to be sure, but still young men of many ranks and backgrounds attended, so that the university did not match up with the more stable and uniform social orders Germans were accustomed to. That has often made social analysis of the university-trained troublesome, but just that gave the university its place in this analysis: it was Germany's place for mixing and for changing.[32] University life and the careers it led to were very nearly the only way to escape one's condition of birth, so that outsiders were anxious to go there: young men who lacked secure social location by birthright, or else who in their ambition had renounced it. There was of course a large proportion of the nobly born there, especially those with political or intellectual aspirations, training in administration or law and the ways of a wider world than the countryman's; probably most of these were from families already engaged in government. There were very many civil servants' sons, and there were sons of urban merchants and patricians. There were even hungry boys on scholarship from small towns and villages, and sons of hometown political leaders, not so hungry, who were trying to professionalize their families' leadership and make it permanent.[33] There was a large and hard-working component of Protestant pastors' sons, outsiders too without communal birthright, who needed academic training if they were to find a place in the world that met their fathers' aspirations: the pastorate was a mobile institution hierarchically organized like a bureaucracy; hometown preachers were not familiar hometowns-men, and pastors almost never Bürger.

Entering students might have been prepared by tutors if their parents could afford them, or by state schools designed to identify promising boys of all backgrounds and train them to be useful citizens and servants of the state; or perhaps they had attended endowed Latin schools of the towns, or church establishments. Hans Gerth, in his study of the German intellectual world at the turn of the century, listed five factors that brought middle-class

[31] Gerth, *Die sozialgeschichtliche Lage*, pp. 17, 30–31, 62.

[32] A great many matriculation lists have been published, mostly in local historical journals, but apart from geographical origins they provide almost no information about matriculants, and I shall not cite any selection.

[33] Bruford, *Germany*, p. 247.

(*bürgerlich*) boys to the university and into the movers and doers:

1) the blocking of economic opportunity by guild monopolies, by patrician control, or by state economic regulations;

2) decline of the family trade, so that the boy could not look forward to slipping comfortably into his father's place;

3) the wish to avoid military conscription;

4) the growing prestige of the civil service, to which university education was the key;

5) the extensive scholarship opportunities that attracted boys with nowhere else to turn nor place to fill; and the possibility of getting a tutoring job with a wealthy family.[34]

For social and quasi-political purposes the students joined together into corps (*Landsmannschaften*), fraternities designated by the presumed geographical origins of their members: the Swabian corps, the Prussian corps, and so on. These organizations, together with the university's legal rights of self-government, separated and indeed protected students from the civil society of the town where the university was located—defense of academic freedom against outraged Bürger. Students moved often, once they had left home for the society of educated men: several times in the course of their educations, from one university, one set of professors, to another. A student's alien and changing environment was probably the reason why he joined together with other students from his own area into his corps, people in whom he recognized his own habits of speech. But by joining with other students in self-conscious exposure to the great world he was making the university his home; he was asserting his difference and an occupational contempt for the quiet little worlds of hometownsmen and countrymen. That was the birthmark of the educated man he was becoming, and the unifying spirit of his caste. Students whatever their origins set themselves over against townsmen as opposites, calling townsmen philistines, *Spiessbürger,* and so defining themselves by the contrast, conceiving themselves collectively as individuals, free of social restraints and prejudices, outside the static dull complexities of Germany's predominant hometown and country life. The student asserted his own natural and uncompromised personality by conventional signs, of costume or of phrase, of his individuality, free-

[34] Gerth, *Die sozialgeschichtliche Lage,* pp. 31–32.

dom, intellectual superiority, and moral breadth: rather like the guildsmen in a way, but still his were antiguilds that tried to be the opposite: an uneasy notion.

The background of university professors was also broader, and the profession easier of entry to ability, than most German occupations of the time. A good proportion came from academic families, sons following their fathers' careers; but probably most came from relatively poor and insecure families and had come to an academic career as a means to social rise. Their educations had been supported by public funds, by tutoring, and by self-deprivation, all of which imposed poverty as well as humiliation; and their pride of place after attaining professorial rank was proportional. Universities were state institutions, and professors were state employees; there was a hot competition among the states for the services of able or at least popular professors who would bring in students and money, so that a successful academic career was a moving and shifting one, self-assertive, without community roots outside the profession and the intellectual world. And an academic career depended heavily too upon the professor's attractiveness to the state as a trainer of useful civil servants, especially in the fields of cameral and police science and of law.[35]

After university training a man might get a job in the civil service, or a pastorate, or a licensed medical position; or failing these he could tutor the children of a wealthy or a noble family. It is remarkable how many of the intellectually dominant figures of the time—Kant, Fichte, Hegel, Schleiermacher, and Hölderlin, for example—had put in terms as private tutors before escaping to other things. It was not a kind of dependency that made them admire their established betters.[36] Or trained intellectuals might, insofar as their energies were not absorbed by their regular jobs, do some writing. There were hundreds of books on law and administration, including matters we should now treat as economics and sociology; there were long systematic descriptions of areas and jurisdictions. Many of these were subsidized by states and commended for pur-

[35] On professors: Paulsen, *Geschichte des gelehrten Unterrichts*, II (1921), 127–129; Gerth, *Die sozialgeschichtliche Lage*, pp. 35–41.

[36] Bruford, *Germany*, pp. 248–249; Gerth, *Die sozialgeschichtliche Lage*, pp. 80–95.

chase to state employees; presumably the writing of them aided one's rise in the official hierarchy. Civil servants, pastors, and professors wrote frequently for periodicals, most of it in moral uplift style but increasingly concerned with civic and political matters toward the end of the eighteenth century.[37] By that time a handful of intellectuals even made their livings by writing, though usually by way of patronage and not from the sale of their publications. One or two literary successes might bring the offer of a position as ornament to a court or a high noble house, with a pension or a not-very-taxing administrative post. Court intellectuals—the Weimar set is the most famous example[38]—were like tutors on a grander scale, and they shared some of the tutor's resentment of culturally inferior employers; but they did not so much resent the state that supported them as they did the people who happened to control it. Like professors they moved from place to place in response to competition for their services. Literary men combined the cosmopolitan world they had entered at the university with often sceptical attachment to the government of a state: one place where there was surely no market for their services was the home town, a solid reason for the contempt they felt for it.[39] Writers lived by choice in centers of literary traffic like Göttingen, Leipzig, and Berlin, to name places with especially high concentrations of writers in proportion to population. They had to be where the news came in—political news, business news, cultural news—and the best channels of information that would interest the reading public were still channels of government. Grist for a writer's mill came where the channels met and crossed: where the state's officials, the professors, the travelers were, at the university towns, at the courts, at the salons, the coffeehouses.[40]

The intellectual was a restless figure in eighteenth-century German society, and often a dissatisfied one. For he shared with mer-

---

[37] Johanna Schultze, *Die Auseinandersetzung zwischen Adel und Bürgertum in den deutschen Zeitschriften der letzten drei Jahrzehnte des 18. Jahrhunderts* (Berlin, 1925), passim; Gerth, *Die sozialgeschichtliche Lage*, pp. 96–97, 104–105.

[38] Bruford, *Weimar*.

[39] Among literary satires of hometown life: Christoph Martin Wieland's "Die Abdoriten" was about his native Biberach; cf. also Heinrich Kleist's "Der zerbrochene Krug."

[40] Gerth, *Die sozialgeschichtliche Lage*, pp. 96–98.

chant and civil servant the wider horizons and the irritant of ambition that were foreclosed to hometownsmen and countrymen.[41] He made his identity through the independent use of his intelligence, or tried to, a principle of identity quite contrary to the communal identity of hometownsmen: he had to distinguish himself.[42] And the intellectual's character, like the official's and the merchant's, was written into the home town's social order if he showed up there at all, or rather written out of it: the "lettered," the "graduated" was expected to live not by town rules but by state rules; [43] or if his status was recognized by the town constitution it was as a member of a special group or guild for persons like himself: the professionals' guilds or officials' corporations that were the devices some towns used to accommodate movers and doers necessarily associated with town affairs while holding them at arm's length, but devices that were awkward misfits in the town's essential guild-based organization of citizenship.[44]

Stability, equality, and democracy

Personal ambition hurt the stability of hometown life, and so the home town suppressed, excluded, or expelled it. Ambition made for inequality, and the home town worked against inequality among its members, whether it threatened from above or below, from outside or within the community. There was a real egalitarianism to hometown life, but it was not an equality of open opportunity but rather equal subjection to limits placed both on opportunity to rise and upon liability to decline. Of course the community knew clear gradations of wealth, influence, and social standing within itself. It expected different things of different people. But it did not tolerate too wide a spread or too rapid a shift, nor did the gradations make differences among hometownsmen even comparable to the differ-

[41] Hegel after 1805 distinguished *Beamten, Kaufmänner,* and *Gelehrten* from communal Bürger by the quality of personal ambition: Franz Rosenzweig, *Hegel und der Staat,* I (Munich, 1920), pp. 189–192; Hegel, *Philosophie des Rechts,* pp. 323–325.

[42] Stadelmann and Fischer, *Bildungswelt,* pp. 54–55, tie this point to Kant's understanding of *Aufklärung* (*sapere aude!*), to the anticommunal individualist estate of *Bildung,* and to romanticism.

[43] Riccius, *Stadt-Gesetzen,* pp. 498–510; cf. the provisions for Seidenburg in Schott, *Sammlungen,* II, 189.

[44] As the constitutions of Rottweil and Aachen, described above.

ences between themselves and the other castes. The home town maintained a steady pressure on all members toward the median. The civic right included a claim on stability and equality of neighborhood. It was a right against the inequality that is felt, when an immediate associate can break loose upward and away from the power of communal regard; and against the inequality that is felt, when one has fallen below and out of it.

Hometownsmen liked money as much as anybody else, and maybe more than most, but their circumstances and their neighbors kept them from getting very much, and they fiercely resented anybody who did get very much. Guilds were conscious and recognized institutions for maintaining a satisfactory degree of equality, by penalizing or excluding the pushy whether rich or poor, and by the mutual agreements among the membership that restrained expansion and that promised security.[45] The civic constitutions and the rights of membership they embodied were instruments of a democracy among members no less fraudulent than those which many polities with more democratic affectations have had. But hometown equality and hometown democracy meant the subjugation of everybody in the community to everybody, to limits set by the whole community. Hometownsmen were neither political theorists nor ideologues, and for the equality and democracy that existed among them, the motives were no doubt a shared jealousy of the stronger and richer and a shared contempt for the weaker and poorer. Their communities—guilds, constitutions, and all—were the kind of polities such motives sustained; and very strong and stable polities they were. An important source of their coherence may have been the suppression within the community of anxiety about standing and place that modern ideas of equality and democracy, which leave the stability out and do not have the hometownsmen's walls, are sometimes thought to have created: hometownsmen directed that against outsiders. Where community sanctions prevailed there was little reason for that kind of uncertainty because there could be little change one way or another. Membership resided securely there. If modern class and racial hostility have developed, underground so to speak, as ways of asserting status and location in legally open and egalitarian societies, then such phenomena were

45 Steinhueser, *Becher*, pp. 34–35.

unlikely to appear where status and location were immediately recognizable by familiarity or law: inside the community, that is, while the alien was outside. While each community's walls held, such resentments and anxieties were directed against people who did not belong, and so strengthened rather than dividing the society where membership was primarily located. Even rules on what clothing who might wear did not actively assert rank and place so much as accept their existence and inhibit the race after status by the display of wealth. "Presumption in clothing not only causes waste," wrote Christian Wolff, "it also arouses the jealousy of others, from which hatred and enmity follow." [46] Presumption can mean either pretending to belong when you don't, or pretending not to belong when you do. Hometown egalitarianism and democracy punished both kinds of presumption.

Still (and at that point in the argument) it seems remarkable that one can even think of applying the same terms, equality and democracy, both to the home towns and to modern liberal aspirations. The difference between the two lies in open membership and the individual capacity to move, to change, to differ; but that is all the difference in the world. I do not think it is the kind of difference that caricature makes; it is not a difference of degree or of maturity, but of kind: not an ordinal but a nominal difference. To ignore or mistake the difference, by identifying liberal ideas with the citizens' community, can and has led to confusion of a most serious kind. At the very least, the social nature of the community must be an important proviso or factor to any such identification. For the conditions of the communities' equality and democracy were the walls and the webs of each of them. It is a confusion—more narrowly now—comparable to that which has come from the use of the term "middle class" in German society.[47] For while both hometownsmen and movers and doers can be called middle class or even *bürgerlich*, between the two lay all the difference.

Any community has its walls and its webs, its resentments with-

---

[46] *Vernünfftige Gedancken von dem Gesellschafftlichen Leben der Menschen, und insonderheit dem gemeinen Wesen* [sic] (Frankfurt/?, 1747), p. 366.

[47] Note the consequences of different uses of the term "middle class" by Lenore O'Boyle, "The Middle Class in Europe, 1815–1848," *AHR*, LXXI (1966), 826–845, and by Edward Shorter, "Middle-Class Anxiety in the German Revolution of 1848," *JSH*, II (1969), 189–215.

out to back up harmony within. But the German home town in the peaceful years from Westphalia to Austerlitz created an unusual mechanism to repel intrusion, and that mechanism became the basis of its political and social life. It is a fairly common modern observation, and a reasonable one, that group consciousness comes in reaction to a threat commonly perceived. "As for the social nature of this reaction," wrote Emile Durkheim, "it comes from the social nature of the offended sentiments. . . . Not only is the reaction general, it is collective, which is not the same thing. . . . Never do we feel the need of our compatriots so greatly as when we are in a strange country; never does the believer feel so attracted to his co-religionists as during periods of persecution." [48] But for the communities of the seventeenth and eighteenth centuries the other side of the coin was the more important: that is, community boundaries severally identified the alien outside, rather than the communities arising as a class in response to a general threat.[49] Aachen's dubious battle, and others I have described, are there to show the relation between the two sides of the identity. Still the hometownsmen's community antedated serious threat, and that distinguishes its posture from the backlash reaction discerned in an insecure "lower middle class" of a more mobile society, the element with which it might be most facilely compared. The peculiarity of a style of life and governance based on familiarity was that it took hold where familiarity was unchallenged. Hometownsmen did not stand perpetual watch at the gates bristling with terror, because they did not need to; if they had, then their response when threat became serious might have been quite different. The customary familiar communal quiet of the hometownsman's life equipped him to identify outsiders and the sources of change, and he was very much aware of the boundaries that separated him from the outside world; but neither quiet nor boundaries equipped him to adapt or to counterattack.

The boundaries then did not arise as defense against outside pressure. They denoted rather the importance of the community for

[48] *Division of Labor in Society*, tr. George Simpson (New York, 1964), p. 102.

[49] For communal emphasis of outside threats to bring internal solidarity, Kai Erikson, *Wayward Puritans: A Study in the Sociology of Deviance* (New York, 1966).

the hometownsman. They told the hometownsman where he was somebody—within let us say the ban mile of guild monopoly in an effort to be concrete, or in some instances the sphere of local fiscal or criminal jurisdiction.[50] There and only there he was a Bürger. Outside, he was nobody. "Within a particular town its particular estate of full town citizens is the most important and most distinguished estate. Thus within his town the citizen is the most distinguished, respected, and honorable person, who for that reason has received the honorable name of honorable and respected person, and enjoys a special rank before others." So wrote Johann Joachim Becher in his treatise on the rise and fall of polities.[51] Perhaps the wholly local nature of the hometownsman's place in the world, for so long as it was that, and his separation from others of his kind in other towns, where others were the Bürger and he the outsider, made him prone to respond to change and uncertainty not by aggressive backlash but by withdrawal within the walls: the journeyman came home to be a Bürger.

The citizen's right

The *Bürgerrecht* meant something both more positive and more inclusive than we are likely to mean by civic right; and unlike the privilege, franchise, or immunity that a sovereign might grant a subject, it was communal, held by grant of one's neighbors. Local control over the Bürgerrecht and participation of the Bürger in the issuing of it was at the heart of the community; a town could undergo a change of masters without disruption while that power stayed in its hands and the Bürgerrecht remained what it was. It was the stem of the cloverleaf, uniting the three capacities of social man: citizen, workman, and neighbor. Consequently all those elements of membership had to be satisfied for the Bürgerrecht to be granted. A man's every transaction participated in all three areas, so that even to speak of them as three is something the hometownsman would have found odd: we see it by contrast with ourselves. The hometownsman did not leave his home and polity to do his

[50] Juridical and fiscal spheres are usually the more appropriate definitions for imperial towns, and economic spheres for territorial towns. To sample the complexity of the problem from the juridical side only, see, e.g., Hanns H. Hofmann's study cited in Ch. VII, n. 2.

[51] *Politischer discurs*, p. 634.

productive work, returning at night to domestic and civic life in another place at another time of day; when he sold a suit of clothes his role as neighbor and citizen was involved. There was no escape from one role to another, no sense of justification by one kind of success despite another kind of failure. The alternatives provided by what a sociologist might call multiple reference groups, wherein success in family life or in friendship might compensate for feelings of professional inadequacy; or the sublimation of moral anxiety a psychologist might see in business drive and political ambition— these were foreclosed to the hometownsman. People knew too much about him. A bad craftsman found neither friends nor influence; the morally deviant found neither customers nor office; political contrariness tainted a man's workshop and the tavern he frequented.[52] Community citizenship was what he had, and he had it all the time, his pride and his prison. If we suppose that a hometownsman's soul at bottom was like what our psychologists tell us of our own, then perhaps it follows that the inescapable totality of his membership (going beyond political or economic description) was correlative to his separation from outsiders or deviants and his reflexive hostility to them.[53] By contrast the wider connections of governing and economic elites, and other members of the movers' and doers' caste, went with their lesser reliance on the familiar community.

The Bürgerrecht, citizen's right or status, was the face of com-

---

[52] For the identity among marriage, mastership, and citizenship see, e.g., the Baden decree of 1751 in Ortloff, ed., Corpus juris, pp. 263–264; and p. 277 for a tentative state effort to distinguish marriage from mastership the Baden decree of 1761. Karl Friedrich Eichhorn, "Ueber den Ursprung der städtischen Verfassung in Deutschland," ZGR, I (1815), 172, held that these related rights emerged together from Germanic community (Gesammtburgschaft): Leben, Ehre, und Eigenthum. Notice that Ehre takes the place of "liberty" in John Locke's formula, and that Eigenthum takes the place of Thomas Jefferson's "pursuit of happiness." Eichhorn of course was aware of that. On Eichhorn see Ch. VIII below.

[53] Christian Wolff put the relation of communal membership with hostility toward outsiders as a kind of social contract in Gedancken, pp. 164–165: "Und wie ferner in einer jeden Gesellschaft das Mitglied einem Fremden vorgezogen wird; so muss auch im gemeinen Wesen solches geschehen, das ist niemand verbunden Fremden zu helfen, wenn dadurch die Wollfahrt derer, die mit uns in einen gemeinen Wesen leben, nachgesetzet werden solte." He goes on then to outline full community as an ideal type: pp. 166–170.

munal membership easiest and most necessary to define in law; one had it or one did not; at the same time the Bürgerrecht was no less a question than what a man's relation with his society was, how far his society extended, and who was in it. It was the place, recovering an earlier theoretical point, where structure most nearly coincided with function: an explicit legal term denoting a real range of working human relations.[54] Therefore any town's citizenship policy and citizenship grants are usually the best place to read its history. There the aims of councilmen, guilds, and social community came together; there political patronage, economic advantage, and familiar influence converged.

Take again the ready example of Rottweil. One could not enter civic community or guild simply by paying a fee; but still entry fees, one gate to membership, reflected the home town's notion of acceptability. A Rottweil butcher's son paid four gulden to enter his father's guild; a citizen's son from another trade paid eight or nine gulden; and an outsider (Fremde) paid twenty-four gulden The Bürgerrecht was free for citizens' sons when they were twenty-five years old, when they married with council approval, and were accepted as masters in a guild; but an outsider paid fees ranging in the eighteenth century from 120–300 gulden for the man, 60–100 gulden for the wife, and 20–35 gulden for each child. If a member of the community married outside it then he or she had to relinquish citizenship unless citizenship was granted to the partner and the customary fees for outsiders were paid. "But except in extreme cases, no one shall be accepted as citizen whose intended marriage into a trade would result in competition within a crowded occupation," according to a 1782 agreement between citizenry and council.[55] The way citizenship, trade, and domestic life combined could hardly be put clearer than that. Membership in any community was normally lost by marriage to an outsider whom the community would not accept, or by entering an occupation that was not a bürgerliche Nahrung: especially the army or the civil service.[56] To

[54] Pp. 34–35.

[55] Laufs, Rottweil, 1650–1806, pp. 25, 146; the quotation is from Hofer, Rotweil, pp. 118–119.

[56] Becher, Politischer discurs, pp. 604–606; Dietrich Kohl, "Das Bürgerrecht in der Stadt Oldenburg," OJ, LXI (1937), 93.

be without citizenship meant to have no right to pursue a citizens' trade, usually no marriage and no right to an established home, no vote, no eligibility for office, no communal protection against the outside (or against citizens), and no share in community property.[57]

The community was a *Bürgergemeinde* of citizens, not an *Einwohnergemeinde* of inhabitants. Simply living in the town space did not confer membership rights. Often outsiders were forbidden to own immovable property in the town, and citizens were forbidden to sell such property to noncitizens (or even rent living quarters to them without special permission), so that physical property itself while not held in common had a strong communal cast.[58] If nobles, churchmen, academics, Jews, or officials owned property in the town they did so by virtue of state privilege or by special agreement with the community, and the property they held fell into a different legal and fiscal category from citizens' property.[59] Not only was it hard to get into a community, it was hard to get out. To renounce citizenship one had to pay an emigration tax: something on the scale of 10 per cent of a citizen's property.[60] The emigration tax was justified on the ground that a citizen's departure removed him from the citizen tax rolls, so that he should leave a share of his property in the communal treasury; the same reasoning applied in prohibitions of property sales to outsiders.

The real social and material costs of leaving a home town combined with the difficulty and expense of entering another to bring uncommon stability in hometown population, especially in civic membership. There seems little doubt that hometownsmen were a less mobile population than either countrymen or movers and doers, and little doubt that this had to do with the communal application

---

[57] Cf. Grönhoff, "Kieler Bürgerbuch," pp. 14–26; Klein, *Entwicklung des Gemeindebürgerrechts,* pp. 11–14.

[58] See the provisions in the Nördlingen and Bautzen statutes in Schott, ed., *Sammlungen,* I, 218, and II, 26–27.

[59] Riccius, *Stadt-Gesetzen,* pp. 567–591. For an idea of the relation among occupation, citizenship, and the status of real property, peruse the lists of Mainz buildings and their owners in Heinrich Schrohe, ed., *Die Mainzer Stadtaufnahmen des 16. bis 18. Jahrhunderts* (3 vols.; Mainz, 1930–1931).

[60] This was the *Nachsteuer* or *Abzugsgeld:* Laufs, *Rottweil, 1650–1806,* p. 26; Schott, ed., *Sammlungen,* I, 212; Moser, *Landeshoheit im Weltlichen,* III (Frankfurt/Main, 1773), pp. 231–244.

of the Bürgerrecht power.[61] But here the relation between hometown institutions and outside threat crops up again, as an egg-and-chicken problem, a historical problem of genesis. In these terms other factors aside: did the relative stability of hometown populations foster membership rules that assumed and relied on stability, or were hometown restrictions and exclusions deliberately designed to protect the communities from a greater and growing mobility in city and country? Which made the Bürgerrecht what it was? Population data are too fragmentary and too crude to provide serious clues. The frame of this study so far has accepted the first: that the hometown membership and institutions statically described in these four chapters could not have assumed such strength and familiarity without the unusual economic and demographic stability of the later seventeenth and the eighteenth century, aided by the constitution of the Holy Roman Empire. So much for the egg, and the incubator. But it can also be argued (the chicken side) that in asserting rights to control their own memberships the communities were recoiling against the active policies of states. Claims put forward in law by communities, to that crucial hometown power to grant the Bürgerrecht, developed quite generally around the end of the seventeenth century; before that the issue rarely arose. Thence the argument is historical and by inference: That state governments in their efforts to recoup from the Thirty Years' War had tried to bring immigrants and industry, and so stimulated the assertion of a special communal citizenship. The persuasive part of the argument, though, is not that the communities were impelled by threat to build up defenses in the Bürgerrecht (for relatively few were actually affected by these policies), but rather that whereas the states and their laws had never seriously been interested in the meaning of the Bürgerrecht before, now a distinction was drawn between state citizenship and communal citizenship; and these two kinds of

[61] See above, p. 31. Erich Keyser, *Bevölkerungsgeschichte Deutschlands* (3d ed.; Leipzig, 1943), pp. 412–415, notes a relatively high and an increasing mobility among countrymen in the seventeenth and eighteenth centuries. For the admissions pattern in a village, where the state controlled Bürgerrecht and no craft or property requirements were applied, see Wolf H. Struck, *Die Neubürger von Grossalsleben, 1604–1874* (Neustadt a. d. Aisch, 1962), pp. 36–43.

citizenship became antithetical even as the states acknowledged, as most of them did, the rights of the home towns to choose their own members.[62]

As in most egg-and-chicken arguments, the difference may not matter much in fact: either way communal membership came to be one thing and membership in the whole society and state another. The incubator and the home town were there. But there are different ways for describing different effects. Narrative history takes over where German affairs lost their dispersed, static, and cyclical character and began to move in a common direction. The thesis of German community consciousness concludes now; antithesis begins with the meeting with autocracy.

[62] Hermann Rehm, "Der Erwerb von Staats- und Gemeinde-Angehörigkeit in geschichtlicher Entwicklung nach römischem und deutschem Staatsrecht," *ADRG*, XXV (1892), the best scholar on the subject, writes (p. 272) of the "gegen den Ausgang des 17. Jahrhunderts auftauchende *receptio civium*"; for the historical argument I have summarized, pp. 195–201.

Part Two

MEETING WITH THE STATE

CHAPTER V

Cameralism and Community

CAMERALISM was a baroque science. That is a description, not an evasion by whimsy of a difficult problem in political theory. It is a way of starting on a theoretical frame for the problems to which this story now turns. Cameralism was a science whose symmetry depended on its being seen for a distance, and whose rationality was in abstract outline seen from the top, subject to giddiness when attention moved from that to concrete detail. It accepted the existence of all the discrete parts of German civil society, each with a set of detailed qualities and rules peculiarly its own, and worked from the assumption that if all of them could be comprehended at once an essential harmony among them would emerge above their apparent diversity. That was a metaphysical assumption and even, to begin with, a religious expression of faith. In cameral practice, the medium of harmony among the discrete parts was the state's fiscal administration, analogously a social abstraction composed of men above and outside the discrete parts of society. Cameralist centralization existed among and within that political element. The home towns were not important to the state fisc, and so they like other social elements that stood outside could live like monads, apart from one another and from the whole, as long as administration was fiscal only and the civil service a social abstraction. While state administration of detail was weak, the cameralist combination of central administration in the state itself with differentiation among places and social estates was not a serious para-

145

dox, soluble (again this is no empty conceit) by means no more material than the pantheistic harmony the philosopher Leibnitz used to encompass the windowless, irreducible, and self-determining entities that inhabited his metaphysical universe.[1] The cameralist paradox could live quietly in the political incubator of the Holy Roman Empire. But when and where the state became strong enough to put the assumption of harmony among diversity and localization to the test, when civil servants reached beyond the fisc into the society itself, then the contradiction within the cameralist assumption became inescapable, and other solutions had to be found both in theory and in practice. But the solutions inherited the proposition that the state was the medium of social harmony and was responsible for it, while differentiation was the essence of society itself.

Harmony, diversity, and the theoretical contradictions of cameralism

Baroque metaphysics and cameralist administration intersected, visibly and concretely, at the German universities: training grounds for the movers and doers who composed the German civil service. German learning, for which Leibnitz was the most characteristic and influential spokesman, made that assumption that there was implicit harmony and system among all the phenomena of the world, and that all things would fit together despite superficial diversity if they were fully and truly understood and were not distorted by error or accident. The goal of learning was to attain the grasp and the overview from which the harmony among all the parts could be perceived, and from which the proper role and nature of each part could be understood. Curriculum and the several academic disciplines were organized, however imperfectly, from that base. Studies in law and administration were encyclopedic, but by that presumption of harmony they avoided the stigma of mere compilations of random data. Their encyclopedic totality resulted in fact from an aim, at bottom, not to impose uniformity, but to understand the true characters of all parts of the society and their

[1] For Leibnitz's political vision (related to his metaphysics) of an organic federative Empire within the European community, based on the Treaty of Westphalia, in which all separate parts participated spontaneously in one harmony: Joachim O. Fleckenstein, *Gottfried Wilhelm Leibniz, Barock und Universalismus* (Munich, 1958), pp. 168–172.

relations with one another. Outside the world of learning, in the world of practice, that kind of overview had to be located in the state, the one secular institution that encompassed the social encyclopedia of diverse parts. In principle the work of administration was not positive reform but the correction of distortions or abuses. If harmony was naturally there, then that task was small enough for the state to take on the whole of it. If the state or civil service was too weak to do more anyway, it was a serviceable principle of government. If steady day-to-day administration was limited to matters peculiarly within state purview—mainly fiscal and military affairs— and did not dig too deeply into the living fabric of the society, then ephemeral state intervention in the home towns restored rather than reformed them: that is what it was meant to do.

The theme of administrative centralization and uniformity commonly discerned in cameralist theory [2] operated within the administrative apparatus itself and the caste that served it, not necessarily within the groups and communities over which they claimed to exercise political sovereignty. Even the assertion of sovereign control did not mean a deliberate leveling of local and institutional differences, but rather assigning to the state the task of sustaining natural harmony. What the massive programmatic treatises of cameralist writers had to say about the home towns confirmed, in doctrine, the state policies described in Chapter II: intervene to remedy distortions like oligarchy and corruption, and thus to maintain the community's essential character. Veit Seckendorff (1626– 1692), state chancellor at a succession of Saxon principalities and then university chancellor at Halle, where cameral science got its fullest and most influential development, thought the common welfare was served best by governance "all in accordance with old tradition and the circumstances of each place." [3] That was not a grudging admission, either, but a position quite consistent with a general political view. Christian Thomasius (1655–1728), professor of law

[2] Typically in Louise Sommer, "Cameralism," in the *Encyclopedia of the Social Sciences*, III (New York, 1930), 158–160. By "cameralist" I mean as a rule of thumb the figures mentioned there by Sommer and those discussed in Albion W. Small, *The Cameralists: The Pioneers of German Social Polity* (Chicago, 1909); but the term is bound to be a loose one.

[3] "Alles nach Maasse des alten Herkommens und jedes Ortes Gelegenheit," quoted in Roscher, *National-Oekonomik*, pp. 244–245.

and philosophy at Leipzig and Halle, extolled German customary law over Roman and canon codes, and described the right of property much as hometown guildsmen might have done if they had been professors of law and philosophy.[4] His successor at Halle, Christian Wolff (1675–1754), professor of mathematics and law and another Leibnitzian, wrote a tract on legal sociology divided into two parts whose titles have become, with some shift of meaning, basic categories of sociology as Ferdinand Tönnies' *Gesellschaft* and *Gemeinschaft*: a first part "On the Societies of Men," and a second part "On the Essential Community."[5] Natural lawyer though he was, Wolff did not suppose laws of social community to be natural to the degree that later historical sociologists (Justus Möser will reappear before this chapter is out) or modern sociologists of anthropological bent have done; for unlike them he looked for natural law where conscious intellect reigned, not where it was absent.[6] Rules of social community were rather, Wolff said, conventional configurations of a set of relations he called power, work, and example. This familiar-sounding trio was, perhaps, natural; Wolff was vague about that; but in the world they were embodied in different structures in different places and different circumstances. Community existed within a group where those three were shared and appropriate institutions governed the sharing of them. The civil laws of a town or a guild derived their force from sovereign authority, to be sure; but their substance was best stated by persons intimately acquainted with each community, and states should exercise their confirmation power only to prevent contravention of the common weal.[7]

Cameral theorists, before the later eighteenth century and growing preoccupation with the police power, understood the home

---

[4] See below, pp. 174–175.

[5] "Von den Gesellschaften der Menschen" and "Von dem Gemeinen Wesen": *Vernünfftige Gedancken von dem Gesellschafftlichen Leben der Menschen, und insonderheit dem gemeinen Wesen* (Halle, 1721; I have used the Frankfurt/? edition of 1747).

[6] For the entry into cameralist administration, through university training, of Aristotelian natural law, Roman code law, and the Reformation idea of calling, see Kurt Zielenziger, *Die alten deutschen Kameralisten* (Jena, 1914), pp. 105–106; and Axel Nielsen, *Die Entstehung der deutschen Kameralwissenschaft im 17. Jahrhundert,* tr. Gustav Barqum (Jena, 1911).

[7] *Gedancken,* pp. 1–2, 415–423.

towns rather sympathetically and had no difficulty accepting their diversity and effective autonomy. One of the best contemporary descriptions of the hometown community (despite its lively title) is Johann Joachim Becher's (1635–1682) "Political Discourse on the Actual Causes of the Rise and Decline of Towns, Lands, and Republics," written in the 1660's and published in several editions through the mid-eighteenth century.[8] Becher argued that "true community" was to be found among those who arranged their affairs so as mutually to live from one another by the bürgerliche Nahrung; authority was a "servant of the community," and its duty was to sustain the social codes "whereby men live together with one another, for the community is not there for authority's sake, but authority for the sake of the community."[9] Governance was the art of symmetry and harmony: Becher, a chemist and economist, gave it the name of beauty (Schönheit). Beauty required that the three economic estates—merchants, artisans, and peasants—have one sovereign in common; but sovereignty was for the coordination of proper roles, literally "beautiful police," not for changes in the nature of them; for each estate, and the subcategories of each, had its own rules and its own reason of being, true pursuit of which ended up in a harmonious whole.[10] Individual selfishness and greed, to be sure, could destroy and splinter community. In the case of the hometown trades, guilds were the right instruments for controlling greed, meaning the prevention both of too many practitioners of a trade and of too few. To abolish guilds (with Holland the dreadful example) would benefit merchants and manufacturers to the ruin of artisans, and render the country subject to uncontrollable fluctuations in foreign economies; Germany's more subtle system of constant internal adjustments in a predominantly domestic economy preserved stability even in the face of war and disruptions in international trade.[11] Becher was quite aware of existing deviations from his harmonious pattern, and he made a long list of them; but he called them accidents and not essences of communal life, and so he was not obliged to say what was to be done if they turned out to be

[8] *Politischer discurs, von den eigentlichen ursachen des auff- und abnehmens der städt, länder und republicken* (I have used the Frankfurt/Main edition, 1759, edited and annotated by Georg H. Zincken.)

[9] Ibid., pp. 23–25. [10] Ibid., pp. 852–885, 1154–1199.

[11] Ibid., pp. 928–980.

in fact essentials of the community. From the perspective of "beautiful police," merchant, artisan, and peasant shared a common interest that Becher found in maximum consumption of material goods. Closer in, though, at the town gates, hometownsmen in fact excluded both merchant and peasant from their communities and thought their communities depended on doing so, and ultimately were correct to think so.

A fundamental error of cameralist theory was its dual faith that all real things were natural and that all natural things fit together. And while that in itself did not urge uniformity or the centralization of power—not directly—it did create a social and political science implicitly encyclopedic and gave the key to it, the index to its harmony, to the state. That gave the state, seriously, a place very like God's, not in a sacramental way but as the place where omniscience and harmony had to be if they existed in the world. Nearly every writer on cameralism has pointed out that cameralism was a state-sponsored science, developed by servants of the state or sympathizers with the state's purposes, and that its goals were fiscal: the accumulation of wealth to benefit the state's treasuries. But that does not invalidate the broader theoretical description: on the contrary it affirms it. For the state's links with society were fiscal; its staff was a fiscal staff; and if the diverse array of German institutions touched each other anywhere it was through that medium. Into the frame of fiscal theory and fiscal administration, therefore, Germany's movers and doers of the seventeenth and eighteenth centuries poured the whole burden of their political, economic, social, and even moral science. And the container affected the content. The goal of that science was, wrote Gustav Schmoller later on, "not only a question of state armies, fleets, and civil services; it was a question rather of unifying systems of finance and economy which should encompass the force of millions and whole countries, and give unity to their social life." But Schmoller from his nineteenth-century stance added something the cameral theorists would not have acknowledged nor civil servants, even Prussian ones, have contemplated: that the issue was the "total transformation of society," summed up in the opposition of the economic policy of the state to that of the town, the district, and the several estates.[12] German government got into that later on, as a way out of the contradictions of cameralism. But while the essential disharmonies of German society could be treated as accidental abuses, the doctrine could remain at once generous in tone and total in subject matter. Baroque inclusiveness of the diversity and separateness of German society could survive while the theory of harmony remained abstract, and while the state as embodiment of harmony barely touched the surface of social institutions for which the home towns serve here as prime example. Cameralist political science was a good idea until the capacity and the will were there to carry it out. But when and where they did, harmony in diversity threatened to become theoretical madness; the effort to shoehorn everthing into system without changing it threatened cameralist doctrine with encylopedic desperation. Baroque painting, sculpture, and architecture, in a modern phrase, "confused the spatial domains of art and reality," an aesthetic solecism.[13] Cameralist theory threatened the state with a task of which no institution has ever been capable, the undertaking of which might be called political blasphemy.

Practical evasions of logical consequences

There were two main ways the logical consequences of cameralist doctrine were avoided in administrative practice. One was simply to leave unharmonious and complicated things to their own devices; that happened to the home towns and guilds of the individualized country. The other was to assert sovereignty over all the divergent elements of a society in the name of harmony without changing the overt structure of any of them; that was the Prussian solution.

The localized economies of the home towns in the individualized country, apart from the difficulty of getting at them, were fiscally unimportant; they lived apart from the whole of society (represented by the state), and could easily be left out of the state's concerns while harmony and purpose were developed within that lim-

[12] *The Mercantile System* (New York, 1897), pp. 43ff, quoted in Small, *Cameralists*, p. 90. Schmoller used the term *Merkantilismus* to give his study a universal cast; he meant cameralist theory blurred together with the Prussian variant of cameralist administration.

[13] *The Thames and Hudson Encyclopaedia of the Arts* (London, 1966), p. 166.

ited and quite separate place: among the movers and doers of the educated state bureaucracy. Officials intervened across the chasm that separated them from the lives of the home towns only against distortions of the essential home town; and that, given the aid of the hometownsmen themselves, was within their capacity.[14]

The political ways in which state government worked to sustain the home towns has already been touched upon.[15] Social and economic policies similarly accommodated their autonomy and diversity. The general cameralist bias in favor of growing populations, for example, was not undiscriminating or limitless. Sometimes it seems so in the generalized writings of cameral theorists, but not in the actions of state officials. At any rate it did not invade the social constitutions of the home towns in the individualized country, nor jeopardize their own population policies. Accept no Bürger unless he has been taken into a guild, ordered the Bavarian government, and above all no foreigners; and never make citizens of "slovenly people who will breed only beggars and idlers." [16] Without citizenship the slovens would be unable to marry and thus presumably unable to reproduce their kind. Keep out the incompetent (a general guildsman's word for unacceptable) ordered a Cologne archepiscopal edict for Westphalia in 1723, suggesting that one way to do this was with high admission fees, another was to hold Bürgermeister and council personally responsible for anybody they admitted who got into trouble, and another was to make sure the guilds had their proper voice.[17] Bavaria too stated a rule in 1782 that if any incompetent was licensed and got the Bürgerrecht, the officials who got him citizenship, whoever they were, must bear the burden of his failure.[18] Württemberg, despite an official claim that citizenship rights were the state's to give, agreed that new citizens could be made only in conformity with local law and tradition, and never

[14] Compare the retreat to appellate jurisdiction of post-Napoleonic liberal bureaucracy described in Chapters VI–VIII below.

[15] Above, pp. 62–72.

[16] Ordinances of 1656, 1676, and 1681 in Meyr, Sammlung, III (1788), 555–563; and the Instruction of 1748 in Kreittmayr, Sammlung (1771), p. 564.

[17] J. J. Scotti, ed., Sammlung der Gesetze und Verordnungen, welche in dem vormaligen Kurfürstenthum Cöln . . . ergangen sind, I (Düsseldorf, 1830), 615, 663–664; also the 1780 edict against the einschleichen of poor outsiders in Schlözer, Briefwechsel, VII (1780), 73–74.

[18] Meyr, Sammlung, II (1784), 991–993.

against the will or the advantage of local trades. Communal membership came normally as local birthright; and when and if, for reasons of local advantage, persons born elsewhere were admitted, the state directed that care be taken that such persons were hometownsmen: people who had learned hometown ways in the places of their birth and who would recognize and accept the ways of the community they entered.[19] And in 1789 the Prince-Bishop of Fulda, citing the dangers of indiscriminate population growth, urged upon his subject communities high property qualifications for marriage, citizenship, and the trades, to hold down the proportion of non-citizen laborers.[20]

The guild question was crucial because here hometown concern with membership interesected with state concern for the general economy and fisc; and the pattern was hardly different from the pattern of civic rights. Hanover, in keeping with cameral administration in the individualized country, upheld the line between hometown trades and rural pursuits, and affirmed guild control over membership and the guilds' right to drive out groundrabbits; Bavaria had a special edict against groundrabbitry.[21] Württemberg produced elaborate guild legislation in the late eighteenth century. It followed contemporary administrative practice by treating local guilds in terms of their own needs and circumstances. But putting that practice into law made such paper work and contradiction as to suggest even to Württemberg district officials that something might be wrong with the system:[22] hometown economies were perhaps ill-suited to state law and administration. Baden officials, though inclined to assert state powers especially in economic matters, accepted the hometown pattern generally when they asserted them: holding the cloverleaf together in 1751, for example, by forbidding journeymen to marry on the grounds that journeyman marriage would tend to extort membership and citizenship before the candidate was ready for them. But the sequence that followed

[19] Moser, *Landeshoheit im Weltlichen*, III (1773), 41–45. Note also the Weissenburg preference for distant outsiders over nearby countrymen, below pp. 221, 224.
[20] In April, 1789: *Patriotisches Archiv*, X (1789), 443–470.
[21] Ortloff, ed., *Corpus juris*, pp. 189–218; Meyr, *Sammlung*, II (1784), 733–736.
[22] Hoffmann, *Das württembergische Zunftwesen*, pp. 35–36.

in Baden, economically perhaps the most vigorous and administratively the most autocratic state of the individualized country, may have been a sign: a decree ten years later forbade guilds to require marriage of masters—guild membership thus was still obligatory, but undomesticated artisans were to be allowed in guilds—and a general ordinance said that while guild officers were to be elected locally by guild members, they should be sworn by state officials and act as agents of the state.[23] Baden had moved halfway toward the Prussian alternative.

The Prussian way of baroque administration in the seventeenth and eighteenth centuries did not suppose that harmony would come from neglect and affirmation of local corporations and estates, but neither did it try to destroy their formal peculiarities. Prussian administrators simply took on, as best they could, effective direction over the components of Prussian society in all their complexity, thus removing their autonomy but not their individuality and variety. There is little sign of any clear thought of changing the society; rather it was a seizure of power by the Prussian administrative corps, closest-knit body among Germany's movers and doers and in many ways their lodestar. Their strength was the organization, skills, and power built up within the areas of royal administration—domains, finance, war. Probably they could not have achieved their position but for the political weakness of Prussian local corporations and relative fluidity of Prussian society; and no doubt they were aided by the energy and ambition of Prussia's rulers.[24] But evidence for the historical model of leveling Prussian bureaucratic absolutism comes mainly from documents that passed among themselves and that had to do with their own organization. It does not

[23] Ortloff, ed., *Corpus juris*, pp. 225–226, 263–264, 277.

[24] Cf. above, pp. 21–26. But to support the position that the civil service, not the crown, was the vital force: some of the most vigorous bureaucratic activity and legislation came in the reigns of kings generally left out of the histories of Prussian autocracy, such as Frederick I, and Frederick Williams II and III, whose relative indolence and timidity perhaps unleashed bureaucratic propensities beyond what was politic for a Prussian ruler. See for example the vigorous immigration, guild, and town policies under Frederick I in Meyer, *Handwerkerpolitik*, I, 109–132; and the drive for administrative unity under Frederick William II to replace Frederick II's calculated confusion, in Hans Haussherr, *Verwaltungseinheit und Ressorttrennung vom Ende des 17. bis zum Beginn des 19. Jahrhunderts* (Berlin, 1953), pp. 146–147.

tell much about how their dominance may have modified the society they governed. Their seizure of power in Prussia, pretty well accomplished by the middle of the eighteenth century, was very real. But in local situations the pattern of seizure appears more political than systematic: they did not crush Prussian social institutions but infiltrated or bypassed them.[25] Political power in the hands of such men was a factor for social simplification and uniformity no doubt, intended or not; yet even Prussian administration accepted baroque variety on the social and institutional scene. To do so was theoretically justified by the academic tenets of cameralism; but more important, the officials were not really equipped to do more. Their political reach exceeded their administrative grasp; the centralization and mobility that existed within their caste could be extended into the society itself only partially, unevenly, and by slow degrees.

Prussian policy toward towns and guilds from the Thirty Years' War until the end of the eighteenth century was to treat communal organizations as state institutions—meaning, insofar as there was resistance to state policies in indigenous corporate bodies, to convert them into public institutions. That overrode, to speak in terms of legal theory, the private-public-law tangle that defended hometown constitutions and bedeviled their analysts in the individualized country. There was resistance, over matters whose importance hometownsmen anywhere in Germany would have recognized; and while it was not serious enough to make the outline anything like social reform or redistribution, still state political control over community policies meant quite different policies from those hometownsmen pursued when left to themselves. Interests diverged on economic and fiscal matters, most dramatically over the Prussian state interest in the immigration of skilled artisans. The reluctance of town magistrates to grant them full economic rights was what led to laws of the 1680's granting to Brandenburg *Steuerräte*, the basi-

---

[25] Compare the study of Hannelore Juhr, *Die Verwaltung des Hauptamtes Brandenburg/Ostpreussen von 1713 bis 1751* (Berlin, 1967), with the traditional descriptions of Prussian bureaucracy developed by Schmoller and Hintze, and with Max Weber's models of rational bureaucracy. Juhr is surprised by the amount of intrigue, corruption, and un-automaton-like behavior on the part of civil servants: yet their defeat of local corporate interests, by hook or by crook, was overwhelming.

cally tax-collecting officers who were the main state agents for town affairs, control over decisions that in the home town were exercised by guildsmen in conjunction with avuncular councils. By contrast with hometownsmen, the Steuerräte wanted their districts to produce high revenues that would do themselves professional credit. Guilds and their statutes remained, but each of them as an act of sovereign will rather than as guildsmen's right, and the Steuerräte spoke the sovereign will. Immigrants still had to enter guilds like anybody else; there was no suggestion of an unregulated economy. But Steuerräte got instructions to make entry into the guilds easier, and into the Bürgerrecht as well.[26]

This immigration of the Great Elector's time was encouraged for the sake of production of goods like cloth for export or for consumption by the state itself. The policy did not depend on a broad purpose of increasing gross population for its own sake. Still in the seventeenth century there was a general feeling that productive population overall had fallen below the number that would best fill available economic structures and facilities: there were unplowed fields and empty houses, attributed to war and what went with it, and nobody knew then that wars were about to become less destructive of productive population. Before the late eighteenth century it was not commonly supposed that population increased or even maintained itself spontaneously; indeed an impression was widespread among publicists and scholars, and thus presumably among statesmen, that the European population had been gripped in a general decline since ancient times.[27] They were not sure, but the question was at least problematical; and cameralist theory entered demography more to treat the causes of depopulation, within existing structures, than it did to seek means to population increase. In fact, though, population was generally growing; and

[26] Meyer, *Handwerkerpolitik*, I, 1–106; Schmoller, "Innungswesen," pp. 64–84.

[27] But Paul Mombert, "Die Anschauungen des 17. und 18. Jahrhunderts über die Abnahme der Bevölkerung," *JNS*, CXXXV (1931), 481–503, overstates this. The greatest German demographer, Johann Peter Süssmilch, thought that although human vital powers had declined since antiquity, still a gradual increase was taking place; but the rate of increase was lessening and thus presumably would turn into a decline if things went on as they were. *Die göttliche Ordnung in den Veränderungen des menschlichen Geschlechts* (2d ed.; Berlin, 1761), I, 16–25 and passim.

towns were probably more aware of it severally, each in its own sphere, than state governments were in their sphere; for townsmen knew more about their own towns than state governments did about their territories. For that reason alone it made a difference whether town population policy was controlled by townsmen themselves, as in the individualized country, or by state servants as in Prussia. But the difference in interest between hometownsmen and state was more important than demographic effects; in any case, direct state responsibility for town society and economy made no incubator for home towns in Prussia.

Prussian baroque administration, an autocratic and ungenerous baroque, got its clearest stamp during the reign of King Frederick William I in the early eighteenth century. The way his government turned the thou-shalt-nots of the 1731 Imperial Trades Edict into measures for positive state control was mentioned in the discussion of that edict in connection with the guild economy;[28] where state officials were "the authorities," guilds were made to be responsive to regional and state interests even as their structures were retained for regulative and training purposes: a dubious mismatch of structure with function that made the officials' task no easier. For guilds were the main institutional cements of the home town, but state control deprived them of just the features that enabled them to be so: favoritism for sons, communal decision on the numbers of permissible masters in a guild or journeymen in a shop, expensive masterworks and long waiting periods, exclusion of retired soldiers —all were disallowed by outsiders' notions of what guilds were for. Prussian eighteenth-century artisans, instead of proposing guild statutes on their own initiative (as was usual in the individualized country), tried to avoid having any at all, because a formal statute was a handle for state control through the Steuerräte.[29] Guilds were still local, and separate; each trade had its own rules, and artisans

[28] Above, pp. 93–96.

[29] On Prussian guild policy generally Meyer, *Handwerkerpolitik;* and Schmoller, "Innungswesen"; for a local application, Heinrich Piesch, "Das Ravensberger Zunftwesen im Zeitalter der Aufklärung," *JHVR*, LX (1958), 56–92; for sources and precedents for German guild policies provided by late Roman law and Justinian Code, which were hostile to guilds for political reasons, A. Bruder, "Die Behandlung der Handwerkerkorporationen durch die Juristen des 17. und 18. Jahrhunderts," *ZGS*, XXXVI (1880), 484–503

lived under different rules from other Prussian subjects. This was a kind of differentiation unlike the localism of the individualized country, but in its own way even more complex because it did not run itself. The different sets of rules came together only in the work of state officials, men with various competencies and with outside responsibilities. The hometown interpenetration of economic and political life was impossible. The dividing lines within Prussian society were drawn clearly, sharply, and in excruciating detail; but they were drawn and guarded by state servants who stood apart from them. While everyday spheres of Prussian small-town life remained presumably local, the operative boundaries were among occupations and castes, not among localities; they were administrative jurisdictions and legal definitions rather than hometown walls.

It is worth at least the conjecture that Prussian officialdom would not have entered the business of detailed economic and thence social regulation at all if it had not been for "mercantile" interests that really had very little to do with the economies of small and middle towns. There was little concrete fiscal advantage to be had from systematically policing the hometown trades, but once state regulation was accepted in principle, it was hard to establish any point of diminishing administrative returns. Efforts to differentiate between what mattered to the state and what did not matter only complicated matters further, because the principle of the system did not allow for any blank spaces in the state's competence and responsibility. If an official let something slide because it did not really matter, he was being remiss in his duty. If there was to be diversity under state tutelage, if there was to be neither uniformity nor freedom, then the state had to pay a corresponding price in legislative complexity and administrative labor.

Prussian administration posed two imperatives: first, that public officials know their districts thoroughly enough for their oversight to be genuine, accurate, and inescapable; and second, that they be detached from and immune to local influence and obstacles.[30] The two did not fit together well. The problem was probably most

[30] On the need for thorough understanding of local circumstances if state police was to be effective see, e.g., Theodor Winkler, *Johann Gottfried Frey und die Entwicklung der preussischen Selbstverwaltung* (Stuttgart, 1957), pp. 21–35, on Königsberg and the Polizeireform of 1752.

serious in places annexed to Prussia through inheritence, treaty, or war. A 1772 general ordinance for West Prussia (acquired in the first partition of Poland) said that competent officials should be appointed at the local level *even though* that sometimes might give an advantage to native inhabitants over outside candidates. But in Silesia only a quarter of the town magistrates were natives of the towns where they served in 1809, half a century after annexation; another quarter were soldiers, mostly from outside Silesia altogether.[31]

The Prussian General Code, begun at mid-century and finally issued in the 1790's, was a kind of climax of baroque political theory, Prussian variant. For it was an effort to capture in coherent legal form all the elements of a whole society, recognizing almost interminable differences of occupation, birth, and privilege (that was the baroque of it); but it founded its categories not on local corporations and clusters of social relations, but on social and legal types marked out and recognized by the state (that was the Prussian part). The respective rights and qualities of each category were carefully defined. The different kinds of people the Code described were to be found in the individualized country too. But the Code, while it recognized institutional variety, did not recognize discrete community. Individuals were identified not as community members but as members of the state orders into which the whole society was divided. Thus the Code was an expansion of the principle that had appeared in the guild legislation of Frederick William I: special rules for every kind of person, but general state rules and not local community sanctions: estate or *Stand* categories in the Code meant class, or at least something much nearer our own idea of class than to the community the hometownsmen knew.

The Prussian Code distinguished the three kinds of townsmen already noted in the larger towns of the individualized country: an "exempted" (*eximirte*) town estate of high bourgeois and rich patricians, primarily state citizens, free of local rules and local

---

[31] Adolf Poschmann, "Die Verwaltung der Stadt Braunsberg, 1772–1808," *ZGAE*, XXV (1933), 623–651; Ziekursch, *Städteverwaltung*, p. 121. Of course international considerations operated in both these cases: but see also Ilse Barleben, "Die Entwicklung der städtischen Selbstverwaltung im Herzogtum Kleve während der Reform Friedrich Wilhelms I," *RA*, XVIII (1931), 131–138.

courts and subject, like nobles, directly to central state jurisdictions; "actual Bürger," meaning artisans, retailers, and local merchants; and tolerated residents without local citizenship. Special regulations for manufacturers and factory workers made them immediately subject to the state along with the tolerated residents and exempted citizens. The highest and lowest townsmen thus joined the nobility as explicit state classes, *Staatsstände;* and special marriage provisions and other devices opened the channels between the exempted high bourgeois and the nobility, while drawing a sharp social line between high bourgeois and small Bürger; for Prussia was interested in its state class, knew where to look for it, and whom to keep out of it.[32]

The hometownsman as a social type thus was recognized in the Code although his community was not; there was even an acknowledgment of existing provincial and other particular laws and rights, and the Code's drafters strove for language that would encompass them all and express them all as parts of a general sovereignty embodied in the state. Still implicit was the assumption that all the particulars really fit together in some overview. The framers of the Code almost certainly knew better, at least by the time they were done: knew that all the elements of Prussian society would fit together as the Code contemplated only if the state obliged them to, or at least broke existing social patterns in the interests of the Code's.[33] For although the Code was posed as a static legal snapshot of Prussian society, avoiding any suggestion of social or even civic reform, its effort to encompass every aspect of life gave to every general statement, every accommodation of one legal practice to another, the effect of reform if given the force of law and truly administered. For everything to fit the Code, the Prussian civil service had to govern everything so it would fit; and the contradiction of cameralism, between the acknowledgment of diversity and the determination that all must be a piece, lurked in every clause.

[32] A good discussion of this is Reinhart Koselleck, *Preussen zwischen Reform und Revolution* (Stuttgart, 1967), pp. 78–124.

[33] For these aspects of the Code, Koselleck, *Preussen*, pp. 1–51; and Wilhelm Ebel, *Geschichte der Gesetzgebung in Deutschland* (2d ed.; Göttingen, 1958), pp. 54, 75–76.

Johann Justi and the police power

Two theorists faced the contradiction of cameralism well before the Prussian General Code was published in the 1790's, and reacted in opposite ways: Johann Justi (1705?–1771) and Justus Möser (1720–1794). The reason they did was the development of police science after the middle of the eighteenth century, and the absorption into it of the older tenets of cameralism. It was mainly a theoretical process, but still a very serious one for the home towns.

Terms are loose and treacherous: but the main components of eighteenth-century state government were *Cameralia*, which had fundamentally to do with fiscal activites; *Oeconomia*, which had to do with the exploitation of the state's (technically the ruler's) own properties; and *Polizeisachen*, which had to do with the economic life of the territory and which in towns was administered locally.[34] Cameralist scholars and working officials of the seventeenth and early eighteenth centuries had been concerned mostly with the first two, where their competence was unquestioned; but the incorporation of Police with that previously more limited sphere of administration meant inclusion of economic practices in detail and outside the state's own peculiar sphere—beyond, that is, fiscal practices, general commercial legislation, and domain administration.[35] And then Police came to dominate the others. With that, administrative science became state science and more: it became political science, a political science whose peculiarity was that it inherited the old cameralist assumption of totality. And whereas the older assumption of totality had been supportable inasmuch as it applied within a body of movers and doers who stood above everything, the new totality, that came from incorporating Police with the other two, would have actually to include everything. It would undertake to treat towns in the way the older branches had been able to treat state fisc and domains.

Justi put the relation of police to the older cameralism thus: "Police is the foundation of true cameral science; and the police authority must sow if the cameralist is to reap. . . . Police is con-

[34] On the relations among this trinity and the absorption of the first two into police, Haussherr, *Verwaltungseinheit*, pp. 26–28, 58, 84–87.

[35] Zielenziger, *Kameralisten*, pp. 101–102.

cerned to maintain the total wealth and substance of the state's internal structure and to increase it; but the cameralist is concerned to abstract from out of this total wealth of the state the most accessible part, without disadvantage to the whole, for the necessary expenses of government." [36] Johann Jakob Moser (1701–1785), a contemporary of Justi's but less enamored of state instrumentalities and less given to theoretical and administrative aspirations, said that "police, as this word is used in practice and understood, means those things which serve to establish and maintain security, good morals and order, which treat poverty and prosperity, and the values of civil life in general—or, whatever people think might do so." [37] Moser's scepticism at so general a notion shows through; but that same wide inclusiveness made the whole compilation seem to most theorists inescapably a province of the state, there being no other institution that could claim it. The officials who *were* the state, along with their academic coaches from the not-too-distant sidelines, were glad to listen. So were princes, and made enlightened despots of themselves.

In the later eighteenth century there was a visible increase in the interest German administrators and academics took in the kind of economic activity associated with towns, even small ones. "Our century is an economic one," wrote Johann Christian Förster, professor of cameralism at Halle, in an "Outline of Rural, Town, and State Science," published in 1782; "We find even insignificant trades worth investigating, and try to find ways of perfecting them; we make systems, to raise the well-being of men." [38] The theorist who suited them best was Justi. His works on police brought what went on in towns to the heart of the state sciences; and that obliged him (though he probably did not think of it this way) to find an alternative to the baroque cameralist contradiction.[39]

[36] Johann H. G. v. Justi, *Grundsätze der Polizeywissenschaft* (3d ed.; Göttingen, 1782), reprinted Introduction to the 1st ed. of 1756.

[37] *Von der Teutschen Crays-Verfassung*, pp. 735 f., quoted in Laufs, *Rottweil, 1650–1806*, p. 94.

[38] *Entwurf der Land-, Stadt-, und Staatswissenschaft*, quoted by Albrecht Timm, "Von der Kameralistik zur Nationalökonomie," in Otto Brunner, ed., *Festchrift Hermann Aubin* (Wiesbaden, 1965), p. 365.

[39] Justi's place as spokesman for the aims of eighteenth-century German administrators is generally accepted: Haussherr, *Verwaltungseinheit*, p. 83; Zielenziger, *Kameralisten*, pp. 101–103; Roscher, *National-Oekonomik*, pp. 444–445. Small, *Cameralists*, builds his study around Justi but often misreads

Johann Justi was born in Thuringia sometime between 1705 and 1720—illegitimately born, according to the kind of rumor that persists because it fits a man's behavior in a satisfying way; but actually he seems to have come from a decent enough civil service family. After some years as a student and a soldier he began to write. His first significant work, a prize essay for the Berlin Academy, was a hostile critique of Leibnitz's monadology. Among his other works was a treatise on the theory of the European balance of power, wherein he urged German rulers to rely not on political balance among the great for their security, but upon maximum development of their own resources: no incubator Empire of windowless souls for Justi. After the Austrian Succession War he was called to the new Theresian Academy for civil administration at Vienna, an Austrian effort to galvanize its government after defeat by Prussia; and his inaugural lecture there was on the "Connection between the Flourishing of the Sciences (*Wissenschaften*) and That of the State." His life thenceforward was spent moving among literary, academic, and administrative occupations in Austria, Prussia, Denmark, and Saxony.

In the 1750's he set himself the task of making cameral and police science, which seemed to be expanding randomly out of all bounds, into a "coherent" academic discipline, one in which servants and citizens of the state could be trained in the useful pursuit of the common weal. That would be the university study in which young men would "gain insight into the whole"; it would bring the scattered elements of public life under a "philosophical head." The state should support it as a practical study because "if someone has no general and coherent grasp of all the activities of governance, then when he tries to serve the common weal in one place, he will harm many others." He thought the study and teaching of Roman law had been "the first step Providence allowed us to take out of the thick fog of ignorance that everywhere surrounded us": now he would make it work in Germany.[40]

---

and even mistranslates him. The best biographical sketch I know is F. Frensdorff, "Über das Leben und die Schriften des Nationalökonomen J. H. G. v. Justi," *Nachrichten von der Königl. Gesellschaft der Wissenschaften zu Göttingen. Philologisch-historische Klasse*, 1903, pp. 355–503.

[40] *Staatswirthschaft, oder Systematische Abhandlung aller Oekonomischen und Cameral-Wissenschaften, die zur Regierung eines Landes erfodert werden,* I (2d ed.; Leipzig, 1758), xiv–xxi, xxv, xxxvi–xxxvii, 31.

Coherence—*Zusammenhang*—was his favorite word and the theme of his administrative theory; police, in a definition he repeated whenever he got a chance, was "that science whose aim it is to keep the well-being of the individual families constantly in precise harmonious relation with what is best for the whole." [41] Well-being consisted, in the first place, in the "perfection of our moral condition," and a necessary means to it was "a good structure and disposition of the state, such that every man may enjoy reasonable freedom and be in a position to acquire, by his own efforts, those moral and material goods that he in his estate needs for a satisfying life." [42] Individual freedom, coherence, and the weal of the whole and of the state all hung together, thus: An industrious and inventive population is vital for any society. Two basic springs (*Triebfedern*) of human action create it: ambition to rise, and the wish for material comfort. All state laws and actions should encourage these individual drives. But since they are natural in men, they develop best when not inhibited by governments: away, then, with rigid despotism and with tyranny. Justi brought the principle to economics; it worked out best there, and on the whole he conceived it economically. Economic policy ought to aim at a large volume of material goods because that would benefit individuals and through them the whole, which was the sum of individuals. It would be achieved by "good coherence among the productive estates of the whole country." Lack of coherence was the cause of stagnation and poverty. It was therefore the duty of government to remove all obstacles to that individual human ambition that brought individual productivity and the coherent prosperity of all. For there would be obstacles, he thought, even in a democracy. [43]

When Justi wrote descriptively of towns he made many of the definitions I have made; but watch for his different emphases and his corollaries. "A town is a coherent body [*Zusammenhang* again] of societies [*Gesellschaften*], families, and individual persons, in a protected place, under the observance and direction of a police

[41] *Die Grundfeste zu der Macht und Glückseligkeit der Staaten, oder ausführliche Vorstellung der gesamten Polizeiwissenschaft*, I (Königsberg, 1760), Vorrede.

[42] *Staatswirthschaft*, I, 65–66.   [43] *Grundfeste*, I, 427–435, 689–695.

college called a town council, or other official persons designated for police administration, living together in order to pursue the more successfully, effectively, and coherently those trades and occupations directly necessary for the needs and comfort of the whole country [*des Landes*] and for the uniting [*Verbindung*] of the country's whole economy." He thought that walls, be they of stone or of police constabulary, were the essential mark of a town; "without them no place can be called a town, however large and handsomely built it is," for a town had to be so constituted that "nothing can get in or get out without police oversight." Villages were quite different because countrymen produced only a few special kinds of goods; "and whereas whole societies, called guilds, exist in towns for the pursuit of the trades, only individual families are to be found on the land." And he distinguished between towns based on local economies and towns based on external commerce: the essence of the former was differentiation of trades, security (the walls), and government, while the essence of commercial towns was communication, on the example of the great cities of antiquity and the towns of America.[44]

Rules for town governance necessarily varied, Justi said, so that he could not give the kind of clear descriptive outline for them that he could for rural governance or state administration. Towns were "naturally" governed by an elected senate or council; that maintained confidence between citizens and government, and citizens knew the candidates for office better than the state could. Major town decisions should be put before the citizenry; the state should preserve the political rights of the Bürger, and intervene to prevent the emergence of patrician oligarchy. The central duty of the council was the administration of police; that power could never be exercised apart from the council, for "they are in essence nothing but police colleges." Therefore the director of local police should always be at the same time director of the town council.[45]

But when Justi turned from describing (conventionally on the whole) the towns as entities to describing the state as *an* entity,

[44] *Staatswirthschaft*, I, 491–493; *Grundfeste*, I, 296–312. Justi thought in 1760 that more than half the German population lived in towns, which would mean perhaps 40 per cent in places of a size I have assigned to the home town: *Grundfeste*, I, 295; cf. above, pp. 27–33.

[45] *Grundfeste*, I, 344–352; *Staatswirthschaft*, I, 490–491, 523–524.

another dimension appeared because the state had the job of maintaining the coherence that made individual and collective weal the same. He admonished the state that "town councils are in essence nothing but *lower* police colleges [my italics]; judicial powers and other rights of their own they have acquired only in accidental ways, and it is very doubtful whether their possession of them is good for town government or well-being." Coherent police administration had to derive from the general authority. Therefore (despite what Justi had said a volume back about the "natural" election of town councils and the avoidance of oligarchy), the periodic election of councils was "foolishness . . . under the fair name of rights and privileges . . . absurdity," for it brought into office men of small qualifications who lacked the broad view, who would be affected by "side issues, emotions, and personal interests." That is, it disturbed the right exercise of the police power, especially in small and middle towns. For there the elected president of the council often bore, by state authority, those police duties that in large towns was exercised by appointed state police directors.[46]

Justi's basic political equation, between the weal of individuals and their aggregate weal in the state, left communal group interests out of account. He rejected the ways in which communities really worked mainly by ignoring them. He recognized diversity; he thought each town government should reflect the particular economic and social composition of its citizenry. But he hedged that, in the interest of universality, with a recommendation that every council include as many "learned persons" as it did members drawn from the natural citizenry.[47] And he insisted that each town had to work coherently with the whole society, and assigned the state the task of seeing that it did, uncontaminated by the "side issues, emotions, and personal interests" that might intervene between individual and common weal. His treatment of guilds was much the same. He had his doubts about them; but without the elabo-

[46] *Grundfeste,* II (1761), 609–612, 614–620, 635, 637–640. Justi was ambiguous on whether a small-town police director was a state appointee or not, because he thought he should be but knew he often was not: typical of the tension in Justi's work.
[47] Ibid., I, 350–351.

rately differentiated guild structures how could there be the detailed economic safeguards necessary if the activity of each was to be kept harmonious with the well-being of the whole? Regulation had to be exercised in such a way as to free the economic aspirations and skills of individuals. "Perhaps it will be said that there will be too many masters that way. But just that is advantageous to the population and the economy." He quite ignored the communal functions of guilds. When, for example, he deprecated the guildsmen's categories of coarse and fine trades, the distinctions he said should be abolished were typically those that distinguished town from rural trades, and landmasters from hometownsmen: rough smiths from locksmiths, or wagoners from cabinetmakers, even though he was emphatic on economic grounds about keeping town trades out of the countryside, farmers out of town, and townsmen out of farming.[48] He thought trades should be organized systematically according to the materials they used. He thought artisans should always stay in one trade, and not spread themselves thin at the cost of special skill; but the distinctions from place to place within a trade (what guildsmen called honor) were, he said characteristically, as absurd as those among religious sects. His example of that was the papermakers' quarrel, between polishers and stampers. Polishers finished one leaf at a time and stampers many; but despite, he said, the superiority of the stampers' method the polishers hated them as though they had violated an article of faith—*Glaubenslehre*. The Edict of 1731 had raised the same dreadful example of guild iniquity, and so had other laws and tracts: professors and bureaucrats were especially sensitive to the technology and cost of paper.[49]

Justi thought persons engaged in commerce with goods not of their own making should not be in guilds. He especially mentioned needles, perhaps with Aachen in mind, though Aachen was not the only place with a needle problem; and perhaps Adam Smith had Justi in mind when he used needles as his example of the division of labor for *The Wealth of Nations*. And Justi distinguished manufacture from artisanry in a novel way (self-evident though it has

[48] Ibid., pp. 480–484; *Grundsätze der Polizeywissenschaft*, p. 163.
[49] *Staatswirthschaft*, I, 503; *Grundfeste*, I, 505–506. See Appendix below, § 13.

come to seem). Artisanry meant the working of raw materials by traditional methods, traditionally trained and organized by guilds; but manufacture implied new processes, not organized into regular guilds, and which required new kinds of training and a new kind of personnel: skilled foreign instructors, and workers who might appropriately be recruited from among the socially dubious inhabitants of orphanages, or from among countrymen—outsiders all, and "for this reason all guild constitutions must be banned" from manufacture.[50] Groundrabbits, he pointed out, were in practice defined not by their individual economic capacities but by their lack of local license to work; rules against them should not be firmly enforced because "the times and the circumstances have changed." It was not simply that groundrabbits were individuals, so that Justi unlike hometownsmen found place for them into his political equation; he thought population and external commerce were growing and economic structures must keep pace: population, time, commerce, and the common weal were all on the side of groundrabbits. Population growth should be augmented by encouraging immigration (but cautiously to avoid arousing native hostility) and marriage (including state provision of dowries for poor girls).[51] Johann Justi at mid-century had begun to sort out all these issues as between new ways and old ways, although most of them were in fact traditional issues. He thought that guild affairs should not be judged by regular judicial courts, which would be credulous of "old guild statutes, privileges, and old traditions," but rather by police colleges; for police science was concerned with today's common weal and therefore was equipped to bypass all that debris.[52]

Still he did not strike directly at the legal structures of towns and guilds. What he did, though, was more serious. He treated them as intermediate mechanisms to transmit harmony and order between individuals and the common weal, between the generality that was

[50] *Grundfeste*, I, 440–459, 471, 486–487.

[51] Ibid., pp. 494–500. Jews, Justi said, should not be subject to coarse prejudice; yet bad legislation and bad customs, and their alien nature, had made them a special problem. They should be encouraged to leave retailing and speculation, in which their alien qualities made them unreliable, and to enter production by their own hands, especially in factories: ibid., pp. 743–751. On liberalizing immigration and marriage, ibid., pp. 204–241; *Grundsätze der Polizeywissenschaft*, pp. 80–88.

[52] *Grundfeste*, I, 492.

the aggregate of individuals "whatever their estate, dignity, and service" and the generality that was the state; whereas the home-town community and guild separated individuals from the gen-erality and the state. He did not suppose "natural coherence" would come of itself, or at least not until the whole society was put on the right harmonious track. It was therefore the place of govern-ment to *introduce* the *natural* free conditions in which all would work together spontaneously: "to regulate each occupation and trade in such a fashion, as it would govern itself in its own self-interest if it had sufficient insight and understanding." The trouble came from insufficient insight into true self-interest. "If we wish to regulate the nature of economic movement correctly, then we must imagine how it would be if it perfectly followed its natural processes and found not the slightest hindrance from the state": the conditions of freedom to be achieved by close regulation.[53] There was a hint in this at a withering away of restrictive laws, or at least conflict, once their task of establishing a free and natural social order was achieved; but to begin with, in the world that was, the task required total control in the name of the common weal. Justi made a remark about obedience to law: when laws are not observed the fault lies not with the citizen, who cannot always tell what is right and good, but with the government that has failed to give enough guidance toward true self-interest and the common weal; in Justi's context at least (perhaps not only in his), the non-responsibility of transgressors led to the total administration of civic life, as distinguished from judicial prosecution and punishment for specific breaches of law.[54] To govern as if self-interest were free: that described the goal of government, but there is nothing in Justi's theory of public authority and freedom that limits the scope of public authority. There is no suggestion that bureaucracy or its power will wither away. Justi did not really say that freedom itself would be achieved by close regulation. Closer to his meaning is that all Germans should come to share the ways of the movers and doers, of whom the civil servants were the pioneering element.

Doctrinal analysis, though, is not the best way to explain the paradox of equating individual freedom with total state sovereignty that appears in the writings of Justi and in the sentiments of the

[53] Ibid., pp. 555–558, 636; II, 576.   [54] Ibid., II, 523–524.

public officials for whom I have made him speak. It only shows that something needs explaining. The German social and political environment is the explanation, for there the state and its staff were in fact the best hope for individual freedom and equal opportunity. It was not at all contradictory for Justi to argue for the suppression of "freedoms" and for individual freedom at the same time—a point that will bear reiteration—but still the argument led, almost inescapably, to the augmentation of state power. The state police power was developed by lawyers to match and counter the total web of community. The way to make communities coherent with the common weal was to take all the levers they manipulated out of their hands. And although Justi clung to baroque acceptance of peculiarity and diversity, still determined to be true to diverse natural conditions, he saw, academically at least, where it was heading. A full corpus of practical police science, capable of taking all variations and detail into account, "would demand an astonishing range," he allowed after twelve hundred pages of getting the general principles down.[55] If German administrative science had been a matter of frank artificial regulation of this kind of behavior and that, then the impossible burden of total governance would not have been imposed. Justi got around it with his fiction: that individual self-interest, and the interest of the whole, and the interest of the state were all the same. The home town epitomizes what forced the equation. It also epitomizes what the equation left out.

The common weal, community, and Justus Möser

Johann Justi's effort to create a "philosophical head" for the state sciences produced not an overview of reality but a body of aspirations.[56] But police science for the common weal provided a caste ideology, instilled by the educational system and sustained by exhortations of government, that was addressed to the structure and suited one of the main divisions of German society. The movers and

---

[55] Ibid., p. 443. Justi quoted Montesquieu (a favorite of his) on the need for conformity to local physical, economic, and political conditions: pp. 482–497.

[56] Thus Haussherr: that Justi avoided mention of the complex hindrances to rational administration, and so produced no descriptive textbooks but rather a *norm-setzende Lehre*, and an *Idealtypus. Verwaltungseinheit*, pp. 83–84.

doers that passed through the fused worlds of German learning and civil service found here a slogan that supported their ambitions and gave them dignity: a watchword, a calling. The principle of the common weal was a justification for their abstraction from the provincial fragmented worlds of hometownsmen and countrymen, and for reentering them on their own terms. It was a guide for action. The welfare of the aggregate of state subjects in this view matched neatly with the aim of expanding the economic bases of the state, and of advancing the careers of its personnel. The common weal meant raising the sum of material wealth; but the encouragement of commerce and industry, the removal of conflicts between town and country, and the unleashing of individual ambitions all contradicted the home town in principle. They contradicted the home town's exclusiveness, and with that the arbitrary moral dogmatism and even cruelty with which the home town defended its exclusiveness. The link among learning, statecraft, and moral humaneness is not happenstance, nor is social environment the only explanation. The same study of antiquity that sustained German humanism sustained the use of Roman law as well (remember the credit Justi gave to Roman law): thus the common weal as a humane aspiration hung together with the legal instrument for unifying and coordinating the interests of all, and with the effectiveness of the state interests.[57] Humanistic individualism, at the time, was the natural morality of a ruling state class.

One definition of the home town is that it was not professionally governed, either by state officials with outside responsibilities, or by the patrician governments of large towns who, unlike hometown councilmen, treated their cities as collectivities, as common weals, rather than as accommodations of corporate group interests. To bring a new and enterprising clothier into a community might indeed advance the economic interests of almost everybody there, or at least the sum of interests, but not of the clothiers' interests; and the hometown system made the interest of the clothiers cancel out the interests of the rest, in the name of social community. Professional governors, state or patrician, might see the public interest as an arithmetical collective sum of interests, but a citizenry organized in guilds and Bürger councils did not total up interests

[57] Zielenziger, *Kameralisten*, pp. 59–69, 76–78.

that way. Communal interest was a mutually canceling-out system of reciprocal protection.

Conflict between the common weal and corporate rights was nothing new. The patrician town council of Bremen in the early seventeenth century licensed a Dutch free cobbler, on the grounds that the town needed good shoemakers like him. In the course of the ensuing quarrel with the shoemakers' guild, the council threatened to abolish the Bremen guilds altogether, citing natural law: "For men of enlightened reason, which nature instills in all men, truly teach that the common weal [*publicam utilitatem*] is always to be preferred over private convenience." [58] On the other hand a rescript of George I in 1716 directed that the rights of Hanoverian guilds should *not* be violated in the name of that same *utilitatis publicae*.[59] Very many of the conflicts between town oligarchies and citizenry came over that difference between the collective interest and the communal interest, bearing particularly on the admission of citizens.[60]

For the civil servants and their theorists to adopt the common weal as the principle of their calling was a claim, by them, that state and society were coextensive (Justi often called the state "republic" in passages abstract enough for safety) and that they were custodians of the whole. But if any government was truly identical with the society it governed it was hometown government; and it stayed that way precisely by excluding all those whose weal was the state's, or the whole society's. On this central issue therefore hometownsmen and civil servants were direct competitors, two conflicting spheres, each claiming full competence. And because bureaucracy (the state) was not in fact coextensive with the society within its purview, but rather something outside it, its claim to speak for the common weal was a dynamic and even an aggressive one—a claim that really could only be satisfied when

[58] "Quare gentes lumine rationis, quam natura omnibus hominibus indidit, egregie docent, publicam utilitatem omnino praeferendam esse privatis commodis, ut ex praeclaris omnium legislatorum sententiis apparet." Victor Böhmert, *Beiträge zur Geschichte des Zunftwesens* (Leipzig, 1862), pp. 31–34, 99–100. Note that this formulation put guilds on the private side of the private-public duality, treating them as associations of individuals without public standing.

[59] Sieber, *Schwierigkeiten*, pp. 5–7.

[60] See the cases in Frankfurt/Main in the 1730's in Moser, *Teutsches Staats-Recht*, XLII (Hanau, 1750), 470–474; and Überlingen in the 1790's, *JM*, V (1795), 432–470.

all Germans did become subject to the same rules of behavior as themselves and share the same style of life. Custody of the common weal seems a better way to describe the attitudes of cameralist civil servants toward the communities than centralization or reform, if only because they did not speak of centralizing or reforming society itself, only law and administration. But consider the logic of the Austrian cameralist Sonnenfels, who regarded the terms "police" and "legislation" as interchangeable: "In a certain sense police is principally defense against either intentional or fortuitous occurrences of a harmful nature; second, every occurrence which hinders the accomplishment of the ultimate purpose of society must be regarded as harmful; third, from this point of view, police regards every transaction which does not *promote* this ultimate purpose as harmful." [61] Every stage of his reasoning cut the edge of state control deeper into the hometown community.

Because doctrines like these existed mainly on paper in the eighteenth century (however many untold reams of it), the home towns were unaffected and critical reaction was limited to a handful of unusual men. Justi offered his alternatives without, perhaps, seeing the problem itself in a practical political way, or at least without stating it clearly. Johann Jakob Moser had too matter-of-fact a head and too much information to talk about harmony; his enormous compilations (the *Teutsches Staats-Recht* alone ran to fifty-three quarto volumes in the 1737–1754 edition, and a 1766–1775 supplement to twenty-one more) are studded with his sense of how ironical it was to undertake a systematic treatment of German constitutional law at all; but he did not take Justi's way out. "Community leaders and officers stand in contrast with sovereign officials [*seynd entgegen gesezt*]; the former are usually chosen by the communities themselves, or their representatives in the magistracy," and their whole posture was quite unlike that of state officials.[62] Administrative efficiency was no excuse for usurping local rights, either;

[61] *Grundsätze der Polizei, Handlung und Finanzwissenschaft* (5th ed.; Vienna, 1787), p. 53. Cf. Small, *Cameralists*, p. 505. Joseph von Sonnenfels (173[2]–1817), a baptized Jew, professor at the University of Vienna after 1763, a humane absolutist considered to have been very influential on Joseph II.

[62] Moser here cited the Württemberg community ordinance of 1758, which he himself had written: *Landeshoheit im Weltlichen*, I (1772), "Regierungssachen," pp. 187–188.

a prince might reorganize within his own administration all he liked up to a point, but "where the whole country or a district [*Amtstatt*] or individual communities gain or lose by it, then it won't do [*da gehet es nicht an*]." [63]

The Württemberger Moser—scholar, civil servant, and one-time political prisoner of his duke—was clear enough about the opposition between community and state, and was sentimental about neither; and that amounted, given the temper of his mind, to a constitutional defense of the community when the state seemed headed for drastic things. The most emphatic defender of the home town against the each and the everybody of the police theorists, though, was Justus Möser of Osnabrück, whose notion of Eigentum helped define what the home town was about in this book's Introduction. The lines of his defense determined, more than anything else did, the conclusions drawn from the crisis of Napoleonic times, and from that the sense later generations of Germans had of their national character and of the nature of community and society.

Möser did not (to pick up the idea of Eigentum again) discover the communal character of property by himself: not in law, fact, or history. Samuel Pufendorf (1632–1694) had postulated (following Grotius) primitive communism in a semihistorical way: barbarians had more of it than civilized people; this was not the social communitarian proposition wherein community renders propriety, though, but a simple kind of communism in which groups of individuals used the same things. Johann Becmann (1641–1717), who was in part a historian, dropped the idea of communism as a historical phenomenon but continued to use the concept as a "scientifically necessary hypothesis," an ideal type for analytical purposes: Möser was not so careful later on. And the great Thomasius, along with elevating German customary law over the written codes of Justinian and the church, had declared the right of Eigentum to be not economic but ethical in its bases; economic activity he deliberately described not as production but as occupations of men,

---

[63] Ibid., III (1773), "Unterthanen," pp. 168–169. Thus local rights were not merely a barrier against state penetration; they even affected the way state administration could be organized: a symptom of the greater reciprocity between state and communal government in the Württemberg Oberamt than elsewhere in the individualized country.

and he denied that there was any natural law governing the prices of things. The nineteenth-century German economist Wilhelm Roscher said these views of Thomasius were a "retrogression after Locke's discoveries"; at any rate the comparison between the two marks a clear divergence of ideas about the relation between a man's work and his place in the surrounding society.[64]

In one sense what Möser did was to unite the attributes of people and of things, distinguished in most written law, in a proprietal idea of community and a social idea of worth. It was an easier thing to sense in the society he knew than it was to write clearly about in academic language, or at least the academic language of the eighteenth century; and Möser was an unsystematic writer, a littérateur who invaded the domains of jurists and philosophers with a sprightly disregard for their canons of evidence and reason. In a very similar sense what Möser did was to assert, between the individual interests and the interests of the whole with which the police theorists represented society, the familiar social community as primary organizer of political, economic, and moral life.

His home town was Osnabrück, a Hanoverian town of some nine thousand souls whose cathedral chapter gave the name of the territory to which it was the administrative capital: the *Hochstift* or High Foundation of Osnabrück, with a population of about 120,000. A peculiarity of the Foundation's constitution since the Treaty of Westphalia, reflecting a political balance between a predominantly Roman Catholic cathedral chapter and a Protestant knights' estate, was that the office of territorial Prince-Bishop alternated between Catholic and Protestant incumbents: during the first part of Möser's career the Wittelsbach Archbishop-Elector of Cologne, and after 1761 a Brunswicker nominated by George III of England. These were the constitutional circumstances of eighteenth-century Germany raised almost to the point of parody; and the towns of the territory were all separately and differently constituted. The constitution of the imperial town of Rottweil will serve well enough to describe the constitution of the territorial town of Osnabrück: the same interpenetration of economic and political institutions, with a complicated government based on guilds composed on mixed occupational and political lines; im-

[64] Roscher, *National-Oekonomik*, pp. 308–309, 319, 342–344.

portant but guarded channels of influence from the common Bürgerschaft; and an apparent institutional arbitrariness that was sanctioned by familiarity. Even the peasant society of Osnabrück, like other parts of Hanover, included prosperous communes more like the home towns than any other German peasantry had, a factor that probably helped Möser associate communal ways with property in land and a remote agrarian past.[65]

In 1747, Möser became *advocatus patriae* of this arrangement, spokesman of the territorial government to outside powers (mainly the electoral government at Cologne) and to internal powers (the chapter, the knights, and the towns); and from the sixties until retirement in 1783 he dominated Osnabrück politics and government. It is easy enough to ascribe Möser's views to his environment and the requirements of his career; but he might have reacted in just the opposite way if his temper had been more intense than sceptical, if he had sought power at the hands of a prince (but which one?) rather than peaceful confidence in his native town and society, or had preferred doctrines for action over literary speculation about the world around him.

Möser believed in the things the home town rested on. He thought social familiarity, habit, and the informal flexible restraints and rewards of communal life were better guarantors of peace and of virtue than laws and punishments were. Large populations of mutual strangers in one place and polity brought with them crime, the gallows, the wheel: the price of losing familiarity and steady communal restraint.[66] Every community should have its own constitutional form, embodying its whole internal substance, but these need not be written: indeed positive law was a symptom of a breakdown of community, a sign that the right social bonds were not operating, that they were not known. Written law was imposed force, not natural participation. And state laws based on general principles would destroy community where they touched it, by ignoring its own peculiar unwritten nature. To do just that was the congenital, and reasonable, professional tendency of those

[65] Havemann, *Braunschweig und Lüneburg*, III, 662; Runge, *Mösers Gewerbetheorie und Gewerbepolitik*, pp. 45–46.

[66] "Von dem Einflusse der Bevölkerung durch Nebenwohner auf die Gesetzgebung," *Sämtliche Werke*, V (1945), 11–22.

who wrote and administered state laws: "to reduce everything to simple principles . . . to let the state be ruled by academic theories and a general plan . . . to make the art of government easier for themselves and to make of themselves the mainspring of the whole state machine." And that, Möser said, had made his age an age of lawbooks designed to serve the vanity and comfort of these gentlemen: as a result "we depart from the true plan of Nature, which shows its richness in diversity, and we build the way to despotism, which seeks to force everything within a few rules." He said it was wrong to promote officials for efficiency and services rendered to the state. That made bad governors of them.[67]

What naturally governed men's affairs, Möser thought, were honor, experience, and what I have called propriety: *Ehre, Erfahrung,* and *Eigentum;* the three ought to be inseparable, and so they were in the familiar and traditional community. Despite the feudal sound of these catchwords, this was no defense of the German nobility, whom Möser disliked and conceived to have usurped and corrupted communal freedom.[68] He was not really explicit about experience. I extract the term to describe his preference for commonplace usage over rational organization, and so as to show the way he related communal familiarity with history.[69] But the main meaning of experience was not necessarily associated with the historical past. Möser really started off (conceptually) with nature, and brought history in mainly to account for the rational imponderability of natural experience, and to dignify it. With experience he meant to say that the making of human consciousness was a subtler and more complex thing than outside rational analysis could reproduce, and that the relations among men were subtler and more complex than outside governments could grasp. In "experience" came together the elements of life that academic

---

[67] "Der jetzige Hang zu allgemeinen Gesetzen und Verordnungen ist der gemeinen Freiheit gefährlich," ibid., p. 22; Roscher, *National-Oekonomik,* pp. 507–508. *Gemeine Freiheit* does not mean individual freedom against state authority in natural-law terms, as some liberal interpreters of Möser have argued; it is a right of communal participation wrapped up with honor and propriety: cf. Böckenförde, *Verfassungsgeschichtliche Forschung,* p. 37.

[68] Böckenförde, *Verfassungsgeschichtliche Forschung,* p. 36.

[69] On the meaning of experience in Möser, Ulrike Brünauer, *Justus Möser* (Berlin, 1933), p. 97.

analysis and systematic governance put asunder; Möser paid the price of conceptual fogginess for the sake of insisting that there was a totality in experience that it was better to describe even foggily (and ultimately historically) than to subject it to the distortions and omissions that analytical simplification must bring.[70] And so of course it was an antiintellectual and antireformist proposition. Experience, moreover, could only serve as a principle of political and social organization within groups circumscribed by roughly the same experience; the larger the group, the more experience splintered, and totalities conflicted. Experience was a way of saying totality, where everything came together in a man's mind, and in social community: there was the link with hometown familiarity, hometown institutions, and hometown membership practices. For social experience could be totally shared only in a little self-contained place—not in a large cosmopolitan state or nation, or even in a big city, let alone the "common weal."

That is not to say that Möser ignored the importance and value of commerce, industry, and large-scale political organization; but he thought them incompatible with the kind of society he defended throughout his writings and administered throughout his career. Life in such places made for a quite different sense of honor, meaning the destruction of the kind of honor and the kind of society Möser cared about.[71] In such places office and perquisites remained; but communal honor, the *gemeine Ehre,* was lost. Honor, the respect of the respected, was "the great mainspring of human affairs" (Justi had called individual ambition and material interest the mainsprings). With loss of honor, "noble love of Eigentum will disappear; reward for public services will always have to be in money . . . and with drifters [literally fugitives: *Flüchtlinge*] mixed together with the established inborn into one estate, criminal law will become savage. The greater and more thorough the mixing, the more dreadful the results; . . . money and service decide everything, and the two between them have destroyed the economy of communal honor in a shameful way." [72]

70 On Möser's aim of total recognition, ibid., p. 5 and passim.

71 Runge, *Mösers Gewerbetheorie und Gewerbepolitik,* pp. 37–38, 42.

72 From an ambiguous satire on clothing laws: "Die Vortheile einer allgemeinen Landesuniforme, deklamiert von einem Bürger," *Sämtliche Werke,* V (1945), 58–59. Möser himself switched the tenses of his verbs.

Möser saw honor and propriety in the values of hometown guilds-men. Maintain the ban mile, he said, and keep bastards out of the community. "Did the authors of the Imperial Edict of 1731 do right when they made all those people legitimate who just weren't?" is the title of one of his essays. The answer: "It is certain that the guilds have suffered seriously from the obligation, imposed by re-cent recess [a 1772 reiteration of 1731], that any whore's offspring legitimized by some count palatine, and practically any creature with two legs and no feathers, must be eligible to enter a guild." He parodied a preamble to a police statute based on such a prin-ciple:

We by the Grace of God etc. give herewith notice, that inasmuch as We and our princely Family and Councilors have withdrawn from human society, the latter consists of Canaille only: Hence it is Our de-sire that all whores' children to whom We under Our seal grant the rights of legitimate birth, shall be received, at pain of a fine of one hundred gold gulden.

Talk of declaring shepherds and the like to be susceptible of honor might sound well in the mouths of philosophers and Christians, but it led to false and destructive government; to make the "class without honor" honorable only destroyed the honor of those who rightly possessed it.[73] Princes who put their legitimation power at the service of their greed for population and productivity, argued Möser, encouraged promiscuity and the growth of an irresponsible rabble, social outsiders and misfits; and they violated a human right that derived from social community, a thing antecedent to the state.[74] Here were some other enemies of community: the "simplification" to which large-scale manufacture tended, because those subject to the division of labor "can have no really sound souls"; the putting-out system, forerunner to the factory, which could succeed only by "making labor a necessity, and industrious-ness a god"; the entrepreneur himself, who "rules his people and overwhelms the richest state with industrious poverty"; the re-tailer, who "spies around the whole world, to see whether there is

[73] "Haben die Verfasser des Reichsabschieds von 1731 wohl getan, dass sie viele Leute ehrlich gemacht haben, die es nicht waren?" ibid., IV (1943), 240–242 and passim.
[74] Cf. Frensdorff, "Zunftrecht und Handwerkerehre," pp. 7, 84–87.

somewhere a poorer nation ready to supply a piece of work a few pennies cheaper; and so he steals the bread from the mouths of his fellow citizens, who burdened with taxes and high labor costs cannot provide so cheaply." [75]

Because Möser conceived economy to be a social aspect of personality, his economic program recalls the hometown cloverleaf: respect the artisans' honor, assure their political voice, and protect their economic security. That was what hometown guilds did, and to succeed they had to be kept free of the propertyless, the dishonorable, the merchant.[76] Cities might have their own ways and states might well favor the ways of cities; but not Möser's Osnabrück. When the Hanoverian government undertook to make the Foundation conform to the 1772 reiteration of the 1731 edict, the towns with their guild-based governments denied its right to do so, and with Möser's help made their refusal stick: his administration worked out, instead of the general code the Hanoverian government wanted, a series of local statutes various and ambiguous on the questions of guild monopoly; all the statutes insisted on legitimate birth, "decent" behavior, and enforced the privileged positions of masters' sons.[77]

No other serious European seventeenth or eighteenth century theorist I know of talked of social relations as Möser did; and it is important to notice that in his preoccupation with the variety of social groups and the peculiar attributes of each he was closer to the German state cameralists than he was to anybody else, even Montesquieu. But he had recognized the contradiction of state cameralism, between endless particularity and unified direction and purpose. He knew the communities were not harmonious participants in a general whole. He saw in the actual social communities a principle that contradicted the orthodoxy of chancellery, study, and lecture hall; and he resolved the contradiction finally by

[75] *Sämtliche Werke*, IV (1943), 156; V (1945), 113–114; VI (same ed., n.d.), 124.

[76] Runge, *Mösers Gewerbetheorie und Gewerbepolitik*, pp. 30–32.

[77] Ibid., pp. 49–53. For the 1772 edict, and the clash it precipitated between the two Reichstag estates of territorial princes and the estate of the towns, Ortloff, ed., *Corpus juris*, pp. 31–48. It went beyond 1731 in efforts to broaden admissibility to the trades, to deny the Blue Monday, that recuperative holiday beloved of journeymen, and to restrict the imposition of dishonor.

turning to history, by adjudging those communal characteristics not explicable by modern statecraft or theory to be remnants of the past persisting into the present and future.

Modern sociologists might not need history to explain social behavior otherwise inexplicable to eighteenth-century habits of thought, although they are often attracted to tradition as an explanation of social institutions that seem odd to them, much as eighteenth-century lawyers grasped at *traditio* in their descriptions of hometown institutions. So perspicacious an analyst as Karl Mannheim commended Möser's proposition that rationally inexplicable contemporary practices are *ipso facto* ancient, and elevated Möser above romantic conservatives for his "empiricism": that Möser actually lived among the social artifacts, the communal institutions and practices, which he explained historically.[78] The historical dimension offered Möser yet another advantage he badly needed. For he knew too much about the unpleasant features of hometown life to present his idealized community as a credible description of contemporary German home towns in the flesh. With history he could blame unpleasantness on the actions of governments and laws, which had split and distorted communal life away from the natural harmony and dignity to be discerned in the surviving artifacts.

Möser's historical work was a commentary on the present and an explication of the political contradictions he saw in the present. He combined the old notion of Germanic freedom found in Tacitus' critique of Rome with the social communities he knew in the eighteenth century. And so the state of nature from which Möser made his political argument did not seem the hypothetical construction of Locke, Hobbes, or even the Book of Genesis. Möser gave the German hometown community, incubated in the Holy Roman Empire, the aura of being natural and primeval. And because he defined it dialectically, in terms of its conflict with contemporary political and administrative theory, his picture of what was natural and primeval included nearly everything that conflicted with the statism and individualism on which the views of Justi, for example, were founded. Möser spoke for that level of organization, the social community, that Justi had left out because it would have

[78] *Essays on Sociology and Social Psychology* (London, 1953), pp. 140–141.

spoiled his convenient axiom that the interest of each accords with the well-being of all.

Möser's "History of Osnabrück" (1768–1780) is a long tale of authoritarian efforts to stifle Germanic communal freedom. That had, in his history, been going on for as long as there were written records. But in a schematic essay called "German History," published by Johann Gottfried Herder as one of a collection "On German Style and Art," Möser seemed clear that the century or two preceding his own time had been the worst: just the time, that is, when I have said the home town took its form. For Möser it was the time when ideal communal forms had been distorted into their contemporary shape. "In this period the old conception of propriety was quite lost: that a person must share the communal law [*einer Rechtsgenoss seyn muss*] to share true propriety [*echtes Eigenthum*]. Just so it went with both high and common [*gemeinen*] honor. The first was transformed almost entirely into freedom; and of the second, *honore quiritario*—citizen's honor— we have only a few hints still left, though they had once been the spirit of the German constitution, and should be eternal. More and more, religion and science [*Wissenschaft*] elevated man over Bürger; the rights of man [*Rechte der Menschheit*] overcame all conditioned and comparative rights [*verglichene Rechte*]. An easy philosophy favored conclusions drawn from general principles over those that could only be made from careful study and insight. And with the help of Christian religion human love became a virtue like Bürger love, so that imperial law itself came near to proclaiming, out of Christian love, that the most dishonorable people should be susceptible of honor and eligible for guild." [79] The turmoil of religious wars had laid the groundwork for territorial absolutism: but to understand Möser's sense and his chronology, note that he was the author too of a paean to the Treaty of Westphalia, praising it for the freedoms its principle of balance defended.[80]

Although Justus Möser delighted to attack the abstractions and the general doctrines of the academic political theorists, his own weapons were theoretical and doctrinaire. He avoided confronting

[79] "Deutsche Geschichte," in Herder, ed., *Von deutscher Art und Kunst* (Hamburg, 1773), pp. 177–178.
[80] Quoted in Dickmann, *Der Westfälische Frieden*, p. 1.

theorists of social contract on their own terms by giving his own theories the label of history and experience; he assumed a guise of intellectual humility before experience ("The old-timers weren't such fools after all" was one of his favorite saws), and in the "History of Osnabrück" dressed his antiintellectualism in the trappings of scholarship.[81] Recall the circularity of the legal defense of customary communal law: that customary law got its legitimacy from acceptance by the community, but community was defined as being those who accepted its customary law. History, a dimension in time, was a way of breaking out of the logical circle, because with history as metaphor he could describe community and custom without the rational justification that a frankly constructed theory of society would have required. In the same way, communities in that dimension were the "plan of Nature," not constructed by the state.[82] Jacob Sieber, writing in the 1770's about communal rights in his dissertation on the Edict of 1731, made a remark that may have been addressed partly to Möser: "If the towns with all their inhabitants had sprung from the earth like mushrooms, or if the latter had lived like savages in the state of nature and subsequently begun to enter social relations," then the state would have no more authority over them than the communities had transmitted to it; but "history shows unmistakably that the towns of Germany did not come into being that way," but rather through monarchic authority, however that may have lapsed.[83] But the communities of Möser's view *had* "sprung from the earth like mushrooms," sometime, or somehow, antecedent to states and their laws and their records: *how else had they got there?* In his histories the chronological frame required him to find primeval and natural community in the pastoral and agrarian past, when the Germans had had no towns; but rural population was not like that now, and by community at least for his own time he meant the home town: honor and propriety dwelt now in small-town guild, citizenry, and council, in the hometown cloverleaf with its de-

---

[81] E.g., *Sämtliche Werke*, X (1968), 133.

[82] See the section entitled "Die Städte sind auch keine Kolonien," in the opening sections of *Osnabrückische Geschichte, Sämtliche Werke*, XII, 1 (1964), 51.

[83] Sieber, *Schwierigkeiten*, p. 172.

fiance of rational separation and analysis, and of outside comprehension and governance.

Möser's work was very popular in his own time, and he infected the eighteenth-century caste of movers and doers with a virus dangerous to themselves, albeit dormant. By finding history embodied in the home town he made it plausible to regard obstruction to change and analysis as something historically primeval and anthropologically natural, and even something morally better and truer than the mobility and coherence implicit in the catchword of the common weal. In his "Patriotic Phantasies," the title he gave to his collected essays, he incorporated the sociology of the home town with the essence of German nationality: not the state of Justi but a contrasting alternative. With him hometown society began to take on an importance disproportionate to its size or intrinsic power. That was his contribution to the idea of the German fatherland, the German nation he perceived through the political fragmentation he welcomed. The idea of German nationality never freed itself from the hometown components that Möser more than any other gave to it. In his own time, though, the officials and their theorists had in their goal of coherence and the common weal another way to treat the contradictions of cameralism; and the two met when the breakdown of the German incubator in Napoleon's time pressed the issue outside the realm of speculation.

CHAPTER VI

Napoleonic Power in Germany.

HOMETOWNSMEN confronted the world outside when the incubator was broken open around the turn of the eighteenth century.* Separate internal community defenses had sufficed before; they had been acknowledged by a cameralist administration that accepted variety and individuality among social institutions. Eighteenth-century government had sought control and harmony but had not contemplated positive reform of a kind that might strike at the essentials of hometown life. The incapacity of state governments actually to grasp the detailed social controls implied by cameralist theory had matched up with the understanding that state intervention was to "remedy abuses," intermittently and unsystematically, so that there had been no general confrontation between different aims of state and community. Möser's polemics against rational administration and reform showed the conflict between local variety on the one hand and the harmony of the common weal that administrative theorists like Justi wrote about on the other. But that contradiction in cameral administration remained latent and abstract until it was energized on a wide front by the territorial changes of Napoleonic times. This chapter means to show how the contradictions of cameralism became apparent to everybody when power was there: how baroque administration thus energized turned to reform, and what alternatives were left

* Parts of this chapter are reprinted, with permission, from *Central European History*, II, No. 2 (June, 1969), 99–113, © 1969 by Emory University.

when state power failed with the collapse of Bonaparte's European imperium.

From administration to reform

The process whereby administration became reform can be described as an extension of state power from areas where state officials had long been managers into areas where they had not. The administration of princely domains and other regalia, where the central power was almost unobstructed, was a bridge from pure administration to social and economic management; cameralist doctrines had grown out of that kind of administrative situation.[1] Extractive industries like forestry, mining and smelting, and often agriculture were "bureaucratic" whether legally parts of the domains and regalia or not: they were governed by state law and civil service and not by guilds and towns, and constituted a malleable segment to which Justi's simple one-track equation of the good of each with the good of the whole might reasonably apply.[2] The idea that actual social change by legal action could be a useful and feasible program infected the civil servants in the course of their work governing the states' agricultural domains, notably in Prussia but elsewhere too. Changes in agricultural technology during the later eighteenth century made reform of rural society itself a serious concern.

Since early in the eighteenth century, proposals had appeared for the free heritability of domain peasant tenures and for the abolition of serfdom, to encourage peasant initiative and energy; but, on the whole, efforts in that direction had stopped short of personal freedom and private property for domain peasants: the peasant was to be ambitious but still he was to stay on his plot and remain a peasant.[3] By mid-century some cameral theorists were going further. Justi recommended independent peasant ownership of small farms for the sake of increased over-all production. Sonnenfels among others urged that large holdings be broken up into

[1] Haussherr, *Verwaltungseinheit*, pp. 1–2.

[2] Ebel, ed., *Arbeitsrecht*, pp. 14–15 and the documents cited thereto; Koselleck, *Preussen*, pp. 123–124.

[3] For eighteenth-century agrarian reform programs in Prussia see Georg F. Knapp, *Die Bauern-Befreiung und der Ursprung der Landarbeiter in den älteren Theilen Preussens*, I (Leipzig, 1887), 81–93.

small, beginning with the domains, to support more people and more production.[4] Proposals like these called for reform: the destruction of vested rights and duties for the sake of individual profit and general growth, the common weal. The analogy to home-town economic organization was open, but developed only in abstract indirect ways like Justi's.

The main force for change in the agrarian constitution came from the improved agricultural techniques that fascinated cam-eralist writers and practicing agricultural administrators in the later eighteenth century, technical changes hardly possible without legal and social reform of the countrymen's world: Germany first learned how technological change might require social change from agricultural issues, not industrial ones.[5] Intensification was the key: intensification would provide higher productivity and support a larger population, and the new technology was especially concerned with the use of intensive crops: turnips and potatoes in the place of grains, and the stall-feeding of cattle with clover in the place of open pasturing. Intensive crops and stall-feeding were far more appropriate to the small independent holding than to the large estate worked by bound collective labor; and the movers and doers who produced a flood of agricultural treatises in the later eighteenth century were not loath to point it out. A great many agricultural societies were formed as large private land-owners began to take an interest in improved technology for the sake of profit. And the editors of their journals, the speakers at their assemblies, and the judges of their prize contests were necessarily the educated, closely connected with university and state and no admirers of noble privilege; so in fact was a large proportion of the membership, and eventually a dissertation on turnip culture almost had to end with a peroration on the evils of the agrarian social structure. With the claim that greater productivity and changes in technique required legal and customary changes, the movers and doers invaded the countryside: a common interest in

[4] Justi, *Staatswirthschaft*, I, 527; Goltz, *Landwirtschaft*, I, 332–333; Roscher, *National-Oekonomik*, p. 544.

[5] For the position that the breakup of the "old order" began on the land and moved from there to towns, Friedrich Seidel, *Die soziale Frage in der deutschen Geschichte* (Wiesbaden, 1964), pp. 58–59 and passim.

production and revenue opened a close relation between them and countrymen that included among its bases a measure of reform —something different from the remedying of abuses. The idea of improving the peasant's character by breaking his bondage mixed in, uniting moral and economic gains into a program of social reform.[6] The first genuine social reform in Germany was the liberation of the Prussian domain peasants in 1799–1805, before Napoleon's conquest of Germany and before the more general reforms of the years that followed.[7]

Agrarian reform was an entry to the kind of change that could reach hometownsmen behind their panoply of particularities. A long-standing simile of German administrative theory was that the governing of a state was like the governing of a huge rural holding —a natural enough description inasmuch as the science of economic administration had grown out of domain management, and insofar as the agricultural economy, especially the domains, was the state's main fiscal resource. Reforms in the domains were changes within the state's own system; but starting with the domains as precedent, it was possible to move further into the outside society by manipulating the relatively pliant countrymen part of it; and the social reform possible in rural society ought, if the whole state was really one big farm, to be applicable to the rest of its subjects as well, to hometown society. This was a transference with important bearing on the meaning of citizenship, for it spread the incidence of state citizenship by stages into the whole society. Domain peasants were directly subject to the state to begin with. The next step—programs of general peasant liberation —made the peasant outside the domains as well as within into a state citizen, a *Staatsbürger*. From there the next logical stage was to extend individual state citizenship to the towns, and convert the

[6] On the relations among rural technological change, state economic policy, and social ethics in the late eighteenth century, Sigmund Frauendorfer, *Ideengeschichte der Agrarwirtschaft und Agrarpolitik im deutschen Sprachgebiet,* I (Munich, 1957), 155–198; for a narrative Goltz, *Landwirtschaft,* I, 389–479. See also Goltz's remarks on Garve, pp. 481–482, and on J. C. Schubart, pp. 358–369. An effective recent study is John G. Gagliardo, *From Pariah to Patriot: The Changing Image of the German Peasant, 1770–1840* (Lexington, Ky., 1969).

[7] Otto Hintze, "Preussische Reformbestrebungen vor 1806," *HZ,* LXXVI (1896), 413–443.

hometownsman into a *Staatsbürger* too. The gain of each added up to the gain of all: the way to individual initiative and high productivity on the land was individual private property, though this be social reform; the hometown analogy to agrarian reform would be the destruction of guilds and the *Bürgerrecht* system. The relative ease of change in the countryside had begun to turn the German civil servant from fiscal administrator to political and social reformer, in his own terms, before the revolutionary legislation in France provided its examples and Napoleonic power in Germany its opportunities.[8]

Another entry from cameral administration to reform lay in the character of the profession of government. This does not only mean that one who has power to coerce others will make them change their ways to suit his wishes, although that is certainly an important part of what it means. Just as important a part has to do, in a contrary way, with the limited range of German government in the era that has taken the name of enlightened absolutism. Let us concentrate now on how what has already been said about cameral administration relates to reform. The rather close limits on government's actual range had two related aspects or consequences: first, that administration did not reach deeply into the society, and second, that within its own sphere the state and bureaucratic interest was unchallenged. If state authority had actually penetrated the society, it could have done its work and satisfied its interest without arriving at the need for reform, or else might perforce have developed a kind of interaction with the society in which the state was only one interest among many. As it was, administration developed within its sphere a body of theory and practice that assumed the ubiquity of state interest; and because the actual state was *not* ubiquitous, the society had to be changed into one that would act as if it was, on its own.

The German civil servant's professional nursery taught him that

---

[8] To discuss the influence of French physiocracy on German administrative and economic theory would carry the subject too far afield; and I think anyhow that in this instance German circumstances and precedents sufficiently explain German developments. There are of course clear parallels, and Germans knew about physiocracy, and evolved a comparable sense of the identity of interests between the peasant population and the state. Cf. Roscher, *National-Oekonomik*, pp. 480–500.

the state was sovereign in all matters, and that impelled him to reform once he reached outside it to places where the state was not. An ultimate stage in German eighteenth-century politics consisted in an effort to extend standards developed within one social or cultural caste—and here it is legitimate to think of the Enlightened fashion of improvement, tolerance, and rationality—to other groups quite undisposed to accept them. That is a general way of saying how the contradictions of cameralism led to reform once they took on flesh: when they were pressed outside the social abstraction that was the administrative corps; when government in the course of its growth came to encompass social entities not at all abstract, entities contradictory in politics and in principle to the society of the movers and doers.[9] Evidence of growing conflict during the late eighteenth century between officials and towns, and within towns, is a sign that governments were becoming ambitious enough to get into trouble, into political thickets they could not discipline. The towns had not changed, but the aims of government had broadened; or perhaps governments were being tricked into overreaching themselves by their innocent theories of omnipotence.

There are several ways of getting at the matter, other than the kind of historical description I am offering: theoretical ways not inconsistent with it though, and some of them quite relevant to the crisis of governance that broke into the open in Germany at the end of the eighteenth century. Their relevance lies in their effort to show contrast in principle between what has made systematic governments behave as they have and what has made social communities behave as they have. Formal sociology distinguishes between state (for this instance the state's ruler and bureaucracy) and social community (the home town) on the analytical point that the state has active goals, whereas the community seeks only to exist. The state is a means to some purpose, and is dynamic, but the community is a way of being; thus the eighteenth-century German state sought after wealth and power, and the home town sought to preserve the ways that gave its members

[9] Compare Fritz Hartung on Enlightened Absolutism as a final phase of absolute monarchy in "Enlightened Despotism," *Historical Association Pamphlet* no. 36 (London, 1957).

being.[10] The German sociologist Ferdinand Tönnies, writing just after the time when this book closes, drew a fundamental contrast between the *Wesenwille* that underlies community and the *Kurwille* of the association, the fluid society and state. I take his meaning of *Wesenwille* to be something poetically between the will of the being and the will to be, between integral group will and existential will perhaps; and that seems a fair way to describe the motives that held hometownsmen together: a will that emanated from the nature of the community itself and aimed at its preservation, no more. By the *Kurwille* of association Tönnies meant deliberate objective choice and purpose, something that could be changed and redirected, the style of living that distinguished the German movers and doers and the German state.[11]

The line of descent from the confrontation this chapter describes to Tönnies' formulations of social will are remarkably direct, and there will be occasion in later chapters to observe the making of that kind of social thought.[12] Max Weber, at a climax of its development early in the twentieth century, described an antithesis between communal social relations on the one hand, based on subjective feelings of belonging together, and associative relations on the other, resting on rational and calculated adjustment of individual interests. But whereas Tönnies sentimentally had placed mutual love at the heart of the community's *Wesenwille*, as its means of transcending conflict, Weber conceded that communal relations might involve coercion to suppress conflict.[13] Hometown community, assuredly, relied as much on coercion as on love. But still this was a different coercion from the formal legal coercion of state law. A very important difference was that hometown standards and hometown means of coercion seem diffuse and

[10] For a general introduction to this proposition, George A. Hillery, Jr., *Communal Organizations: A Study of Local Societies* (Chicago, 1968). I shall not here venture historical critique of the typology beyond remarking that a state apparatus can as well become an end in itself, intent only on its own preservation: there is a circularity in defining as an entity with dynamic goals the kind of state that has dynamic goals.

[11] Tönnies discussed *Wesenwille* and *Kurwille* in *Gemeinschaft und Gesellschaft* (Leipzig, 1887), pp. 97–194.

[12] Especially Chapters VIII, XI, XII.

[13] *Theory of Social and Economic Organization*, tr. A. M. Henderson and Talcott Parsons (New York, 1947), pp. 136–138.

unspecialized, imposing sanctions productive of unnecessary conformity for its own sake, whereas the sanctions of state law and civil service aimed, at least, to adapt specific sanctions to specific ends, and make the punishment fit the crime in a uniform and objective way. Hometown coercion was applied mutually by all members of the community against each; legal or government sanctions were applied by a professional staff against persons who were not on the enforcing staff—by outsiders. The home town suppressed conflict by imposing total conformity, almost indiscriminately (recall the mad morality of the guilds); law regulated conflict by punishing certain kinds of unconformity that were identified as injurious by officers who were not personally engaged. Here we are back with the home town as a place that is not professionally governed. Hans Gerth (of the generation of German sociologists that succeeded Weber's) and C. Wright Mills, writing *Character and Social Structure,* put the difference between law and convention in just that way: "Laws differ from conventions in that they are enforced by a staff. Orientation to convention is guaranteed by socially diffused sanctions, whereas orientation to legal codes is guaranteed by organized sanctions." [14] Where coercion is communal, even formal fines and penalties work not through their direct material effect, but by the notoriety they give to anticommunal behavior. Conversely the important thing about transgression of convention was not the immediate material damage done but the contempt exhibited for the community: in that light perhaps communal coercion was not so diffuse nor guild morality so mad as appears at first.

Effective conventions or traditions, though not necessarily very old, are continuous and familiar, and sometimes for continuity's and familiarity's sake do not make the penalties fit the crimes. Even conventions are modified, perforce, by the mere act of conceptualizing them; and for outsiders to try to make their own sense of them, according to anthropologists who ought to know, imposes unaccustomed social concepts and images where they don't fit, and there is trouble.[15] Germany's governors were bound to arouse

14 (New York, 1953), p. 260.

15 J. G. A. Pocock, "Time, Institutions, and Understanding," in Preston King and B. C. Parekh, eds., *Politics and Experience* (Cambridge, England, 1968), pp. 215 and passim.

that kind of trouble whenever they tried to conceptualize the conventions of hometown life even without hostile intent or thought of reform. Make the distinction between function and structure again, as it bears on the turning of administration to reform.[16] Only by working through the legal structures of the society could government get at its functions. But the structural diversity epitomized by the home towns meant that there were no general handles (concepts) with which to do this; and in practice, government could not in fact be everywhere at once. A contrast between Justi and J. J. Moser puts the problem: the legal encyclopedist Moser described structures, made no serious effort to impose uniformity upon them, and implicitly ascribed to each a kind of *Wesenwille;* the police cameralist Justi talked always of function, and ascribed a common *Kurwille* to individuals and state by ignoring the disparity of structures. But to bring functional "coherence" about, if it did not come by itself that way, meant that the structures had to be grappled with; and the consequent need for general handles, even, initially, just so as to locate where authority lay, was a strong inducement to substantive reform.

These are better theoretical distinctions than they are descriptions. I am inclined to think that the German events do more to explain the present existence of formulations like these than the formulations do to explain the events. But either way they describe a potential: theoretical distinctions may fairly do that. They are too general to make a description of those disjoined and fragmentary events in Germany before Bonaparte came, into which they can retrospectively be read, or to emerge before that time. For them to take on flesh and to happen, there had to be political change on so broad a front as to affect all the communities of the individualized country together and bring them into phase, to raise the same issues in all of them at once, and highlight them as an identifiable common body despite their diversity: all the things that the constitution of the Holy Roman Empire had served to prevent. The entry of Napoleonic power into Germany brought German politics into phase, exposed the contradictions of cameralism—and led to resolutions that still seem curious—even after all this preparation for them.

[16] Cf. above, pp. 34–35, 139.

Breaking up the incubator

The Holy Roman Empire in its European setting had kept German politics since Westphalia out of phase, with its mechanism of localized political cycles and of balance; that had insulated the towns from the world, had fostered the development of baroque administration, and had kept the states from developing administration into reform. French power overturned the German balance by overturning the balance of Europe, and the internal effects of the overturn meant more to German politics than did the presence of French soldiers, governors, or military requisitions. Justus Möser had put a speech in the mouth of one of his primeval "Sassen," at a point in his history where the question arose of entering the empire of the Carolingian Franks: "In this there would be the great danger that soon the magistracy would fall to rootless people and in the course of time even to foreign scholars; and the honor, the body, and the life of a true man would come to depend on the legal opinion of a hireling"; and Möser recounted how "the demise of communal freedom" (one of its repeated demises) came when the Saxons did join.[17] Neither to Möser nor to hometownsmen did rootless officials and foreign scholars necessarily mean Frenchmen: there were plenty of them nearer to home. The role of the French appears in a parallel among the chronology of French policy in Germany, the chronology of German legislation and administration, and the chronology of the experience of the home towns.

The first phase of French policy was a period of compensations; it began with the French victories of the 1790's and lasted until about 1805, including and beyond the Conclusion of the Imperial Deputations in 1803 that changed the German map, and to the eve of Austria's defeat at Austerlitz. During this stage the French were concerned with transfers of jurisdiction within Germany to make compensation to German princes for territories lost to French expansion, but they did not much care what the German princes

[17] "Daher sei es sehr zu befürchten, dass das Amt der Schöpfen bald solchen unangesessenen und wohl gar mit der Zeit fremden Gelehrten zuteil werden [*sic*], und Ehre, Leib und Leben eines Mannes von der rechtlichen Meinung eines Mietlings abhangen würde." *Osnabrückische Geschichte* (1964), pp. 233, 239.

did with their acquisitions. In this phase, to assume the outward trappings of rulership over the places promised them by treaty was the most the German states could manage, and sometimes more than they could manage. Moreover, state officials were still acting in accordance with the old administrative principle: assert sovereignty, but do not try to change the essential character of the society. They could not in any case. Before 1805 the old Empire was not dead, despite reports to the contrary and despite the compensations; and the result was growing confusion and complexity in Germany even as the maps were made simpler. Even Austria joined the game of territorial expansion, trying first to assert old imperial jurisdictions as territorial sovereignty, thus garbling its two perennially mismatched roles, that of imperial protector and that of territorial state.[18] With things moving the gears were grating. The young Württemberger Georg Friedrich Hegel (whose first political tract, written in 1796, had been "That the Magistracy Should be Elected by the People") published a treatise in 1801 on "The Constitution of the German Empire," beginning with the assertion: "Germany is no longer a state. What can no longer be comprehended [*begriffen*] no longer exists."[19] Samuel Pufendorf, trying to describe the German Empire a century and a half before, had called it a logical monstrosity, a freak, *monstro simile;*

[18] Alfred Rambaud, *L'Allemagne sous Napoléon Ier (1804–1811)* (3d ed.; Paris, n.d.), pp. 17–19; Erwin Hölzle, *Das alte Recht und die Revolution: Eine politische Geschichte Württembergs in der Revolutionszeit* (Munich, 1931), pp. 326–327; Schell, *Reichsstädte an Baden*, pp. 15–19, 122–126; Max Miller, "Die Organisation und Verwaltung von Neuwürttemberg unter Herzog und Kurfürst Friedrich," *WVL*, XXXVII (1931), 141–142; Gustav Merk, "Ravensberg unter bayerischer Verwaltung," *WVL*, XXIII (1914), 405–422. For a similar pattern in an area occupied 1803–1805 but not annexed by France, Friedrich Thimme, *Die inneren Zustände des Kurfürstentums Hannover unter der französisch-westfälischen Herrschaft*, I (Hanover, 1893), pp. 59–83. Article 27 of the Reichsdeputationshauptschluss of 1803 provided that the free cities annexed should be treated "in Bezug auf ihre Municipalverfassung und Eigenthum auf dem Fuss der in jedem der verschiedenen Lande am meisten priviligirten Städte . . . so weit es die Landesorganisation und die zum allgemeinen Besten nöthigen Verfügungen gestatten." Ernst R. Huber, ed. *Dokumente zur deutschen Verfassungsgeschichte*, I (Stuttgart, 1961), 12.

[19] *Die Verfassung des deutschen Reichs*, ed. Georg Mollat (Stuttgart, 1935) p. 1; Hans Lotheissen, *Der ständisch-korporative Gedanke . . . in den Schriften Hegels und Lists zur württembergischen Verfassungsreform* (Giessen, 1928), p. 62.

Hegel said it just wasn't there. The communities, like other privileged bodies, could play the usual game of conflicting jurisdictions while the old constitution remained, but among the changing and precarious territorial states this was a provocative and dangerous game, arousing sharp hostility among the states, and between the states (Austria included) and the imperial constitution.

The second phase was one of centralization, of administrative reform to break through the confusion that territorial consolidation had only aggravated. It began with the War of the Third Coalition in 1805 and lasted roughly until the Russian campaign at the end of 1812. In the treaties Napoleon made with the German states in the summer and fall of 1805 he ordered internal administrative centralization and reform and promised French support for it against internal and imperial resistance, "because," quoting the text of the treaty with Württemberg, "of the difficulties the Elector might [otherwise] experience in fulfilling his obligations to the Emperor [of the French]." [20] After Austerlitz came the Confederation of the Rhine, in 1806, joining together nearly all the individualized country in a league of states under French tutelage. The act establishing the Confederation declared that all imperial laws affecting or constraining the relations of the princes with their subjects were nullified.[21] Napoleon believed that efforts by the Rheinbund princes really to incorporate and exclusively to control the annexed places would make them politically dependent on him, because they could not do it on their own resources. But there was a real quid pro quo in the arrangements of 1805–1806, and a real community of interests: French support and protection was provided for the internal control the German governments wanted and which in turn was needed to generate the military and financial contributions Napoleon wanted. French demands stimulated the administrative energies of the German states and French power was lent to them; and implicit was the threat

[20] M. De Clercq, ed., *Recueil des Traités de la France*, II, 1803–1815 (Paris, 1864), 121–123, 126–127; August von Schlossberger, ed., *Politische und militärische Correspondenz König Friedrichs von Württemberg mit Kaiser Napoleon I, 1805–1813* (Stuttgart, 1889), pp. 11–12, 39–40, 48; Hans K. Zwehl, ed., *Die bayerische Politik im Jahre 1805* (Munich, 1964), pp. 179–180, 197–198, 203–204, 271–273, 284.

[21] Huber, ed., *Dokumente*, I, 27.

that if the German governments did not get their territories and towns to respond, the French army would move in and do its own requisitioning and its own governing.[22] To signalize the new phase Count Maximilian von Montgelas, who had presided over Bavarian annexations to sovereignty as Foreign Minister since 1799, now took over as Interior Minister to see to the new territories' incorporation and their institutional reform.

Hegel, pondering all this, made a new scheme of political sociology. In 1803 he had divided German society into two main components: a noble upper estate composed of landowners and army officers, and a lower estate apparently including everybody else. But in 1806 he replaced the noble estate with a "general estate," *Stand der Allgemeinheit,* corresponding closely with the movers and doers of the eighteenth century, whom recent events were bringing to the forefront of German political life. It was an estate of general*izers,* dominated by the civil service and distinguished by its separation from local Bürger and peasants. The merchant class, inasmuch as its activities freed it from "ties to the earth and to the locality," did not "realistically" belong to the Bürger estate, either socially or ethically; "by his rootless character [*unbodenständigen Art*] the merchant blends systematically over into the general estate, the estate of the officials." The world of learning was in it too, since officials "are simultaneously men of learning." The quality of personal ambition set civil servant, merchant, and scholar off from actual Bürger. Hegel ultimately sorted German social spirits or ethics into three: the peasant's ethic was trust, the Bürger's was righteousness, and the merchant's and official's was "cold heartlessness, the hard law." [23]

---

[22] For the relation of Napoleon's Rheinbund policy with the internal reorganization of the German South and West, Erwin Hölzle, "Das napoleonische Staatssystem in Deutschland," *HZ,* CXLVIII (1933), 277–293; Napoleon's letter to Talleyrand in *Correspondance de Napoléon Ier,* XII (Paris, 1863), 266–268; Wilhelm Hausenstein, *Die Wiedervereinigung Regensburgs mit Bayern im Jahre 1810* (Munich, 1905), passim; Marcel Dunan, *Napoléon et l'Allemagne: Le système continental et les débuts du Royaume de Bavière, 1806–1810* (Paris, 1942), p. 68 and passim.

[23] "*Vertrauen,*" "*Rechtschaffenheit,*" and "*gänzliche Unbarmherzigkeit . . . das harte Recht.*" Rosenzweig, *Hegel und der Staat,* I, 188–192, noted this evolution of Hegel's political thought and studied it in unpublished writings; he associated it directly with Napoleon's victories and their political effects in

This second period (the one that began with Austerlitz, the end of the Empire, Montgelas' assumption of the Interior portfolio, and Hegel's discovery of the general estate) became the critical time for the hometown communities. It was the time when the civil servants learned that administrative control required reform of local institutions, not just sovereignty over them exercised by a symmetrical state apparatus. It lasted as long as Napoleon's continental hegemony was unquestioned on the international scene, and for so long, on the domestic scene, as the states remained hopeful that they could in fact impose direct bureaucratic control over their territories from the center. It ended when failing confidence, growing recognition of the limits of German administrative capabilities even when backed by foreign armies, and finally the defeats of Napoleon in 1812–1813 led into a third phase, lasting through the teens and early twenties—a restoration phase of European politics, a phase that restored local autonomy to the communities, and that left the civil servants looking for other ways than direct control to bring change into the communities and make them participate in the life of the whole society and state.

There is one important departure from this chronology: that is in the individualized areas occupied by Prussia before the Treaty of Tilsit in 1807: in Ansbach-Bayreuth where Karl August von Hardenberg worked in the nineties, for example, and in Westphalia where Baron vom Stein worked in 1802–1803. There comparable stages are apparent but they came earlier: the Rheinbund states had to await the power of France to move from annexation to centralization, but Prussian power was enough to start the process right away in its new territories. Hardenberg's report on his administration of the Franconian territories annexed to the Prussian crown, for example, rings the successive changes of experience and tactics with local institutions that officials of weaker

---

Germany. It seems fair to note that I had already arrived at the analytical scheme outlined in Chapter IV before I discovered that Hegel came to agree with me. Note also that Hegel's discovery of the general estate coincides with the Prussian reformers' discovery of themselves as the true, and the only possible, constitutional representatives of the whole Prussian nation: Koselleck, *Preussen,* pp. 153–162, 217–283, and passim.

states, dependent on French initiative and support, passed through later and more slowly. "After long and fruitless efforts to come to terms in a friendly way, I confess it had to be done by our own authority, once and for all and emphatically; for nothing at all was possible by constitutional means and the imperial courts, so that self-help in terms of *ius gentium* became the only possibility, because it was absolutely necessary to act consistently and with the greatest firmness, or else give up on everything." [24] But then Bonaparte awarded Ansbach-Bayreuth to Bavaria; Prussia did not enter the Rhine Confederation, and already after its defeat at Jena in 1806 began the kind of administrative retrenchment that the Confederation states began after Bonaparte's defeat in 1812. The variant is evidence that it was not uniquely the influence of revolutionary France at work here; the contribution of France was to lend power to a German process.

The shock of reform and change experienced by the communities, especially in the middle stage, had two general origins: first, the technical administrative necessities that the takeover imposed, requirements of government *per se;* and second (following partly from the first), social and economic policies applied to the communities by their new masters. Centralization, long a familiar theme in the organization of state service itself, became a theme of hometown life when the civil service entered the communities of new territories. For one thing, incoming officials had to show they represented authority that was going to stick; but the real problem was not bureaucratic bombast. More serious trouble came from the incongruity between bureaucratic processes of professional government, and the home towns. This came partly from an incoming official's own unfamiliarity with the unwritten institutions and standards of the communities he governed; but more important, the individuality of the communities made it impossible for government to do its work in all of them without violating the character of each of them. If the society had been more fluid

---

[24] Christian Meyer, *Preussens innere Politik in Ansbach und Bayreuth in den Jahren 1792–1797* (Berlin, 1904) prints Hardenberg's report, pp. 37–210; the quoted passage, p. 43. I have translated Hardenberg's *Völkerrecht* as *ius gentium* because he seems to have meant not international law in the modern sense but the law of nations as applied to aliens and to war, in contrast with existing local law.

or its institutions more uniform, either one, then the states could have got along without the harsh disrespect for local self-determination that the civil service learned in Napoleonic times. On the hometown side, centralization became anathema not because of any dispute over the location of sovereign power, nor because state government was worse or cost more, but because it meant violation of the accustomed right. Hometownsmen usually accepted new regimes with equanimity at first. Hostility arose from the ways in which state officials were obliged to govern. The demands of that task pressed them from administration to centralization to disruption and reform.

Territorial change on a large scale revolutionized governmental procedures by making baroque administration impossible. An official's very first professional duties in an alien territory impelled him to reduce, if he could, the procedures of the communities within his responsibility to a simple and uniform pattern. For a hometown regime, merely to expose its resources and its political structure to an outsider was a shocking enough experience, and those were the first things a new governor wanted down on paper. "Purification," Hardenberg called it: *Bereinigung*, getting things straight and simple. None of the procession of new governors the communities got—many changed hands two or three times—could afford a leisurely process of getting acquainted with local idiosyncrasies, nor the occasional leisurely reports of curious events that made up the files of eighteenth-century local administration. Each new governor had to understand the community in clear and standard ways he could report to harried superiors, harried by high politics and wars and by Bonaparte. He had to try to make the community into an institution that could be understood and described in such ways, to bring it into the state and make it produce revenues for the high politics and the wars, and for Bonaparte. His professional duty joined with his training and his personal background to make him an enemy of the familiar and the particular, and of the hometownsmen whose identities rested on familiarity and particularity.[25]

[25] The effect was the same in the secularization of an ecclesiastical town, the mediatization of an imperial town, or the rationalization of a territorial town. Compare the examples in Walter Breywisch, "Quedlinburgs Säkularisation

"Purification" was the main reason why the civil servants became eager to adopt the Napoleonic Code or something similar—again, urged upon them by Bonaparte for purposes that matched their own: to bring local affairs under a manageable procedure and make local society and government responsive to the demands of the state.[26] Or as Montgelas said, introducing the Bavarian constitution of 1808: "to bring all subjects into a beneficent union with the common [Bavarian] fatherland, and provide for them the advantages of nearer association with administrative authority."[27] Karl Friedrich of Baden ordered the drafting of a Code because it would be "both useful, and for political reasons advisable." Simplification could come now that German politics had been brought into phase by a single motive power, so that the protection of peculiar privilege by appeal to outside jurisdiction was ended. From Nassau in 1808, Hans von Gagern proposed to Baden and to Hessen-Darmstadt that all three cooperate in preparing a single code on the Napoleonic model, on grounds of "the similarity of political considerations."[28]

But to say that uniformity was possible now that the diffuse localism of politics under the empire had succumbed to Napoleonic power is to say that the codes were a different kind of law from the old law: they were not Moser's compilations but Justi's systems of norms. With codification, law ceased to be a statement of what rules and rights existed—even the Prussian General Code had clung to that assumption—and became a statement of what the

---

und seine ersten Jahre unter preussischer Herrschaft, 1802–1806," SA, IV (1928), 207–249; Sebastian Hiereth, "Zur Geschichte des Landkreises Landshut . . . ," VHVN, LXXXVIII (1962), 1–66; Schell, Reichsstädte an Baden, passim; and the observations in Paul Darmstädter, Das Grossherzogtum Frankfurt (Frankfurt/Main, 1901), pp. 77–78; and in Preuss, Entwicklung des deutschen Städtewesens, pp. 294–295.

[26] For Bonaparte's pressure for their adoption in Hanse towns, Hessen-Darmstadt, Bavaria, and Baden, Willy Andreas, "Die Einführung des Code Napoléon in Baden," ZSSG, XXXI (1910), 194–195; for other instances and for German receptiveness, Hölzle, "Staatssystem," pp. 284–289; and Charles Schmidt, Le Grand Duché de Berg (Paris, 1905), pp. 115, 134–139.

[27] BayReg 13 VII 1808.

[28] The quotations from Karl Friedrich and from Gagern in Andreas, "Code Napoléon in Baden," pp. 198–199, 204; there also the view of the Bavarian professor Gönner that a uniform code was far preferable to the spuckenden alten Comitialgeist.

legislator thought ought to be. That gave unprecedented power to the lawgiver and the administrator, but a kind of power which brought with it a political peril: that the governor did not need to know nor share his sense of right with the governed.[29]

Reform was implicit in system and generalization. German codes and laws based on the Napoleonic pattern directly revoked the old slogan *Willkür bricht Landrecht*. The 1809 Baden law introducing the new code there put it flatly: "Herewith all force is removed from existing state and town laws and all customary laws." [30] The principle of equal rights under the law embodied in French revolutionary legislation and the Napoleonic Code offered the civil servants a mandate for the clean administrative sweep it was their job to bring about: it meant the same rules applied to everybody. It amounted to a constitutional statement of Justi's equation of the sum of individuals with the state, half a century before; and where Justi had achieved this in theory by ignoring intermediate institutional and social bonds, the civil servant could achieve it in practice only by destroying them. To free individuals of those bonds was the way to simplicity and symmetry. In Paris people talked of liberty, equality, fraternity. In Germany freedom and equality accorded power to a reforming state apparatus over against the eccentricity and complexity that guarded the hometownsman's Eigentum; and they compelled him to accept fraternity with people he did not know at all, a notion he could hardly conceive, and with people moreover whose brotherhood was repugnant to his own self-respect. These were principles of state autocracy, as Justus Möser had said. And of German autocracy: what such words might mean in French could not register with hometownsmen even if they heard them, and the French connection was indirect, a coincidence.

All the same, many of the administrative reforms ostentatiously adopted French models and even used French names; and this was especially true of the change that affected hometown government

[29] A good discussion of this point is in Ebel, *Gesetzgebung*, pp. 75–76.
[30] ". . . ist damit . . . die Kraft aller Land- und Stadtrechte und alle Rechtsgewohnheiten . . . aufgehoben." The Prussian General Code of 1794 had said to that point (Einl. § 21): "Übrigens stehen . . . die allgemeine Gesetze den Provinzialgesetzen, diese den besonderen Statuten . . . nach." Ebel, *Gesetzgebung*, p. 54.

most: the systematic introduction of municipal constitutions, *Municipalrecht*, to replace the *Stadtrecht* of German council and collegial government. Where imitation of the French model was closest, in the immediate French satellites along the northwest perimeter, from the Hanseatic departments to the Grand Duchy of Frankfurt, the very office and title of Bürgermeister were abolished in favor of the *maire*, who stood in a direct chain of command from prefect and subprefect and who was appointed by the state or by electors named by the state.[31] Not only was the chief officer of local government thus formally converted into a state officer under state discipline: he was further separated from the social community by the reorganization of municipal districts to include several towns, and countryside as well. The territorial aggregation of communities into administrative districts or cantons served also to break down the distinction between town and land that was so important to the Bürgerrecht. When it came to breaking into the economic privileges of townsmen, state interests agreed with countrymen's, and officials could expect peasant support.[32]

Local magistracies surrendered their judicial capacities to state courts, which in many instances simultaneously assumed administrative direction of local government. A separation of justice from administration, a long-standing aim of administrative reformers and widely undertaken in Napoleonic times, ended the useful blend of the two in communal councils. But it was a lop-sided reform: with it came the principle that any conflicts over what officials did as state agents came before administrative boards rather than an independent judiciary—the French principle of *Le Roi est juge en sa propre cause,* if the German bureaucrats needed it. Consequently

[31] For the introduction of the *Municipalverfassung* generally Maurer, *Städteverfassung*, IV, 301–313; for Möser's Osnabrück, Werner Hömberg, "Über Verwaltungseinrichtungen während der französischen Zeit im Osnabrückischen," *OM*, XXXVIII (1913), 135–145 and passim; Thimme, *Hannover*, II (1895), 102–110; Erwin Hölzle, *Württemberg im Zeitalter Napoleons und der deutschen Erhebung* (Stuttgart, 1937), pp. 92–93; Darmstädter, *Frankfurt*, pp. 102–110. For the replacement at higher levels of collegial bureaucratic structures, Haussherr, *Verwaltungseinheit*, pp. 189–195; and Stephan Elsberger, "Geschichte des Rezatkreises (1806/08–1817): Eine verwaltungsrechtsgeschichtl. Studie," *JHVM*, LXVII (1931–37), 69–70.

[32] Cf. Miller, "Organisation von Neuwürttemberg" (1931), pp. 130–131; Ziekursch, *Städteverwaltung*, pp. 20–24; Reichard, *Ansichten*, p. 44.

the main effect of the reform was to end hometown control of local police powers and give them over to the administrative channels that already controlled them in city and country.[33]

The device lawgivers of the individualized country found for describing the new relation of state with community was that of trusteeship: the communities were conceived still as legal entities, but as something like minor persons under the legal guardianship of the state, not competent to make independent decisions or contracts. This legal metaphor comported, perhaps, with a notion of maturing communal citizenship into state citizenship, although it did not seem to imply that communal corporations themselves would ever be released from state tutelage: on the contrary it was often made clear that for the communities this was a permanent condition.[34] During the earlier, annexation phase there had been an effort to metamorphose old local notables into state civil servants in their localities, for reasons of political and administrative expediency. States also tried to appoint lawyers and merchants, where they could find them, into town councils. But that had never worked out; hometown leaders remained what they had been; and so strangers were deliberately brought in for the business of organization and reform—trained and ambitious newcomers, young men fresh from their legal studies, from the pool of the central civil service, as their numbers allowed, to clear up the self-centered, the corrupt, the *sloppy* procedures of native communal government.[35]

Men like these in their alien jurisdictions depended on just the uniform codes and centralized procedures that were a mortal as-

[33] This treacherous subject deserves more scrutiny than I can give it here. Cf. Reichard, *Ansichten*, pp. 34–35; Darmstädter, *Frankfurt*, pp. 111–112; Wilhelm Horn, *Erfurts Stadtverfassung und Stadtwirtschaft in ihrer Entwicklung bis zur Gegenwart* (Halle, 1904), p. 21. On the prime concern to keep the police power in state hands, however local administration was organized, see Montgelas' own *Denkwürdigkeiten . . . über die innere Staatsverwaltung Bayerns (1799–1817)* (Munich, 1908), pp. 161–166; and Hiereth, "Landshut," pp. 9–11.

[34] E.g., BayReg 19 X 1808; BadReg 14 VII, 11 VIII 1807; *RB*, IV, Heft 2 (1807), pp. 526–547; or any number of other constitutions and community ordinances (many printed in *RB*) especially of the period 1807–1810.

[35] Miller, "Organisation von Neuwürttemberg" (1931), pp. 140–142, 302–303; Darmstädter, *Frankfurt*, pp. 78–79; Schmidt, *Berg*, p. 145 and passim; Schell, *Reichsstädte an Baden*, pp. 123–126; Hömberg, "Französische Zeit im Osnabrückischen," pp. 167–168.

sault on the home towns, and so they, like the codes they administered, became the home towns' mortal enemies. In that circumstance their procedures became policies. It is hard to distinguish
a point where administrative requirements blended into policies of
civic and social reform because their direction was the same, but
some state policies toward the home town took on a momentum
of change that exceeded the procedural impulse. The critical ones
had to do with citizenship rights, social rights and services, and
the organization of economic life.

Breaking down membership

To break communal membership down analytically was to break
it up socially. The state could not distinguish among individuals
except in very general, simple, and systematic categories, beyond
which it did not care; but the home town could distinguish more
subtly, uncategorically, and it did care. The community had been
able to function as it had by careful selection of who its members
should be, by the imposition of indirect tests and long scrutiny
to make sure of a candidate's conformity and familiarity with community ways. But now an outside civil servant armed with general
laws took over the Bürgerrecht and admitted citizens by the book:
as taxpayers, as state subjects, or because they chose to live there,
and admitted them freely; or else he applied laws giving all residents rights equivalent to citizenship. The bias of state administration was to bring new citizens into the community; they were after
all state subjects and had to be located somewhere, and the fewer
the distinctions among them the better. Fees laid on new citizens
took on another character when imposed by civil servants: the
communities had applied membership fees selectively to help safeguard their integrity, by discriminating against unwanted misfits;
but now such fees became an important source of revenue for
the state and encouraged wholesale admissions instead. Financial
penalties the communities had imposed upon people who moved
were either abolished or deliberately converted into a headtax on
everybody. Conscription and other obligations to the state were
imposed equally on everybody (mainly excepting civil servants)
and on everybody's sons. And although such measures could not
be uniformly applied, the officials tried to apply them, and they
were a clear signal of what happened when state citizenship took

priority over communal membership. Sometimes the communities grumbled and resisted; in some places there was violence, military intervention, and imprisonment; but mostly they seem to have drawn in closer unto themselves.[36]

Second, local citizenship rights were social rights, including the right to marry and settle as community members, and including the right to call on the community which was one's home for support in case of need. To ease marriage suited the state's bias (especially in wartime) in favor of growing population; to restrict and control it had been one of the community's main ways to stability and security. The state moreover had no interest in protecting the communities against the entry of the poor, whether by marriage, birth, or migration; on the contrary its interest was to see that its poor subjects were settled somewhere and taken care of, and encouraged not to be shiftless; and this obligation it obliged the communities to assume. But at the same time the states seized or took control of the charitable and religious endowments that supported social services like poor care, churches, and schools, both for the sake of the wealth they produced—almost certainly far more than was actually spent on charity, religion, or education—and because of their political importance. For these social funds had been not only a major part of community revenues, but also an important resource for patronage, budget-juggling, and the granting of favors; and so the seizing of them by strict professionals dissolved a cement on which the community relied. The Württemberg decree absorbing local endowment income to the state spoke of returning these funds to their "original purpose," and the use of other community properties was put under strict supervision; for "individuals should have property," declared Frederick of Württemberg, "but communities [*Kommune*] should not." [37]

36 Thimme, *Hannover*, II, 583–596; Darmstädter, *Frankfurt*, pp. 237–248; Karl von Beaulieu-Marconnay, *Karl von Dalberg und seine Zeit*, I (Weimar, 1879), 203–217; Miller, "Organisation von Neuwürttemberg," WVL, XXXIX (1933: a later installment of the article already cited), 232–235; Schlittmeier, "Landshut," p. 14; Willy Kohl, *Die Verwaltung der örtlichen Departements des Königreiches Westphalen, 1807–1814* (Berlin, 1937), p. 86; Klein, *Entwicklung des Gemeindebürgerrechts*, pp. 20–23.

37 Miller, "Organisation von Neuwürttemberg" (1933), pp. 245–247; Thimme, *Hannover*, II, 583–589; Elsberger, "Rezatkreis," pp. 105–106; Merk, "Ravensberg," pp. 420–421; Hölzle, *Zeitalter Napoleons*, pp. 93–94. On the

The economic organization of community life (thirdly) was of course directly threatened by state efforts to open the door to citizenship and social rights, for they disrupted the process of civic-economic decision by which the home towns had controlled their membership. The trades guilds were guardians of the social and moral qualities of the citizenry; conversely the interpenetration of guild leadership with political leadership defended the balance and integrity of the hometown economy. State assumption of the police power, or at least direct supervision over its exercise, replaced community control with state control over economic standards and thus over determination of who might carry on a trade and how. Now state licenses issued directly to individuals in effect replaced communal mastership conferred by guild in conjunction with local civic authorities. The civil servants issued very many licenses to persons who could not have got them from the communities. In Württemberg where local police was centralized at the capital in 1808, word went down that Jews and resident aliens should be admitted to the guilded trades.[38] It was simpler to be even-handed that way, but more than that: state economic policy aimed to develop a body of productive workers, while hometown economic policy developed the master guildsman—not the same creature at all, any more than state citizen was the same creature as communal citizen. Admit landmasters "to increase the sum total of work and production," the Bavarian government told the reluctant townsmen of Bamberg in 1807; it spoke of "raising the welfare of Our loyal subjects" by "a systematic division of labor" in the trades, and ordered local citizenship to be conferred on all state-licensed artisans.[39] Interest conflicted, along a line separating two quite different ideas of what social membership was and what economic organization was for.

In the Kingdom of Westphalia and in the Rhineland areas annexed directly to France, guilds were legally abolished in favor of

---

Bavarian Stiftungswesen, start with P. Fries, *Das Nürnberger Stiftungswesen vom Ende der reichsstädtischen Zeit . . . etwa 1795 bis 1820* (Nürnberg, 1963).

[38] Klein, *Entwicklung des Gemeindebürgerrechts*, pp. 22–23; Friedrich Wintterlin, *Geschichte der Behördenorganisation in Württemberg*, II (Stuttgart, 1906), 207–213.

[39] BayReg 10 I, 31 I, 15 VIII, 22 VIII 1807.

full occupational freedom. Elsewhere they were eviscerated, or reduced at least in theory to instruments of the state.[40] Bavaria, where guilds were not abolished, offers the clearest instance of systematic efforts to eviscerate and use them. Local guild monopolies, the *Zwangs-* and *Bannrechte* that had required consumers to patronize local guildsmen and had forbidden outsiders to enter the local market, were abolished: a confiscation of property in communal membership that Möser would have recognized, but a liberation of the rights of individual private property as the civil servants saw it. Rural, noble, and state-licensed artisans were allowed into the communities over the protests of hometownsmen (though the consumer populations of great towns like Munich welcomed the change). The so-called *Realgewerbe,* meaning a heritable property right in the exercise of a trade, was sharply restricted and put on a cash basis; and insofar as property right in a trade was an extension of the customary automatic entry to a guild by masters' sons (although the *Realgewerbe* is a very intricate and technical topic), to cut it back was to attack the social continuity of the communities as well as the rights of their members; and the towns called for a defense of their "Eigentum" against liberal theorists. When the deluge of trade licenses issued by provincial and state authorities brought direct conflicts with towns and guilds, Montgelas decided in 1807 that his reforms could only succeed if all Bavaria's complicated economic jurisdictions were clarified, by transferring all local powers to a "higher police" administered from Munich; with that the volume of new licenses grew all the faster. With state assumption of licensing powers, state supervision of guilds grew sharper and more detailed. Economic control required, in its turn, more administrative centralization.[41]

General economic developments of the Napoleonic period probably did not affect the home towns in any unusual way. Neither

[40] Thimme, *Hannover,* II, 594; Miller, "Organisation von Neuwürttemberg" (1933), pp. 110–127; Elsberger, "Rezatkreis," p. 101; Wolfram Fischer, *Der Staat und die Anfänge der Industrialisierung in Baden, 1800–1850* (Berlin, 1962), passim, and his "Ansätze zur Industrialisierung in Baden, 1770–1870," VSWG, XLVII (1960), 207 and passim; Darmstädter, *Frankfurt,* p. 291; Scotti, ed., *Cöln,* II, 2, p. 589; Hölzle, *Zeitalter Napoleons,* pp. 109–110.

[41] The best description is Ernst Anegg, *Zur Gewerbestruktur und Gewerbepolitik Bayerns während der Regierung Montgelas* (Munich, 1965), pp. 92–170.

did the efforts states made to encourage manufacture in large-scale enterprise—not directly. The economic sectors affected by the wars and the Continental System—luxury goods, export goods, and textiles—were the same ones that had attracted state interest and support in the past, and they had little relation with the hometown economies. Indicators of industrial activity during the period, such as they are, rise and fall listlessly in accordance with ephemeral circumstances: there were as many industrial failures as industrial foundations. At any rate it seems clear that the state-licensed and state-regulated manufactories of Napoleonic times were not the onset of nineteenth-century industrialization.[42] But the desire of the states to encourage this kind of manufacture was one reason for their attacks on the guilds, and upon the socially conceived practices of community economic control. It was a reason for the large volume of specific trade licenses they issued to private individuals independently of the guild system altogether, and in defiance of it. The intense fiscal pressures experienced by the German states during the Napoleonic period strengthened the link between the civil servants and those kinds of economic activity which, unlike the hometown trades, seemed capable of fast expansion (faster than population or social institutions) and of high revenues. They wanted to bring that kind of manufacture into the towns, and to do so they had to control or bypass or break by some other means the mechanisms that towns both large and small had used to prevent the upset that might bring. Werner Sombart once wrote of the "rusticalization of industry in the early capitalist epoch," by which he meant the era of putting-out industry, state manufactories, and other forms of organization kept out of towns by guilds and other communal regulative systems.[43] The countryside, some suburbs, and a few capital cities had been the state's sphere; there it could by its license exempt enterprises from guild monopolies, from the limitations on the size of enterprises and the number of

[42] A number of studies, encouraged notably by Friedrich Lütge, have developed evidence of a growth of large-scale enterprise during these years. I think they demonstrate the favorable state attitude, but no lasting or important economic effect. Reuter, *Manufaktur im fränkischen Raum*, pp. 5–23, 152–158; Slawinger, *Manufaktur in Kurbayern*, pp. 10, 66–67, and passim; Forberger, *Manufaktur in Sachsen*, passim.

[43] Above, Ch. III, n. 41.

employees, from the elaborate preparation for mastership and the unproductive qualities the guilds demanded of candidates for the mastership. It had not been hard to control industrial activity in those areas, where there were no strong guilds, no close-knit communities based upon them, and where the state was unquestionably dominant. But now administrators brought that same cameralist assumption of control to their economic policies of Napoleonic times. Now they were extending their power, or trying to, from city and countryside into the community.[44] Control was harder to achieve there. By 1812 the Bavarian Interior Ministry in Munich found itself contending with 9,800 separate guilds.

So matters stood when the phase of centralization and control ended. The failure of centralizing reform came with the decline of Bonaparte in Europe. The officials caught that political signal immediately, for by that time they were ready for it. What made them ready for it, and made Bonaparte's fall decisive for German domestic politics, was that the civil servants everywhere were finding detailed grasp and control of the communities beyond their powers. The main reason was the built-in resistance of the communities, their unmalleability, and the persistence of their terrible variety. Not everything could be foreseen by a code; the result was impossible floods of litigation and administrative inquiry, and the machinery stalled and broke down. Bureaucratic resources were not enough to master the detail of local life: state officials succeeded neither in reconciling local issues with general policies nor in forcing local affairs into a uniform pattern. Bavarian "higher police" found that the 9,800 guilds defied all efforts at rational administration; even the licensing system had turned into a monstrosity, quite incapable of flexible informed responses to economic needs. Decentralization began about 1811, and soon the volume of state licenses declined. Control over local endowments and services, assumed by Munich in 1806–1807, already began to be decentralized in about 1810.[45]

[44] Besides the citations in n. 42 above, Miller, "Organisation von Neuwürttemberg" (1933), pp. 110–127; Wolfram Fischer's article and book cited in n. 40 above; Anegg, *Gewerbepolitik Bayerns*, pp. 86–9f

[45] Anegg, *Gewerbepolitik Bayerns*, pp. 143–146, 170; Montgelas, *Denkwürdigkeiten . . . über die innere Staatsverwaltung*, pp. 50, 159. In many other places where full destruction of guilds was at least contemplated the idea

Even in the Kingdom of Westphalia it turned out that central state control of community property budgets was impossible. Prefects could neither understand nor supervise local finance without the cooperation of local leaders, and they did not get it. Detailed budget instructions did not find or keep track of the money. Efforts to enforce the state system required every community budget to pass from locality, to sub-prefect, to Interior Ministry, to State Council, with endorsement at every stage; and each local budget got legal validity only by royal decree. The Westphalian state, smothered in a mountain of paper, gradually gave up the struggle. In Berg, the prefects found that where they had been unable to put in their own outside officials the communities simply went their own ways and the Napoleonic Code was a facade.[46]

After the Battle of Leipzig in 1813 the royal Westphalian *maire* was renamed Bürgermeister, and the old Town Council was restored, on the grounds—so it was argued in Göttingen—that participation by the Bürgerschaft was the only way to master the problem of local administration. In the Grand Duchy of Frankfurt, plans to abolish the community as an administrative unit and to destroy the guild structure had been dropped by 1813, when instead the German office of Bürgermeister was revived to stand alongside the *maire*, together with a local collegial board—the old town council—to handle community finance. When the Austrians entered the Grand Duchy they abolished all the middle-level administrative positions that had been the backbone of Karl Theodor Dalberg's Rhine Confederation state in favor of a direct relation between the Austrian governor-general and local authorities. "The general national interest requires," according to a New Year's proclamation of 1814, "that German laws and customs, whose beneficial effects are proven, shall take the place of an alien lawbook." With that the Grand Duchy fell to pieces and disappeared.[47]

---

was dropped at about this time. In Bremen where the French had abolished the guild system in 1810 it was restored in 1814, and *Patentmeister* licensed in the interval were forbidden to operate: Böhmert, *Zunftwesen*, pp. 52–53, 136–137.

[46] Thimme, *Hannover*, I, 383–448, and II, 137–139, 596–605; Schmidt, *Berg*, p. 145; Koch, *Göttinger Honoratiorentum*, pp. 177–178.

[47] Mohnhaupt, *Göttinger Ratsverfassung*, pp. 124–125; Darmstädter, *Frankfurt*, pp. 124, 287–290, 401–404.

The consequences of confrontation

In 1805–1806 the officials had moved from annexation to control; now in 1812–1813 even control had failed. The Baron vom Stein had pointed to the problem in 1803 from Münster; he had come there, after earlier work in domains, forests, mines, and factory regulation, to incorporate certain Westphalian provinces, individualized country, into the Prussian monarchy. He did not see, finally, how this could be done by the kind of centralized administration that worked in the old Prussian state core. The superb Prussian system of administrative control relied, he said, on every officer's having full knowledge of his district and subordinates, and easy communication with them; in an alien and more complex jurisdiction, with the consequent piling up of business, this was lost, control was lost, and the genius of Prussian administration thwarted.[48] As Napoleon's star sank, the Rhine Confederation princes of the individualized country turned toward Stein's principle of local self-government; otherwise they were threatened with territorial collapse like Frankfurt's, as Prussia had been after Jena.

That opened the way to a restoration of the home towns.[49] Unity through control had failed. The communities had come out of the reforming decade, with all its laws and its bureaucratic flurry, almost unaffected except that now they knew they had an enemy, and who it was; and all of them knew it. Their tenacity and resiliency was reason enough to call them rooted and natural, organic and historic, and real; and beginning with the Napoleonic experience, they came to be described with words like these. That is a matter for the next chapter but one, on restoration, historical jurisprudence, and the places Germans began to look to see what

48 H. Kochendörffer, "Territorialentwicklung und Behördenverfassung von Westfalen, 1802–1813," WZ, LXXXVI (1929), Abt. I, 198–200; R. Wilmans, "Der Freiherr vom Stein und die Organisation der Erbfürstenthümer Münster und Paderborn in den Jahren 1802 bis 1804," ZPGL, X (1873), 660–679.

49 Willy Andreas, *Geschichte der badischen Verwaltungsorganisation und Verfassung in den Jahren 1802–1818*, I (Leipzig, 1913), 356–357; Darmstädter, *Frankfurt*, pp. 401–404; Daniel Klang, "Bavaria and the War of Liberation, 1813–14," *FHS*, IV (1965), 22–41.

their own society really was. For the confrontation of Napoleonic days posed a serious problem to German politics and German thought, and to the law, that linked the two: it laid out a contradiction between system and the particular, between forward motion and the stubbornly concrete. Could there be state power, and unity and progress, without change? Could this apparently distinctive German particularity, its variety and its tough social roots, be reconciled with the goals of a dynamic and vigorous society? In one form or another these have been the central questions of modern German politics.

The use of history was one way of accommodating particularity with change: a better way, it appeared now to the chastened German intellectuals, to explain the way Germany was and where it was going, than the eighteenth-century analysts had offered. The kind of community whose near-extinction Möser had lamented had survived after all, down underneath, silently and unnoticed in the unwritten ways of the people. It must have; there it was! It had defied now the assault of the new Rome, of the new Franks and their minions.

There was another effect of the Napoleonic experience, another set of conclusions that could be drawn from it and another posture that might be assumed; and its connection with the Napoleonic confrontation ought also to be noted here. I mean a conversion of the German civil service especially in the individualized country from cameral to liberal principles, and so ultimately a corresponding hostility to liberal principles on the part of hometownsmen. Whatever world-ideas may have been in the air breathed by some administrators, the head-on clash with the home towns was something experienced by all. The detailed control taught by the chairs of cameralism and urged by eighteenth-century statesmen seemed to have reached the limit of its possibility and failed. It was dropped from university curricula now. But yet that oddly necessary offshoot of cameralism, the doctrine of the harmony of individual wills, still had a way open to it. It was mainly a change in emphasis and political method, in a sense not more than a change in tactics: but a very important one. Liberalization appeared as an alternative weapon to control, another way to break up the impenetrable and immovable communities, and to integrate them with the larger life and purpose of the society and the state—to make them enter the general estate of movers and doers.

If the state's servants had been unable to assume and direct all the social powers exercised by the communities, then an alternative was to block and destroy those social powers. If the state could not make and enforce its rules, it could deny the home town's rules. In practice, liberal administration meant that where once the civil servants had tried to permeate the society with executive power, saying "You must do this," now they retreated to the appellate jurisdiction and said "You may not do that." In such a way the walls defending community integrity might be breached, and its frustrating particularity dissolved by a stream of social and economic movement. This was a position quite different from the neglect and sporadic intervention to correct "abuses" in earlier times, because now nobody could reasonably suppose the communities were part of a harmony. They had been recognized. They were rather the disrupters of harmony by their suppression of free individuality, and free individuality was therefore the principle their bureaucratic enemies found to turn against them.

Liberal ideas are easiest to trace out of Napoleonic times (and earlier) in economic matters; there fiscal connections were direct, and the interests of civil servants constantly engaged; but everybody knew, by now surely, that economic life was inseparable from local governmental and social practices. The idea of occupational freedom was not new, but it had meant freedom from guild restraints, not from the state's own right to regulate the economy. Out of the conflict with the communities—in almost no instance before then—arguments for a fully free economy began to be taken seriously.[50]

50 But still with many reservations about how much freedom to do what there should be for whom. Hardenberg's Ansbach-Bayreuth report is a neat example of an official's economic liberalism: C. Meyer, *Preussens innere Politik in Ansbach und Bayreuth*, especially pp. 148–149, 168–169. Montgelas' inability to decide for economic freedom even after deciding all other systems unworkable shows in his report on his administration: *Denkwürdigkeiten . . . über die innere Staatsverwaltung*, especially p. 159. I do not find it necessary, in the light of this chapter and the preceding one, to enter the belabored question of Adam Smith's influence in Germany: according to Wilhem Roscher, few Germans had paid any attention to Smith before Napoleonic times, but the genera-

It is important to remember that the force and substance of this liberalizing impulse from the beginning came not from a desire to reduce the strength of the state and of the men who embodied the state, but to enhance it. It had nothing to do with popular control over those men, or popular rights to defy them. German bureaucratic liberalism was mainly addressed to the ways whereby the organic communities had repelled change, and had repelled the state that had sponsored change. And that points to its limits; beyond that point lay confusion, confusion for the bureaucrats and townsmen, and for historians as well, not to mention liberal politicians of the nineteenth and twentieth centuries. German civil servants arrogated to themselves the mission of representing all the people—Prussia offered the clearest example of that notion—on the grounds that corporate institutions by their manifest nature could not represent all the people or join together to represent them.

Hegel was able to say in 1805 or 1806, about the time he devised his category of the general estate, that although local affairs might be left in local hands, the "general will" was to be expressed not by public participation but by the civil service; and the Napoleonic experience was enough to show bureaucrats the rightness of that way of thinking.[51] They were bound to accept local self-administration, given the experience of the Napoleonic period and immediately thereafter. And yet—although the distinction was rarely clear to them—they could not really accept local self-government.[52] For local self-government, in the individualized country of the communities, was a contradiction of the goal of progress through the unimpeded rational movement of individual persons and impersonal commodities that was the concrete basis of German bureaucratic liberalism. Free movement of persons and of impersonal commodities was a denial of Eigentum.

Cameralism had fulfilled its contradiction: Harmony was impos-

---

tion of statesmen and bureaucrats that came out of that decade were all Smithians: *National-Oekonomik*, pp. 598–601. See also Anegg, *Gewerbepolitik Bayerns*, pp. 86–90.

[51] N. 23 above.

[52] Heffter, *Selbstverwaltung*, passim. For a different interpretive theme for official liberalism, based on the Prussian experience, Hans Rosenberg, *Bureaucracy, Aristocracy, and Autocracy* (Cambridge, Mass., 1958), especially pp. 204–206.

sible without reform, reform without autocracy, and autocracy strangled in the web of its own directives, reports, and tables of organization when it tried to extend itself into the whole society. "Enlightened despotism" disappears from the history books with Napoleon Bonaparte. "Thus it was impossible," wrote Franz Schnabel, "for the great historic mission of Absolutism, the uniting of all forces for a common purpose, to be fulfilled among the German nation." [53] For neither of the two alternatives that appeared now out of the conflict resolved it: not veneration of the past, if the past meant all that baffled ambitious and generous men, nor a bureaucratic liberalism against which hometownsmen now must defend their freedom of the familiar as they had defended it against bureaucratic autocracy. The Napoleonic encounter brought no resolution to German political society but rather exposed the lines that divided it.

[53] *Deutsche Geschichte im neunzehnten Jahrhundert,* I (Freiburg, 1933), 88; see also pp. 99–100.

CHAPTER VII

Weissenburg, 1780-1825

WEISSENBURG is a walled town in Middle Franconia, lying on the checkered border between Roman Catholic and Protestant Germany: the confessional line at the core of the individualized country. In the meadows a mile or two southwest of the town is a great unfinished ditch that Charlemagne caused to be dug; from one end the water flows into the Rhine and the North Sea, from the other into the Danube and the Black Sea. Charlemagne gave up the project, says the chronicler, because mud kept sliding down into the channel during the night.

High windy plains, planted mostly to rye, overlook the town from the northeast; along the plateau's edge the Limes run straight as a draughtsman's rule, the wall and road Roman military engineers laid out in Hadrian's time against migrant barbarians. Eighteenth-century essayists discovered that local folk quaintly called the wall the Teufelsmauer, the Devil's Wall, and that has been its name ever since. After the building of the Teufelsmauer, local topography was afflicted with no other straight lines until the coming of the railroad and high-voltage power lines after the middle of the nineteenth century, for there was nobody in the neighborhood with enough political capacity, or wide enough interests, to draw any.

A steep hill stands directly above the town to the southeast; it is crowned by a fortress called the Wülzburg. The Wülzburg had been a monastery in medieval times; the Weissenburger burned it

217

in 1449; the Swedes besieged the Imperials there in vain during the Thirty Years' War. For centuries a cloister and hospital that lay within Weissenburg's walls was in the jurisdiction of the Wülzburg, or rather in the jurisdiction of whomever the play of dynastic politics had made the Wülzburg's master. The town did not get control of the cloister when Weissenburg turned Protestant in 1530, by which time the monks had already left it; and that is where the territorial officials attached to the Wülzburg lived and worked in ordinary times. Now it is owned and occupied by the state government of Bavaria.

Weissenburg was a free imperial town. It was so described in the Treaty of Westphalia; and it was kept free by the Empire's incubative internal balance, by the town's unimportance to anybody powerful outside the walls, by its insulation from foreign entanglements and trouble, and by following the lead of its stronger neighbor Nürnberg in the Empire's affairs. The account that follows of its experience in Napoleonic times is not intended to stand as typical, for it was not in the nature of any home town to be typical of the rest; nor does Weissenburg by any means conform in detail to the generalized description of the home town I have made in earlier chapters and will resume in subsequent ones. Some of the deviations from the general description can be anticipated from its free imperial status; that rendered its magistry, legally immediate to the Emperor, more independent of the citizenry and of nearby territorial rulers than the political leaders of a territorial town, similarly constituted in other ways, normally would have been. But Weissenburg's experience suggests the kind of thing that could happen to any home town; more important, it can show how and why certain issues mattered, some of them general issues which however might, without intimate examination of a single place, escape attention or be misunderstood. And it can animate conflicts of principle with people one can come nearer to seeing, walking around about their own affairs.[1]

---

[1] This chapter owes more than I can acknowledge to the work and perceptions of others: to former Weissenburg Town Archivist Brun Appel; to Lawrence G. Duggan, Ronald A. Fullerton, Steven W. Rowan, Frank B. Tipton, and Timothy Wright, all members of a graduate seminar at Harvard in 1966; and to my wife Irma, whose participation in it is at least as great as mine.

The free town

Weissenburg's walls, late in the eighteenth century, enclosed about five hundred dwellings and a population between three and four thousand, mostly citizens and their families, with a smattering of *Beisitzer* (tolerated residents) and of *Schutzverwandten* (protected aliens), most of them apparently servants or dependent relatives of citizens, with inferior civic and economic standing.[2] Rarely —no more often than coincidence would allow—did any male *Beisitzer* or *Schutzverwandte* bear a surname any Bürger bore, notably excepting one Simader who somehow got born in the cloister; resident non-Bürger rarely crossed the line that separated them from citizenship. But they were too few and too scattered, and too dependent, for them to constitute a distinct group in the community.[3]

The town was governed by an Inner and an Outer Council, mainly by the Inner, whose members divided up most of the important administrative offices and at least one of whom sat on each of the important administrative committees. The Councils were renewed by an Electoral College nominated by themselves from among themselves; legally there were annual elections, but ordinarily new members were chosen only to fill vacancies caused by deaths. Other important bodies like the Tax Office, the Forestry Office, and the School Board were similarly organized and similarly staffed. It was unusual for anyone whose surname was not familiar in local politics to achieve high office, and the community had got used to seeing certain families there, and so had the families; to that extent it will be possible to speak of leading political families, but not of familial oligarchy, let alone a closed patriciate. The most important office the town did not dominate in this way was that of

[2] Hanns H. Hofmann, *Historischer Atlas von Bayern,* Teil *Franken,* Reihe I, Heft 8: *Gunzenhausen-Weissenburg* (Munich, 1960), p. 177; "Kirchenlisten der Reichstadt Weissenburg im Nordgau, vom Jahre 1760 bis 1790," *JF,* II (1791), 445–449; partial and inconclusive evidence scattered through contemporary records support these population figures for the later eighteenth century.

[3] It is never easy to learn about noncitizens; the best source I know for Weissenburg's only lists them irregularly by name to record payment of their weekly residence fees to the town: Stadtarchiv, Weissenburg (hereafter StAW) B76.8: Beisitzer-Register 1718–44.

the town pastor, for he was nominated by officials at the cloister: that is to say the Wülzburg, which in the eighteenth century was in the hands of the Hohenzollerns of Ansbach.[4] Not one eighteenth-century town pastor was Weissenburg-born; they all came from the surrounding territories of Ansbach and Bayreuth. Meanwhile all deacons, church offices that the town directly controlled, were born Weissenburger of prominent name. There was one exception: a man from Rothenburg who got to be a citizen and then deacon by marrying a Bürgermeister's daughter late in the seventeenth century; but he joined a protest against the Councils and was dismissed from office and driven out of town in 1703. No such experiment with high office was made again.[5]

Most of the population worked at the customary local crafts and services, largely organized into guilds under the eyes of members of the Inner Council. Many of the less common occupations were left outside the guild structure, for Weissenburg guilds had little constitutional importance. Income from outside came from the agricultural population nearby, from sporadically successful weaving and needle-making, and from the making of gold and silver lace. The town owned very valuable and extensive forests in the hills to the south. There had been no acknowledged Jews in Weissenburg since a 1520 pogrom, but there was a colony in a village not far outside the walls, and a prosperous community in Treuchtlingen, an Ansbach territorial town five miles to the south, on the Augsburg road. Jews entered Weissenburg's affairs only through the cattle trade, and on occasions of financial stringency as creditors.

The best introduction the records allow to the civil composition of the town is the *Bürgeraufnahmen*: admissions to citizenship. Ordinarily citizenship came simultaneously with the *Meisterbrief* that granted full status as practitioner of a trade; or it might come with appointment to administrative office; occasionally it was bestowed on a member of a prominent family who was studying law or theology. The last two instances are rare, and the table below of civic admissions 1780–1805 does not distinguish them. It shows

---

[4] The cloister officials had *ius praesentationis;* the town had formal *Kirchenhoheit* and control over church administration as well as over the property secularized in the sixteenth century.

[5] Friedrich Blendinger, "Weissenburg," in Matthias Simon, ed., "Pfarrerbuch der Reichsstädte Dinkelsbühl, Schweinfurt, Weissenburg i. Bay. und Windesheim, . . ." *EKB,* XXXIX (1962), 61–82.

Civic admissions to Weissenburg, 1780–1805

Year	New citizens		Outsiders		Per cent sons of citizens
	Absolute	(Rate)	Local	Distant	
1780	13		1	2	77
1781	12	(15)	1	2	83
1782	21	(21)	0	2	86
1783	29	(23)	3	6	69
1784	20	(22)	2	2	80
1785	18	(20)	1	5	67
1786	21	(21)	2	4	71
1787	23	(19)	2	4	74
1788	13	(16)	0	2	85
1789	13	(14)	0	3	77
1790	17	(16)	1	4	71
1791	17	(19)	1	3	77
1792	22	(18)	1	2	87
1793	15	(24)	2	1	80
1794	35	(23)	2	5	80
1795	18	(24)	1	4	72
1796	18	(16)	2	4	67
1797	13	(19)	3	1	69
1798	25	(22)	1	5	76
1799	27	(22)	5	5	63
1800	13	(21)	1	1	84
1801	23	(18)	1	3	83
1802	17	(22)	1	2	82
1803	26	(23)	4	4	69
1804	26	(22)	3	4	73
1805	13		0	3	69
Totals	508	(20)	41	83	76

the number of men admitted each year, and distinguishes two kinds of outsiders from the sons of Weissenburg citizens. "Local" outsiders means either inhabitants of Weissenburg who were not of citizen family or else were natives of villages in Weissenburg's immediate sphere; they paid three times the customary fee to the town upon entering unless they married a citizen's widow or orphan, and often when they did: that was very nearly the only way for a local outsider to attain citizenship. "Distant" outsiders means persons from other territories, mostly to the north: Saxony and

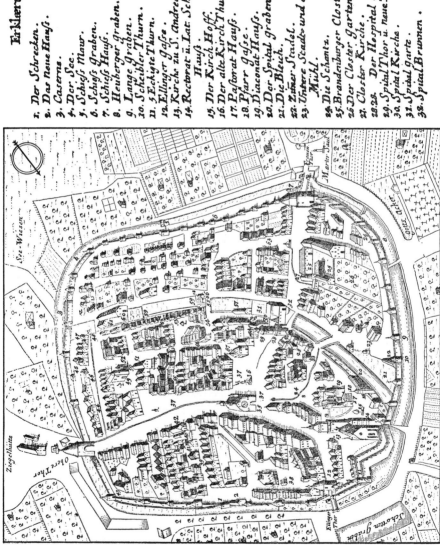

Weissenburg in the eighteenth century

Weissenburg in the Eighteenth Century

The original descriptive meanings of many names had already been forgotten by the eighteenth century, so that some translations (although most of the names are still in use) are guesswork.

1. The fright
2. New House
3. Barracks
4. Pond
5. Gun wall
6. Gun ditch
7. Gun house
8. Heuberg ditch
9. Long ditch
10. Slice tower
11. Five-cornered tower
12. Ellingen lane
13. St. Andreas' church
14. Rectory and Latin School
15. Churchyard
16. Old churchtower
17. Parsonage

18. Preacher lane
19. Deaconry
20. Hospital ditch
21. Bleachery
22. Carpentry shop
23. Sawmill
24. Redoubt
25. Brandenburg cloister
26. Cloister yard
27. Cloister church
28. Hospital
29. Hospital gate and new tower
30. Hospital church
31. Hospital yard
32. Hospital well
33. German boys' school
34. Court

35. Town Hall
36. Pretty well
37. Market
38. Chapel
39. Paved lane
40. Convent
41. German school
42. Convent church
43. Horse mill
44. Brook
45. Brickyard
46. Jail
47. Poorhouse
48. Coppersmith
49. Granery
50. Salt-house
51. Administration

52. Town Clerk
53. Rose hill
54. Bubbling spring
55. Meadow
56. Laundry
57. Slaughterhouse
58. Scales
59. Fishpond
60. Baths
61. Upper town mill
62. Hatters' lane
63. Pig market
64. Hell alley
65. Beer alley
66. Jew lane
67. Meat market

Thuringia (and a mysterious Friedrich Rex from Stallopin in Prussia), presumably persons able to provide services the town needed (Friedrich Rex married the Widow Bub). They paid only double the entry fee that the sons of citizens paid. The "rate" figure—technically a moving average—represents an effort to even out the eccentricities of calender years by calculating an average for three years of which the named year is the middle one.[6]

During the whole of the eighteenth century, incidentally, there seems to have been a gentle rise in the rate of admissions, something under half a per cent a year, probably not enough to be perceptible but enough to bring a slight rise in citizen population. Meanwhile the number of outsiders admitted had not risen, and thus the proportion of citizens' sons had: genealogically Weissenburg's population had tended to stabilize during the eighteenth century.[7] But during the quarter-century before 1805 the pattern of admissions did not vary significantly. About three quarters of the new citizen-masters were regularly the sons of citizen-masters. Of the remaining quarter, the outsiders, about two out of three came from some distance (thus one new citizen in six), probably appearing in Weissenburg first as journeymen, from places very like itself. One out of three outsiders (thus one new citizen in twelve) came from the villages or the lower orders within.

A list of the family names that appear most frequently begins to show the relation of family to citizenship in the community; they are worth looking over, for they will recur.

Roth	25	Bösswillibald	8
Schnitzlein	17	Häusslein	8
Oberdorfer	17	Beck	7
Wägemann	14	Guttmann	7
Preu	13	Hirschmann	6
Pflaumer	11	Pfahler	6
Fleischmann	10	Eckert	5
Staudinger	10	Hoffmann	5
		Rauenbusch	5

Among the 508 new citizens between 1780 and 1805 there were 216 family names. Eight names accounted for 23 per cent of the

[6] StAW B25.3: Bürgeraufnahmen 1706–1806.

[7] Cf. Frank B. Tipton, "Structure and Recruitment of the Town Council of Weissenburg during the Eighteenth Century" (MS seminar paper, Harvard, 1966), pp. 18–20. I am not concurring exactly with Tipton on this point.

entries. Sixteen, including those eight, accounted for over a third, leaving about two hundred names to account for the other two-thirds. The common names were not necessarily the most important politically. Roth, Preu, and Staudinger were both common and very eminent names. So to a lesser degree were Pflaumer and Häusslein. But some of the most eminent eighteenth-century names do not appear at all often on the citizenship entry lists for 1780–1805: Freyer (four times), Döderlein (twice), Lotzbeck (twice), Sonnenmeyer (once).[8] These last four were very old names, antedating the Thirty Years' War and still important: families with inherited prestige that had been maintained, but with low birth rates. Conversely some of the commonest citizens' names were not important in public affairs: Oberdorfer, Bösswillibald, Fleischmann, Guttmann. Some of these were old names, some relatively new.

Hence it does not appear that the simple size of a clan made its members politically important. About one eighteenth-century Weissenburger in ten reached one of the Councils before he died. If his name was Roth he had one chance in 6.6; if he was a Preu, one in 5.3; the Oberdorfers, fruitful of family but politically impotent, reached the Councils one time in 52, and the Schnitzleins one in 17; the Wägemanns one in 10.3; but the Lotzbecks one in 2.5, and the Sonnenmeyers, with four Council positions among nine citizens in the eighteenth century, one in 2.2. The common but politically unimportant names show no growth in political strength toward the century's end, either; on the contrary if there is change it is slightly in favor of the traditional names, including the scarce ones like Sonnenmeyer and Freyer.[9] Although neither the familial stabilization (or concentration) of leadership nor the increasing proportion of the citizen-born among new citizens is more than faintly

[8] I identify these nine eminent eighteenth-century names by their appearance at least twice (for persistence) in at least two (for versatility) of the following categories of public office: 1) Bürgermeister, Inner Council; 2) Bürgermeister, Outer Council; 3) *Stadtschreiber* or *Syndicus;* 4) teacher, Town Physician, Cantor, or organist. Compiled from Georg Voltz, *Chronik der Stadt Weissenburg im Nordgau und des Klosters Wülzburg* (Weissenburg, 1835), pp. 11–16; and Blendinger, "Weissenburg . . . Pfarrerbuch," pp. 61–81.

[9] StAW B25.3; StAW B24.1: Wahlbüchlein von Ao. 1504 . . . Ad Annum 1791. Tipton, comparing the *antiquity* of families with their share of eighteenth-century Council seats (as I here am comparing general eminence), similarly concludes that the older families grew stronger in the course of the century: "Town Council of Weissenburg," pp. 11–16, 20–21.

apparent, still taken together they are enough to suggest at least a growing consolidation of the community. Such a tendency might be ascribed to a recoil by the community to general population growth (a nineteenth-century explanation) or to the intramural jelling of the community (an eighteenth-century explanation), and it would be useful to decide which; but the tendency is too weak and the evidence too sparse and indirect for that; the latter seems more plausible.

In 1693, 1754, and 1795 there were electoral disputes, imperial interventions, and political reorganization in Weissenburg, and ordinarily in the course of them the newer and weaker families got greater Council representation—probably not so much because they wrung it out of a monolithic leadership as because of competition between Council factions which turned to them for support. But despite these moments of greater fluidity (perhaps, through the cyclical balancing effect proposed in Chapter II, with their aid), the civic pattern did not change; and when the pressure was relieved and harmony restored the older and stronger families were able to reassert themselves. Their bases in the community lay deeper than ephemeral political alliance or the formalities of political organization.

The normal pattern of a political career in Weissenburg was to rise from citizenship to Outer Council to Inner Council to Electoral rank. But there were variations. Some rose faster than others, and some—the perennial elders of the Outer Council—never rose above a certain level. That makes it possible to work out the relation between family and political influence in another way:

First: the nine most eminent political names amount to 12 per cent of all new citizens, 1706–1805 (15 per cent in 1780–1805);

Second: but they account for 33 per cent of the accessions to total Council membership, 1699–1791. Thus 67 per cent of the Council membership still came from outside the chief administrative and political families (only 50 per cent in 1774–1791).

Third: once on the Councils, 41 per cent of the strong-family members reached the high positions of Inner Council and/or Electoral College, whereas 35 per cent of the weaker-named Councilors did so. As a result,

Fourth: just half the eighteenth-century entries to the Inner

Council and Electoral College came from those nine families (and that is the figure for 1774–1791, too).

At successively higher levels of civic responsibility and power, then, the participation of the strong families grew—12 per cent, 33 per cent, 50 per cent; and in a few pages it will appear how in critical and unprecedented situations they were likely to take control pretty much into their own communarchal hands, and take responsibility on their patriarchal shoulders. Still the nine families, even though defined by their frequency in high office, held no more than half the places on governing and appointing bodies; and as one moves down the scale of eminence, office diffused progressively and rapidly into the citizenry. Neither the figures nor any other local evidence that comes to hand suggests persistent or structural cleavage between citizenry and Councils, or between Inner and Outer Councils.[10]

Economic organization shows a pattern very like civic organization, though there are some curious features. The constitutional weakness of the guilds probably delivered much of the usual guild role—lower-level political organization and reciprocal representation between citizenry and leadership—over to the elected ward chiefs, the Viertelmeister. Each guild was assigned to an Inner Council member for oversight; and although he acted as rapporteur for that guild's affairs before the Council, he seems to have been on balance the Council's man and not the guild's, if only because he usually supervised more than one guild. But constitutionally organized or not, the Weissenburg artisanry participated fully in local government, especially after mid-century: before 1747 half the Council members were artisans, including a third that were guild members; and after 1763 more than two-thirds were artisans, and half from the guilded trades. The rest were merchants, lawyers, or

---

[10] But outside lawyers for formal reasons, and historians who have followed them and have added the predisposition to think in terms of class stratification, have described Weissenburg's disputes that way: see, e.g., Moser, *Von der Reichs-Stättischen Regiments-Verfassung*, pp. 442–443; *Zusäze zum Teutschen Staatsrecht*, III (Leipzig, 1782), 710–711; *Reichs-Stättisches Hand-Buch*, II (Tübingen, 1733), 851–872, all cited by Tipton, "Town Council of Weissenburg," p. 5; and Gustav Mödl, "'Weissenburg contra Weissenburg': Ein Beitrag zum Verhältnis zwischen Rat und Bürgerschaft," *Uuizinburc/Weissenburg, 867–1967* (Weissenburg, 1967), pp. 105–110.

their occupations were not listed; and although their representation on the Councils was distinctly greater than their proportion of the whole population, still they never constituted a majority on the Councils.[11] But neither for that matter did guildsmen.

New citizens, 1780–1805, show this distribution in the larger trades; [12] guilded trades are marked with asterisks:

*Metzger (butchers)	69	*Hutmacher (hatters)	9
*Schuhmacher (shoemakers)	34	Handel (commerce)	8
*Bäcker (bakers)	28	*Müller (millers)	8
*Weber (weavers)	23	Drahtzieher (wire drawers)	8
*Tuchmacher (wool weavers)	22	*Wagner (cartwrights)	7
*Bortenmacher (braidmakers)	18	*Seiler (ropemakers)	6
*Schneider (tailors)	15	*Schreiner (joiners)	6
*Schmiede (smiths)	14	Knopfmacher (buttonmakers)	6
*Zeugmacher (cloth workers)	12	Weissgärber (tawers)	6
*Rotgärber (tanners)	11	Färber (dyers)	6
Brauer (brewers)	10	*Säckler (pursemakers)	5
*Maurer (masons)	10	Gürtler (beltmakers)	5
*Schlosser (locksmiths)	9	*Zimmerer (carpenters)	5

The large number of new butchers implies that there must have been well over a hundred master butchers operating at once in a town of five hundred households. Probably many of them operated taverns in conjunction with their butchershops; and of course the large meat trade with the villages brought income from outside the town. Many of the butchers would have been called swine merchants if an occupation so named had been acknowledged and respectable. But clearly there were too many butchers toward the end of the century; the guild tried to limit the number of new masters. It did little good; butchery was an elite and profitable trade, closely related with town police administration and attractive to important families who went ahead and established businesses anyway; the guild limitation seems mainly to have excluded those not influential enough to ignore or overcome it.[13]

[11] StAW B24.1; StAW B25.3; Tipton, "Town Council of Weissenburg," pp. 24–25, n. 57. Note that the guilds' lack of constitutional status made it unnecessary for citizens to join guilds for political purposes, as sometimes happened elsewhere.

[12] Smiths and cartwrights were organized together into one guild, and four established guilds admitted fewer than five new members 1780–1805: Kirschner (furriers), Nagelschmiede (nailsmiths), Hafner (potters), and Büttner (coopers).

[13] See below, pp. 244–245.

There were twenty-two organized guilds, with a total of fifty-six publicly recognized officials—*Viermänner, Geschworenen, Alt-meister,* and so on.[14] Their lack of constitutional powers did not render them meaningless. The degree of internal self-government they possessed is not clear and varied probably with guild, time, and circumstance. Sometimes they seem to have chosen their own officers, and sometimes the Councils or Electoral College seem to have chosen them; very likely guildsmen proposed candidates and civic authorities confirmed them, with the responsible Councilor as intermediary; probably there was little disagreement over who the obvious candidates were. Constitutional status apart, they played the usual guild civic and social roles. A citizen's son paid one gulden apprenticeship fee to the butchers, and outsider's son ten gulden; outsiders put in six years *Muthjahre,* waiting for mastership after all other conditions had been met; natives put in three, and often escaped those.[15] Among the tanners, only one non-native was made master between 1700 and 1750, out of 24; and there were no outsiders at all among the new tanners 1750–1790. But though they were citizen's sons, the new tanners were not all tanners' sons: a third came from within the guild, but another third from other guilds, and a third from nonguilded occupations.[16]

Guilds had the civic responsibility for training and certifying the economic credentials of new citizens in the trades most important to the community; they had the social responsibility to care for poor masters and to help marry off the bereaved; and their exercise of low-level justice guarded community social as well as economic behavior. Here are some decisions of the butchers' guild court, taken (almost) at random. Johann Georg Jordan was fined in 1763 for not attending the burial of a fellow master, "while letting himself be seen peeping around the gate." Christian Döderlein was next thing to a groundrabbit: in 1766 he was fined for slaughtering more than the limit the guild had established, in 1767 "for that his wife sold meat other than his," in 1768 for extending credit

[14] StAW B23.6: Ämter Büchlein, de Anno 1771.

[15] Karl Kirchmeier, "Die Entwicklung des Metzgerhandwerks in Weissenburg bis zur Gewerbefreiheit 1868" (MS Studienarbeit 1961, at the Weissenburg town archive), pp. 12–13.

[16] Lawrence G. Duggan, "The Fortunes of the Tanners of Weissenburg i. B., 1750–1869" (MS seminar paper, Harvard, 1966), p. 7.

to a customer, an offence he repeated in 1772. Johann Georg Grasser was fined for allowing a peasant laborer to carry meat from the slaughterhouse to the place of sale; Johann Michael Schnitzlein for adulterating the bratwurst. The heaviest fine that comes to eye was imposed on Johannes Guttman in 1763, at the end of the Seven Years' War, for speculating in pork: "that he re-sold to a stranger three pigs that he had bought here." Probably the commonest penalty was for abusive language: *Schand- und Schmähwort.*[17]

During the period 1780–1801 (when the necessary records end), the three guilds always listed first in official documents—the butchers, the tanners, and the bakers—were consistently headed by Weissenburg political families. These were not the small-but-powerful eighteenth century families, though (like Sonnenmeyer and Lotzbeck), but rather the larger ones (Roth, Preu, Schnitz-lein), plus other sizeable families of consistent but secondary po-litical weight (such as Wägemann, Hirschmann, and Pfahler). Rarely did either large but unpolitical families, or small but pres-tigious ones, provide officers for those guilds. An Oberdorfer was *Viermann* in the butchers for a time; but a very large proportion of the butchers were always Oberdorfers. A Bösswillibald was *Viermann* in the bakers—the Bösswillibalds had been bakers for centuries—until he was suspended from office in 1801. But of the thirty men who held office in the three first guilds in protocol be-tween 1780 and 1801, twenty-one bore traditional eighteenth-century political names. Eight of the ten who took office after 1789 had old political names. Every one of the five that took office after the Prussian occupation of 1796 bore political names.

In sharp contrast with these three guilds, though, almost no names of political weight appear among the officers of the other nineteen. Here are the most important of them:

In protocol:
> *Schneider* (tailors)
> *Kirschner* (furriers)
> *Schuhmacher* (shoemakers)
> *Nagelschmiede* (nailsmiths)

[17] From StAW B285: Register und Ordnung der Meister eines Handwercks der Metzger aufgerichtet Anno 1757.

Schmiede (smiths and cartwrights)
In size:
Schuhmacher (shoemakers)
Weber (weavers)
Tuchmacher (wool weavers)
Bortenmacher (braidmakers)
Schneider (tailors)

Of the sixty-one men who held office between 1780 and 1801 in those eight guilds at the second level of prestige and importance, only five bore the names of political families, and two of those took office after 1798; all five, moreover, were from large families with many branches, who could hardly have helped producing that many *Viermänner*. This quite clear division of guild organization along political lines—or vice versa?—cannot be accidental; and yet we find nothing in the records to explain it or to say whether it is part of a larger pattern; the Weissenburger knew, and so they did not write it down, and so we do not know. The guilds on one side, or one level, did not exclude from their trades members of the families that ruled on the other; ordinary membership was mixed; only the leadership hardly overlaps at all. That is enough to show that Weissenburg's guild organization was interlaced with political institutions in some persistent, quasi-constitutional manner, through the familial structure, despite official silence on the matter. It was not reported to the Prussian crown or the Bavarian electorate when the time came for that.

One more institution needs mention before the narrative of the crisis years begins: the *Pflegamt*. This body administered most of the old imperial and ecclesiastical fees and endowments that had fallen to the town over the years, such as those for the maintenance of the church, poor relief, and education. The sources of most of its income lay outside the walls, so that the Pflegamt collected some of Weissenburg's most important external revenues and exercised some of its most important external powers, reaching well outside the town limits strictly defined; but by that same token Pflegamt resources were more vulnerable to the outside too. Town subjects (but not citizens) who lived outside the walls, in the nearby mills, farmsteads, and villages, were within its fiscal and judicial competence, though there was constant conflict between the Weissenburg Pflegamt and the officials of Ansbach and of other jurisdictions over this. Annual income to the Pflegamt amounted to about a quarter as much as the town's regular taxing system collected; and except in times of unusual demands upon it —notably the time of the Seven Years' War—income ran ahead of expenditure, far enough ahead for the Pflegamt to show a cash balance by 1800 equivalent to Weissenburg's total annual budget.[18] But features of Pflegamt funds even more important than their size were their independence and their flexibility; for they were not extracted from the citizens in the form of taxes and were not subject to the kind of Council oversight and public complaint that periodically afflicted the regular Tax Office. Pflegamt money was raised outside the town and spent inside, a happy situation. Moreover, the Pflegamt's power to lease the endowments it controlled and set the price, to influence food supply and prices through allocation of the produce from its farms, gave it an influence hard to call to account; and by the end of the century it was making sizeable loans to citizens and to the town treasury, as it chose and at the interest rates it set.

But no Weissenburg institution can truly be called independent of the communal order; rather, the Pflegamt was a special and very useful part of it. It was administered by a body of four men, on effective life appointment; only eight men held the office in the last half of the century, and from 1780 until 1801 there were only five: Freyer, Pflaumer, Sonnenmeyer, Preu, Huber. The first four were from the most important of the political families, and Huber was a man without family who held an extraordinary number of political and administrative positions during those years, presumably by virtue of unusual talents and energy. The affairs that these officials undertook to administer were when reduced to paper such an impenetrable tangle that with the best of intentions it was possible only to muddle through without becoming altogether clear—again on paper, financially—about what was being done, let alone explaining it to others. Weissenburg book-

---

[18] Such computations are most treacherous; I rely here mainly on two MS 1966 Harvard seminar papers: Timothy Wright, "Weissenburg from the Pflegamt: 1750–1801," and Steven W. Rowan, "The Steueramt of the Reichsstadt Weissenburg im Nordgau, 1760–1801."

keeping was designed to record, to supplement memory, not to analyze or explain. But that is not to say that the Pflegamt's administrators did not know what they were doing. In Weissenburg the guides to everyday administration were long detailed experience and adherence to precedent, shaded by an intimate grasp of where interest and influence lay, of how the town worked as a community and a polity: for laws were not there to say. But the rest of the community was. The Pflegamt's independence was conditioned by its interlocking through family and through multiple office with other community institutions; what happened to its money was a matter of public concern.

If the main implements of political coherence in a civic system are at the same time the main opportunities for corruption; if politics is stylized favoritism, bribery, and intimidation: then in Weissenburg such opportunities were limited mainly by the personal standards of the town's leaders. But their politics were stylized by the community. Their personal standards were of a kind that such a community developed, and they were appropriate to it. Moral standards are inculcated by the consequences of violating them; we usually behave well in those areas of our lives where ill behavior will bring retribution: "Honesty is the best policy." Weissenburger dealt only with one another and with all of one another, all the time; to cheat was to invite destruction because there was no place to go without serious loss; and so they were honest in the "small ways" that are the ways of such a place, and they were well-behaved toward people like themselves. I should never suggest that the Weissenburger loved one another; rather I suspect they abominated one another, although that probably made them feel guilty, because their moral consciences were developed in ways to make it possible for them to live together as they did. And when a political leader took office he assumed the same kind of responsibility a butcher did when he sold a sausage, and for the same kind of reason. Colleagues, neighbors, and customers were circumscribed within the walls and hardly changed in a lifetime. But that circumstance, consequently, was vital to the town's civic and even its moral life. So were the men and the families that incorporated that circumstance into their exercise of authority. Within the circumscription conscience served. Their powers of leadership, reciprocally, bound the citizens: citizenship, mastership, family. It was a system that worked remarkably smoothly for so long as no important alien element entered the scene.

Town into territory

In 1790 Karl August von Hardenberg became first minister to the aged and indolent Hohenzollern prince of Ansbach and Bayreuth. In 1791 that prince, having sniffed the wind, abdicated in favor of the Prussian branch of his house and retired with his mistress to England. Hardenberg became King Frederick William II's first minister in the Franconian principality, and thus master of the Wülzburg and the cloister, and Weissenburg's antagonist in the eternal but theretofore desultory jurisdictional controversies. He was a personality of a kind the Weissenburger had not encountered before, except perhaps for occasional imperial lawyers to whom they had paid little attention and who had behaved casually toward them. And it was he who then negotiated the separate Treaty of Basel with France in 1795, whereby Prussia gave up its territories west of the Rhine in return for French support in taking compensation within the Empire.[19]

While those arrangements were being made in high places, Weissenburg was having an administrative reform, urged by an imperial commission. This had no obvious connection with outside events, nor was there any important internal reason why it should be a more serious matter now than on some earlier occasions, nor any evidence that anybody thought it was. If events outside were causing any special uneasiness, then in Weissenburg the reflex was to emphasize the avuncular regime. A committee of twenty was set up in March of 1794 to reorganize the administrative structure. Twelve members of the committee were deputies of the two Councils, six from each, and all of these held important administrative offices as well. Four more were deputies of the Viertelmeister, the precinct leaders, and four were citizens'

---

[19] The following narrative will be composed of local events in Weissenburg, to minimize duplication of materials presented in other chapters. Two excellent studies describe events at an intermediate level: Elsberger, "Rezatkreis," and Hiereth, "Landshut."

representatives chosen by the Viertelmeister. About a third of the reform committee was named Roth (Weissenburg's largest clan). A Freyer, a Sonnenmeyer, two Preus, and a Pflaumer made up another quarter. Those traditional names account for all the representatives from the Councils except for two technical administrators: Town Recorder (*Stadtschreiber*) Hirschmann for the Inner Council and Town Treasurer (*Stadtkammerer*) Stadelmeyer for the Outer.[20]

The committee accepted reforms proposed by the imperial commission: the Councils were reduced in size and some of the administrative offices were consolidated.[21] The imperial rationale was to professionalize and simplify administration, and to economize, by reducing the number of town officials. Something similar had happened during the last imperial intervention forty years before; but in the interval the Weissenburger, whose notions of local government were different from those of the imperial lawyers, had expanded the regime again. Shrinkage would be a better name than reform for the changes of the nineties in any case: the same men exercised the same powers, whatever the names of the multiple offices they held. The Pflegamt administrators disappeared from the election rolls, but they held their titles and continued to direct Pflegamt functions along with their other duties. From all appearances the public business of Weissenburg was conducted just as it always had been; and there was no reason within the walls or within the imperial system why it should not go on functioning as before.

But there was an alien outside, moving closer. During the night of July 29–30, 1796, signs inscribed *Royal Prussian Territorial Limits* sprouted all around the close perimeter of Weissenburg's undisputed jurisdiction. Two villages and a smattering of endowments lay behind the signs, although Hardenberg respected the town's immediate galaxy of mills, gardens, and outbuildings. Some officials were not so indulgent, or perhaps they had confidential instructions: just before three in the morning the chief of the cloister administration, with a party of peasants, drove in a sign just outside the north gate, facing in: *Territoire Prussien.* An emergency session of the Councils decided to ask the Empire for

[20] Voltz, *Chronik*, p. 173.   [21] Hofmann, *Atlas*, p. 72.

help, and issued warnings to the townspeople not to become excited and stir things up. But a week later Prussian soldiers appeared at all the town gates, pushed the feeble Weissenburg watches inside, and took up guard on the bridges. That night a new sign appeared to confront the double eagle emblazoned on Weissenburg's gates: a black eagle with a single head, and with initials over it that signified *Frederick William, King of Prussia and Count of Nürnberg.* The outlying villages were occupied, and the peasants were told that thenceforward they must pay their regular taxes, and all dues not indisputably Weissenburg's, to Hardenberg's officials. In the villages the houses were numbered —even the houses belonging to undoubted Weissenburg subjects.

At that time the French armies moving against Austria were at Schweinfurt and Würzburg. All the Franconian Circle of the Empire lay open to them, except the parts now held by the Prussians; Prussia and France were at peace and implicitly allied. The Circle tried to buy off the French with protection money. But after some negotiation and expense Marshal Jourdan rejected their offers of cash, food, and horses; he could collect more effectively than the Circle anyway; he would march. The Weissenburg Councils saw only one way to escape French occupation and forced tribute: they must ask for the protection of the Prussians. A delegation made up of four Roths and Bürgermeister Sonnenmeyer went to Ansbach to see Hardenberg. They returned on the evening of August 20 with Hardenberg's promise that Prussian troops would enter the town next day to protect it from French requisitioning. Other aspects of their negotiations with Hardenberg, said the delegates, still required clarification. The Viertelmeister were dispatched to their districts to quiet the population with this good news. They were warned not to discuss any possibility of the town's subjection to the Prussian crown. For on the whole the leaders (possibly excepting Bürgermeister Sonnenmeyer) were readier to submit to Prussia than the citizenry was. Hardenberg had been courteous and careful with them, and they stood to lose the most financially from French requisitions and the consequences of hostile military occupation. The situation needed not be, after all, very different from the normal patterns of German politics, and their response was normal: turn to one prince for defense against another. There is no hint of any politically radical pro-French party in the town; anti-Prussian sentiment among the townspeople cannot be interpreted that way, even though it tended against the communarchs insofar as they were ready to negotiate with the Prussians. The Prussian troops entered peacefully. Two days later Prussian and now French cavalry were riding quietly about the town stirrup to stirrup. That was not the way it was supposed to work. Perhaps the situation was not so normal after all.

But then in September the French were driven back to the Rhine by the Imperials and normalcy seemed to return. The Weissenburg Councils received a note from Hardenberg thanking them for their "voluntary submission" but reporting that the government in Berlin did not think it wanted Weissenburg after all and had ordered the troops withdrawn, along with those in Nürnberg and Windesheim. Berlin, to Hardenberg's disappointment, had become nervous now about its relations with Austria, and its enthusiasm for Franconia had cooled accordingly. Hardenberg still commanded his bureaucracy from Ansbach, though. The single-headed eagles remained on the walls, and the cloister became administrative center for the surrounding county. In the hands of the officials there the "purification" process drove deeper into the murky tangle that had protected the town's perquisites and powers—within the town as well as without, because the Weissenburg regime and the properties and status of its citizens could not be neatly marked out at the wall.[22] Not to Hardenberg's satisfaction, anyway. Only half the half-million population of his principality considered itself directly subject to his territorial government,[23] and Weissenburg's contribution to the cloudiness was for him no different from the rest. Vienna was far away, so

[22] So far the narrative of internal events has relied mainly on L. Götz, *Die Beziehung Weissenburgs zum Fürstentum Ansbach und zu Preussen, insbesondere in den Jahren 1796 und 1804* (Weissenburg, 1904), and on Voltz, *Chronik*, pp. 174–181; the jurisdictional maps in Hofmann, *Atlas,* clear up a number of gaps and inconsistencies in those accounts. For Hardenberg's policies at this time see Fritz Hartung, *Hardenberg und die preussische Verwaltung in Ansbach-Bayreuth von 1792 bis 1806* (Tübingen, 1906); C. Meyer, *Preussens innere Politik in Ansbach und Bayreuth;* and Hans Haussherr, *Hardenberg: eine politische Biographie. I. Teil: 1750–1800* (Köln, 1963).

[23] Reuter, *Manufaktur im fränkischen Raum*, p. 5.

was Berlin for that matter, and both of them had more than Weissenburg to think about; besides, plenty of old assertions of territorial rights and sovereignty could be dug out of the archives. Purification from the cloister meant that many citizens found themselves paying to Prussia taxes they had never heard of before, or paying other taxes twice because both the town and the cloister claimed them. About that time the Bürgermeister began to complain of growing disrespect from the citizens.[24]

Under such conditions domestic political life seems to have grown steadily more unpleasant during the later nineties; then in July, 1800, French troops appeared again and demanded a large contribution in money and in horses. The asking price was reduced in return for a cash *douceur* paid the officer in charge out of the pockets of the negotiating uncles; but the French returned again and again with ever-greater demands, naming sums really beyond the town's capacity to pay. The Councils thought they would have to turn to Prussia again; but because such a step was now openly a constitutional question, involving the imperial privilege, the issue was put to a general vote by the citizenry. The town voted 306–98 (really a substantial dissenting vote as Weissenburg balloting went) that they should seek Prussian help.[25] This time the government at Ansbach (Hardenberg himself having moved on to Berlin) put it to them squarely and publicly: if the town wanted Prussia to intervene with the French on their behalf they must submit to all the claims of the King of Prussia and unanimously beg his protection. The substantial "No" vote, though, apparently ruled that out; at any rate Weissenburg undertook to pay the French. A Jewish banker appeared on the scene with an offer to lend the appropriate sum, but the Councils found the interest rate too high, or perhaps they reasoned that the French would take all they could scrape together anyway: they determined to pay out of their own resources. Meanwhile Prussia increased pressure for acknowledgment of its full sovereignty beginning at the walls. Successive efforts to play the two powers against one another increased the pressure from both. In the end the French did occupy the town until quite large levies had been collected: an amount about three times the normal annual

[24] Voltz, *Chronik,* pp. 182–184.   [25] Ibid., p. 187.

budget, not counting what the French absorbed in less formal ways. Apparently the troops behaved well; that was Weissenburg's experience throughout the wars. But many citizens put their valuables in the cloister or fled with them to the Ansbach-controlled villages during the occupation and the raising of the levies by town officials. Quarreling over how the burden was to be distributed caused the sharpest dissension within the town for the whole period; probably this was the most ticklish time for the uncles. Fiscally as well as politically the strain was severe, and took its toll. But even so the community structure held.[26] On one occasion the citizenry, or enough people to look like the citizenry, appeared before the town hall and demanded that the Councils lead them forth to uproot the Prussian turnpikes outside the gates; the Councils demurred. Town Attorney Friedrich Wilhelm Roth mysteriously disappeared with his family. He came back in the baggage of the Bavarians and resumed office on the day Weissenburg surrendered its imperial status: September 19, 1802.[27]

The general nature of the bartering of the Imperial Delegations at Regensburg was well enough known in the summer of 1802 for it to be clear that Weissenburg was about to become subject to some prince; the only question was which. The answer came when troops of Montgelas' Bavaria entered the town at the end of August. A month later, after the publication of the German territorial settlement, a very brusque Bavarian commissioner appeared with new detachments of soldiers, who were quartered on the town; he was escorted to the town hall by a reception committee of three Roths, a Preu, a Schnitzlein, and Pflegamt administrator Huber. Town officers and citizens were summoned "in black dress" to hear his pronouncements: all documents thenceforth would be phrased as coming from Bavarian authority; there would be no trafficking with non-Bavarian courts, especially imperial ones; the Bavarian arms would be put on church, town hall, and gates. The commissioner put public treasuries under Bavarian seal, took the keys to archives, files, and offices, and confiscated the town seal. He further required a detailed inventory of town

[26] Rowan, "Steueramt," pp. 18–28, describes the fiscal methods used.
[27] Voltz, *Chronik*, pp. 188–196.

resources and their management (what consternation that must have caused, and one hopes some mirth as well), and a list of town officers—with biographies. He asked about the town militia, and was told there had been none since 1800: it had proved useless and the town had needed money that year. All civic officers were sworn to the Bavarian Electorate, down to gutter clearer and shepherd. But they were the old officers. The popish Elector at Munich was put into the official prayers at the churches. But the deacons sworn in as secular administrators were two Roths and a Preu.[28] The traditional Friday evening door-to-door begging was abolished in favor of systematic support for the "genuine poor."[29] But little else of consequence seems to have occurred during this first Bavarian period; less than a year after their arrival the town was turned over to Prussia again, in a boundary treaty of 1803.

The Weissenburger had some experience at changing masters by now; they knew what mattered, and put it in a petition they had ready for the entering Prussian territorial commission. They asked to keep the forest, with hunting rights; they asked for freedom from conscription, quartering, and labor levies. They asked that the sale of local real estate be forbidden to "foreign persons, not of this community," and that Jews be forbidden to trade or live in the town. They asked for Prussian guarantee of town debt, and full pensions for all officials, amounting to their customary receipts from all sources when in office. They asked for town administration of local affairs, of the church, endowments, and taxes, a town court, and legal immediacy under Ansbach— as it had been, they said, under His Majesty the Emperor—rather than administration by those busybodies right there in the cloister. And they asked for a new grain storage and exchange and a new cattle market. The conveniently named Friedrich Wilhelm Roth, Town Attorney and now Town Recorder as well, the man who had returned with the Bavarians the year before, was named representative to the Prussian commission, and went to meet them

---

[28] Narrative of this first Bavarian takeover is mainly from Ludwig Götz, *Der Übergang der ehemaligen Reichsstadt Weissenburg a. S. an Kurpfalz Bayern am 9. September und 29. November 1802* (Weissenburg, 1903).

[29] Voltz, *Chronik,* pp. 202–203.

in the company of Bürgermeister Sonnenmeyer, Pflegamt Administrator Huber, and Chief Forester Roth.[30]

The Prussians paid no apparent attention to the petition. Ansbach told the uncles to consult county officials at the cloister respecting their future duties. The clergy was ordered to put off its customary white ceremonial costumes and put on black; new Prussian prayers replaced the old ones. All special local holidays were abolished, and Thanksgiving moved from a Tuesday to a Sunday; Good Friday on the other hand, which had been a minor holiday in Weissenburg, was elevated now to a major one. A professional bureaucrat was installed as Director of Justice and Police (so much for separating justice from administration), with Town Attorney and Recorder Roth, whose relations with the Prussian commission were altogether friendly, to help him out. Weissenburg did get its local court, but it was staffed and run by officials with outlandish names. A workhouse was opened in the former Latin School, and fire insurance introduced. The grain market was built, but seems to have done little business, probably because not much grain found its way casually into Weissenburg in those years. The precincts were lettered and the houses numbered; Weissenburger had addresses now: nobody had needed them before. All sons of citizens were measured and registered for conscription. Meanwhile all town officers were provisionally retained, with full pay and perquisites. Street-corner politicking and the trappings of office remained theirs, and in the end no doubt that proved important. But they were neither in the courts nor in the county administration where decisions were made nor in the police—except of course for Town Attorney and Recorder Roth. Then in February and March of 1806, Weissenburg, along with the rest of the Ansbach territory, was occupied by French armies for transfer back to Bavaria. Church school director and organist Staudinger came home from church and shot himself dead; Town Attorney and Recorder Roth somehow got a hasty appointment as Police Director of Weissenburg, just ahead of the Bavarian resumption of sovereignty.[31]

The new Bavarian commissioners followed much the same

---

[30] Götz, *Weissenburg und Preussen,* pp. 25–28.
[31] Ibid., pp. 26–31; Voltz, *Chronik,* pp. 203–231.

pattern the Prussians had, but carried it further. The eight major annual markets were moved from Apostles' days to Sundays. There was smallpox vaccination. Town commons were divided: each householder eventually got a little snippet for himself, and paid the treasury for it. Most town officers retained their titles and their pay, and a town militia was set up, with sons of the better families as officers, in uniforms two shades of blue. Then in 1808 came the new state legislation for communal organization. Weissenburg was thrown into a juridical and administrative district whose seat and weight was in Catholic Eichstätt, over beyond the Wülzburg; and the town court was abolished in favor of a Catholic professional judge who refused to live or sit in Weissenburg and held court in a small Catholic town nearby. A new tax office was set up in the cloister, directed by professionals sent in by the state. Police administration—detailed oversight of the trades, public order, and welfare—was located in the state administrative hierarchy, and entrusted for the time being to Friedrich Wilhelm Roth, whose principal aides were a young civil servant and two former soldiers, none of them Weissenburger.[32] There was a single Town Council, now called a Municipal Council, of five (recall the lush days when the Councils had numbered dozens); it met under the direction of the Police Director and was explicitly forbidden any judicial function. And now Town Attorney, Recorder, Commissioner, and Police Director Roth was promoted and transferred to Munich, and so disappears from this story—the one figure in all of it who had a foot both in the old local regime and in the administrative state. By now he was a most unpopular man in Weissenburg, and was regularly slandered by the townspeople. His powers, and the direction of all town administration, were delivered over to the state court.

All in all it was a strong attack on the communarchy. And the 1808 ordinance struck at nepotism, oligarchy, and abuses from below as well as above: the Municipal Council over which the Police Commissioner presided was to be elected, at frequent intervals, by the whole citizenry. But when the people spoke it was for the familiar eminent names: the only names on the Council were Staudinger, Pflaumer, Roth, and Schnitzlein. Elections were

[32] StAW A. 19/20 Jh. 191.1: Personal des Stadtmagistrats, 1806–1808.

carried out under the direct supervision of state inspectors; it is hard to doubt their legitimacy. Their results were yet more communarchal than the cooptive elections of the old days; it would be hard to find better proof of the rubbery resiliency of the political community than that. And with declining confidence at Munich the assault weakened. In 1813 Weissenburg was allowed to have its own Police Bürgermeister, with an important administrative and judicial role, and a Commune Administrator who managed town properties; these two officers, together with three other Councilors, constituted the Magistracy, another name for the old (but reduced) Inner Council. Their names were Roth, Staudinger, Schnitzlein, Pflaumer, and Fleischmann. In 1817 Weissenburg even got its own town court back, separate from the county, although Munich defiantly sent one Xaver Müller, of Kempten and Munich, to be its chief judge. Three days before he arrived in Weissenburg, Montgelas finally fell from power.[33]

The Bavarian town

A month after Montgelas' fall a royal order returned to the "political community" full control over town property and local endowments. The Bavarian Constitution of 1818 and the Community Ordinances that came with it generally limited state powers in communities like Weissenburg to oversight through judicial review and administrative appeal. All Weissenburg citizens shared in the indirect oral election of a representative council of Community Deputies of twenty-four, which in turn elected by written ballot a collegial administrative magistracy of eight, with a Bürgermeister and a neo-Pflegamt. Through these bodies the town again controlled the admission of new citizens, the licensing of trades, and most church, school, and welfare matters. The grain market was handed over to the town government and entrusted to two members of the magistracy; it began to prosper.[34] All seemed very much like old times.

The half-dozen years that followed were quiet ones; it hardly

[33] Hofmann, Atlas, pp. 196–201; Voltz, Chronik, pp. 218–238.

[34] Hofmann, Atlas, pp. 200–208; Voltz, Chronik, pp. 44–45, 225–238. The Gemeindeordnung is in BayGes 1818, pp. 49–95; and the Wahlordnung on pp. 477–555. For a more general description of this Bavarian legislation, see below, pp. 271–273.

pays to recount the continuing recovery of internal equilibrium. Indeed it was so very much like old times that it seems to go against the grain of the story to find that in 1821 only three of the eight members of the inner or administrative council bore the names of eighteenth-century councilmen. Two more bore eighteenth-century citizens' names of lesser import; the rest were people who had arrived in the past twenty years. And that composition did not change in the 1824 elections. Confusion, though, would be unwarranted. For thirteen of the twenty-four Community Deputies of 1821 had eighteenth-century council names, and twenty-one of them had old Weissenburg citizen names. In 1824, when the number of Deputies was reduced, the number of eighteenth-century council names rose to fourteen out of eighteen, and every one of the eighteen was of eighteenth-century citizen family.[35] These are figures that would have seemed right for the Councils of the eighteenth century. The uncles' regime was located now in the representative council of Community Deputies, a stronger Outer Council by virtue of holding the former Electoral College's right to appoint the administrative magistracy, and a veto power over lesser town offices. That is was orally elected at large does not seem to have changed it much.[36]

The strongest evidence that the community had come through the political crisis without changing its ways was the trades licenses issued—Gewerbe-Concession now took the place of Meisterbrief. Licenses were issued by the magistracy, which received and almost always followed the recommendations of "those engaged in the trade," though on occasion the magistrates were more liberal than the guildsmen, and the infrequent appeals to the state court show that it was likely to be more liberal still. The records run from 1819 to 1825, when the power to license trades was taken over by state officials again; and during that time the town licensed an average of twenty new tradesmen a year—exactly the rate at which it had admitted new citizen-masters in 1780–1805. The trades are much the same as in 1780–1805, too, except that some who might

35 StAW A. 19/20 Jh. 93: Gemeinde-Ersatzwahlen 1819–22; 19/20 Jh. 94: 3. Gemeindewahl; BayMF 1822, pp. 299–301; and 1824, p. 2537.

36 About six hundred citizens had the franchise in 1824, in a population of four thousand souls in five hundred houses. StAW A. 19/20 Jh. 72: Statistische Notizen 1824; StAW A. 19/20 Jh. 94.

have appeared as butchers then appear now as swine merchants; there are more brandymakers; and the almost total absence of new braidmakers and wiredrawers marks a sharp recession in the gold-lace trade. The pattern is clear in the following summary figures;

Trades licensing in Weissenburg, 1819–1825

Year	Total	Old family	Old family (%)
1819 (first half)	26	21	81
1819/20	9	8	89
1820/21	18	17	94
1821/22	18	16	89
1822/23	18	16	89
1823/24	18	15	83
1824/25	25	19	76
1825 (second half)	11	8	73

it does not vary much from year to year. The eccentric figure for 1819 reflects the prompt simultaneous licensing of fifteen established and middle-aged butchers from traditional Weissenburg families.[37]

The record does not show whether the slight relaxation toward the end of the period is significant or not. Taking the period as a whole, the striking result of comparing this table with the table on page 221 is that Weissenburg's political economy seems if anything to have become more ingrown and restrictive than ever.[38] Seventy-six per cent of the new masters (and citizens) in 1780–1805 had been the sons of citizens, but now that same group of names, a generation later, accounted for 85 per cent of all trades licenses, which still ordinarily were required for full civic rights. Rejected applications show that this was not caused by natural demographic stagnation: of the twenty-one applications rejected in 1819–1825, ten bear names that do not appear on the 1780–1805 citizen-master lists.

[37] StAW A. 19/20 Jh. 1503.1: Die Quartalanzeigen über die ertheilten und abgeschlagenen Gewerbe-Concessionen, 1819–1825. "Old family" here means a name that appeared on the *Bürgeraufnahme* lists as citizen's son between 1780 and 1805.

[38] It is impossible to say whether this is related to the gold-lace decline and contemporary changes in the structure of German textile industry.

Outsiders got half the rejections but only 15 per cent of the concessions. There having been 120 applications from insiders approved, and only 23 from outsiders, it follows that an outsider was four times as likely to have his application refused than a native, even though one might expect an outsider to have a better objective case before presenting himself to the uncles. And of the ten insiders who got rejections (one of them twice), five were accepted within the period after fulfilling certain conditions, such as marriage, imposed by the magistracy or by "those engaged in the trade." One outsider was turned down twice, and the second application of another approved by order of the state court; no other outsider tried more than once. The outsider who tried unsuccessfully twice was a cutler from Baden; and although he had the unusually high capital of eight hundred gulden he was turned down on motion of the Poor Board: there was no cutlers' guild in town. The community was learning to use other institutions. The very next applicant was a butcher named Roth who was licensed although he had no capital at all; and another Roth a little farther on was licensed as a brewer with only the entry "Unnecessary" in the column designated for professional references.

The acquisition of civic rights was now a separate legal transaction from the economic license, and it bore a formidable title reflecting an effort to analyze out what the old Bürgerrecht had consisted in: Settlement, Marriage, Home, Citizen, and Forest Use Rights.[39] No statistical analysis of this new Bürgeraufnahme is possible because of the tangle the new categories caused: in place of the laconic entries in the old Citizens' Book are the helter-skelter piles of sworn testimony to this and to that, and of protocol that the rules called for and that might be needed in case of appeal outside the town. Sampling suggests that the criteria for admission were much like those of the eighteenth century: sons of citizens were admitted regularly, while the best entry for an outsider was to marry a citizen's widow (or, as it turned out, to keep the application alive until the state changed the rules in 1825).

Yet the political and social barriers to membership, though still

[39] StAW: Repertorium über Ansässigsmachungs-, Verehelichungs-, Heimat-, Bürger-, und Waldnutzungsrechtsverleihungsakten.

applied, showed signs of weakening. That may be a reason why the economic ones were being strengthened. If outsiders were in fact penetrating the civic community in greater numbers, that was something the Weissenburger had call to talk about, and we may be sure they did. Among claims to citizenship rights by outsiders is this one: I must be let in so I can marry and legitimize my children, and support them. One Adam Schreiner from a nearby village appealed a rejection by the magistracy to the county court, and the town countered in support of his exclusion with a list of "Day Laborers," *Tagelöhner,* now resident in the town, arguing that their number was already too great for the community to lower its defenses. Their number bore almost exactly the same proportion to the citizen population that resident aliens had borne to citizens at the end of the seventeenth century.[40]

They were indeed the old *Beisitzer*—names alien to the citizens' lists, plus a sprinkling of dependent female relatives and widows, and a few outcasts, with Weissenburg names. But now they were called Day Laborers. Now the cutler from Baden was turned down by the Poor Board. In the early 1820's it seemed that Weissenburg had got through thirty years of European revolution, war, and administrative turmoil without undergoing any serious change in its habits or in its communal structure. But the names of things had changed, and that was changing the rules a little.

[40] Friedrich Blendinger, "Die erste Volkszählung in Weissenburg im Jahre 1688," *Uuizinburc/Weissenburg,* p. 101; Schreiner's folder under the Repertorium cited in note 39 above.

CHAPTER VIII

Community Identified

NAPOLEON'S fall seemed a cosmic event to Europeans, cosmic in the literal sense of signifying a pattern encompassing everything. All are present at Armageddon. "World history is the world court," declared the philosopher Hegel, a man of those days. *Weltgericht* is the word Germans use for the Last Judgment, and the earnest shoemakers of Bremen used it in a petition of January, 1814, to abolish the occupational freedom that Napoleon's Code had enstated. "Events have shown, to everybody's cost, what that vaunted freedom has meant; . . . the World Court held on the plains of Leipzig has decided the fate of our good town too"; and its Júdgment called for "the return of our honorable, centuries-old associations, the restoration of the rights and privileges won by our fathers." The Bremen guilds were restored.[1]

Along the range connecting Hegel with the shoemakers, many others sought in their own ways a universal key or dimension within which to locate their affairs. German religiosity and German metaphysics both were preoccupied with the meaning of Bonaparte's rise out of revolution, his power, and his fall. German scholars looked to the past, to history, to learn there what had condemned the empire of universal reason. They turned to history in a frame of mind that a century and a half before might have attracted them to astrology, or a century and a half later to sociology or anthropology. Everybody was in history now. Intellec-

[1] Böhmert, *Zunftwesen,* pp. 135–136.

tuals were no less set on finding total and coherent pattern in history than the eighteenth-century members of their general estate had been on finding it in reason and logical system, and in the search of those years they framed the German intellectual tradition that is still quite alive, although shaken by the effects of the two great wars of the twentieth century.

The characteristic historical schools of German scholarship taking shape then—in law, philology, economics, literary criticism —acknowledged their mutual relations and their common birth.[2] Nearly all of them did obeisance to Justus Möser of Osnabrück. Among them they made the community into a kind of German Adam. Meanwhile German lawgivers and administrators were obliged for political reasons to concede to the home town a primordial right to exist for its own sake.

Home towns as the German Adam: Karl Friedrich Eichhorn

Law was the chief link between scholarship and society, and among the historical schools probably jurisprudence had most to do with the affairs of the hometownsmen, as towns and general estate emerged from the Napoleonic encounter. Friedrich Karl von Savigny is called the founder of German historical jurisprudence, but his fame rests more on his public leadership and his polemical achievements than on his scholarship. His student Karl Friedrich Eichhorn did more than Savigny to work out the implications of historical jurisprudence for contemporary society and law.[3]

Eichhorn's great work, *The History of German Politics and Law*, began to appear in 1808, two years after the formation of the Rhine Confederation and the end of the Holy Roman Empire; and it was finished in 1823.[4] In the midst of this work he took time to

[2] The brothers Grimm studied law under Savigny at Marburg, along with Eichhorn; and there they became friendly with Savigny's brother-in-law Clemens Brentano and with Brentano's friend and collaborator (in *Des Knaben Wunderhorn*) Achim von Arnim. The latter two became chiefs of the Heidelberg Romantic Circle, and Eichhorn acknowledged the contributions of Jakob Grimm's researches to his own understanding of German law.

[3] Albion Small begins his *Origins of Sociology* (Chicago, 1924) with the German historical school of jurisprudence, and describes Eichhorn's *Rechtsgeschichte* as the cornerstone of modern social history: pp. 63–79.

[4] *Deutsche Staats- und Rechtsgeschichte*. My page citations below are to the

write a long essay, a hundred and seventy-five pages, on "The Genesis of the German Town Constitution" for Savigny's new "Journal of Historical Jurisprudence."[5] In that essay, an indication of how he prepared and how his mind was set for the major work, Eichhorn put forward a description of the early medieval German communities that amounts to the home town of his own time: here is the familiar interlocking relation of community, propriety, and honor; here is the "freeman" who, because he is without those attributes, is subject to a territorial sovereign unless he can gain acceptance to a community; here are birth within wedlock, socially sanctioned marriage, and legitimate heirs as conditions, because they are bonds, of communal membership; here is the contradiction in principle between sovereign official and community; and all the rest. Where his German sources grew too thin for all conscience, Eichhorn supplemented them with Hume's *History of England* and English legal collections from the times of Edward the Confessor and Canute, for after all the Anglo-Saxons were Germanic too.[6] He did not quite reach the position of so many hometown historians from his time to the present: that the earliest towns before records appear must have been like presently visible home towns because, as is well-known, hometownsmen cling stubbornly to tradition. But there is no doubt of the present-mindedness and more important the future-mindedness of his work, especially that part for which he took special time out to help inaugurate Savigny's journal: the primal nature of community. Eichhorn was neither a political conservative nor an antiquarian in quest of quaint legal artifacts. He wanted to know and to show how the communities had got there.

Eichhorn had addressed himself to the critical task of his generation of jurists and politicians: to reconcile the kind of social relationship that persisted independently of the positive codes of lawgivers and defied them, those extant communal relations that Möser had loosely identified historically and that the Napoleonic era had thrown into high relief, with larger groupings of men and

---

4th ed. (4 vols.; Göttingen, 1834–1836); I include §§ citations that seem to have been consistent in all editions.

[5] "Ueber den Ursprung der städtischen Verfassung in Deutschland," ZGR, I (1815), 147–247; II (1816), 165–237.

[6] I (1815), 176–180.

families, towns, countryside, and state: to see the relation between the familiar community and what Germans still distinguish as the greater home, *die grössere Heimat*. It was the task of reconciling *Gemeindebürgertum* with *Staatsbürgertum*, community membership with state citizenship; and the cosmopolitan Justi's easy abstractions about wholes and individuals, now they had been tried, would no longer serve. Like most historians Eichhorn wrote his story forward like a chronicle, from the earliest time to the most recent; but even more than most historians he thought it backward, trying to master the contemporary problem that concerned him by tracing it toward its beginnings; and I shall describe his work that way, starting with the last parts of it and moving toward the beginning parts. For Eichhorn was seeking a central unity, seeking it within German law and custom now that conquest and code had failed to provide it; and he thought he could find it at the heart of a bulb whose overlayers were the accidents and corruptions and divisions that time had brought. The peeling outside of the bulb seemed stained, irregular, and scarred; but if he could work back, identifying the causes of corruption and irregularity as he went along, he might eventually reach the pure heart of the thing, in its earliest existence; that would be what the later stages and the contemporary eccentric shapes had, underlying them, in common, and that would be their essential nature.

It was a procedure very like Jakob Grimm's philology: both men worked toward a distant past where pure and single law, or language, existed; variations of dialect, or of local institutions, were to be explained by intervening events; the variants were comprehensible and legitimate insofar as they could be traced historically back to the common origins. Grimm argued, for example, that "history teaches us to recognize in language, the farther we are able to follow it up, the higher perfection of form, which declines as culture advances," and that "people of simple customs everywhere maintain a coherence [*Zusammenhang*] in faith, law, and custom; it is a free commonality, which allows many differences and variants." [7] The peculiar quality of German ways was variability of form in place and time without loss of essential unity.

[7] *Teutonic Mythology*, tr. James S. Stallybrass, III (4th ed.; London, 1883), vi (preface to the 2d ed., 1844); *Geschichte der deutschen Sprache*, I (3d ed.; Leipzig, 1868), 81.

Like history; like the home towns. *Historical* unity did not require uniformity. History could encompass things and show relations among them that static analysis could not. Through history, variety could be reconciled with unity; there unifying principles could be found that did not violate the true essentials of the variants. Grasp of historical evolution would supplant systematic grasp. It would be possible to understand and to govern Germany without contradicting its nature: what enlightened autocrats from Justi to Bonaparte's minions had failed to do. Of course the pure white part of the bulb is the most recent part, not the oldest, so that the metaphor (which is mine and not Eichhorn's) has significant defects; but so had the method. Eichhorn knew when he began writing that he would find something like the home town at the historic heart of German society.[8]

Both the German Rhine Confederation experience of 1806–1813 and the French Revolution that introduced it, Eichhorn said, had been political disasters, and they derived from a pair of related general errors: the transformation of rules made for administrative convenience into constitutional law, and a misuse of social contract theory. Territorial changes had begun with a pretense of constitutionality, but giving the new rulers free hand in civil and military administration had opened the way to unconstitutionality: a trampling on legitimate institutions and duly acquired rights by the "raging haste" of the bureaucratic class which in those days reached its pinnacle of power and independence. No doubt administrative unity was necessary; no doubt territorial sovereignty had to be acknowledged; anybody who denied that was a fool. But it ought to have been done by adaptation, not by leveling destruction. And so it might have been done if the essentials had been understood. Towns should not have lost their local administrative and police powers, their corporate property, their capacity to discriminate wisely in the imposition of taxes and punishments. The separation of justice from administration violated Germanic institutions [certainly it violated a home-

[8] On Eichhorn's contemporaneity Böckenförde, *Verfassungsgeschichtliche Forschung*, pp. 49–73. In the margins of the copy of Eichhorn's history that I used in Cornell University's Olin Library are these exclamations in a nineteenth-century hand, where Eichhorn describes the earliest Germanic communal institutions: "also *damals* schon . . . war *damals* schon. . . ."

town institution]; but it was not applied where it ought to have been applied: against the nobility.[9]

Eichhorn pointed to a tradition of historical study of German law dating from the early eighteenth century that ought, he thought, to have developed a base for constitutional procedures consistent even with the administrative demands of the time. Why had it not? Because of superficial and sloppy scholarly entrepreneurship. To compose a body of state law compatible with the peculiar institutions of localities meant a lot of work. "The more intensive the research had to be, to serve as a basis for a theory of territorial law created out of those sources, the happier the scholars of public affairs [*die Bearbeiter publicistischer Gegenstände*] were to save themselves the trouble of such labor, and preferred to get their principles out of general state law," administrators' law; and when territorial changes opened the way, these were the principles applied within the territories.[10] Eichhorn's resentment was not the familiar sour envy of scholarly opportunism, not altogether anyway; he truly believed and seemingly never stopped believing that if only everything concrete was known, and understood historically, it would fit together harmoniously without artificial constructions. He did not doubt the need for doctrine if that meant positive general descriptions based on true institutions; but he condemned the use of principles to make consistency, as being a facile way of papering over ignorance. Legislation based on principle led to the erroneous notion that laws and constitutions could be independently created by the lawgiver, in the same way that intellectual analysis made theory. That was the overweening pride of the revolutionary bureaucrat.

The fatal pride of the political revolutionary, French style, had been quite similar and had a comparable source in error. Social contract theory had begun as an effort to reconcile political sovereignty with a true existing society: so far, in its English and Dutch forms, so good. But the turn contract theory took within the quite different French social and political circumstances was the ruin of it; for there it was used to overthrow the existing order rather than to demand that laws and government reflect it: just what the bureaucrats had then gone on to do in Germany. The

[9] § 616: IV, pp. 729–739.   [10] § 616: IV, pp. 728–729.

fault lay not in Germanic law, with its emphasis on "the individuality of social circumstances," nor even with Roman law properly
understood. The danger and the disaster had come when contract
theory lost sight of the Germanic principle from which it had derived: the basic truth that "every state is a finite, given social condition"—living and flexible, but concrete. The American Revolution, conservative and customary though it had been in fact, had
opened the abyss when it was falsely theorized to mean a historic
step toward abstract freedom, a new society created by men.[11] In
French hands contract theory had been used to disrupt and destroy: the German counterpart misuse of contract theory (appearing in Germany under the name of Natural Law) was its creation
of a fictitious sovereign distinct from the society; that made of
administration a state machine, unmoved and unaffected by existing social corporations and *their* law; it freed the bureaucrats from
history and society at once. Legal changes were needed to be sure,
in Germany as well as France: for example, German society was
no longer really feudal, and German law needed reform to reflect
that reality. But the coarse practice had grown up of regarding
every historic institution as "feudal," even those that did in fact
still have social reality. Everything that was "traditional, national,
and individual" had been labeled feudalism by comparison with
easy abstract system. And the conservative reaction against this
was coarse and excessive too, ignoring the difference between
"the maintenance of founded right [*die Erhaltung des begründeten
Rechts*]" and "clinging to the contrivances [*Einrichtungen*] of a
past time." Eichhorn did not really explain how to distinguish between founded rights and past contrivances; but he opined that
failure to make the distinction had led to the confusion and crimes
of German youth movements, as well as to selfish reaction.[12]

Eichhorn's description of the Prussian General Code was less
wrathful because he sympathized with its aims and properly admired Frederick the Great, but his line of argument was the same;
and he saw the seeds of disaster in it. Frederick had avoided the
worst consequences of abstract sovereignty based on contract, for
though he had been absolutist still he had controlled his bureaucracy, allowing them to be no more than executive agents of himself

[11] § 614: IV, p. 703.   [12] § 614: IV, pp. 703–721.

as embodiment of the whole law; and his governance showed "the highest respect" for what he thought he recognized as "the existing constitution and traditional right." [13] The General Code was a culmination of long seventeenth- and eighteenth-century efforts to bring the coherence of Roman law together with the particularities of German law. But few scholars—none, really—were capable of true reconciliation of the Institutes with the infinity of real German laws and customs; nor was there any high German court capable of building a united system, after the imperial courts were driven out of the territories. The German jurists had arrived at the supposition that only foreign and imperial law could be called general and consistent, and that they encompassed, by principle and content, a different juridical world from German customary and local law. Even "codes" of German law like the one Bavaria had issued in 1756 were compilations, not codifications.[14] The Prussian Code had begun, under Cocceji (who died in 1755), the same way, as a compilation of German law in contrast with Roman codes that were too distant and abstract. But Frederick wanted something systematic, to speed and clarify justice; and the two aims combined, laudibly enough, in a project to take the Roman principle of systematic law, and make it specific and reconcile it with existing institutions—not to change legal institutions, let alone social ones, but to provide their organic form and mutual reference. Study of the legal sources, though, was too superficial (weak scholarship by other professors again) to support the project. The ground was not prepared for it (in the half-century the Code was in preparation). Thus the reconciliation between detail and system into German legal doctrine was not achieved; they could only approach each other.

That might not have been serious if care had been taken not to do any violence to true laws for the purpose of codification. But the authors of the Code had departed from actual law whenever they needed to fill gaps or to insert structural provisions to hold the whole thing together; that meant the intrusion of abstract theory wherever real material was not known to them. If they had identified the right local material the job could have been done then. Eichhorn was quite specific about it: true German law and

[13] § 613: IV, pp. 699–703.　　　[14] § 618: IV, pp. 758–765.

institutions were not intrinsically irrational or contradictory; they only seemed so because of insufficient respectful study, from which "abstraction" and "theory" were the fatal escape, the bad layers. But now, concluded Eichhorn with professorial passion, we can do it: now our experience with trying to apply general principles has *brought out* the particular into full view.[15]

To describe the particular in a coherent way, peel another layer off the onion, and now the late medieval and Renaissance town appears. The formal distinction between imperial and territorial town had developed then, but Eichhorn took little stock in it; whether the Emperor kept sovereign rights himself or delegated them to another affected a town far less than its internal political vigor and its capacity to exclude outside interference.[16] The important constitutional event of that period had been the development of artisans' associations into true guilds, with political roles commensurate with their economic functions. This happened in one of three ways, or a combination, or an evolution from one to another. First, a separate administrative section or a specified share of offices might be allocated to the artisan organization. Or (often following from the first), the whole citizenry might be divided up into political guilds, perhaps with patricians in one and with the others organized by trades, and with Council seats distributed among them all. Or an Outer Council might be set up, either as an alternative to the other forms of guild participation or together with them.[17]

The blending of guilds into community raised a historical problem, though, for the legal origins of guilds were actually to be found in Roman laws that grouped workers by trade, as a sovereign police measure. "But that," Eichhorn shrugged, "by no means belies the fact that the root of the institution can as readily be sought in the original German custom [*der ursprünglich deutschen Sitte*] of fraternal combination of individuals [*der Verbrüderung einzelner*] for given purposes."[18] Original German: that was reminiscent of Möser's agrarian communes; but Eichhorn

---

[15] § 618: IV, 766–787. [16] § 431: III, pp. 303, 308.

[17] § 432: III, pp. 309–312.

[18] § 312: II, pp. 493–495. See also § 243: II, pp. 157–161, for the blending of Roman and German law, and of artisans and magistrates.

was careful not to let visible countrymen represent community. Rural communes, he said, had been dissolved and the peasantry subordinated to the state, leaving commoners no escape from state domination but in towns: "for that reason no actual rural community could ever again come about." [19] Medieval community was described thus: "The immunity of the town community and its goods from the territorial court, and the right to choose its own officers for the administration of communal property, to exercise the community's corporate rights and the special rights conferred upon it, the maintenance of requisite order in general and oversight over pursuit of the town trades in particular (police), and the direction of communal affairs generally." [20]

With the destruction of rural Germanic community its essence had migrated to the towns then; into the town community Roman and German institutions blended, and authority blended with artisan guild. With the help of imperial immunities they had become "independent corporations, i.e., governed by their own unrestricted common will." [21] Their populations had grown as "freemen sought the fellowship [*Genossenschaft*] of such community"; and their quarrel with state power reached back to struggles in Carolingian times to regulate the entry of alien freemen into fellowship and into the trades.[22] Here Eichhorn's chronology became awkward, as Möser's had; he found particular community brought out into full view wherever he found a strong state apparatus. And here the old ambiguous freedom problem was becoming troublesome too, as it had for Möser but now in a more sophisticated way; and its connotations lay closer to Eichhorn's time (closer indeed to our own problems of civil freedom) than to early medieval servility and freedom: "Every kind of unfreedom could be ended by a declaration by the Master that he relinquished his rights. But that kind of *liberation* [*Freilassung*: Eichhorn's emphasis] could not by itself give full freedom, for it did not make the freedman a member of a people's community." Freedom to participate and to be somebody—work, marry, share—did not come automatically with civil liberation; such freedmen only became protégés of the

---

[19] § 345b: II, pp. 620–621.   [20] § 310: II, pp. 486–487.
[21] § 243: II, pp. 157–161.
[22] § 224: II, pp. 79–80; § 173: I, pp. 743–745.

state.[23] For "full freedom still depended on a fellowship of rights within a people's community." Here Eichhorn seemed to be talking about late Roman times; there is a touch of Tacitus and the un-Roman character of Germans; and his term now was *Volksgemeinde*. I might almost as accurately have translated it as "national community," for the German does not distinguish between the two meanings of *Volk;* and just here, writing of *Volk* and freedom, Eichhorn found his bridge between the communal particularity of the German people and the essence of German nationality. "The condition of true freedom was proof that one stood within the fellowship of rights of a recognized free *community* . . . full freedom was acquired [*erworben!*] by legitimate birth to free parents, or by the acceptance of an imperfectly free person into a free people's community: but never through any kind of liberation." [24]

The historical portrait Eichhorn had now achieved was a blend of the Roman privileged city with Justus Möser's socially enclosed primeval commune—a hybrid being that Pufendorf might have called a monstrosity even as he had the Holy Roman Empire of the German Nation itself. But it was manifestly the home town. Eichhorn did not, of course, confine his history of German law and politics to local law. There were plenty of emperors, nobles, and kings. The emphasis does not mislead, though, respecting either Eichhorn himself, or the corporative assumptions of German social and legal thinking. The communal town is a better place to seek out those assumptions than feudal estates or Roman corporations, if only because the Germanists who founded the tradition had little liking for nobles, kings, or Roman law. Nor had they any liking for a cool contractual view of social relations, because they did not think society was really like that.

A more recent constitutional historian puts the point (or problem) thus: "The point of departure of German law is the free, but morally bound, the *moral free will,* thus a *unified* conception of will, that reciprocally includes the marks of freedom and confinement, the being-for-itself and the being-for-others, of the individual and the communal." [25] Jakob Grimm, writing in 1810, alleged that the basis of real societies is love, and the more societies like

---

23 § 51: I, pp. 330–333.   24 § 48: I, pp. 314–318.

25 Lotheissen, *Der ständisch-korporative Gedanke,* pp. 6–7.

that there were, the better; universities recognized that in their *gemütliche Gemeinschaften,* he said, and trades guilds were another place to look for it. Apropos love he offered then an answer to Möser's rhetorical question of forty years before: should communities be forced to consider people honorable who just aren't? "It is a fact" (thus Grimm) "that ever since the guilds have been forced to accept illegitimate children the number of the latter has so increased, that far more people than usual are unable to get into any trade." [26] Guild moralism was on its way to the "social question." But more important, both guild moralism and embryonic social question were tied into the sense of nationality and of freedom the Germanists were developing. They tried to transfer the communal freedom of Möser and the home town, which was specifically and necessarily localized within the sphere of familiarity, into a national communal freedom: to make Bürger into *Staatsbürger* without changing him. But *Volksgemeinschaft* is a contradiction in terms: a whole people cannot have community: *monstro simile.*

The xenophobia attendant upon foreign wars, in which German states were made and unmade but communities remained, helped the notion along that German law was communal and bureaucratic law was alien, but did so along lines of a division that had long existed in the law and that reached crisis together with the foreign wars and the territorial change. The very typography of published legal documents had always changed back and forth between Gothic and Roman print with switches between German and Roman or French concepts. "We didn't become Romans," wrote Friedrich List in 1818, of the Napoleonic period, "but we stopped being Germans"; and to rectify that he called for a restoration of Germanic communal self-government.[27] Germany came to a national communal ideal by exposure to its opposite, and the Germanists made their critique of the Rhine Confederation in terms of a converse norm, which they found in national historic community.

Hegel, who had a clearer and more prescient mind than most of the historical school, found another way out: local corporate self-government was truly and rightly the townsmen's business, but

[26] *Über den altdeutschen Meistergesang* (Göttingen, 1811), p. 10.
[27] Lotheissen, *Der ständisch-korporative Gedanke,* p. 23.

common Bürger participation in state government was untrue and wrong, for that was the business of the general estate which bore the collective aim and spirit, restrained only by sovereign above and corporate resistance below.[28] Reinhart Koselleck has observed a split in German law and administration during the early nineteenth century: an academic branch that followed the historical school of Savigny and Eichhorn, and practicing administrators and jurists who followed Hegel.[29] That practical men followed the philosophical idealist Hegel, and academics the "concrete" historical school, bears thinking about; that German public life should have to choose between Savigny and Hegel, between the idealization of the past and the reification of ideals, seems misfortune enough; that they should ever have been combined seems predictably disastrous—intellectually, anyway, to begin with.

Old constitutions for new

The communal politics of the teens did draw on both: the restoration of "historic" local rights and the deliberate separation of the communities from general public affairs. In the circumstances of the time, the two amounted in practice to very nearly the same thing; and in the teens the home town was restored in a way that almost exaggerated its eighteenth-century character, for now the communities were recognized as a common form of government and social organization, not a random tangle of peculiar statutes and odd customs. In a way the hometown experience of the generation past had recapitulated the cyclical process that had operated severally in the eighteenth century: from outside intervention and pressure on local regimes beginning around the end of the century to reconsolidation in the 1810's. But the communities had gone through the process in step, in the same rhythm all through the individualized country, and so had the civil service, so that the hostility of motives between the two was recognized and the communities were acknowledged as general political phenomena to be reckoned with. Their history thenceforward entered into the history of the states. Before Napoleonic times there were

[28] Rosenzweig, *Hegel und der Staat*, I, 188; Hegel, *Philosophie des Rechts*, pp. 323–328, 403.
[29] Koselleck, *Preussen*, p. 143.

statutes and customs; afterwards there were community ordinances and state constitutions.[30]

The first place to see the continuity of Germany's eighteenth-century circumstances into the conjoined phase of hometown politics is the South German constitutional movement. Prussia's way was distinctive (but there will be more to say about that) and Hanover issued no constitution nor general community ordinances, reverting instead to a patrician-aristocratic political order with individual town statutes.[31] In the German South and West, where the greatest stability and variety had prevailed in the eighteenth century, the territorial changes had been the greatest too, so that the administrative challenge and the political tensions were doubly great there. The Vienna settlement of 1814–1815 generally retained the territorial arrangements of Rhine Confederation days for that region, but brought with it a reversion to eighteenth-century political styles; and the South German constitutions and provisions for local government were an outcome of that combination.

On the continental scale, the Treaty of Vienna and the German Act of Confederation restored the old principle of the Treaty of Westphalia: the interrelation of the European political system with the German internal constitution; Germany's federative balance and the not-quite-sovereignty of its several principalities.[32] The home towns, to be sure, had lost the power to appeal to outside jurisdictions, relying on tangled imperial laws and privileges, that had defended their autonomy in the old incubator. But the withdrawal of French power from the Rhine Confederation states restored this ability, albeit in a different political form. Jealousy among states, and between states and the new Bund, still served the home towns, but now it worked territorially rather than jurisdictionally; and now it got them general constitutional guarantees

[30] Cf. Lorenz von Stein, "Das Gemeindewesen der neueren Zeit," *DV* (1853) I, 41.

[31] Heffter, *Selbstverwaltung*, pp. 186–207; Meier, *Hannoversche Verfassungs- und Verwaltungsgeschichte*, II, 640–641, lists 106 Hanoverian town constitutions, and attempts a general description, pp. 450–555, enraged by the absence of clear general principles.

[32] See above, pp. 14–15 for the approving views of Arnold Heeren, historian at Göttingen. Compare his treatment in *Handbuch der Geschichte des Europäischen Staatensystems* (1st ed., 1809; I have used the 5th ed., Göttingen, 1830), I, 11–13, 159–160; and II, 78.

of their autonomy and integrity in place of individual state acknowledgments and outside protections. Imperial jealousies were supplanted by territorial anxiety among the rulers and the responsible ministers of the still-new states that lay over the individualized country like fragile political membranes—states which, as far as anybody knew, might be doomed relics of the era just past, doomed to disappear as the Grand Duchy of Frankfurt had done when the French and Dalberg's bureaucracy had disappeared. The danger was both domestic and foreign, and both at the same time as it had been (much more mildly) in the eighteenth century, but with two alterations. For one thing, governments did not know how strong or how "national" the new Bund was to be, nor how far central institutions or national appeals might be put to use by rival states to challenge them for the loyalty of their subjects and the integrity of their territories. Second, with German politics in phase the problem of fragmentary internal disaffection was now generalized and extended to include, out of recent experience, fear of revolution. During the teens internal disaffection still seemed an opportunity for rival states, even a greater one than before. Prussia was the main source of this kind of anxiety for so long (until about 1820) as Prussia maintained a constitutional posture, and until the Confederation was under the control of Metternich's Austria; but territorial rivalry among the South German states, for example between Baden and Bavaria over the Rhine Palatinate and between Württemberg and all its neighbors, operated similarly. Nobody knew in the teens that the Metternich era of territorial stability lay at hand; and the South German constitutions were the political instruments of the rulers to keep their acquisitions by popularity and concessions now that executive power was gone. Leopold von Ranke said the constitutions were adopted as necessary means—temporarily and unfortunately necessary—for holding restless and unfamiliar lands together in the absence of Napoleonic patronage.[33] He was prejudiced, but he was right.

[33] "Ueber die Trennung und die Einheit von Deutschland," *HPZ*, I (1832), 346–351. The essay is unsigned but undoubtedly the work of Ranke, the journal's editor. See also Montgelas on the need for a representative constitution "pour consolider le repos" in *Denkwürdigkeiten . . . über die innere Staatsverwaltung*, pp. 76–79.

In order to keep all the places they had obtained, the princes restored *to* the places they had obtained much of their local autonomy.[34] To the degree their executive sovereignty was insecure, princes had to act as politicians. The high hostility between bureaucracy and home town demanded a choice between the two on issues of local government, and the rulers chose the hometownsmen. It was the Bavarian Foreign Ministry, not Interior or Justice, that first ordered a restoration of local judicial powers to the town councils that had lost them.[35] The governments needed support from the kind of town leadership that "naturally" embodied communal "organisms." The Montgelas system, argued the ambitious Bavarian Privy Councilor Friedrich von Zentner before the Council of State, had rendered such local leaders "without influence and without effectiveness, subjected to the contempt and reproaches of their fellow-citizens." [36] Growing disrespect from fellow citizens had in truth been the commonest complaint from the avuncular magistrates absorbed or bypassed in Napoleonic times, not the technical loss of legal powers, for their authority had always depended more on civic respect than on laws; yet the blatant removal of their legal independence, and their incapacity to resist power intruding from outside, had undermined local government to a degree that now seemed politically dangerous, as well as administratively out of hand.

To get political unity and security (that is, to keep what they had got), the statesmen sacrificed uniformity and directness of administration, and the freedom of action of their bureaucracies. The political decision for the home towns forced the officials to retreat into political eclipse, or at least silence. Such a policy might speak of binding people to state and sovereign, as it had in Prussian reform thinking. Self-government seemed to some a happy combination of the two post-Napoleonic alternatives of popular government and historic rights, and many intellectuals were caught up with the idea: it seemed liberal inasmuch as it was antiautocratic,

[34] On the political motives, including fear of Prussia and of a strong centralized Bund, for the Bavarian Community Ordinance of 1818, Horst Clément, *Das bayerische Gemeindeedikt vom 17. Mai 1818* (Kassel, 1934), pp. 64–75.

[35] Ibid., p. 24.

[36] Bayerisches Hauptstaatsarchiv, Munich, Staatsrat (hereafter BHM Staatsrat), 2340. *Organismus* is Zentner's word.

and yet it fit together with the notion of historic corporate roots. It was not a synthesis, though, but a garble, and a naive one: in operating substance, in South and West Germany, it meant leaving the communities to their own devices, and in the hands of the cooptive-elective communal corporations, more than it did binding them to the state or the state to them. And there was another aspect of the policy of granting local autonomy, apart from acquiring popularity that way. It was not just a matter of giving people what they wanted, and what hometownsmen wanted was the home town. There was a constitutional ambivalence deriving from the political motives of the statesmen: They were ready to restore local privileges to the localities, but not to balance that with an accrual of political power outside the walls, in the affairs of the state at large; and the resurrection of the walls was a price states paid hometownsmen to keep out of state affairs, now that the states had failed to subordinate them. In the South German constitutions, unlike the system planned by Stein for Prussia and partly erected by his successors, there were no intermediate representative bodies lying between community and state levels, linking communal institutions by stages with general state institutions (allowing the Württemberg district assemblies as a partial exception). State-wide diets, though they often became arenas for the identification and defense of hometown interests and for occasional checks on bureaucracy, were not true legislative bodies nor yet estates emanating from corporate interests at successive governmental levels.[37] Consequently any autonomous powers the communities got in the teens severed their links with the state rather than integrating their political worlds into it—leaving, by the way, the scorned bureaucracy still the only effective "general estate," and still alien to local society.[38]

Prussian institutions of local government had come at the hands of the state, in the Stein legislation of 1808. Prussia again provides a foil: "Before 1808," wrote Savigny, "the constitutions of the Prussian towns, whatever their differences in detail, were alike in that the magistrates were very dependent upon the state officials

[37] The point is developed in broader terms in Loss, "Status in Statu," Chapter IX.
[38] Cf. Heffter, Selbstverwaltung, pp. 125–127.

and conversely very independent of the citizenry." [39] That describes the relative success of Prussian administrative autocracy and the passivity of Prussian local politics; and in such a context local self-government could be a reasonable means of invigorating political life and civic participation. In the individualized country by contrast, where the social communities had not been leveled by their brief Napoleonic encounter with autocracy, local self-government even when justified on the same principles meant not participation but separation of the communities from politics.[40] Even provisions for broadly based local elections and prohibitions of open cooption did not threaten hometown regimes as long as social controls and familiar status held; rather they strengthened the regimes' positions against the outside. The political direction of local self-government in Prussia was opposite to the political direction of local self-government in the individualized country because the starting points were different. Prussian town corporations had been too weak to link their populations into politics; hometown regimes were too strong.[41]

Consequently the Prussian reforms not only provide a foil, they began a process whereby Prussian local government and the home towns grew more like one another in the following decades. One must be careful not to exaggerate; at the beginning at least it was more a matter of direction than substance. Still the communal constitutionalism of Stein's Town Ordinance of 1808 reiterated many elements of the hometown constitution: citizenship consisting in the right to carry on town trades within the police district and to vote; an Outer Council bearing the name of Town Representatives and the exclusion from it of intellectuals, free professionals, and state officials. And even the elective pyramid leading from citizenry to magistracy tended to produce, with the passage of time and with long terms for town offices, stable avuncular regimes very like the home town's—almost certainly more like it than the old Steuerrats' regimes had been.[42] It can even be argued that the Stein reforms of local government paradoxically separated community from the whole society to a pernicious degree by

---

[39] "Die Preussische Städteordnung," *HPZ*, I (1832), 392.

[40] On the contrast see also Klein, *Entwicklung des Gemeindebürgerrechts*, p. 24.

[41] Koselleck, *Preussen*, p. 560.   [42] Ibid., pp. 567–568.

allowing insufficient state engagement in local affairs, especially inasmuch as the planned representative superstructure was not fully achieved.[43] But that separation is more a matter of which functions the bureaucracy reserved to itself and which it left in local hands. The state retained control over justice. In the larger cities it controlled the office of Chief Bürgermeister, and the police. The Prussian Revised Ordinance of 1831 combined strong bureaucratic features in some respects with further concessions to local corporate autonomy and individuality in others, coming on the whole closer still to the South German arrangement of leaving townsmen in control of their own nests while excluding them from the affairs of the generality.[44]

The sharpest difference between Prussia and the individualized country—it was a very significant difference, and the overcoming of it would be more significant still—had to do with economic organization. Stein's law of 1808 had provided that town districts would be the primary electoral units; it explicitly denied that role to guilds (to Stein's own later regret). Hardenberg's establishment of occupational freedom in 1810 then deprived the 1808 Bürgerrecht of one of its most important components, and encouraged fluidity of movement and occupation.[45] And the 1831 revision, while allowing local elections to be organized by occupational "classes," an updated turn toward hometown political patterns,

[43] Albert Hensel, *Kommunalrecht und Kommunalpolitik in Deutschland* (Breslau, 1928), p. 16.

[44] About that time the home towns of the individualized country began to change toward the Prussian pattern: see below, pp. 343–345. For the evolution of Prussian local government in a hometown direction, 1808–1831, Loss, "*Status in Statu*," pp. 418–420, and the sources cited there; also Reichard, *Ansichten*, pp. 52–57; Hartlieb von Wallthor, *Selbstverwaltung Westfalens*, I, 111; Savigny, "Städteordnung," passim; Friedrich C. Dahlmann, *Die Politik, auf den Grund und das Maass der gegebenen Zustände zurückgeführt*, I (2d ed.; Leipzig, 1847), 250–253. For a different and more democratic emphasis, rather like Preuss' for the eighteenth century, in which bureaucratic equals illiberal and in which avuncular regimes are bureaucratic, Heffter, *Selbstverwaltung*, pp. 92–98, 213–220; Koselleck's description mainly considers cities and the general estate, but outlines the neo-corporate character of Prussian local government ordinances: *Preussen*, pp. 560–637.

[45] But Ziekursch pointed out that in Silesia the artisan element, on the basis of the 1808 law, drove out the old (Protestant) state officials and took control of local government at the very moment when their economic organization was destroyed by Hardenberg: *Städteverwaltung*, pp. 152–165.

simultaneously raised property or income requirements for the suffrage, as distinguished from the simple, ungraded, local trade or property provision of 1808.[46] But in Prussia the local government issue did not arouse the kind of confrontation between bureaucracy and townsmen that it did elsewhere, because local self-government there was a bureaucratic gift to apathetic townsmen, and because the Prussian bureaucracy reserved its chief hostility for the nobility, who were not an important problem in the South. Besides, Prussian territorial gains did not raise the serious constitutional problems that the expansion of the South German states did; they were relatively much smaller, and the constitutional issues they produced were worked out within the administrative system itself, as a kind of bureaucratic federalism.[47]

In South Germany the recovery of hometown autonomy from the benumbed hands of the bureaucracy there took a number of forms, but the pattern is clear. The local rights individual communities had lost to the general laws and the territorial consolidation of Napoleonic times were now to be restored to them by general state constitutions and ordinances. Among the states that got constitutions in the restoration period—Nassau (1814), Württemberg (1819), Bavaria (1818), Baden (1818), and Hessen-Darmstadt (1820)—only little Nassau, the first, maintained a liberal bureaucratic regime, keeping French municipal government and occupational freedom; and that was more a victory over the constitutional movement than through it.[48]

In Württemberg the question of community rights over against the state was part of the struggle over the "Good Old Law" of pre-Napoleonic constitutional conservatism, which saw the government at Stuttgart pitted against hereditary privilege and against the organized power of corporate estates to influence the conduct of

[46] Contrast Savigny's description of these provisions, "Städteordnung," pp. 395–400, with Heffter's, *Selbstverwaltung,* pp. 213–220; and in between Koselleck, *Preussen,* pp. 574–577, who argues that the 1831 law, while introducing the *Einwohnergemeinde,* still not only confirmed but sharpened the distinction between *Staatsbürger* and *Stadtbürger.*

[47] On this very complex question, Koselleck, *Preussen,* passim; Heffter. *Selbstverwaltung,* pp. 117–123, 127–136.

[48] Heffter, *Selbstverwaltung,* pp. 117, 125. The Nassau Gemeindeordnung of June 5, 1816 is in Julius Weiske, *Sammlung der neueren teutschen Gemeindegesetze* (Leipzig, 1848), pp. 319–339.

government.[49] Württemberg was strong hometown country, and the Württemberg communities had an effective champion in the energetic and brilliant young Friedrich List from Reutlingen, a near-model home town with markedly effective and almost democratic institutions.[50] In the Napoleonic period Württemberg town magistracies had become state-appointed bodies, their judicial powers had been removed, and local endowments placed under state control.[51] That would seem on the face of it to place the hometownsmen on the side of the Good Old Lawyers in the constitutional struggle, and such was the initial impulse of many of the community leaders, probably most of them. Still if the home town had no love for bureaucracy it had none for privileged nobles or provincial potentates either, nor had the latter any interest in hometown autonomies: consequently by reducing its own presence the crown was able to split the townsmen away from its more serious enemies, the Good Old Lawyers. A state ordinance of June, 1817, established local bodies called Community Deputies (*Gemeindedeputierten*) "for the preservation of their interests against the magistrates" (at that time still state appointees); the Deputies had the right to speak for the town and all its citizens to the government if there was conflict with existing magistracies. The Deputies were to be elected by all full citizens, with signed paper ballots, and all Bürger petitions were to pass through them. At the same time the magistrates' terms of office were changed from the biennial appointments of mobile and removable state administrators to the life tenure of avuncular civic leaders grown into the lives of the communities where they served.[52]

The Good Old Lawyers opposed the strong Community Deputies —in effect the old outer councils—so as to gain the support of

[49] I cannot faithfully reproduce the complexities of this struggle here; standard descriptions are Albrecht List, *Der Kampf ums gute alte Recht* (1815–19) *nach seiner ideen- und parteigeschichtlichen Seite* (Tübingen, 1912); and Hölzle, *Zeitalter Napoleons.*

[50] Lotheissen, *Der ständisch-korporative Gedanke*, pp. 231–232; above, p. 50.

[51] Alfred Dehlinger, *Württembergs Staatswesen in seiner geschichtlichen Entwicklung bis heute*, I (Stuttgart, 1951), 268; and the many citations to Württemberg affairs in Chapter VII, above.

[52] WbgReg 18 VI 1817; Wintterlin, *Behördenorganisation in Württemberg*, II, 185–192.

provincial and local authorities whose powers the Deputies were designed to limit or replace. But the government's political ploy succeeded: despite election boycotts organized by the Good Old Lawyers, hometown civic leaders rallied to the royal measure because they correctly expected to be elected to the new offices.[53] As the constitutional struggle continued, the government pressed the tactic further: in 1818 the formerly state-appointed upper magistracy was replaced by a town council elected by the citizenry from among the citizenry, with a life-tenured administrative head chosen by the council and appointed by the state. The theory was that this chairman would act as a state official in matters within state jurisdiction and as a local officer in communal affairs. The size of the town council was between seven and twenty-one, depending on the size of the community, and practically all citizens were eligible to sit on it. The term of office was an initial two years, and then life tenure if reelected—a small modification of the old council systems, providing for citizen participation but very much the same stable composition as the more formally cooptive councils of the past.

Significantly, the ticklish and vital question of who had the right to grant the communal Bürgerrecht, bearing with it the right to vote, set up in a trade, marry, and so on, was left unsettled in these ordinances, or rather evaded with vague allusions to general legislation to come; but the Deputies got veto rights over budget and tax affairs which included imposition of the citizenship fee. Control over church, school, and poor endowments was returned to Council and local pastors, acting together, and administered by a lifelong local body subject to state oversight. Should there be conflict between Deputies and Council over any measure, then conditions were to remain "as they had been before [im vorigen Zustand]," unless that prevented officers from carrying out their duties, in which case there could be appeal to the state. Local judicial powers were entrusted again to the Council. There were some mild restrictions on the simultaneous presence of close relatives on the

[53] Württembergisches Haupt-Staatsarchiv, Stuttgart (hereafter WHS), E 31–32: G 585, Geheimer Rat, II, Gemeinde-Deputirten, 15 and passim. The political analysis seems to have come from Justinius Kerner, an associate of List's.

Council, but these were relaxed within a year: provincial courts were ordered to give dispensations in almost all cases.[54] And the Constitution of 1819 that culminated the Good Old Law controversy, while it declared that every state citizen (with certain special exceptions) must be a full citizen or a legal resident (Bürger or *Beisitzer*), said also that the acceptance of citizens was exclusively a community affair except in case of conflict, when the state could mediate "in accordance with existing law." It is not clear whether these laconic provisions between them meant that every Württemberg subject had to be placed in some community, or that the communities through the local acceptance power would exercise control over Württemberg citizenship; and the reason it is not clear is that both principles were present and they were contradictory. Neither did the constitution venture to say where existing law was to be found. But it forbade state officials to meddle with community property.[55]

The Bavarian constitutional struggle was quieter than Württemberg's, for it took place mainly within the ranks of government, in the form of intrigue and bureaucratic politicking around the faltering figure of Montgelas; but in the end the community "organisms" emerged in a similar position. While Montgelas remained first minister, the Bavarian government was divided and deadlocked. Projects to restore local judicial rights and control of endowments were beaten back by Montgelas' unwillingness to reconstitute the old town councils. The lower and middle bureaucracy with liberal views, and those who represented them in the higher councils of government, backed the absolutist Montgelas. The best historian of the Bavarian Community Ordinance, Horst Clément, wrote critically of Montgelas' "stubborn inability to adapt himself to new tendencies and forces," and describes his bureaucratic allies as "the most conservative and least reformist inclined of all," even though they knew better than anybody the difficulties of local administration—a puzzling situation that he attributes to "subaltern nervousness and skepticism" among junior officials.[56]

[54] WbgReg 1819, Ed. I, III, and IV; 23 I, 27 VIII 1819; Maurer, *Städteverfassung*, IV, 329–331. In 1818 the *Gemeindedeputierten* were renamed *Bürgerausschuss*.

[55] WbgReg 27 IX 1819.

[56] Clément, *Das bayerische Gemeindeedikt*, p. 33.

I cite the view to show the danger of conventional labels in this matter, and the need for describing administrative events in detail. For it was precisely the immediate professional experience and interest of rank-and-file administrators that made them unwilling to return local powers to the hometownsmen of the old days; and to call their position conservative and anti-reform begs the issue where it does not invert it. The frustration of their efforts to reform, to rationalize, to open up and thus to liberalize the local "organisms" made them look upon local magistracies and the communal societies that supported them as the stubbornest enemies of the state as they knew it, of their own professional success, and so of themselves—political enemies, class enemies. But now those enemies had been joined by politicians of high estate: King and State Councilors. It was a coalition of political men, in Munich and in the home towns, against administrators in the middle.

The deadlock was resolved by the fall of Montgelas on February 2, 1817. The first consequence for the home towns had to do with social controls and social endowments. A Poor Law of the preceding November, issued under the pressure of the harvest failures of that year, had insisted that the native community of every candidate for relief, his *Heimat*, must be responsible for supplying it; the law stipulated that no marriage of "unsettled [*unangesässenen*] persons" could be allowed without simultaneous acceptance of responsibility for poor support; any official who neglected this provision would be held financially responsible. These rules were to be administered by a board (*Pflegschaft*) composed of local officials: police commissioner, town physician, pastor, Bürgermeister, and representatives from the councils and from other categories of citizens in accordance with local circumstance.[57] Other laws on beggars, wandering tinkers and sharpeners, players, musicians, peddlers, Jews—the old dishonorable wanderers—reiterated the need to protect the community against such people: specifically that they should not be allowed to settle or marry unless accepted into the practice of one of the settled trades.[58] These were matters close to the hometown heart; and within weeks after Montgelas' fall a royal ordinance restored local endowments and communal property to the "political communities," explicitly

[57] BayReg 23 XI 1816.   [58] BayReg 23 X, 7 XII 1816.

revoking all the relevant Montgelas legislation since 1807. A difference of form between the 1817 law and the Montgelas ordinances it revoked is instructive. The bureaucratic edicts had categorized endowments thus: 1) for religious purposes, 2) for educational purposes, and 3) for charitable purposes, looking vertically down lines of administrative function; but the 1817 law drew horizontal political lines among 1) local and communal endowments, 2) "general" endowments, and 3) "other" endowments.[59]

The Bavarian restoration process went on through 1817 and 1818, in the seven provinces east of the Rhine; in the separately administered Palatinate, where French administrative law prevailed, the provincial administrators on the contrary assumed stronger control over community affairs.[60] The Community Ordinance that these measures had anticipated was finished in May, 1818; and it proposed, in the words of the general state constitution it accompanied, "the revival of the communal bodies through restoration of the administration of those matters most closely affecting their weal." [61] It did not apply to the Palatinate. On the whole it was a victory for the communities and the anti-Montgelas ministers and Council of State over the working officials of the Interior Ministry. State Councilor Maximilian von Lerchenfeld, one of the triumvirate that had replaced Montgelas (Thürheim and Rechberg were the others) described the kind of community contemplated by the ordinance as he repelled a bureaucratic effort to consolidate communities into district units: "The formation of larger composite communities would indeed make it easier for officials, but it does not follow [*geht nicht . . . hervor*] from the nature of true community: the living together, dwelling together, for centuries bound together, the sharing of the same communal interests among the heads of families." [62] The Council agreed that there would have to be a local administrative magistracy which

[59] Fries, *Nürnberger Stiftungswesen*, pp. 10–12.

[60] BayReg 12 III 1817, 12 X 1818; and Bavarian provincial Regierungsblätter 1817–1818, passim.

[61] BayGes 1818, pp. 49–95, 103.

[62] Clément, *Das bayerische Gemeindeedikt*, pp. 35–54, describes the debate within the government; the quotation is from Anton Schmid, "Gemeinschafts- und Gemeinderecht im altbayerisch-schwäbischen Gebiet," *ZBL*, IV (1931), 386.

had professional skill and at the same time the confidence of influential townspeople; the device used to accommodate these conflicting ends was a Magistrates' Council partly professional and partly nonprofessional in composition, affirmed by the state but chosen and overseen by a body of Community Spokesmen (*Gemeindebevollmächtigten*), with powers much like those of the Württemberg Deputies plus this elective one.

The Spokesmen were made to be strongholds of the familial leadership of the socially eminent, through oral and direct election by "real members of the community," as citizenship was defined. The police power over local social and economic life was turned over to the Councils, except in certain specified larger towns with more cosmopolitan economies and populations, where the Interior Ministry retained uniform control. In working out details for promulgating the law (a function they found most valuable), Interior Ministry officials tried to subvert it by inserting state commissioners with veto power over the Councils, but were defeated by Lerchenfeld. They also tried to insert a high wealth qualification for membership in the Spokesmen on the one hand, and a very wide suffrage for electing them on the other, an apparent effort to strike at the hometown regimes from above and below: communitarians by contrast wanted free and equal eligibility into the Spokesmen, for anybody who could get elected by the votes of Bürger homeowners, tradesmen, and artisans, excluding from the ballot academics, free professionals, and financial occupations, not to mention wage earners who rented their quarters or lived with their employers. Ultimately, eligibility to the Spokesmen was compromised so as to give wealth special weight in the largest towns and progressively less down the scale to the smallest, another recognition of how the nature of communities varied with their size; and the communitarians got their way about who was to elect them: "real citizens" only.[63]

[63] BayGes 1818, pp. 477–555; Clément, *Das bayerische Gemeindeedikt*, pp. 54–63; Wilhelm Imhof, *Die geschichtliche Entwicklung des Gemeinderechts im rechtsrheinischen Bayern seit dem Jahre 1818* (Munich, 1927), pp. 7–29. The bureaucratic case here was argued by Zentner, now Interior Ministry Director and later State Councilor, fervid spokesman of "organic" community when the ground was crumbling under his chief Montgelas in 1816–1817, but all bureaucrat when it came to writing promulgation ordinances in 1818: cf. Max Doeberl,

In Baden the communal body corresponding to the Bavarian Community Spokesmen and the Württemberg Community Deputies was called the Community Citizens' Committee (*Gemeindebürgerausschuss*), established by an "Emergency Decree" in 1821 to smother noisy confusion within the state administration and in the Diet. The lower chamber of the Baden Diet was dominated by a mixture of state administrators and local officers chosen by hometown constituencies; they were and are hard to sort out because many local officers whose political roots were communal had state appointments and were formally designated state officials.[64] Also, the Opposition in the Baden Diet was usually led by liberal civil servants, which confused both the hometownsmen's reflexive hostility to the state and the bureaucrats' natural distrust of local regimes; and the government was often able to use hometown issues to keep these two kinds of opposition from consolidating.[65] Diet debates over local government reflected the ambiguity. It could not resolve, nor did it even fully acknowledge the inconsistency between the two principles of local self-government: the one that saw it as a means of incorporating responsible citizens with the purpose of the state, and the one that saw it as defending corporate autonomy against leveling state domination.

As a result Baden got no general community ordinance in the teens or twenties; the administrative magistracy remained formally at least state appointees; and the hometownsmen had to make the Committees do. The liberal Interior Ministry official Ludwig

Entwicklungsgeschichte Bayerns, II (Munich, 1912), 416. Edward Shorter, "Social Change and Social Policy in Bavaria, 1800–1860" (unpubl. diss., Harvard, 1967), describes these processes differently, in a steadier continuum of modernization and politicization.

[64] On bureaucratic participation in the South German Diets—a lively issue involving political advantages nobody was sure about, and also the constitutional question of distinguishing the roles of representation and administration —the standard work is Wilhelm Clauss, *Der Staatsbeamte als Abgeordneter in der Verfassungsentwicklung der deutschen Staaten* (Karlsruhe, 1906), but his political analysis is weak; pp. 62–66, 88–91 for Baden in the teens and twenties.

[65] Lothar Gall, *Der Liberalismus als regierende Partei: Das Grossherzogtum Baden zwischen Restauration und Reichsgründung* (Wiesbaden, 1968), pp. 32–34.

Winter in the teens proposed an ordinance which would have endowed all inhabitants of a town—bureaucrats, teachers, "capitalists," the poor, Jews, and the rest—with full citizenship rights, the same as real citizens; Bürgermeister would have been removable by the state. But in violent debate the Diet rejected civic equality and state definition of communal rights. It concluded that communities ought to have full control over the extension of citizenship rights; and the control, along with veto power over fiscal actions by the state-appointed local magistracies, was handed over to the Community Citizens' Committees in the state decree of 1821. A three-class voting system was devised that made sure the Committees represented all the citizenry evenly, as follows: one third of each Committee was to be chosen from among the highest-taxed third of the citizenry, one third from among the next highest-taxed third, and the last third from among the lowest-taxed citizens, which guaranteed equal representation for the least prosperous (who however were still economically independent townsmen) against the natural gravitation of communal ballots toward the well-to-do and the prominent.[66] State officials and other noncitizen residents were excluded, and of course Jews.

The Baden Committees, like their counterparts elsewhere, were hometown bodies. Politically this was self-government; but socially there was nothing liberal about it, and it hardly seemed to draw hometownsmen into the whole society. All very puzzling: the liberal political publicist and theorist Carl von Rotteck averted his eyes from the strange "illiberality" of the views manifested in the Chamber in these debates, a result of "a lamentable misunderstanding, or temporary division, between the *intellectual leadership* and the majority of the Chamber." Rotteck decided to "draw a curtain" over the scene and not to examine it further in his history of the Diet.[67]

[66] BadReg 5 IX 1821. Recent work by Loyd Lee, pursuant to his unpublished Ph.D. dissertation, "The Civil Service of the State of Baden, 1815–1848" (Cornell, 1967), would revise my estimate both of the Baden constitution of 1818 and the decree of 1821 in a liberal direction. See also August-Wilhelm Blase, *Die Einführung konstitutionell-kommunaler Selbstverwaltung im Grossherzogtum Baden* (Berlin, 1938), pp. 59–93.

[67] Carl von Rotteck, *Geschichte der badischen Landtage von der Einführung der Verfassung bis 1832* (Stüttgart, 1836), p. 128. Rotteck's *Sperrdruck* here as italics.

Who shall say who belongs?

For anyone willing to see, though, it was becoming apparent that the communities were stubbornest about the right to control admission of new members: the *Bürgeraufnahme*. In one legal form or another that was the main issue between the communities and state officials during the first half of the nineteenth century, though the diversity of forms and channels often obscured the unity of the political issue. It was the one state-wide, public issue that intimately affected every community, for whom the administrative and social questions it involved were the heart of politics. It was an issue on which communal affairs and state affairs could not be kept in wholly separate compartments. And while the middling and small communities were ready to accept the convenience and even the need for professional administrators in the town hall —administrators of a kind cities and countryside had always known—they were determined to hold control over their own composition in the hands of leadership emerging from the towns' social organization. Officials whose responsibilities and whose institutional ties were above and outside the communities, of course, had to find places—and not just physical room—for persons whom the communities did not want. In periods of tension and uncertainty the nervous state political leaders were likely to favor the "real citizens," whose resources and influence were independent of them, over their own administrative officers and over politically dispersed outsiders. In Baden, for example, the first such period lasted through the Emergency Decree of 1821.

In Hessen-Darmstadt, a Community Ordinance of 1821 gave the role of community self-preservation to a Community Council (*Gemeinderat*) elected by all citizens. All citizens were eligible for it: categorically excluded were nobles, soldiers, pastors, teachers, and state officials. An administrative Bürgermeister was appointed by the state from among three candidates chosen similarly by the citizens. The Council, with nine to thirty members depending on the size of the community, was empowered to admit or refuse citizens. It was expected to accept all adult Christians, but had the right to deny membership on either of two grounds: inability to support a family, or "bad reputation." The meaning of neither was elaborated in the ordinance.[68] Bad reputation conventionally meant sexual promiscuity, morally distasteful and leading to irresponsible procreation, but it could have other meanings that needed no clear definition. As an economic description it could mean laziness, or predictable failure at a trade (regardless of skill or capital) because of community mistrust or dislike. Really it was a direct descendant of the guildsman's dishonor known to the home towns, moved half-a-step toward a manageable general definition. It was a versatile standard indeed for the hometownsmen, but an unfortunate one for persons they might choose to reject for reasons they did not care to specify or that the law did not allow, and a hard one for the law to come to grips with.

The legal battle of the hometownsmen in Hessen-Darmstadt over control of membership was fought mainly in the area of economic and guild legislation. The family-support standard provided in the Community Ordinance made that critical. For the customary way for an applicant for citizenship to prove he could support a family was to present a certificate as a master in a trade. In the "Old" Hessian provinces east of the Rhine (Starkenburg and Oberhessen), the certificates were issued by the local guilds, socially interlocked with the political communities. But in the newly acquired province of Rheinhessen there were no guilds, as a consequence of sometime French administration; there artisans and tradesmen were liberally licensed by state officials on the basis of uniform tests of skill. If these licenses were made valid throughout the Grand Duchy by general economic legislation, even the Old Hessian communities would lose their ability to control membership through the guild system. There would be the general threat of immigration: but the Old Hessian communities seemed less worried about that than lest local outsiders whom they were blocking from guild, citizenship, and all that went with them could go to Rheinhessen, get state licenses there, and then come back with them to demand places in the community and its economy.

In the Diet their spokesmen fought against any general law, talking of the rich variety of indigenous customs and local situations, which called for local treatment. No state law could cover them all. But in 1821, and with an economic issue at stake, the

[68] HDReg 9 VII 1821.

Hessian officials began to show determination of their own.[69] That summer the government, with support from Rheinhessen and a large bureaucratic delegation in the Diet, succeeded in getting a law of maximum simplicity accepted, explaining that complex local situations were best handled in the administration of a law, not in the law itself. It forbade local guild limitations on where a duly certified master might work, and on how many journeymen and apprentices he might employ. But the government promised to uphold in practice the other rights and the integrity of the guilds in the old provinces.[70]

For the detailed attack on the guild form of communal defense, though, the Hessian officials avoided the political process of constitutional legislation, with its public debate and excitement. They used the camouflage of an administrative order on fiscal reorganization—ostensibly a technical matter concerning only themselves—to move into the area left open by the taciturnity of the Community Ordinance on family support and the advised brevity of the Trades Ordinance, both of which had had to pass the Diet. By ministerial decree, a new High Chamber of Finance assumed responsibility for all state revenues, including among others "guild monies and guild fees." [71] There had been no constitutional legislation assigning general control of such fees to the state, as far as I am aware. Two weeks later another order went out through administrative channels: a "promulgation order" for the first. By virtue of the fiscal reorganization decree, it read, henceforth "guild affairs [Zunftwesen]," dispensations from guild requirements (the hometown method of lowering, for the benefit of their own, barriers held high against outsiders), and marriage permits (which required proof of self-sufficiency and thus had been controlled in the same way citizenship had)—all fell within the jurisdiction of provincial officials, who were directed to act accordingly.[72] Now, the first organizational edict had in literal fact given none of these powers to state officials, and assuredly the public legislation on communities

[69] On the participation of middle-level civil servants in the Hessian Diet, encouraged by the government after 1820, Clauss, Der Staatsbeamte als Abgeordneter, p. 93.

[70] Hessen-Darmstadt: Verhandlung in der zweiten Kammer der Landstände (hereafter (HDVerh) 1820/21: 17 II, 26 II 1821; HDReg 18 VI 1821.

[71] HDReg 16 VII 1821.   [72] HDReg 30 VII 1821.

and on the trades had not. Neither of the latter was even mentioned in this order, despite their obvious relevance: that omission is enough to show what the officials were about. And then finally another order, two months later, began: "In accordance with [the decree organizing the High Chamber of Finance] the awarding of all licenses to practice trades in Starkenburg and Oberhessen [the Old Hessian provinces] belongs henceforth to the provincial governments." [73] These powers were to be exercised, that is to say, from the level of government best shielded from political pressure from above or below. From such middle-level administrative redoubts the officials, though they had failed to force the communities into the general estate, could quietly help open the way for the general estate into the communities.

[73] HDReg 17 IX 1821.

Part Three

MEETING WITH THE
GENERAL ESTATE

CHAPTER IX

Undermining the Walls

THE decade of the 1820's was so quiet that it hardly finds its way into the histories of Germany at all.* Political drama and public controversy were deliberately muted, or shunted into the sterility of literary rebellion, or surrogated into the dubious cause of faraway Greeks. Hometownsmen surely had no objection to the suppression of political demagoguery and rabble-rousing by misfits and outsiders through the Metternich system that took hold in Germany with the Carlsbad Decrees of 1819, nor for that matter had the officials. The concession into hometown hands of their familiar communities in the teens, and together with that the retreat of bureaucracy into the intermediate levels of administration and judiciary, also contributed to political quiet.

But the quiet twenties have an important part in this story. The civil servants carry most of the action. They did not work bluntly or publicly, so that what they did appears in a mosaic of detail, most of it indirect and most of it covert. They began a silent siege of hometown walls whose structures and perimeters were now recognized. The reason for concluding the last chapter with so close a look at their procedure in Hessen-Darmstadt is that to legislate through administrative reorganization, and by juggling jurisdictions, became the bureaucratic tactic for opening up, modifying, and directing community life. What Hessian officials did

* Parts of this chapter are reproduced with permission from the *Political Science Quarterly*, LXXXII (March, 1967), 35–60.

there with their new High Chamber of Finance sets out both the method and sector of their attack. It was a tactic suitable both to the conditions of political quiet and to the positions bureaucracy had taken up in German politics and government after the rebuff of the teens.

The decade of the twenties holds within it the continuity between the conflicts of Napoleonic times, and the Biedermeier dualism that underlay the conflicts of the pre-March and the disillusions of 1848. It was a period of bureaucratic recovery between the hometown waves of the teens and of the early thirties. The experience of the decade restated the lines of political division in ways that gave another dimension to the relations among government, home towns, and a changing general estate, at a critical interval. These years at the beginning of Europe's liberal century gave a distinctive and troubling cast to the question of what freedom meant in Germany: what freedom was for, where it was to be found, from whom it was to come, against whom it must be maintained.

The subterfuge of liberal bureaucracy

The constitutions and systems of local self-government of the teens had papered over the gap between the state and the society, and in that gap bureaucracy was lodged. If the home towns or some social equivalents had not been there, those measures might have bridged the gap; as it was, they accepted the gap and even widened it, inasmuch as the self-government they provided meant hometown restoration and withdrawal. The strength of the historical communitarian movement was its recognition of the tough social substance of community, identified with the home town; but that had been its weakness too, for to dwell on the importance of "organism" was to leave out what was outside it. Community, as always, implied outsiders. That essential exclusiveness was the moral weakness or at least the illiberality that accompanied the community's social and emotional strength. Or leaving morality and liberality quite aside, the exclusion that went with recognition was a bar to political resolution. The sorting out of politics into liberal and conservative sides caused part of the trouble. The liberal ideologists who favored self-government were less aware of that aspect of community than conservatives were, or rather they avoided the moral inconsistency by supposing hometownsmen to be the people, who by definitions of the time could not be illiberal. The greater the remove from state authority, they supposed, the freer the society and the individuals in it. That was not true, and nobody knew it better than the professional administrators, the bureaucrats.

The political eclipse of the officials in the teens was part of the general eclipse of restless outsiders to stable social estate. Bureaucracy was not a social estate, in that stabilizing sense; or perhaps it would be better to say that it was a very peculiar estate whose principle was the dissolution of other estates into a generality, so that the hostility of other estates toward it was built into them and into it. But behind the political papering and plastering the officials sat athwart the channels connecting the several parts of the society, and the lines of force connecting society and state. It was not a spectacular location, not a place for dramatic political action, but one from which they could impose blockages and prohibitions at strategic points linking home town with state government and policy. The skills of the officials and their control over political communication and over the promulgation of laws assured them steady influence even from within the sanctuary of the chancellery and from behind the judicial bench. The quieter things were, the more effective these persistent skills and controls of theirs were. Between waves of political crisis, when the hubbub died down and others turned away from what was after all bureaucracy's full-time occupation, their influence grew in proportion. The fiscal and administrative needs of the states (though less pressing now than they had been) tended to tip state policy in their direction when the heads of state thought they could get away with it politically.

The bureaucratic resurgence of the twenties differed from the Napoleonic variant on the same theme in three important ways, all relating to its silence. First, it was not connected with historic political events on the Napoleonic scale; that drama and that justification were denied it. Second, there could be now no open application of rude power, so that instead of frontal assault the officials now had to use their indirect means and apply leverage at their selected points. And third, they were sealed off ideologically into the retreats whither they had been driven politically. They had no public ideology. The liberal position that took form in the early nineteenth century, expressed in Germany by such a person as Carl von Rotteck, took patronage over constitutional and communal positions in the name of restraint on autocracy by public participation in government, thus confounding the progressive position, which theretofore had been associated with state autocracy; doctrinally, such a position was likely to blur together natural-law and historical theories of self-government.[1] Neither public participation in government nor restraint upon autocracy comported with the position of bureaucracy in the scheme of things; and recent bitter experience and professional instinct both told them that public constitutional politics conflicted with their freedom of action, and with their aim of progressively opening and galvanizing German society. It would inhibit the expansion of that segment of society where their aims and interests did prevail.

And so in the twenties, in contrast with Napoleonic times, the officials were working in political seclusion, whenever they could "unpolitically." During their next resurgence, in the later thirties and the forties, issues of economy and population brought what civil servants were attempting to the forefront of public affairs, much as territorial politics had done in the days of the Rhine Confederation. There they found allies against the home towns more powerful—and more dangerous to themselves—than Bonaparte's armies had been. But in the twenties they pursued their ends almost alone, in the deliberate obscurity of administrative processes until their activities came to light later in the decade, and even then shielded from public understanding by the kind of doubletalk the Hessian government had inflicted upon the Diet at Darmstadt in 1821.

The political forms taken by economic and social issues in the later decades might have been quite different but for the positions civil servants took in the twenties. Because of the concealment that was the precondition for bureaucratic achievements during

---

[1] On the blend of historical and natural-law theories of self-government, Heffter, *Selbstverwaltung*, especially pp. 180–199; and Krieger, *German Idea of Freedom*, pp. 239–240 and passim.

that decade, they widened the cleft between German society and German government; and because of it their campaign can be followed only through the paper labyrinth that was the bureaucrats' natural and chosen terrain.

Infiltration, 1821–1825

Probably the best-concealed process of all was one followed in Württemberg. It was the most successful, too, though the success owed more to the political skills of the Württemberg *Oberamtmann,* the state official nearest the communities, and his professional need to reconcile the confidence of the communities with the demands of his superiors, than it did to the origins of the rules he administered—though their obscurity surely helped. Neither the Community Ordinance of 1818 nor the Constitution of 1819 had managed to decide where to locate the power to accept new citizens. The decision came in an order of June 28, 1823, "Respecting the Simplification of Procedures within the Department of the Interior," [2] and the materials surrounding it were officially labeled "Chancellery Affairs"; but the government knew it was making important substantive law. The officials had just found procedural ways of hiding it. That made it different from the open legislation of fifteen years before; but another difference was that the officials were now disenchanted with the total administrative centralization that had seemed the answer in those days, and no doubt distrusted the crown as well.

The history of the order begins indeed with an effort to halt the proliferation of paperwork: the government ordered administrative officers throughout the kingdom to submit their views on how this could be done. The unanimous answer was that the main cause of bureaucratic paperwork and delay was the thousands of appeals in cases of community citizenship and trades certificates. Jurisdiction and policy were not clear, and the situations were various and complex. This had come of the restorative measures of the teens, where the government had left law uncertain and fallen back on appeal mechanisms. But the Oberamtmänner stood out against clearing away paper by giving first and final decision in these matters to the communities, where local prejudices and

[2] WbgReg 5 VII 1823.

private interests would imperil the general welfare (and the authority of the state and the interests of individual applicants). At the same time they declared that community entry was a transaction peculiarly unfitted for systematic written presentation. It was too intimately individual and too subtle—*gefühlsmässig* was one Oberamtmann's word for it. On one hand was a need to clear the report-clogged channels of government, and on the other was a need for equity, sense, and flexibility: the eternal riddle of home-town administration that always came down to the question of who should exercise local authority. And the solution offered was administrative power to the Oberamtmann, who was held to be in touch with local situations but free of community prejudice and self-interest. Acceptance of new citizens, the estimate of whether they could honorably support a family—who but the Oberamtmänner, asked the Oberamtmänner, could promptly and justly and inexpensively judge this? Marriage permissions for minors? Tavern licenses? Dismissal of malfeasant local administrators of town properties and endowments? Permission for close relatives to sit together on Community Councils? Appointments to minor church and town offices? Decisions to allow periodic public markets, open to outsiders? All the practical administrative arguments for independent local procedures were made to support the powers not of the communities, but of local state officials.[3]

For anyone at all acquainted with the home towns, of course, these were far more than procedural issues. They were questions of substantive and even constitutional law, and so eventually somebody asked whether they should not after all be treated as legislation, not as administrative clarification. But the Interior Ministry, after five years of keeping these matters out of the political spotlight, wanted no such candor. The Privy Council itself, reporting to the King, said that it would be wiser not to communicate the proposals to the Diet, which was turning over some notions of its own for laws on communities and on trades that were repugnant to the Ministry.[4] By this time the government had no doubt it was legislating, nor that it was legislating in a

---

[3] Württembergisches Staatsarchiv, Ludwigsburg (hereafter WSL), Ministerium des Innern, Kanzleisachen, Generalia, E 146: 705/1, 6, and 8.

[4] WSL E 146: 705/23.

direction hostile to the communitarian tendency of the teens, still prevalent in the Diet. But King and Privy Council, under the cover provided them by bureaucracy, had by the end of 1823 been brought back to the bureaucratic side.

When the procedural order emerged finally from the hands of its editors, it included all the powers over the communities the Oberamtmänner had asked for, plus some others they had hardly brought up: for example, the power "to assign places of residence to homeless persons [legally homeless, meaning without community membership] in accordance with existing rules," and over "dispensations from the trades regulations . . . from the limitations on the number of artisans who may be employed in a single enterprise; from the prohibition against the simultaneous pursuit of two guilded trades; and from the preparation of the masterpiece; also the granting of permission to buy one's way into the guild as a master"; and over most of the other flexible instruments of hometown guild politics.

The Diet was trying to draft a law on community citizens' acceptance through its own committees and procedures; but, the Privy Council told the King, the Interior Ministry was alert and would get its hand in first if the Diet showed any signs of reaching a conclusion. Interior officials prepared their own position and laid it before the King "because for one thing the Diet will probably bring the matter up for discussion anyway, and because proposals for the trades and on the civil condition of Jews will come up for discussion in Diet committees, and they are related to this [the *Bürgeraufnahme*] in many ways." But the Ministry made no proposals to the Diet, preferring to follow the procedural path it had found for as long as it could. For they thought chances were good that the Diet would never get down to cases; and although, they said, one should avoid giving the appearance of reluctance, still one should not openly raise questions "which the government has in fact no interest in causing the chambers of the Diet to pursue." [5] A swift series of departmental orders in January, 1824, set up rules whereby state officials would assign the homeless to communities, the guildless to guilds, and state licenses would be granted to unpropertied and untrained peddlers—all based on the

[5] WSL, Ministerium des Innern, Bürgerrecht, E 146: 644/15.

order of June, 1823, to simplify procedures in the Department of the Interior.[6]

In Baden the party alignment was obscured by that ambiguity in the idea of self-government that Rotteck preferred not to think about: community as participation, and community as insulation.[7] Partly because of this, the strong liberal bureaucratic element in Baden politics and in the Diet managed, in its struggle to stay there, to assume the mantle of people's tribune against a despotic government. In debate, what I am calling ambiguities often seemed an accommodation of political interests, among liberal intelligentsia, liberal bureaucracy, and home towns; some people no doubt hoped that would come about. And so it might have: but the liberal Baden bureaucracy was at the same time the most powerful bureaucracy in the individualized country, with the fewest restraints upon its operation, and the least reliant on formal legislation. It got along without any law on communities at all in the twenties, after the "emergency decree" of 1821.

But in Baden too, there was toward the middle of the decade a visible movement against the powers and the privileges of the home towns, a current running against the communitarian tide that had held through 1821. It appeared mainly in low-level decisions on individual cases, but sometimes these came out of the administrative machinery with the status of state law. In 1825 a rural official asked if an elderly and poor countryman might work as a glazier, so as to make a living, despite the existing rule that reserved this trade, like most others, exclusively to townsmen. The Interior Ministry said he could; the old law had never been fully promulgated and so was without force. The ruling caused some consternation among those officials who had been enforcing the law for years, and the outcome was a Grand Ducal order of 1825, by handwritten circular notice to officials affected (and never published as far as I can tell), that *all* rules limiting the rural population to specified rural trades were abolished. The reason given was that country people no longer needed to be protected against entering trades which could not succeed in the countryside. But that was a disingenuous and perverse notion of what the restrictions on rural artisanry had been about—at least of

[6] WbgReg 31 I 1824.   [7] Above, pp. 274–276.

what hometownsmen, reasonably, had supposed them to be about. For it was really the small townsmen who here were denied their protection against competitors who might set up in business outside the walls and thus be free of the informal price-fixing and restraints on production that prevailed inside: competitors who might even succeed in getting inside on the basis of licenses that in rural areas were issued by state officials alone.[8] A few months later rules forbidding artisans to sell and deliver goods outside their home districts, the ban miles that preserved local markets for local people, were nullified.[9] Local state officers were given the power to forgive the masterpiece and journeyman travel requirements, especially for poor candidates: liberal assertions of what communities might not do merged inevitably into what civil servants could.[10] A series of "fiscal clarifications" in 1825 removed, with state bonds as compensation, most of the old complex, manipulable, scattered incomes of the communities, thus removing community jurisdiction or fiscal influence over the persons, funds, and transactions upon which the fees had been levied. Implements of communal favoritism and exclusion were clearly the target: unequal local sales taxes and trades certification fees, and special taxes on Jews and other nonmember residents of the communities got special mention in the orders.[11] In 1828 the Jew tax was entirely abolished: nobles got compensation, communities got none, but thenceforth Jews were to pay regular local taxes instead.[12] In Baden as elsewhere, state ministries in those years pressed wherever they could toward the assimilation of Jews into the civil society, with measures for legal equality and for stabilizing residence. There were measures to inhibit the entry of Jews into such unguilded occupations as peddling, or speculation in livestock and real estate, and to encourage their entry into Christian hometown trades instead. All efforts like these were resisted by hometownsmen when they came, severally, to their attention.[13]

In Bavaria the counterattack of the officials after the setback and compromise of the teens was opener and ruder. The hometown

[8] Badisches General-Landesarchiv, Karlsruhe (hereafter BGK), Ministerium des Innern, Generalia, Gewerbe, 236/5818.

[9] BadReg 9 XI 1825.   [10] BadReg 25 VII 1825.

[11] BadReg 16 IV 1825, 22 VI 1826.   [12] BadReg 16 V 1828.

[13] Regierungsblätter, passim.

provisions of constitution and Community Ordinance had been leveled categorically against Montgelas and all his works; but the bureaucracy he had trained still staffed the channels of government between communal and ministerial levels, and their professional problems and aspirations had not changed. Moreover, the Rhenish Palatinate was governed by the liberal bureaucratic law of earlier days, and although (unlike comparable provinces of Baden and even Hessen-Darmstadt) the Palatinate had an entirely separate system of law and administration, officials there delighted in needling their colleagues and superiors in Munich and in the seven provinces to the right of the Rhine, telling how much simpler, cheaper, more orderly, liberal, and humane Palatine administration was, and how much faster its economy was growing.[14] And during most of the twenties the Bavarian Diet was rather firmly under noble and government control, affording at the capital at least the political peace the officials needed, as long as they did not provoke the sleepy Bavarian nobility. But Bavaria was sharply divided all the same.

The economic features of the division are clearest. An Interior Ministry analyst described it in November, 1821, in a memorandum on trades regulation. There were two opposed "parties," he wrote. The first, made up of the existing independent tradesmen, always lamented bad economic conditions "and see the only desirable help, for their own survival and that of the trades generally, in further tightening the guilds and their restrictive powers, re-establishing the pursuit of a trade as a legal property right, and ceasing to issue new licenses." The other party was composed of "the public, new applicants for trades licenses, and most of the lower and middle officials concerned with trade regulation. . . . The working officials complain of the great labor caused by economic affairs," and the burden of that labor encouraged their belief in economic freedom, which they hoped would lead to "the attainment of that system of natural freedom which has become all too popular in the past thirty years; and to the general welfare through subordination of private interests." [15]

[14] For example, BHM, Geheime Raths Acta, Ministerium des Innern, Gewerb und Zunft, MH (= Ministerium des Handels) 6127, unnumbered.
[15] BHM 6127, unnumbered.

From the outset, provincial and local state officials had in practice reinterpreted the communitarian laws of the teens with rulings of their own that restrained or undercut the powers Munich had granted then to the hometownsmen. Dispensations from journeymen's travels, customarily allowed to local masters' sons, were brought by procedural directives into the jurisdictions of state courts. Communities were ordered to regularize their treatment of "beggars and paupers" (community outsiders but Bavarian subjects) and to file a report on each case with the state. There might be clerical fees upon the acceptance of new citizens, but no charges for the acceptance itself. Communal magistracies and Spokesmen—Inner and Outer Councils—must stop meeting together: mingling the two bodies was constitutionally improper.[16] The indignation of communities and guilds at these prohibitions reached the Diet and caused sharp debates in 1819 and 1822, enough to show the lines of division; but the only conclusion there was that there ought to be a law.[17]

The Bavarian Interior Ministry at that time (like Württemberg's at the same time) wanted no formal legislation on guilds if it could help it, but prepared for the eventuality. It asked the advice of provincial administrators, lecturing them first on the evils of guilds, but warning them that full freedom of entry to the trades was politically impossible. The officials replied overwhelmingly, but with varied reservations, in favor of as much occupational freedom as could be attained, arguing especially that people already engaged in a trade should not be allowed to influence the admittance of others—above all, said one Franconian province, in the instance of overfilled trades. The administrative chief in the Rhenish Palatinate said in his reply that in his seven years in office there he had not heard a single complaint against occupational freedom, nor did his province know the permanent war of public interest versus guild that buried Right-Rhine Bavarian tribunals and chancelleries in paper. The strongest statements came from the government of Upper Bavaria, seated at Munich and responsible for administering the communities to the south and

16 BayNB 16 II, 23 II 1820; BayUM 23 III 1820, 7 VII 1821.
17 August Popp, *Die Entstehung der Gewerbefreiheit in Bayern* (Leipzig, 1928), pp. 67–78.

east. Certain *theorists,* wrote the administrative head, favored strong guilds (in Munich the epithet could include both Catholic corporatists and liberal advocates of self-government, whose views blended together in such a figure as Josef Görres). But practical men like himself and his colleagues knew that every restraint on freedom endangered the natural order of things and hindered the development of individual citizen and state. Between theory and practice, he would always choose practical administrative experience and thus individual freedom.[18]

The officials understood now that any steps to stimulate the trades involved themselves in the whole complex of community life (the home towns knew it too). So while they were organizing their position on trades, they were preparing other legal areas too: on rights to marry and settle in a community, and a new *Heimat* law, on standards for determining where people belonged for the purpose of poor support. They made no public legislative proposals during the early twenties. Then they picked up an important political ally. Count Karl von Thürheim had been one of the triumvirate that had replaced Montgelas. He had become Interior Minister, and had presided over the laws of 1817 and 1818 that had attended Montgelas' fall. Now after eight years in the ministry he was ready to reverse them. "There are various reasons to believe," he told the Council of State in the summer of 1825,

that openly liberal ideas might now have the upper hand in the Chamber, so that proposals by the *Gouvernement* for greater mobility in the relations among state citizens will find better reception than heretofore. . . . The spirit of the times seems resolved to press forward as it were with violence, though the dead weight of customary institutions and the traditional rights of exclusion [*Ausschliessungsrechte*] struggle against it.

Put legislature proposals before the Diet, then; in any event that would distract them from other kinds of foolishness; and if the laws could be approved they would give the officials stronger bases from which to defy public opinion. Keep the laws brief, vague, and general; with enough elbowroom the officials would do the rest.

18 BHM MH 6127, unnumbered.

There would have to be a simultaneous legislative effort on all three fronts, for the communities would find ways to get around any piecemeal laws, using the rights they held in one legal area to frustrate liberal legislation in another.[19] A cloverleaf of new laws on marriage and settlement, on trades, and on Heimat were pressed quickly through a compliant Diet and published simultaneously in November, 1825. They applied only to the provinces right of the Rhine (remember these included the important individualized Franconian and Swabian provinces acquired some twenty years before) because, as the ministerial rapporteur told the Diet, this kind of law was not needed in the Palatinate.[20]

The law on trades was designed, said the preamble, to strike a compromise between "serious reservations which for the time being persist against unrestricted freedom in the trades, but on the other hand a desire to remove deterrents to diligence and initiative, to raise the level of competence in the trades, and to raise Bavarian industry to a higher level of perfection." Every independent tradesman was to be licensed on the basis of ability alone; and if he was "competent" and could meet the settlement requirements (treated in the simultaneous marriage and settlement law), certification could not be denied. Once licensed he could not be forbidden to diversify his enterprise into related fields, no matter how that affected the established trades. Guilds might continue to exist, as educational and social institutions under state oversight; but the state could split or combine them at will, and could at its discretion declare trades requiring no elaborate training to be open and free. Patents for new processes were to be issued independently by the state: trades guilds had nothing to do with such things.

The law on marriage and settlement was frankly designed to ease the formation of families, "for the moral and civil well-being" of Bavarian subjects. It obliged communities to allow domestic rights to any person who was of good reputation (here the law left a loophole to quiet Diet opposition), who had learned a

[19] BHM Staatsrat 2163, unnumbered. At one stage the program included a fourth area, liberal land reform, but that had been dropped for fear that noble hostility would jeopardize the campaign in the communities.

[20] [Karl] Christian E. v. Bentzel-Sternau, *Baiernbriefe, oder Geist der vier ersten Ständeversammlungen des Königreichs Baiern*, III (Stuttgart, 1831), 268–359.

trade (by the terms of the trades law), and who had a minimum capital. And finally the Heimat law said that everybody had a home: it granted the right to dwell in a community, and to invoke its aid in case of impoverishment, to anyone born there or who had settled or married in conformity with the accompanying law; moreover, any Bavarian subject could stay and work in any Bavarian town he liked, provided he stayed within the law and supported himself.[21]

There was no treatment of the Bürgerrecht itself; not one of the three laws ventured to attack head-on what the communities had insisted on in the teens, the right to choose their own citizens. But the government assigned a novel breadth to the conception of that Heimat which every Bavarian had a right to have. It had been a police criterion for assigning beggars and vagrant paupers. Now the Heimat, declared the government in its presentation to the Diet, was "the cradle of complex and beautiful [manchfaltiger und schöner] relations and sensibilities from which the sense of cooperation for common ends develops; and the nursery of civic virtues and order, whose foundation and whose cultivation shall be regulated by this law." [22] That would change the police definition into a subjective and communal right of membership that home-townsmen understood well enough, but one ominous for them indeed if the state succeeded in making it, by this process, into a general right of all individuals.

The government had grasped the nature of the cloverleaf, with its three interlocking laws designed to take hold of the whole thing at once. The officials had their mandate. But the laws were silent on the question of who should decide whether an applicant for rights in a community was "competent" to carry on a trade. On the trades license, marriage and settlement rights depended; and Heimat (for anybody coming to a new place) depended in turn on marriage and settlement. This issue, between the bürgerliche Nahrung of the hometown tradition and the common weal of bureau-

21 BayGes 1825, pp. 103–142, for the texts. I owe the term "cloverleaf" to the 1825 discussion of these three laws.

22 Quoted by Emil Riedel, Commentar zum bayerischen Gesetze über Heimat, Verehelichung und Aufenthalt vom 16. April 1868 (1st ed.; Nördlingen, 1868), p. 26.

cratic tradition, consequently became the crux of the matter; [23] and in Bavaria, as in the other constitutional states of the individualized country, it was decided in the twenties by an administrative instruction, this one issued in December, 1825. The government ordained new administrative districts for the trades, and required that guilds be split up or amalgamated to conform to the districts, so as to break up their contiguity with the social and political communities. Only the "immediate" towns already subject to state police direction were exempt from the reorganization. The new associations were to be called "trades associations [*Gewerbs-vereine*]," and each was to be headed by a state official, aided by two elected leaders whose statutory duties were to do what the state commissioner told them to do. The tradesmen of the district were to meet once a year to hear what new rules there were and who had been admitted to the trade—something very different from the familiar gatherings at the Red Ox where they customarily made their own convivial decisions.

The Community Ordinance of 1818 had given local magistracies the authority to issue trades licenses in their communities, but this economic redistricting superceded that. Now by executive order district testing commissions were to determine the "competence" of new applicants, with all the ramifications of that decision. The commissions were to be composed of the two elected members of the trades association, the state commissioner, and two judges selected by the applicant himself, so that the commissioner held the balance between opposing interests, and so that commissioner and applicant between them had a majority. Only the commissioner was allowed to put questions. No applicant was to be rejected for reason of birth, class, or religion; there was to be no distinction between townsmen and countrymen. No one could be excused from the wandering requirement: wandering was one traditional practice that struck the officials as a good one, and now no sons of local masters were to slide into the hometown trades without experiencing it. In deciding whether to issue a license, the commission might consider in purely economic terms the level of local demand, but not local sentiments; and commercial enterprises or

[23] On the bürgerliche Nahrung, above, p. 101; on the common weal, above, pp. 170–173.

factories whose markets extended outside the local district were exempted from the demand factor altogether. A licensed tradesman might have as many employees as he wished, might locate where he chose, and buy and sell wherever it suited him.[24] And the duties of a royal Bavarian official, ran another instruction appearing at about the same time, were "to assure to every single state citizen within his district the freest possible development of his powers within the limit of the laws." [25]

Hand to hand

As soon as the hometownsmen began to feel what had happened in 1825, trouble began; the bureaucrats were caught in the open, up to their old tricks. Local guilds began to pour complaints into Munich that the state-controlled licensing procedures were letting too many new people in, and the wrong kind of people.[26] They discovered too that Interior Ministry officials, with a mandate to develop Bavarian industry, were issuing a great many "patents" to nonmasters which permitted them to set up shop in competition with guildsmen who produced virtually the same things.[27] Patentees, from the hometown perspective, were the old race of freemasters hybridized with open industrial privilege—groundrabbits turning into monsters.

As local resistance grew it became apparent that district officials were having a difficult time promulgating the liberal rules of 1825; construction of the new trades associations and the ruin of the guilds stalled.[28] The communities had some tricks of their own. They found they could use the good-reputation provision of the marriage and domestic settlement law to frustrate much of the 1825 legislation, including that which had liberalized economic settlement. Or they levied fees for citizen acceptance so large that applicants could not pay them and still meet the property and self-support provisions of the domestic settlement law. They burdened large families with especially high "registration fees." But

---

24 BayReg 18 I 1826.   25 BayReg 24 XII 1825.

26 Popp, *Gewerbefreiheit*, citing appendices to the Diet proceedings of 1827/28; Riedel, *Heimat*, pp. 32–33; G. Döllinger, *Sammlung der im Gebiete der inneren Staats-Verwaltung des Königreichs Bayern bestehenden Verordungen*, XII (Munich, 1837), 1046–1048; Bavarian provincial Intelligenzblätter, passim.

27 BayReg, passim.   28 BayUM 20 IV 1826 ff.

the officials did not retreat as they had in the teens. From their politically insulated strongholds in the provincial governments and in Munich offices, they goaded the embattled district officers and judges. They brought a state tax law (also of 1825) into play to set uniform limits on permissible communal entrance fees. Again and again they ordered district officers to report any new devices communities had found for getting around the 1825 laws and reasserting their customary ways, so that everybody in government could be alerted to them and forbid them.[29]

In Württemberg and in Hessen-Darmstadt, too, conflict broke toward the open after 1825 in public debate over new legislation. In Hessen it was a matter of a law for uniform taxation of the trades, drafted by the government—a draft so long, so technical, and so complex that the Diet could not puzzle out what its social and economic effects would be,[30] and that was what they wanted to know. The government did not tell them what they expected the law to do, but the Diet suspected that it was designed to favor large factories and big towns at the expense of the home-town trades. After a long and fruitless struggle with the details of the draft, they proposed that local tax assessment be put in the hands of local people, rather than in the hands of bureaucrats armed with those hundreds of pages of impervious and undecipherable tables. The government made its usual reply that special situations would be met in the administration of the law; the ministerial promulgation order would make appropriate provision. Of course that bureaucratic promulgation was just what the old-Hessian members of the Diet were afraid of; and they were afraid of any law that treated them together with Rheinhessen. They had learned in 1821 how fiscal reorganization could lead to administrative social controls. But worn down with hopeless worrying about details, they could present no alternative. They even conceded that officials would need the power to manipulate the tables for equity's sake.[31] In 1827 the government got its law; and the promulgation order, as anticipated, increased the powers of civil

[29] Bay OD 30 III 1829; BayNB 15 IV 1829; other Intelligenzblätter, passim.
[30] Neither can I, and the records of the government's own deliberations were destroyed with most of the rest of the Darmstadt archives in World War II.
[31] HDVerh 1826/27, II: 23–30 XI 1826, 30 VI 1827; HDReg 30 VI 1827.

servants over communities well beyond the law's own provisions.[32] For good measure the government quietly put out an administrative edict for the old-Hessian guilds at about the same time: they were to be reorganized into districts on the pattern planned in Bavaria, away from communities and under state control. Closed guilds were abolished.[33]

In Württemberg by this time there was no doubt what the debate was about. The Interior Ministry had tried to keep hometown questions out of the public political arena. But its hand was forced in 1826 by a sharp order from on high—precisely from where is not clear—to edit and place before the Privy Council an enclosed draft for a law on "The Fellowship [*Genossenschaft*] of State Citizens with Communities," presumably to settle the contradiction between the kinds of citizenship, state and communal, that the constitution and ordinances of the teens had left open. The draft proposed to settle it in a communal direction, giving the decisive powers in hometown matters to town councils and important influence to guilds. Ministry officials, then engaged in drafting a vigorously liberal trades law, were clearly reluctant to deal with this one. But they felt obliged to treat it with respect, reflected in reams of technical commentary and many successive redrafts, which progressively altered and even reversed its import. In the course of a year's journey through the chancelleries, *"Die Genossenschaft der Staatsbürger mit Gemeinden"* became a sober "The Law of Community Citizenship and Residence [*Das Gemeinde-Bürger und Beisitz Recht.*]" Article I of the original draft had read "The communal societies [*Gemeinde Gesellschaften*] are limited exclusively to state citizens . . . fellowship is a personal right." When it emerged from the Interior Ministry the article read "The communities are basic elements of state association. Therefore every citizen must belong to some community as a citizen or legal resident." Fellowship had become citizenship right; and a restriction of fellowship to Württemberger had become a demand that the communities must accept civic responsibility and afford a degree of membership for every Württemberger. The officials had edited out most of the difference between Bürger and

[32] HDReg 12 XI 1827.   [33] BGK 236/5819: 159–164.

Staatsbürger, and in a direction contrary to the draft's apparent intent.

The Privy Council, noting that the Diet would have to approve the measure, restored some of the corporatist features the officials had removed. The King approved most of the restorations, but not one that provided that community membership could be refused if any present member's well-being might be endangered by it. This, he said, would "undermine the whole system of this law and the [forthcoming] trades law as well, and open very dangerous latitude to the chicanery of the parties and the arbitrariness of community councils and to government officials as well." [34] The political tide was turning.

The Diet was already debating an ordinance for the trades. The Württemberg Diet after 1825 was elected under strong administrative pressure and included a high proportion of disciplined state officials. The Good Old Lawyers of the teens had left the arena, and so had several disturbing figures like Friedrich List.[35] The Committee on Trades had received scores of petitions from guilds and community councils, but their own report dwelt instead on English and French economic growth, which they alleged had come from economic freedom. But full occupational freedom might be bad, they allowed, because it would allow incompetents to set up in business with the aid of family connections, a doctrine that must have flabbergasted those whose traditional objections to occupational freedom bore quite the contrary social expectation: that it would reward entrepreneurial aggressiveness and skill at the cost of the familial hometown economy. Therefore, the Committee went on, there had to be qualifying tests and licenses; but only state officials were disinterested enough to administer them.[36] It was the formula found for the hometown rule issue of 1823: the Württemberg compromise between freedom and control in the trades, too, turned out to mean more power to local state officers.

A remarkably strong attack on guilds was developed in the Diet,

[34] WSL E 146: 644/18–36; WHS, Akten des K. Geheimen Rats. Gemeindebürgerrecht. E. 33: G 112, I, 25.

[35] Walter Grube, *Der Stuttgarter Landtag, 1457–1957* (Stuttgart, 1957), pp. 512–514.

[36] WbgVerh 1828, Beilagen I, pp. 113–221; IV, p. 1051.

and in the end a generally liberalizing law was approved there. Most of the guilds survived in form, but under state control. Their funds were firmly separated from community properties and endowments, so as to break up the hometown financial complex. Communities were obliged to grant an applicant a license for his trade when he had his mastership and community membership (membership was treated in a simultaneous new law). The mastership was issued by the state, at the instance of a testing commission something like the Bavarian one: its chairman was the head of the guild, but the head of the guild was appointed by the Oberamtmann, could be dismissed at will—and might under no circumstances be a practitioner of the trade of whose guild he was the head! He and two other persons chosen by the Oberamtmann dominated the testing commission of five, the other two being elected guild officers; for good measure the applicant himself could name a sixth member if he chose. Mastership thus attained was valid everywhere in Württemberg; there could be no restrictions on how many or what assistants the master could hire, nor where he could sell. Merchants were enabled to compete freely with guildsmen everywhere: no more ban mile. Factories were freed of all local jurisdiction whatever; they came under provincial (*Kreis*) oversight.[37]

Württemberg hometownsmen never recovered their control over trade masterships. Accordingly the main instrument left to them for self-protection was the community acceptance right. The provision of the government's Community Law that all state citizens must be members of some community was quickly identified in the Diet of 1828 as the crucial one (the similar statement in the constitution having been contradicted in that very document, and in the confusion evaded and contravened ever since). With such a mandate in a new, constitutionally approved law, the officials could write themselves promulgation orders enabling them to force unwanted citizens on any community. Hometownsmen in the Diet claimed that public opinion was more aroused against this legislation than against any since the Diet's creation. No doubt they were right:

[37] WbgReg 5 V 1828; Ludwig Köhler, *Das württembergische Gewerberecht von 1805–1870* (Tübingen, 1891), pp. 111–141.

for here were concentrated the most serious domestic issues of the twenties. They pointed to the 1819 constitution's guarantee to the communities of the right to decide whether to accept a new member. They argued that *good* men were always voluntarily accepted by the communities; to force bad and antisocial members upon them amounted to social and moral confiscation. And what else was this law for? Who would these strangers be? they asked. Could a man who had failed in one place be expected to succeed in another? The government, after the manner of governments, was trying to encourage people to wander around aimlessly all the time, said the hometownsmen. After a time Interior Minister Schmidlin lost his poise. "Up to now I have not allowed myself to speak of the narrowness and prejudice that can prevail among community councilors; I shall never accuse any single community, but the opportunity for unjust influence from personal interests is obvious." The fact was, he said, that the more able and prosperous a new man had shown himself to be, so much the more community emotions and interests were aroused against him. Württemberger did not wander around without good purpose, he said; there was indeed the emigration overseas, but that was entirely different from internal migration; nobody sought El Dorado in a home town on the Neckar.

The legal point then was whether and when a community might reject an applicant on grounds of "bad reputation." The government proposed the theory that it was a good thing for someone who had developed a bad reputation in one place—not always justifiably —to move to another place and start over fresh. And the government wanted "bad reputation," insofar as it remained a bar, to be fully spelled out in the law, as specific actions, identified and judicially condemned by state courts. What other fair and uniform criteria could there be for an idea like bad reputation? The hometownsmen knew: a person's reputation is bad "when the town council and the community deputies agree that it is."

The government (or Interior Ministry) won, and hailed the law as a liberal measure that would facilitate social movement and so aid economic development: "We shall hold the gates open." Opponents warned of what might come of violating the natural and constitutional rights of communities "to keep themselves pure of unsuitable members."[38] The law of April, 1828, ordered that all citizens (but not nobles, and not most civil servants) must become members of communities, either as legal residents (*Beisitz* and *Heimatrecht*) with the right to live there, carry on a trade, and claim poor support; or as full citizens, with the right to vote as well and share in community property. Thus resident status, now belonging to everybody, had taken over a large share of the old communal Bürgerrecht, essentially all but the political part and the commons. A community was legally bound to admit a new member if he was able to carry on a trade (as determined by the state commission established by the simultaneous trades law), if he had minimal property in amounts specified in the law, and if he had a good reputation; bad reputation was specifically defined as conviction for a crime, dismissal from public office—or vagrancy. No one could be excluded on the grounds that the community, or the trade, was overpopulated. Wherever there was conflict, state officials would have the final say.[39] Another law of April, 1828, declared Jews to be the same as Christians before the law: they could join communities under the same conditions, were placed in the same tax system, and might travel and change residence freely (but officials were to keep an eye on them). Jews could enter all trades freely (except that community councils could forbid new Jewish retailing establishments, or an expansion of the Jewish proportional share of any trade).[40] Follow-up instructions through the spring of 1830 extended, as usual, the liberalizing authorities of the officials beyond the provisions of the laws.[41]

Then that summer the political situation changed drastically. But by the end of the twenties the situation was already highly charged. The seizure of socially liberalizing powers by the civil servants was meeting growing, more coherent, and more self-conscious resistance. Something like public political opinion was being formed among agitated hometownsmen throughout the individualized country. It was a kind of public opinion harder to see than were

---

[38] WbgVerh 1828, pp. 218–331, 615–618; Beilagen I, pp. 1–112; Ausserordentliche Beilagen IV, pp. 3–14.
[39] WbgReg 24 IV 1828; WSL E 146: 644/51.   [40] WbgReg 8 V 1828.
[41] WbgReg 25 I, 2 III 1830.

the published views of prominent and educated men. Prince Metternich had identified the "agitated classes" for Tsar Alexander I in 1820: "wealthy men, paid State officials, men of letters, lawyers, and the individuals charged with the public education"—the movers and doers, leaders of the general estate.[42] Hometown "agitation" had nothing like the unity that mutual communication gave intellectuals, or that organization gave the civil service. If it were not for the administrators' own denunciations we should hardly know where to look for it at all. The unity of hometown political opinion came as shared antipathy to what these better-organized people were doing and saying: a fuzzy reverse image of themselves. But that was enough to line up hometown opinion into a pattern, ready to precipitate out when German politics became public again in 1830.

During the distracted Napoleonic time the communities had got into phase without really knowing one another; in the teens they had been sorted out as a kind of institution and their working principles recognized. In the silent struggle of the twenties, the commonality of "real citizens" got an identity and an articulation it had not had before. Probably the governments' increased willingness to enter Diet debates, after they had recovered confidence, contributed to a hometownsman's awareness of a shared partisan position there, though my illustrative use of the debates should not exaggerate their political importance or clarity, nor the attention hometownsmen paid to them. Hometownsmen learned who they were in the course of a general but oblique infiltration of their positions, that probed and exposed now one aspect of their community, now another.

Still theirs was a unity of piecemeal resistance, hand to hand. The devious means bureaucracy used in the twenties was partly responsible: the issues were not fully and publicly joined where the officials could avoid it, and frankly declared only on such rare occasions as Schmidlin's outburst in the Württemberg Diet. The close essential relations among the different kinds of law, and how they focused together on the home towns, were almost never mentioned publicly. Hometownsmen did not become politically en-

[42] Clemens L. W. Metternich-Winneburg, *Memoirs*, tr. Mrs. Alexander Napier, III (London, 1881), 467.

gaged on a common front over the issues that affected them because the officials, so as to have their way with a minimum of
trouble, shielded those decisions from politics whenever they could.
Had the assault been autocratically blunt and open—like the
Napoleonic one but now in frankly domestic terms, in which
present awareness of what home towns were like replaced the
earlier territorial or foreign connotations—then hometownsmen
might in the twenties have found their place in the larger scheme
of politics. But the characteristic style of the civil servants combined with the limits they discerned to their own power to prevent
this. The communitarian baggage of both liberal and conservative
political doctrine was another hindrance to them, and another
reason for following their own subpolitical procedures.

There was a slogan going back to Montgelas, that the German
people were ready for civil rights but not for political rights. When
the pendulum swung back to the hometownsmen in the political
uncertainty that followed the July Revolution of 1830, and the
officials retreated back behind their own lines again, that slogan
described a social perimeter as well as a political one. The home
towns were to be left alone again in their local spheres of social
relations and community life, a kind of world marked off while
a new world with a different face and different rules grew up
around them. The officials were not sure how to cope with that
world either. That is the story of the Biedermeier and the failures
of 1848.

CHAPTER X

Biedermeier

THE Biedermeier style was called forth by its opposite. So
much can be said of a great many cultural and intellectual styles,
perhaps all those of conservative tendency. Its unique quality
among styles, though, was its provincial homeliness and quiet social
familiarity. It was a style of withdrawal, and what it withdrew
from was the massing of forces and the pervasiveness of change
that marked public consciousness of the nineteenth century from
its beginning. Biedermeier culture was a tense and precarious culture because its essence was the containment of opposites: the
quiet style itself in the foreground, and the Biedermeier sense of
radical change, in the middle distance but inseparable from the
foreground's insistent quiet. In the background, to persist in the
simile, lay a hazy representation of Nature.

The Biedermeier was a hometown style, even when it took hold
in the mansions of the rich and the palaces of the mighty. There
have been other cultural forms in which the upper levels of society
have imitated the styles of lower levels rather than the other way
around, but the Biedermeier was neither pastoral nor proletarian:
it was *bürgerlich*. It was a hometown style because at the baseline
of withdrawal stood the home town as an obvious symbol of
permanence and stability. The hometown principle of enclosed
familiarity, adopted into the general culture to contain and explain
sharp division and instability within the actual society, was the
Biedermeier principle. The conflict that produced the Biedermeier

was the one traced here by way of the home town, from the community of the eighteenth century through the Napoleonic assault, the restoration of the teens, and the liberal bureaucratic undermining of the twenties.

In the history of that confrontation lies the difference between Germany's Biedermeier and England's Pickwickian early Victorian style, and also between Biedermeier Germany and the France of Stendhal and the July Monarchy. An important reason for the difference was the initiative and strength of the German civil service, which England did not know, and their sub-political methods of bringing coherent rationality and change, methods very different from what France had come to know. In England and in France, rather different elements with very different styles held the historic initiative, and imposed their different reverse images on the respective societies. Both comparisons help render the peculiar hometown flavor of the Biedermeier. Of all important modern cultural styles, only the homely Biedermeier bears a specifically German name and tone (unless one grants Romanticism as a partial but instructive exception). Its conscious quiet homeliness is inseparable from the confrontations between state and community around the turn of the century, and carried within it the conflicts laid bare in the pre-March and the Revolution of 1848; for the heart of the Biedermeier was the meaning and preservation of home. The emerging questions of industrialization, capital formation and proletariat, of population growth, and of national unity of the individualized country with an administratively and economically dynamic Prussia—all stimulants to the Biedermeier—fed into existing alignments, and produced there the emotional and legal issue of the Heimat, the home.

The New England poet Robert Frost wrote about home in "The Death of the Hired Man." "Home is the place where, when you go there, they have to take you in," runs his dialogue. "I should have called it something you somehow haven't to deserve." [1] Those two succinct points are the foundation of a diffuse and complex body of law peculiar to the individualized country of Biedermeier Ger-

---

[1] From "The Death of the Hired Man," from *The Poetry of Robert Frost*, edited by Edward Connery Lathem. Copyright 1930, 1939, © 1969 by Holt, Rinehart and Winston, Inc. Copyright © 1958 by Robert Frost. Copyright © 1967 by Lesley Frost Ballantine. Reprinted by permission of Holt, Rinehart and Winston, Inc.

many: Home Law, the *Heimatrecht*. Home Law developed out of efforts to get past two quite contradictory alternatives: either to insulate the home towns from massive changes everybody thought under way, a policy with which the thirties began; or, to make hometownsmen into *Staatsbürger*, which liberal bureaucrats and intellectuals again attempted at the end of the forties. It was a very difficult question to sort out, let alone solve; for in the Biedermeier era belief in nature, the home, and social peace were almost obligatory even for those of the general estate whose inevitable tendencies were to destroy them.

And so Home Law never really was sorted out, and disappeared with the Biedermeier. "To write about this home question is an undertaking of a quite singular kind," began the author of the one systematic contemporary effort to do so, A. Vahlkampf in an article published in 1840 and reissued as a pamphlet in the spring of 1848. "One can hardly imagine a subject matter of greater practical importance," none for which evidence and experience were more voluminous, nor one "to whose exploration the statesman, the scholar, and the humanitarian find themselves more urgently drawn by the present structure of public life and the direction of the times." But neither was there any issue in which "the language is more confused, the number of direct contradictions between theory and practice greater, or political intolerance more sharply divisive." Whatever one tried to say or do about Home Law, he was likely to get lumped together with his political enemies and to reap epithets from his friends; on this matter "one sees the bellwethers [*Koryphäen*] of liberalism fraternally trooping together with the reactionaries, seeking the same ends; absolutist governments strive for the progress of the times and liberal Chambers put spokes in their wheels." [2]

The Thirties: Self-government, the trades, and the Biedermeier division

Vahlkampf saw confusion because he saw clearer than most; and besides, when he wrote at the end of the thirties, that decade's events and changes had thrown the Biedermeier home problem into

[2] *Ueber Heimathgesetze: Der Streit der Interessen und Ansichten in Beziehung auf das Heimathwesen* (Frankfurt/Main, 1848), p. 1; the essay had appeared in Cotta's *Deutsche Vierteljahrsschrift* in 1840.

sharper and fuller relief than it had in the political years at the decade's beginning. The liberal July Revolution in France and the German repercussions—the "bursting of a dike," Metternich feared —brought a new wave of constitutions and communal legislation to the individualized country. That served to alleviate the tensions that had grown up in the later twenties over the authoritarian liberalism of the bureaucracy there. Governments made new and larger concessions of autonomy to the home towns, as they had in the political crises and uncertainty that had followed Bonaparte's fall. Local self-government was conceived to be a bulwark against revolution. Channeling political interests and energies into local administration was a diversionary alternative to citizens' participation in state government, participation that had democratic and radical political implications and that would have posed a threat to the general estate's hegemony in the state governments. This was a rationale and a policy that suited the aims of hometownsmen perfectly well.[3]

New concessions of hometown autonomy, although they were extracted from authoritarian government structures by political fear, might fairly be called liberal only if the powers the home towns sought were sought and exercised for liberal ends. But given the nature of the home towns, to equate local self-government with political liberalism was—and is—to repeat the ancient error of German politics and history this book is about. "Liberal" laws of the early thirties, where they affected the home towns, for the most part reiterated the "restorations" of the teens, affirming local rights the bureaucrats had usurped in the later twenties. The constitutional movement now spread further, though, to the north and east of the constitutional country of the teens, and communitarianism spread with it. Hessen-Kassel's 1831 constitution promised a Community Ordinance that would give the communities the right

---

[3] On this motive for the Prussian Revised Ordinance of 1831, Heffter, *Selbstverwaltung*, pp. 215–217, and Karl-Georg Faber, "Die kommunale Selbstverwaltung in der Rheinprovinz im 19. Jahrhundert," *RVB*, XXX (1965), p. 139, both citing Savigny's 1832 article "Die Preussische Städteordnung" in Ranke's *Historisch-politischer Zeitschrift*, I, 389–414. I do not read Savigny's article, though, to be as explicit on this point as Heffter and Faber interpret him to be. Note also that it was at this time that Ranke gave his similar interpretation of the politics of the teens: above, p. 262.

to elect their own officials, to administer community property themselves, and to "exercise the power of acceptance into the communal union"; the state government would issue no more economic "privileges"—it would exempt no more enterprises from guild rules—without Diet approval; community and state fiscal resources were never to be consolidated.[4] The Ordinance itself, when it came in 1834, allowed each community to choose its own membership, and to write its own constitution within the following guidelines: the assembled citizenry elected an Outer Council (*Gemeindeausschuss*), the Outer Council elected an Inner Council (*Stadtrat*); and the two Councils together elected the Bürgermeister, who was constitutionally responsible to the community, not to the state. The Inner Council's duty was to "represent the social interest of the community," and the state was to intervene only in instances of notorious maladministration.[5] Thus the ordinance recapitulated the communal ordinances of the constitutional states of the teens, which in turn had been general restatements of much older principles of communal government.

The Kingdom of Hanover still got no general communal ordinance, standing by the restored individual statutes of the teens; and the Constitution of 1833 included a barrier against intrusion by bureaucracy and nobility: the communities were guaranteed corporate control over acceptance to citizenship, over local police, and over communal property.[6] Hildesheim, sometime home of the

---

[4] Huber, ed., *Dokumente*, I, 201–223.

[5] Carl W. Wippermann, *Kurhessen seit dem Freiheitskriege* (Kassel, 1850), pp. 262–263, 330–333, 358–376; Maurer, *Städteverfassung*, IV, 333–334; Eduard Schübler, *Die Gesetze über Niederlassung und Verehelichung in den verschiedenen deutschen Staaten* (Stuttgart, 1855), pp. 123–130.

[6] Meier, *Hannoversche Verfassungs- und Verwaltungsgeschichte*, II, 489–495; Heinrich A. Oppermann, *Zur Geschichte des Königreichs Hannover von 1832 bis 1860*, I (Leipzig, 1860), 346. This was the period of the rise to eminence of Johann C. B. Stüve, hometownsman of Justus Möser's Osnabrück. Hanover's political and social constitution, its predominantly rural character including prosperous farmer communities and a landed aristocracy closely aligned with high levels of government, distinguish it from the individualized country to the south. In Hanover the communitarian movement emphasized rural communities along with home towns over against bureaucracy and against a kind of aristocracy more like the Prussian than the South German. For the comparison I am indebted to Christa Graf, "The Hanoverian Reformer, Johann Carl Bertram Stüve, 1798–1872" (unpubl. diss., Cornell, 1970); see also Heffter, *Selbstverwaltung*, pp. 205–206.

tinsmith Flegel, had played an important part in Hanover: a Hildesheim guild revolt in 1830 against an "excessive licensing of rural masters" had established contacts with guildsmen of other towns and with other political dissidents. The government moved sharply against student troublemakers and other radicals of that stamp, but simultaneously offered Hildesheim a guild constitution with a firm ban mile encompassing a dozen nearby villages, and with a rule that no masters should be licensed under thirty years old. The Hildesheim Outer Council assumed a predominant power in town government. "Everywhere in the German Fatherland," Hildesheim's chief historian writes of the early thirties, "the old Bürger pride of days past awoke, and demanded its right." [7] The Thuringian home towns, in the little Saxonies, recovered from a strong bureaucratic attack of the later twenties with successful assertions of local rights to control local government and property, and to wield the instruments of communal social defense.[8] The Sachs-Weimar Home Law of 1833 gave communities an unchallengeable right to reject any applicant for membership by whom the existing community felt threatened.[9] The Kingdom of Saxony's first general town ordinance, in 1832, promised the towns their own judiciary and police, and a local magistracy elected by a kind of double Outer Council of which one part was elected directly by the citizenry and another indirectly by an electoral college of community leaders.[10]

Of the older constitutional states of the Southwest, only Hessen-Darmstadt seems to have escaped a hometown counterswing in the early thirties against the bureaucratic twenties. The home-townsmen's Community Ordinance of 1821 stood, but so did the economic powers the government had got with its tax laws of the later twenties: one of many signs that concrete economic issues were not seriously at stake at the beginning of the thirties. And

[7] Gebauer, *Hildesheim*, II, 323–328, 340–341.

[8] Maurer, *Städteverfassung*, IV, 344–346; Egbert Munzer, "Die Entwicklung der Gemeindeverfassung im ehemaligen Herzogtum Sachsen-Meiningen," *SVSM*, LXXXV (1927), 17–27, 35–36; Heinrich G. Reichard, *Statistik und Vergleichung der jetzt geltenden städtischen Verfassungen in den monarchischen Staaten Deutschlands* (Altenburg, 1844), pp. 50–51.

[9] Vahlkampf, *Heimathgesetze*, pp. 70–72.

[10] Heffter, *Selbstverwaltung*, pp. 201–202; Maurer, *Städteverfassung*, IV, pp. 343–344.

it was an early example of how, consequently, the Biedermeier gap was widened, between the communities' political autonomies on the one hand and the governments' furtherance of the higher economy on the other, once governments succeeded in separating the two. But Bavaria in 1831 ordered provincial officials to call off all pending efforts to form the supracommunal trades associations ordained in the twenties, and to be sure to consult with whole town councils, not just a few favored magistrates, when cases arose over marriage and settlement.[11] Powers given communal Poor Boards in 1816 to veto community membership, marriage, and economic rights—powers abolished in 1825 and 1827—were emphatically restored in 1832: a most important restoration because in the course of the next few years the issue of poverty became the main arena of Bavarian communal defense.[12]

Württemberg hometownsmen rose up in the Diet of the early thirties to demand revisions in the laws on citizenship and the trades, to protect "seated" citizens against immigration from the countryside and from other floating population that they said the liberal legislation of the twenties had set loose.[13] Some places, it appeared, were sending people they did not like over to other communities, using public funds to provide them with the capital resources stipulated by law for civic acceptance, and further equipping these cuckoos' eggs with affidavits of good reputation to get them into the other nests.[14] The government agreed to return to the communities many of the powers over citizenship that administrators had seized in the twenties. It conceded in particular that the question of poverty strengthened the communities' claim to authority over domestic rights, and so altered the meaning of the marriage side of citizenship; still the Interior Ministry insisted that the rules of the twenties, though defective in some of their

[11] BayUM 9 VIII 1831, 7 III 1832.

[12] BayUM 1 VII 1826, 29 VIII 1833; above, p. 271, and below, pp. 336–340. The Bavarian Community Ordinance of 1834 fits the pattern: generally it reasserted the Edict of 1818 in matters affecting this study, over against the actions of 1825, except for certain provisions to be discussed below in connection with other legislation.

[13] Köhler, *Das württembergische Gewerberecht*, pp. 141–150; WbgVerh 20 V 1833, p. 2; 1 VI 1833, pp. 11–14.

[14] WSL, Ministerium des Innern, Bürger- und Beisitzrecht, Generalia, 1807–1847. E 146: 642/32.

detail, were right in principle: they served the interests of "the individual and the totality." Shades of Justi: that was no way to talk to hometownsmen. But the government accepted the pre-eminence of communal membership over that catch-phrase of the general estate: nobody without local membership (Bürger- or Beisitzrecht) could marry, carry on a trade, or own a home.[15] University Chancellor Autenrieth of Tübingen wanted to know, in the Diet debate, whether that meant town councils could decide whether or not a writer could get married, and was told that in such a case academic tenure would probably have the effect of a master artisan's certificate. Oh, said Autenrieth, and how about master beggars? Unamused hometownsmen carried point after point against the government with the support of such liberals as the powerful publisher Cotta, who prefaced his vote in favor of communal exclusion powers with the declaration: "Community itself is the goal and not the instrument of the state: therefore Yea!" [16]

A hometown champion warned his fellows in the Württemberg Chamber not to be satisfied with a mere citizenship law that left the trades question open. For "many a person has been able to sneak into a community under the pretext of practicing a trade." [17] The government was able to keep trades licensing out of the 1833 law on communal membership, while in all other respects reversing the direction of the twenties. Civic membership was not to be acquired by the purchase of land (for some undesirable people had been able to "sneak in" that way too). An applicant could be excluded for begging or for having received public support in recent years; and to the concrete 1828 judicial definitions of bad reputation was added a right of town councils to determine that an applicant was "to be regarded as a bad householder." Property requirements in monetary terms were systematically raised, especially for large families (and contributions from the applicants' former communities were *not* to count!) Marriage depended on civic rights plus proof to community authorities of economic self-sufficiency; and if there was any doubt about that, then the "will" of the Citizens' Committee (formerly the Community Deputies)

15 WbgVerh 1833, III, pp. 89–107.
16 WbgVerh 1833, IX, pp. 3–89; X, pp. 44–46.   17 WbgVerh IX, p. 76.

made final determination, and might overrule the administrative Inner Council in favor of an applicant as well as against him. State oversight and appeal jurisdiction extended only so far as to see that the communities did not act illegally; and given the autonomous powers the communities had got, it is really hard to see what they could do in the way of civil and social exclusion that would be illegal.[18]

The liberal Württemberg trades regulations of 1828 had got past that Diet as purely economic legislation. Now in the thirties hometownsmen attacked them for what they did outside economic life narrowly conceived. Trades laws were not purely economic in their application or their effect, they said, and only persons with economic blinders, like Interior Ministry bureaucrats, could pretend they were. Objective economic criteria of competence and capital had proceeded from a false principle, and poverty, said the hometownsmen, was misunderstood. Poverty was not primarily a matter of being poor. They were not against the industrious poor, but against irresponsible behavior on the part of people they had to live with; that was why the towns wanted good reputation, or a definition of economic competence that included something like it, to replace inflexible objective standards of capital or skill. Success did not come from skill alone, nor was a home something that rested on economic bases alone. Competence really meant about the same as reputation; there were plenty of *potentially* bad people who had not yet done the actual deeds that in the government's view would justify exclusion; but the communities, unbound by a rule book, could identify such people before the damage was done.

The communities complained (accurately) that the government had been following a policy of recognizing more and more unguilded trades: all such trades must be put under community control lest a "horde" of unskilled outsiders flood the communities, an "army of poor, low, misfits." The free movement of populace that bureaucratic arbitrariness was forcing on Württemberg was unconstitutional; *Staatsbürger* just were not *Gemeindebürger*, either legally or socially. Governments talked of communal "arbitrariness" because, in their eagerness to spread the sphere of the in-

[18] WHS, E 33: G 112/II 25; Klein, *Entwicklung des Gemeindebürgerrechts,* pp. 38–39; WbgReg 27 XII 1833.

dustrial economy into the communities, they were determined to break communal control over communal membership. Governments were bent on destroying self-government. The common good: well, it was not at all certain "that the true weal of the fatherland can in fact and can only be served by the gradual dissolution of the old German town constitution, by the establishment of an easy but barren system of state citizenship and occupational freedom." [19] That was the revived hometown argument. But the government was able to delay action on the trades until after the middle of the decade and thus past the moment of communitarian initiative. On the economic issue liberals outside government split away from hometownsmen and joined bureaucrats; and the Trades Edict of 1836, with its Instruction of the next year, hardly retreated from the position achieved in 1828.[20] Between Württemberg's citizenship law of the thirties and its economic law lay the Biedermeier disparity in social direction, with political liberals supporting the communities on civic self-government, but supporting the officials in seeing that hometown protective rights were kept where they could not cripple that other economy of the general estate. Communal and economic rights had generally traveled together since the pendulum had been set going in Napoleonic times; but here, despite hometown efforts to hold them together, they were drawing apart.

Half the Chamber that produced the Baden Community Ordinance of 1831 were civil servants.[21] That famous law ranks as a showpiece in the history of German self-government because it

---

[19] WbgVerh 1833, Beil. VIII, pp. 99–130. An instructive inquiry was launched that year into the relation between *Bürgeraufnahme* fees and the annual usufruct of a Bürger's share of communal property. The government proposed as a rule of thumb that entry fees should amount to twice the annual usufruct; but community practices varied widely, and there was strong opposition (especially in the Schwarzwaldkreis) against transforming a fee based on "the social composition of each individual place" into a calculated local tax. WSL, Ministerium des Innern, Bürger- und Beisitzrecht, Generalia, 1848–1866. E 146: 643/64–65.

[20] WbgReg 5 IX 1836, 25 X 1837; Köhler, *Das württembergische Gewerberecht*, pp. 149–156. The main achievement of the guildsmen was a ranked system of limited masters' rights for secondary or semiskilled trades.

[21] Clauss, *Der Staatsbeamte als Abgeordneter*, p. 103.

delivered the most extensive powers of local self-administration of any legislation of the time. For the Baden bureaucracy's control over state economic and social policy, in its administrative role, was so unrestricted that it could easily afford, in its parliamentary and political role, to be popular champions of the Baden communities. There was as much demand from the Baden communities for a new trades ordinance as there was for a community ordinance, or more; guildsmen wanted a trades order to replace what they called the "trades disorder" of unrestrained bureaucratic decisions and liberal permissiveness, but they never got one: they never got the autonomy in the trades that liberals were glad to hand them in civic government. A sample of guild petitions collected by the Diet and sent to the government shows why.

From Offenburg: a plea for a new trades ordinance and complaints about the unfair use of market days by outsiders. Offenburg shoemakers made special complaint about the intrusions of state-licensed rural masters.

From the nailsmiths of Ettlingen, Karlsruhe, Bruchsal, and Mannheim: to stop peddlers, retailers, and Jews from trading in nails.

From the guildsmen of Neckargmünd: a strengthening of guild powers and no occupational freedom.

From the wigmakers of Mannheim: against women making wigs.

From the potters of Rastadt and of Baden-Baden: that masons be forbidden to make stoves.

From the brewers of Villingen: restoration of the local brewers' guild.

From the artisans of Weinheim and Heidelberg: a new trades and guilds ordinance to replace bureaucratic arbitrariness and the system of state license.

From Wertheim and Sinsheim: a new ordinance to replace the occupational freedom which they deemed presently to exist.

And so on. Nearly every petition for a new ordinance lumped occupational freedom together with arbitrary bureaucratic domination of economic life, as the same evil. Of twenty-nine petitions filed only three supported occupational freedom: one from Mannheim, one from Baden-Baden (neither of them mentioning any specific trade), and one from "twenty-one citizens of the District of Lörrach" on the Swiss border.[22] Clearly any effort to legislate in that sphere would have exposed the essential hostility within the hometown-liberal alliance that produced the Community Ordinance; and the government preferred "disorder" to guild order; so no trades laws were undertaken, and the cleft between local political rights the communities did get and the economic rights they did not get was allowed to develop.

The Community Ordinance was based on a draft that had been prepared in the teens but not used then; during the twenties the government had buried it.[23] It was a remarkable piece of compromise legislation whose unblemished reputation comes from its apparent success in making communal self-government compatible with political liberalism after all. Bürgermeister and Council (*Gemeinderat*) were to be elected by the whole citizenry, and not— explicitly—by guilds. The Bürgermeister was to be confirmed by the state; but if the state would not confirm, he became Bürgermeister anyway after three successive ballots by the community in his favor. The Citizens' Committee (*Bürgerausschuss*) was to meet regularly with the administrative Council to safeguard citizens' interests and check oligarchy. It was elected by the three-class system of 1821: one third of the Committee to be from each third of the citizenry ranked by local tax liability. That guaranteed representation to citizens at all economic levels, but in so doing— and this side of the system got an emphasis now that it had not had in 1821—it made sure that a poor majority among the citizenry would not be able to shut out the wealthier altogether. The Committee's approval was required for administrative appointments, building permits, and most fiscal decisions. When Council and Committee disagreed, the citizenry assembled to decide between them.

---

[22] BGK 236/5819: 46–50. BGK 236/5821 includes twelve more for 1846, and a number of later ones are in 236/5822.

[23] For a general discussion, Heffter, *Selbstverwaltung*, pp. 160–186, especially 180–184; Fritz Dürr, *Die geschichtliche Entwicklung der Gemeindevertretung in Baden* (Heidelberg, 1933), pp. 5–12; Blase, *Selbstverwaltung im Grossherzogtum Baden*, passim; Maurer, *Städteverfassung*, IV, pp. 331–332; Werner Obermayer, *Die Beteiligung der badischen Gemeinden in der Polizeiverwaltung* (Heidelberg, 1930), pp. 18 and passim.

This polity was given direction of all communal affairs: community property, the local police power including "lower trades police," and the "acceptance of new citizens and the incidence [*Antritt*] of born citizenship", the latter a novel phrase. The Bürgermeister had certain judicial powers—fines up to five gulden or 48 days in jail—but could not exercise them against schoolteachers, pastors, or state officials for actions taken in connection with their official duties. Nor could the community tax factory buildings or factory capital, though it could demand compensation for services rendered to a factory enterprise. But the Government's most important achievement was to abolish the distinctions among the kinds of community membership, converting former semi-citizens (*Orts-* and *Schutzbürger*) into full communal citizens, with the right to vote, marry, pursue a trade, share in community property, and of course to bear a full citizen's fiscal and political responsibilities. Still a category of outsiders was preserved: "state citizens with the right of permanent residence, or *Insassen*." For neither state nor community was quite ready to equate physical presence with membership.[24]

The extension of community citizenship to former sub-citizens was surely an important reason why the three-class system was now described as a defense for the prosperous against the poor, and why in the preparation of the law there was much more talk about relative wealth and poverty than was usual in questions of hometown governance. The expansion of communal citizenship brought with it a change in the meaning of citizenship, and a different way of ranking membership; there will be more to say on this important point shortly. Taken as a whole and by itself the Community Ordinance was a liberal law indeed; those who drafted and defended it could, and did, boast of its combination of communal self-government with civic responsibility and an equality of civic rights. The ordinance had somehow got past the hometown stumbling block: communal citizens were state citizens now.

But another law, published the same day, explains the place of this law in the early thirties and the reason why it was accepted by hometownsmen without serious demur. This one was called a "Law

[24] BadReg 17 II 1832. The edict was dated 31 XII 1831, to be effective 23 IV 1832.

on the Rights of Communal Citizens and on the Acquisition of Citizenship," a law the politicians did not talk about and that historians of local government seem not to have noticed. The citizenship law might have come out of an altogether different body from the community ordinance, an altogether hostile body: here is the Biedermeier duality again. For no eighteenth-century hometownsman could have wished a better town statute for privileged social defense than all Baden communities got in the citizenship law of 1831, which capped off the political rights they got in the community ordinance and compensated (with some new twists) for the abolition of former categories of semi-citizenship. All the particular rights of Bürger were named: vote, eligibility for office, share of communal property, trade rights, marriage, poor support. These might be acquired by citizen birth, except—and here is the reason for the peculiar wording on admission in the community ordinance—even the adult sons of citizens, to be admitted, had to prove that they could support a family, with property or a recognized occupation; and that determination was for the Council to make. Entry fees for the citizen-born (rather high ones) were stipulated in the law, but the stipulations turned out to be little more than guidelines: Council and Committee could remit them in whole or in part, and could erect additional fees if there were unusually valuable public facilities in the community.

By these provisions the communities got discretionary powers over the entry even of the citizen-born, now that former semi-citizens had become full citizens. The meaning of communal citizenship had to be sure been diluted with the extension of its incidence; but to match that, avuncular control over membership was if anything enhanced. So much for native citizenship. The acceptance of outsiders was also the community's own business, not the state's, with the Citizens' Committee here holding the final say. "Good reputation" was required of an applicant, meaning that nobody with a criminal past or a "reputation as a bad householder" should be admitted. The outsiders' entry fee was set high, up to ten times as high as the natives'; and a large property requirement, expressed in money, was added to the usual "accepted occupation"; but the uncles might waive these requirements too if they chose. Entry fees were automatically reduced by half if the applicant married a citizen's widow or daughter. Besides the entry fees specified by the law, a community could levy other "heretofore traditional" ones, and introduce new ones if it saw fit.

Appeal from a community decision had to be made on the basis of this hometownsman's law; and as in the Württemberg case it is hard to see how a community exclusively empowered to judge an applicant's reputation and his economic competence could be overruled. But there was special provision even in this law for the *Insassen,* those resident state citizens that the community ordinance had exempted from communal citizenship. The community might accept their presence voluntarily or the state might order it; in either case they had full economic rights and a claim on poor support, but no regular voting franchise, no share in community property, and no right to marry.[25]

The two Baden laws of 1831 on communities, though produced together, ran in opposite directions; taken together they show that the contradictory tendencies of the home towns and the general estate of Baden had not been resolved, though each side brought home its trophy from the Diet's deliberations: the liberal his accommodation of local self-government with a generalized citizenship, the hometownsman his control over local membership. Conflicting laws are common enough in legislative history; in this instance, though, home towns sought and got in their law provisions to prevent just what the chamber liberals thought theirs achieved: the entry of the communities into a general open sphere of public life. The coexistence of contradictory principles is evidence enough of the problem's irresolution. One political reason the conflict was not met head-on and worked into one law (instead of these simultaneous separate ones) was surely that Chamber liberals thought the philistine fussiness of the citizenship law made it insignificant alongside their larger goals, while hometownsmen no doubt were confident that the autonomy they got in the one law, on self-government, put together with armor they got in the other, on citizenship, was security enough against the liberal provisions of the first—as

[25] BadReg 17 II 1832; and an election decree in 14 VI 1832. This was a difficult law, with significantly complex phrasing ("Citizenship may not be denied unless . . .") and with provisions that seem contradictory and probably were. Neither the status of the *Insassen* nor whom they were generally thought to be is at all clear, and caused considerable administrative confusion then.

much or more security, at least, as they had had in law before. Community and general estate still lived in different worlds; the 1831 ordinances did not change that. As for what bureaucracy itself thought this was all about: the Baden government a few months after these laws appeared forbade local political bodies to debate state affairs, hear public speeches, or write petitions: their business was *local* government.[26]

That was the hometownsman's natural milieu. The concrete effects of this Janus-headed legislation I take to have been small; it is more important as an instance of the peculiar Biedermeier capacity to hold within itself the tensions that created it, which is not, after all, quite the same thing as inconsistency, irresolution, or even internal conflict. There was a real relation between the Biedermeier style and these legislative technicalities, a relation that appeared in the phrasing of the laws as well as their substance. The link between style and law was the terms, of social analysis and of value, through which the home towns were perceived and provision made for them. The communities enjoyed a strong political position in the Biedermeier period. But they had too a cultural and aesthetic justification. They were "natural." No legislative program could frankly give priority to the "artificial" over the "natural." Hometown communities had got a claim on *Naturschutz*: they were to be treated, socially and politically, as something like German natural (and even national) preserves.

Nature, the home town, and Biedermeier culture

The principle of the German Biedermeier was the identification of the home town with nature and identification of both with virtue. Both Nature and the home town got their visibility in those years by contrast with what was new and therefore unnatural —and thus defective in virtue. We cannot explore here the full metaphysical import of Nature in German culture, beyond the general remark that Nature necessarily stands nearer to divinity than what is man-made and hence artificial. It is there by itself. To Nature is attributed a higher reality than the man-made; and anyone who doubts the persistence of that notion in the German world need only read advertisements for drugs, cosmetics, or tobaccos, or

[26] BadReg 22 V, 7 VI 1832.

the labels on German wines for domestic consumption. In such matters to be natural means, on the whole, to be fabricated out of materials or by processes familiar in the early nineteenth century. But one facet of Nature's higher reality, and I think psychologically the most important one, is nature's unchangeability, or rather the predictability and the repetition of its cyclical changes. Though a tree lives, grows, and dies, collectively the forest remains the same. So permanence partakes of divinity too, under the name eternity, and not only in Germany: "Change and decay in all around I see. O Thou Who changest not, abide with me," runs the English hymn of the 1840's.[27] Nor does one encounter Nature in Germany by crashing through the underbrush. It is a quiet and familiar thing, fields and forests regularly observed from comfortably trimmed and trodden paths.

Biedermeier culture extended Nature socially, to include the small town. One might even put the equation: Biedermeier as a combination of the nature cults in science and literature of the later eighteenth and the nineteenth centuries, with the historical school of society and law; for the latter too described community as something more nearly of natural and divine origin than of human construction. It was there by itself: *Stadtrecht geht vor Landrecht.* Thus in both its Natural and its communal aspects the Biedermeier ideal arose out of an awareness of man-made change as such, and in some degree arose against it. The idea of home, too, has changelessness in it for nearly everyone (at least it used to), a sentiment deriving probably from the long slow childhood years at home, among furniture and parents that have always been there since the beginning, the place where "they have to take you in," the eternal peace. The Biedermeier was a culture of the quiet and orderly interior, posed as a snapshot of eternity. There is indeed a retrogressive childhood-seeking about it, albeit a childhood that may never have been; people preoccupied with the problems of adulthood forget the fears and insecurity of childhood and think of it by contrast as a time of gentleness, security, innocence, simplicity, and whimsey—all hallmarks of Biedermeier expression.

The gentle aspect of Biedermeier culture, like the gentle aspect of nature, came from its surface changelessness, its subdual, and often

[27] "Abide with Me," by the small-town Anglican pastor Henry Francis Lyte.

its hazy distance from the eye of the beholder.[28] That same subdued quality that enabled the Biedermeier to become the official culture of pre-March Germany has always attracted the sharpest criticism: epithets like "philistine," or *spiessbürgerlich*. Both these epithets were aimed against hometownsmen from the seventeenth century onward, by students, bourgeois patricians, and nobles, to describe communal defensiveness and timidity: there seems to be a peculiarly German association of *Bürger* with *Geborgene*, of citizenship with shelter.[29] More recently Alfred Weber, in his "Cultural History as Cultural Sociology," called the Biedermeier a "townsman's [*verbürgerlichte*] Old Regime, whose analysis I shall pass over, because its consequences, insofar as they are now visible, have had no fundamental cultural effects." [30] Weber wrote in the 1930's, and I am surprised that he discerned no effects: perhaps because of the Biedermeier's gentle haze, perhaps because of an elevated and benevolent notion of what constitutes culture. According to an ill-tempered critic of the German Biedermeier writing in the 1960's, "If there is a German soul, it nests in the small towns, or better: it turns ever back, with its yearnings and hopes, its disappointments and frustrations, to that nest—to the nests the German *Bürgertum* of the late eighteenth and early nineteenth centuries pasted over a political and human abyss: homely shelters against the winds and storms of a radically changing world." The small town has been the German national idyll; and yet "in reality the small town has always been from time out of mind that sociocultural location where inertia and malice, pendantry, prudery, and spiritual narrowness have grown rank out of a marsh of stunted souls." [31] Such invective is not new. "The *Kleinbürgerschaft*," wrote Young Hegelian and manufacturer's son Friedrich Engels in the 1840's (he meant the hometownsmen), "is, next to the peasants, the most miserable class that

---

[28] Cf. Friedo Lampe's story "Septembergewitter," in which the narrator rises above the old town in a ballon: "How peaceful it lies there . . . it only looks that way from up here." *Gesamtwerke* (Hamburg, 1955), p. 121, quoted in Herman Glaser, *Kleinstadt-Ideologie: Zwischen Furchenglück und Sphärenflug* (Freiburg/Breisgau, 1969), pp. 59–61.

[29] Hans-Gerd Schumann, "Spiessbürger-Philister-Spätbürger: Kulturzerfall oder Dekadenz einer Klasse?" *AK*, XLIX (1967), 120, and the citations therein.

[30] *Kulturgeschichte als Kultursoziologie* (2d ed.; Munich, 1935), p. 415.

[31] Glaser, *Kleinstadt-Ideologie*, pp. 65–66.

ever sneaked its way into history." Engels' verb, *hineingepfuscht*, is the word hometownsmen used to describe what groundrabbits did: hometownsmen were the groundrabbits of Engels' historical scheme. Hometownsmen to him were the fragmenters of society and the frustrators of purpose; and anyway he did not like the breed.[32]

But other social critics took an opposite position, or rather they put in the place of invective a kind of fond irony toward Biedermeier foibles over which Biedermeier virtues easily prevailed—as in the small-town paintings of Karl Spitzweg, for example. Biedermeier fiction was preoccupied with the wholeness of the provincial community, set over against the hurrying great world: one thinks of Immermann, Auerbach, Stifter. That racing world was really to blame for the fragmentation of society and of soul. "Let the world refuse us everything else," wrote Karl Immermann about *Münchhausen* to a bookbinder friend, "it cannot shut us out of Nature and History;"[33] and in *Oberhof* his Hanoverian kulak retained communal rank and status despite the historical dubiety of his symbolic Carolingian sword, because they were natural, which amounted to the same thing as historical and social validity. Communal society could fabricate traditions, and still the traditions would be true and natural because communal society was true and natural. Berthold Auerbach—so he wrote in the 1842 introduction to his *Schwarzwälder Dorfgeschichten*—thought he had a choice between history and locality as a frame for representing German national qualities. History, he thought, might have given more freedom to his fantasy. But he had chosen locality because it offered in the end a truer, though analogous, opportunity for what he wished to say. For the essential Germany needed a kind of description and understanding different from what served in "the lands of centralization, of historical unity and uniformity. . . . Englishmen, Frenchmen have each grown up under the same laws, similar conditions of life and historical influences; their character has a similarity not only in the tendency toward the general, but also in details, in customs, attitudes, etc. But we, divided by history, represent rather the culture of provincial life." German literature like the study of

[32] "Der Status Quo in Deutschland," *Marx/Engels Gesamtausgabe*, Erste Abt. Bd. VI, p. 238.

[33] *Werke*, I (Leipzig, 1906), 44.

German history must therefore be progressively localized, not generalized. German cultural unity could only be achieved (recall Eichhorn) by a full grasp of all locality; the provincial kernel survives and must survive the oscillations of the times and even territorial consolidation.[34] Germany, he wrote in *Die Frau Professorin* (the story of a small-town girl who married into the general estate), is like an untuned piano; only the artist can bring it into tune and play upon it. The problem was that still-unsolved German dilemma, he went on: that sharp discontinuity between communal life and the world of city and court, of "lawyers, doctors, merchants, and technicians." The very languages were different: "the whole world of reflection, of generalizing thought, can find no real home in dialect." With that theme of community and general estate Auerbach mingled metaphors associating nature, with community, with history: the intellectual's delighted discovery in the provinces—Auerbach could put his tongue in his cheek—of a fossil. Here were nature and history in one piece. And the intellectual's labors, after looking at the provincial community about him—to tune a piano.[35]

Quite possibly fiction, and especially the nineteenth-century novel, was a better medium for getting at the nature of the home town than the more formal intellectual and legal disciplines. Wilhelm Heinrich Riehl suggested in the 1850's that "the time has come when statesmen should add novels to their program of instruction," to fill the gaps in their understanding of society, which had become very apparent.[36] The novelist's frame was analogous to the community's frame. The novelist who knew his characters, like the hometownsman who knew his fellows, could escape the categorical distinctions that the lawyers, scholars, and the drafters of the laws and administrative structures that have taken up so much space here were obliged to observe. Analytical media found it difficult to represent the relation of the individual to his community; their representation was "artificial"; the failure of laws to come to grips with the home towns, reaching back into the seventeenth and eighteenth centuries, was a facet of the Biedermeier contradiction. The poetic oppor-

[34] *Gesammelte Schriften*, I (Stuttgart, 1857), vii.
[35] Ibid., III (Stuttgart, 1857), 101–295.
[36] *Bürgerliche Gesellschaft*, p. 22.

tunities fiction afforded for synthesis and association had real advantages. Fiction need not be a truer medium for representing the Biedermeier or the home town, but honest fiction could be. There is another parallel between the life of a hometown community and the life of a successful novel: that the action of the story and the interaction among its characters take place without powerful intrusion from outside. Epic novels, or even historical novels into which epic personages intrude, almost always fail or at least have something uneasy about them. Heroic figures are too singular and opaque for either novel or community, and they cannot be contained.[37] The life of the home town was not epic, nor was it high drama, for its Biedermeier existence was within itself and all that was epic was its enemy. It stayed inside the covers. Its virtues were the converse of the vices its critics have described, a morality not *bourgeois* as historians customarily use the word but *bürgerlich;* and insofar as the high bourgeoisie of the movers' and doers' world assumed the cultural and moral style of the Biedermeier without living that way, without living in the milieu that enforced it, they were subject to the kind of ambiguity that Anglo-Saxons call Victorian hypocrisy.

The hometown *Weltanschauung*—a good Biedermeier word, apparently introduced by Immanuel Kant—shared with the jaded romantic conservatism of a Burke or a Novalis a strong sense of hierarchy and status, but included too a sense that variation in status was submerged into a kind of moral equality with submergence into the stable community, much as the equality of eternity is said by theologians to submerge differences of merit. Here in Biedermeier dress is that troublesome problem of equality again. The important thing about status was location. Location in the hometown hierarchy, by comparison with other hierarchies of wealth or power, was more qualitative than scaled; rank, again by comparison, meant differentiation more than it did competitive level.

---

[37] Thus Leo Tolstoy denied that *War and Peace* was a novel: "it is not a novel because I cannot and do not know how to confine the characters I have created within given limits." Ed. George Gibian (New York, 1966), p. 1365. I owe these reflections initially to Edgar Quinet's Introduction to his epic poem "Napoleon," translated in Mack Walker, ed. *Metternich's Europe* (New York, 1968), pp. 169–179.

The hometownsman's opportunities to rise were after all very small, and a competitive attitude was a social vice. He had no liking for indiscriminate equality as outsiders might mean it; but neither did he have to rule his community to enjoy its benefits and dignity. Another Biedermeier word is *Gemütlichkeit:* a sense of well-being attained only in a familiar company, the hometownsman's enclosed well-being. He spent his evening in the tavern with men he had seen and talked with during the working day: what price the approving attention he got with his familiar weighty jokes and comments about the affairs of the town! All he had to do in return was listen approvingly to his neighbors' familiar weighty jokes and comments, and it was satisfying to know what they would be. To keep that meant keeping the community as it was: one in which he was listening to. It would be easy to lose that to the powers of numbers, of wealth, of wit. With those he could not compete on equal terms; he was not equipped for it. Hometown attention and respect were the power and the wealth he knew, and only his community would render them. He understood without thinking about it that they could not survive the death of the town: its absorption into another faster world, or its inundation by hungry strangers. The community was his life; and in his instinctive fear, from the twenties onward, he knew this. The Biedermeier was its cultural style.

But there is in the end an important difference between the attitudes of Biedermeier artist, historian, or liberal politician toward the community and the hometownsman's own position. The hometownsman was not sentimental about it; his posture was a most realistic one. He lived there, with other hometownsmen, and he knew how it behaved. He knew the home town was not at all gentle toward those who had no secure place in it. His commitment to the stable structure of familiar communal status came from a full harsh knowledge of how much he depended on it, of how ruthlessly and contemptuously the world of his experience, and he himself, treated those who did not share in it. The tenacity with which he clung to hometown ways in the Biedermeier era was an acknowledgment of the increasing fragility of the social web that sustained him. He had every reason to believe that if that web dissolved, if those strands tying him together with community were broken, he would face alone a world of indifference, cruelty, and contempt.

He would be homeless. That was and is the other side, the hysterical side, of Biedermeier *Gemütlichkeit*.[38]

Raising the tension: Population and economy

I have already remarked that a difference between the German Biedermeier and the counterpart cultures of England and France was the history of the separation and confrontation between the home town and the general estate, especially the civil service, that dominated state politics. Cession of local controls to the townsmen in the teens and the thirties, and in between those waves the subversive bureaucratic liberalism of the twenties, hardened the division. Then the economic issues of the second third of the century charged this separation into a highly polarized field of force, containing the Biedermeier tension.

Economic legislation in the individualized country was at crosspurposes. On the one hand it sought to free the economy from the grip of artisanal institutions and practices; and on the other it sought to protect the artisanal estate, in its social and political embodiment as hometownsmen, from the consequences of social fluidity and ultimately of industrial growth. Therefore the economy (quite apart from its own spontaneous evolution) was quite consciously split into two antithetical entities.[39] The separation between the two worlds was not new; it was traditional in local government, and recognition that manufacturing and commercial enterprise operated by a different set of rules from hometown artisanry went back at least as far as Becher's seventeenth-century *Diskurs*.[40] Thus the lines of economic distinction, home town from general estate, had been well laid out and the first administrative encounters had occurred before concrete economic and demographic changes added their charge and made the distinction into a conflict.

[38] Cf. my description of German emigration in the 1830's and 1840's in *Germany and the Emigration, 1816–1885* (Cambridge, 1964), pp. 42–69. What I have learned since about the emigration, from the home towns, offers this confirmation of what I wrote then: that the characteristic emigrant until the forties at least was not the regularly excluded outsider (as I had feared he might turn out to be) but rather the man of respected family name who had come to doubt that he could attain the secure place traditional in his family.

[39] Cf. Stadelmann and Fischer, *Bildungswelt*, pp. 56–58; and Fischer, *Handwerksrecht und Handwerkswirtschaft*, p. 65.

[40] Above, pp. 121, 149, and the citations there.

Still—until the middle forties at least and really until the fifties—it was mainly a political and legal conflict, wherein the material consequences of change fell into predisposed political patterns.

The hometownsmen's economic principles were summarily these: to prevent entrepreneurial expansion at the social cost of the small independent tradesmen, and to uphold restrictions on occupational mobility so as to enable local trades organizations, guilds, or their equivalents in local government, to protect their members' security. Such principles were necessarily local in their conception and application. The bureaucratic goal was an economy of the general estate: an economy in which, unlike the hometown economy, the individual worker would produce a margin of profit beyond his own needs (or consumption), and in which the sum of production would provide a margin of profit and growth over the sum of local needs (or consumption). Individual economic enterprise in which expansion and profit would be unrestricted, and which would allow the diversion of work and capital from less profitable to more profitable activity, was the immediate and general aim; a factory system of wage labor and venture capital would be its natural culmination, and became a more explicit goal in the course of the Biedermeier era.

The Württemberger Robert von Mohl, in many ways the last of the Cameralists, tried to sort out the relation between that mobile economy of wages and profits and the hometown economy in a book on "Police Science According to the Principles of the Legal State [Rechtsstaat]," published in 1837. Knowledge of local circumstances, he wrote, was a reason for delegating the police power to the localities. Local economies should be organized and defended locally. But that delegation should not inhibit the well-being of the whole. "Therefore all establishments whose success is conditional on the higher insight of the officials, on uniformity of structure, and on harmonious development, must remain directly under the state; and also those requiring the application of sizeable effort, or that affect the whole more than they affect the inhabitants of individual places; finally those that are significantly related with other arrangements of the state." The factory (Fabrik) was a direct concern of the state by its nature; but where it entered guild territory these rules ought to be observed:

1. Only those enterprises should be licensed as factories that clearly involved large-scale production, division of labor, and the application of machines and natural power resources not present in the usual artisan enterprises.

2. A factory might spread its activities over several guild districts, by contracting work out: but not to the regular guilded artisanry.

3. A factory might have any kind of employee, guilded or not: but factory work should not count as guild training.

4. A manufacturer was not obliged to enter any guild. If he chose to do so he ought to be accepted: but he should not be enabled thereby to influence any guild decision affecting artisan interests.[41]

The actual building and operation of factories did not directly affect hometown tradesmen before the middle forties, and not seriously for some time after that. Even then, industrial growth did more to open new economic areas than it did to destroy old ones.[42] But though it did not directly invade the home towns, its relative importance grew. Its organizational principles and its novelty demanded a personnel, a labor force, different from the hometown artisanry. It summoned for its growth the kind of rootless outsider that in traditional society had appeared as an irresponsible pauper, so that poverty and irresponsibility were firmly associated with the factory well before factory industry itself had social consequences.[43] It contemplated the individual/state society that Justi had described and that bureaucracy had tried to slip past hometownsmen in the twenties. And insofar as the successful hometown political resistance of the early thirties made it necessary to develop this other society and its rules without them, the cleavage became all the greater. Liberalizing change in social and economic organization—preconditions or at least concomitants of industrialization—were not a victory of town over country, they were an outflanking of small-townsmen by cities and countryside; for hometownsmen could not

[41] I have used the 2d ed. (Tübingen, 1844) of *Die Polizei-Wissenschaft nach den Grundsätzen des Rechtsstaates:* I, p. 15; and II, pp. 319–320.

[42] Schmoller, *Kleingewerbe,* pp. 166 and passim.

[43] Cf. Manfred Erdmann, *Die verfassungspolitische Funktion der Wirtschaftsverbände in Deutschland, 1815–1871* (Berlin, 1968), pp. 109–127; Erich Angermann, *Robert von Mohl, 1799–1875* (Neuwied, 1962), pp. 214–215.

prevent them from taking effect in city and countryside. Economically and legally, factories were set up outside the walls, and in many ways hometownsmen were able even to strengthen the walls against them. But in other ways the walls were already weaker. German population was beginning to move, and the shit-hens were getting over the walls.

A greater proportion of the German population lived in small towns during the early nineteenth century than at any other time —another and ironic reason for calling the Biedermeier a hometown era, and another indication of the kind of tension it contained. Figures are hard to come by and harder to compare; but during the first part of the century the small-town population was growing faster than either rural or urban. Between 1792 and 1819 the population of German cities of over twenty thousand (Germany here meaning the area of the later Second Empire) rose by 51,900; that of towns from twenty thousand down to five thousand rose by 186,700. The size of the two categories being roughly the same, each about a million and a half, it follows that the populations of the smaller or better the middle towns were growing at about four times the rate of city populations around the turn of the century; and there is no reason to suppose that ratio would be reduced if the figures included the great mass of home towns below five thousand. Put another way: the population of the Germany that entered the Second Empire in 1871 grew by about 10 per cent in 1792–1819, thus:

in places under 5,000 (countryside included)	10%
in cities over 20,000	3%
in towns 5,000–20,000	13%

Growing population and freed peasantry at least in those years were going not to the cities but to the smaller towns; and when in fact one considers only the population of places over five thousand, then the proportion living in middle towns as opposed to cities (over twenty thousand) was greater in 1871 than it had been in 1792.[44]

Up into the thirties, German population grew quite evenly among the different landscapes, but then clear differences developed in the rates of growth; and it was precisely in those areas with the

[44] Compiled from figures in Franke, "Volkszahl deutscher Städte," p. 110; cf. Dieterici's supporting conclusions from Prussia, 1840–1855, cited in Schmoller, Kleingewerbe, pp. 191–193.

highest density of small towns, the individualized country (look back at the table on page 32), that population growth began to slow, most sharply in Württemberg, Baden, and Bavaria.[45] This

Average annual growth of German population, 1816–1858
(in percentage)

Place	1816–1837	1837–1858
Prussia	1.7	1.21
Bavaria	1.01	.33
Württemberg	1.01	.24
Baden	1.26	.27
Upper Saxony	1.54	1.07
Lower Saxony	1.34	.64
Hessian states	1.24	.41

oddly neat set of correlations calls for explanation, and economics is as good a place as any to begin.

The small town was the home territory of the master artisans. Even Prussian figures for 1828—faute de mieux—show only about half as many masters proportional to population in the thirty-nine largest cities as in the smaller towns, and only a third as many proportionally in the country as in the small towns.[46] Master artisans were twice as thick, then, in the small towns as they were in city or country. The home town's main economic and civic component, unlike city or country, was its artisanry; consequently the artisan's fate is one key to the home town's fate.

A traditional statistician's way of getting at the changing circumstances of the artisan economy (for the kind of figures that can be developed for industry and commerce obviously do not arise out of hometown exchange) is with the ratio (not absolute numbers here) of apprentices and journeymen to masters within the guilded trades. A growing ratio of hired help to masters is taken to mean good times: the masters are taking on new hands to meet growing demand. But that comes of thinking of the artisan economy as though

[45] Georg v. Viebahn, *Statistik des Zollvereinten und nördlichen Deutschlands*, II (Berlin, 1862), 40. The percentage is average growth per year; Prussia means the whole state; Upper Saxony is mostly the Kingdom plus the Thuringian states; Lower Saxony means mainly Hanover.

[46] Schmoller, *Kleingewerbe*, p. 278.

it were a capitalist economy of entrepreneurs and laborers, with elastic payrolls and occupational flexibility, which it was not. It comes from applying the general estate's economic models and categories to the home town.[47] For the hometown economy of masters and journeymen, that same statistical pattern can have the opposite meaning: the proportion of apprentices and journeymen is growing because in the local spheres times are hard, they are being excluded from mastership. Actually the well-being of the hometown citizen-master-father artisanal structure was not a question of good or bad times in the ordinary modern sense; it was a question of whether young men could properly be absorbed through the guild system into the community; and if there were more apprentices and journeymen awaiting mastership than were being absorbed, then the system was in trouble, whatever the "times" had to do with it. Hometown society called for some roughly appropriate ratio of pre-master to master artisans. That is how the communities' health is reflected in shifting ratios. Any general computation of that appropriate ratio must be so imprecise as to be almost imaginary; regions and trades varied widely. But just to lay out the home towns' "social problem" in these terms: Suppose an apprentice began his training at about age fourteen, with the expectation of becoming master, citizen, and husband at about thirty, then remaining an active master into his early sixties. Within this pattern of expectation (subject to variations of life expectancy and length of the training period) there ought to be half as many help as masters to keep the system stable: enough to meet the community's economic needs, but not more than it would absorb socially, allowing journeymen to enter the community at the time of their maturity. Modify this now to include gross population growth during a Biedermeier master's career, 1820–1850. German population grew by about a third in those years,[48] so that at the end of that time there should

---

[47] For example Schmoller, *Kleingewerbe*, regularly uses this interpretive scheme, and those who follow him have accepted it. Note that 1) Schmoller's statistical experience was mainly with Prussia, where the fullest figures are to be found and where that interpretation of them was more nearly valid than in the individualized country; and 2) all such figures were assembled with an eye to industrial expansion and to general unemployment, not hometown economies.

[48] Lütge, *Deutsche Sozial- und Wirtschaftsgeschichte*, p. 420.

have been four masters where there had been three; consequently the right proportion of hired help rises to sixty-seven for every hundred masters. Rural artisans ordinarily had fewer help than that, urban masters considerably more.[49] When that approximate ratio is exceeded, then either must wage-earning journeymen be allowed to marry, or they must be socially depressed and excluded. For them to marry on the speculative basis of wages, without full acceptance into the community, is unsafe in the home town, for the community and for themselves.

But alternatively, with their exclusion grows the illegitimacy rate, probably less from sexual promiscuity than from *wilde Ehen*, the unsanctified cohabitation that produced children whose parents, then, could and did escape domestic responsibility far more readily than settled and socially accepted Bürger parents could. Moreover, with the frustration of sober domestic expectations journeymen stop saving and start living, indulging the "passion for luxury and plea-sure" that Biedermeier opinion indignantly applied to those who spent beyond what was safe and what was fitting, and who seized the day and present satisfaction rather than taking thought for the morrow and for community approval.[50] The ratio of help to masters rose quite steadily after the 1820's; and as for the 67:100 figure, Prussia passed it in the 1830's, Württemberg in the 1850's:[51] a chronology that lends serious credibility to that ratio as a critical point along a scale of social tension and change.

Hometownsmen generally discerned the threat of a growing extra-communal, wage-earning class by the early thirties. As of that time, paradoxically, their own restrictive communal practices had done more to create it as a separate and hostile entity than statesmen or factories had done. Hometown policies, looking at them as a whole, only swelled the ranks of hometown enemies. But the communities still did not think as a whole even when they thought alike, or even when they acted the same, with their petitions and their political pressures. To the home town, outsiders were still the groundrabbits, the land and state artisans, or the "incompetents" and beggars it had

49 Schmoller, *Kleingewerbe,* pp. 257–390 and passim.
50 Shorter, "Middle-Class Anxiety," passim.
51 Schmoller, *Kleingewerbe,* p. 331; Köhler, *Das württembergische Gewer-berecht,* p. 331.

always known, except that there seemed to be more of them; and its response was what it had always been: shut them out, drive them out, and don't worry about where they go then. The trouble was, all the other communities were trying to shut them out too, and urban industry had not developed to where it could absorb them. The new class was becoming something quite different from the scattered bastards, tramps, and dogkickers of yore, although from the perspective of the home town its members were their direct social heirs. Biedermeier preoccupation with the family arose at least in part from awareness of the domestic implications of the social division, as the wage earner gradually inherited the role of the old irresponsible outsider, and with it his marital and sexual reputation. The hometown master artisan retained his shop and home in one building, for example, and in his native neighborhood; the mobile wage worker left his family (if he had one, or whatever served as one) when he went to work. The wage-worker family took on a morally inferior quality along with its economic insecurity, inasmuch as it violated (and escaped) the triune ethical integrity of the guildsman: socially enforced domestic, economic, and civic decency—*Redlichkeit*. For the unsettled wage worker's domestic affairs did not affect his economic function; his place in society was not bound into the community.[52] State law had tried to distinguish between his private and his public life, treating marriage, for example, as an individual right (which produced more people) rather than as a communal act and a sacrament—as a communal sacrament of the home town. But from the thirties onward the states were obliged to yield to a communal resistance in which the name of Poverty became a rallying signal for local autonomy.

The social problem: Outsiders and poverty

The Bavarian New Poor Law of December, 1833, was one of several elements in the restorative swing to hometown autonomy around that time, and perhaps the most significant one. Where poverty was the issue the communities had a decided advantage over bureaucracy that they did not enjoy on other issues: the states had no wish to assume the burden of poor support nor the task of distributing it. Thus the new law declared an intent "to free the

52 Cf. above, pp. 137–138.

communities from excessive state intervention"; the crown put its trust in the "proven public spirit [*Gemeinsinn*]" of its subjects and of community leaders. The local Poor Councils of the teens, administratively dissolved in the promulgation of 1825 legislation, were reestablished (with an uneasy pretence that they had never gone away), and given the duty of distinguishing the "true poor" from the shiftless, and of overseeing all charitable activities. Each Poor Council was to be composed of Bürgermeister, two or three Town Councilors, all pastors in the community, the town physician (a local office), and three to six tax-paying citizens elected by the Community Deputies.[53]

Figures collected by the Bavarian government in connection with this legislation show the dimensions of the problem there: 8,155 communities reported 81,061 "paupers" in receipt of an average fourteen gulden a year apiece, a small sum betokening intermittent grants to persons in distress, not standing family relief rolls. The Palatinate, the only Bavarian province with occupational freedom, reported a much higher incidence of "paupers" than Bavaria right of the Rhine, twenty-five per community, instead of the over-all average of ten, but a much lower per capita cost, less than two gulden instead of fourteen. Bavarian local income for poor support was still markedly higher than outlay. Most recipients were described as incapacitated or untrained persons—that would include elderly widows, orphan children, and the like, of which every community had its share—and only a very few "unemployed"; the "unemployed" got practically no stipends from the communities. Charitable establishments contributed well over half the whole amount; and even though these figures might mean substantial sums in a small community's budget, they do not show pauperism to have been a desperate problem in Bavaria.[54] But the law's intent and the Poor Coun-

[53] BayUM 1 VII 1826, 20 III 1834. The latter law contemplated a *Kreis* Poor Commission to coordinate the local Councils, but this was shunted aside in the interest of local autonomy (BayUM 1 V 1834).

[54] BHM Staatsrat, Act. des Königlichen Staats-Raths, Die Ansässigmachungen und Verehelichung betreffend, 1825 (sic), 2316:F. Comparisons within these figures can only suggest tentative conclusions; the several provinces raised and developed them in different ways, and do not relate community size with incidence of pauperism. It is not clear whether the category "charitable establishments [*Wohltätigkeits Anstalten*]" included communal social endowments or not; I think generally it did not.

cil's role were broader than the maintenance of the existing poor; they were, said the royal order of promulgation, part of a whole pattern of local social rights, especially the rights of communities to prohibit the entry of persons whose futures were doubtful, "so that the communities, legally bound to support their own poor, shall in return be equipped with protective instruments against an increase of the rootless [*bodenlosen*] population and against the impoverishment of fellow citizens already established." The local poor were declared to be "in moral and economic respects subject to the supervision of the Poor Councils, and are bound to obey them." [55]

The Bavarian Law on Marriage and Settlement of July, 1834, produced by Privy Council and Diet under strong pressure from communities and guilds, was part of the same galaxy. It too reversed the direction of the legislation of the twenties where it did not categorically revoke it. Even the government had lost confidence in the 1825 policies; the Interior Ministry had supposed, for example, that liberalized marriage and settlement laws would reduce the volume of illegitimate births—one in five in the kingdom between 1824 and 1833, one in ten in the liberal Palatinate—but that had not worked out.[56] A reason why it had not worked out appears in another defect the government now found in the 1825 law: that although policy control had been in bureaucratic and judicial hands, effective individual decisions had remained in local hands, and the two levels had worked at cross-purposes.[57] The new law then acknowledged the home towns' capacity to resist social liberalization and accepted, as quasi-state policy, hometownsmen's means to social cohesion. It raised property qualifications for marriage and settlement, especially for outsiders, and gave the communities the power to forbid marriage by anybody who was not already in effect a community member. "Adequate income" was to be determined locally in terms of local conditions, in consideration of the "personal situation [*Verhältnisse*] of the applicant." Community consent to marriage and domicile rights was to come from the Community Deputies; sharing in the decision were the restored Poor Councils

[55] BayOB 20 X 1835.

[56] Ludwig Zimmermann, *Die Einheits- und Freiheitsbewegung und die Revolution von 1848 in Franken* (Würzburg, 1951), pp. 171–172, 467 n. 24. Statistical efforts to relate illegitimacy with religious confession seem fruitless.

[57] BHM Staatsrat 2613: E; Riedel, *Heimat*, pp. 39–41.

and "other applicants for the same category of settlement, if they think their rights are reduced by the issuance of that right to a third party." Communities could waive the high statutory standards for property and entry fees if they chose to indulge an applicant with little property, one of their own. On the other hand building a house or buying land did not in itself found a claim for domicile and marriage rights.[58]

A license in one of the guilded trades did found a marriage right; but that license could only be issued after careful consideration of the circumstances of existing masters as well as the applicant's. In pursuit of that point, a series of royal orders replaced the promulgation order of the Trades Law of 1825, in order to combat "the tendency of many officials to act in a way contrary to the intentions of King and Diet": their assumption of excessive jurisdiction and their issuing of too many trades licenses on their own. The ban mile was restored: no one could sell his wares outside his own community unless the members of the same trade in the other community assented.[59] Trades associations, whose formation had been stalled at the end of the twenties by local resistance, were promptly to be established wherever they did not exist; but although the name "guild" was not restored, the associations were now to be guilds, not guild breakers as they had been designed to be in 1825: their size, location, and jurisdiction were to revert to pre-1825 "historic" principles; they were to have maximum authority on matters affecting their trades, "so as not to destroy the organic life of these institutions at their heart"; they were to "restore the needed real content to that vital corporative principle that is the foundation of all social configurations." [60] Trade competence was still to be tested by a commission where the state's voice was strong and sometimes dominant, but the interests of existing masters and of the com-

[58] BayUM 16 IX, 30 IX 1834; 28 II, 3 III 1835; 1 IV 1837.

[59] BHM, Acta des Ministerial-Bureau des Innern, Den Vollzug des Gewerbs Gesetzes von 1825, nach aufgehobener Instruktion, 1834, MH 6145; BayReg 3 VII 1834; BayUM 9 XII 1834; BayOB 29 IX 1835.

[60] BayNB 20 VIII 1835. The Bavarian Interior Ministry of 1831–1837, under Prince Öttingen-Wallenstein, was led by enthusiastic corporatists. Recall that this legislation was contemporaneous with the politically repressive measures of 1832 and 1834, by the German Confederation and the Vienna Ministerial Conference, as the similar legislation of the teens had come with Teplitz and Karlsbad.

munity were to be part of the test; and the question of "competence" was legally to mean not only whether the young man would be able to make his way but also whether, contrarywise, by successfully making his way he would hurt the interests of the old hands: if that seemed the case he was incompetent.[61] And to knit in any possible loose ends: a trades license, which *conferred* a settlement right, could be issued only to somebody *entitled* to settle in a community.[62]

The communities found it quite easy to forbid marriage and settlement even to persons who had got past these tests of economic competence.[63] The state was unwilling to relinquish its domination of the economy of the general estate; but that determination, because it stopped where it met communal insistence on local social controls, reinforced legally the literal, physical separation of the two economies. The "free trades," outside the guilds and licensed directly by the state, basically included certain highly skilled infrequent arts plus the unskilled labor of factories, textiles, and rural occupations; but piecemeal declarations of the twenties had steadily expanded their scope to include more and more activities. Now in the thirties the communities struck back at that evolution in the trades through the marriage and settlement laws and the theme of poverty: for a free trade license to found a right to settle it had to get community approval, not subject to appeal; and no free trade license could be issued to anybody already settled in a community unless the community approved.[64] The general economy could develop, but it was to be kept out of the home town.

The issue of poverty, meaning a growing number of persons not integrated into the hometown trades, had a significant political effect on the home towns in Baden: a new stage in the process that had begun with the conversion of semi-citizens into citizens, with its ramifications for the meaning and foundation of citizenship. An electoral law of 1837 now compensated for that extension of citizen-

[61] BayUM 9 VII 1834; BayReg 22 VIII 1834.

[62] At least I think that is what an Interior Ministry directive of 22 VII 1834 means: it falls back on the settlement provision of the trades law of 1825, but settlement, by the removal of the 1825 promulgation edict and by the Marriage and Settlement law of 1834, had been restored to communal hands.

[63] Provincial Regierungsblätter, passim.   [64] BayOD 18 I 1836, 3 I 1837.

ship by devaluing the votes of the poor—in effect, making local political rights a function of relative wealth or poverty, in place of the old hometown criteria of civic membership.[65] The three-class voting system was now revised into a plutocratic standard for the communal franchise, an accommodation between state interest and communal structure, between general estate and home town, that identified communal outsiders with the economic poor.

The Baden government's aim in extending full communal civic rights to semi-members, the old *Beisassen* and the rest, had been the individual economic and social liberation of them, in accordance with liberal bureaucracy's traditional aims—not wholesale political enfranchisement of the poor. In its 1831 local government draft it had proposed a flat property requirement (calculated from local taxes) for the vote in sizeable towns; the Diet had rejected that. The hometownsman's citizenship law with its local rights of exclusion was produced instead.[66] Then by 1833 the Interior Ministry was back on the trail of a property qualification for the franchise, to alleviate the political effects of that extension of citizenship rights to the lesser civic orders, and on the other end of the scale to increase the political weight of the makers and holders of wealth (many of them also former *Beisassen*) with whom government had common interests of long standing. The expansion of civic rights together with anxiety about poverty had made bureaucracy readier to modify its traditional alignment with outsiders against hometownsmen if the right terms for accommodation could be found. Ministry officials argued within the government that the enfranchisement of so many people across the board was having evil political effects: it had got so that a man had to be poor, or pretend to be, in order to get elected. Remembering their defeat in 1831, though, they held off until the last minute before the communal elections of early 1834, too late for public proposals or debate in the Diet, and issued then a "Provisional Electoral Ordinance," establishing high tax qualifications for the local franchise: the right to vote for Bürgermeister and Council. Anything the Com-

[65] Wintterlin, *Behördenorganisation in Württemberg*, II, 288, argues that Württemberg, by retaining the Beisitzer category and reserving full civic rights for Bürger exclusively, was able to remain democratic when Baden went plutocratic in 1837.

[66] BGK 236/13530.

munity Ordinance of 1831 said to the contrary was declared void, by decree. The effect was to disenfranchise about half the Bürger of Baden communities.[67]

That was too many. Baden communities were outraged by the high qualification, especially the smaller towns, where the former *Beisass* element among the citizenry was smaller, where ordinary Bürger income was lower, and where the economic distance between rich and poor was smaller. The Lower Rhine provincial government described the political situation as dangerous. The government tried to play on hometown sentiments and self-esteem, arguing in the Diet that noncitizens traditionally (the recently enfranchised *Beisassen!*) had no voice in the election of local officers, and that the rootless poor were a political threat; that the right to vote was not a right to vote for one's own interest but for the common interest, and the poor would be more tempted to vote for their own interests than would the securely established.[68] With this argument the government was equating citizenship with wealth, and subcitizenship with poverty.

But the communities were not persuaded they wanted this rich man's law that excluded so many respectable hometownsmen from the franchise. Generally the provincial state officials too recommended a restoration of universal citizens' suffrage, though with serious reservations about the larger towns. "After all," argued one of them against the property qualification, "everybody knows there are means of persuasion that do not consist in cash and that are more readily available to the higher classes of citizens than to the poor." [69] The outcome was an electoral law which, in the government's words, compensated the wealthy for the larger number (especially in cities) of the nonwealthy, without excluding any citizen from the franchise altogether. Thenceforward Bürgermeister, Council, and Citizens' Committee in the larger towns were to be chosen, with secret ballot, by an electoral Greater Committee whose num-

[67] BadReg 13 XII 1833. The qualifications were stated as capitalizations of annual taxes paid (*Gesamtsteuerkapital*): for the franchise that had to amount to at least 2000 fl. in the four largest towns, 1500 fl. in other towns over 3000 population, and 800 fl. in all smaller communities. BGK 236/13531 for an Interior Ministry analysis of the law's effect, July, 1835.

[68] BGK 236/13531: the government's preparation for Landtag debates.

[69] BGK 236/13531: results of an inquiry of early 1837.

ber would be about one-tenth the size of the citizenry; and a third
of the electoral Committee would be chosen by the one-sixth highest
taxed, a third by the next third highest-taxed, and third by the
lowest-taxed half of the citizenry.[70]

One might actually do worse than take the Baden 1837 communal
election law as an arithmetical equivalent for the distribution and
channeling of political authority in the home town of the eighteenth
century: the formulation that all citizens had some place but some
had more place than others, the elaborate staging and ranking
of political influence from citizen through Inner Council and Bürgermeister, and even the recognition that relative wealth amounts to
something but not everything. The difference lies in the legal act of
formulation and in the adoption of a purely fiscal basis for the
distribution of political weight among the citizenry, in place of the
flexible imponderables of the old home town. The hometownsman
and his regime were still there, but they had become something
different. Though wealth had given political weight before, here
wealth was its formal justification and its index. The bureaucracy's
association of its interests with economic wealth was penetrating
hometown forms, and communal exclusiveness was taking on the
language of the general estate. The evolution of a new communal
citizenship, by the interaction of state and community, shows in the
compressed Baden legislative microcosm of the 1830's: the assertion of local autonomy accompanied by the extension of civic rights
to partial outsiders; the translation of "outsiders" into "poor," and
the reassertion of communal rights against them *as* the poor; thus
the reassertion of a hometown regime now formally based on relative wealth. Perhaps that was the way out of Germany's Biedermeier
contradiction.

I remarked earlier that the development of Prussian local government through the Revised Ordinance of 1831 was a movement toward the hometown political autonomy of the individualized country;[71] now the home town was closing the gap that separated it
from the Prussian community. For Prussia had already made that

[70] BadReg 16 VIII 1837; government draft and argument in BGK 236/13531;
Dürr, *Gemeindevertretung in Baden*, pp. 17–18. The law was aimed especially
at towns over 3,000, where such electoral committees were made in effect
obligatory; elsewhere general citizens' assemblies continued to elect directly.

[71] Above, pp. 266–267.

kind of fiscal approximation of the home town to compensate for social and economic mobility. Interpretations of the evolution of Prussian local government and especially of the law of 1831 differ radically, and the law's promulgation is problematical, but this much seems clear: that at the same time the Prussian state was strengthening and extending its control over the local police power it was granting greater political power to local ruling groups, over the citizenry as represented in Stein's local assemblies; and that when (in 1831) it abolished the economic distinctions between first- and second-class community citizens it established high qualifications in wealth for the right to vote or take office.[72] The theme of poverty and its converse, local plutocracy, in either case economic standards for political rights measured in the general terms money provided, were bringing Prussia and the individualized country closer together. The Prussian Rhineland towns, which generally had clung to the French municipal administration after their annexation into Prussia in 1814 and then refused the autonomy offered them in 1831, began about 1840 to press for more self-government and together with it a plutocratic local political organization: the weighted three-class system reconciled Rhenish Bürger to self-government.[73]

With that evolution in Prussia, the political liberalism that had been a credible alliance there between popular and bureaucratic dislike for noble privilege and power (in the absence of home towns) underwent a modification toward an alignment of bureaucracy with local, wealth-defined oligarchy [74]—the same end to which the individualized country, or Baden at least, seemed to be moving from a different point of departure. No comparably sound basis (to Prussia's) for political liberalism had ever existed in the individualized country, because of the absence of an energetic nobility and the pervasive presence of the home towns, so that the liberal principles of individual freedom and of self-government had been contradictory there. Changes taking place in the individualized

[72] Heffter, *Selbstverwaltung*, pp. 212–220; Savigny, "Preussische Städteordnung," passim; Reichard, *Statistik und Vergleichung*, pp. 52–57; Dahlmann, *Politik*, I, 250–253.

[73] Emil Zenz, "Die kommunale Selbstverwaltung der Stadt Trier seit Beginn der preussischen Zeit, 1814–1959," *STLV*, V (1959), 31–37.

[74] Comparable situations involving powerful nobilities in the nineteenth-century political equation existed in Hanover and Saxony. Cf. Heffter, *Selbstverwaltung*, pp. 186–207.

country during the thirties, and especially the issue of poverty, were an avenue of accommodation between bureaucracy and home town that combined the least liberal features of the positions of each: the state's predilection for wealth and the community's for social exclusion. Just as Prussia and the individualized country had moved closer together along those avenues, so had bureaucrats and hometownsmen within the individualized country. But it was an accommodation on local political structures only, and behind it lay only a very general agreement that poverty was dangerous and evil. It was an illusory accommodation because of quite different conceptions of what poverty actually was and of what ought to be done about it, and most especially over what the role of technological change and industrial development out to be. There was no agreement on economic policy, only a standoff. For it was not directly poverty as an economic phenomenon that both feared. What the communities meant by poverty and feared in it was penetration and social expropriation, not to mention a rising poor tax to support people toward whom they felt no obligation. They wanted to keep the poor out of society. The states feared mass alienation from society, the growth of a socially unintegrated and unproductive class which because it was kept out would eat into the substance of the economy; and ultimately they feared revolution.

Different perceptions of poverty made for different reactions to it. The home town's instinctive policy of exclusion, though self-defeating collectively, at least made local sense. The states were subject to a dilemma that appears in their efforts simultaneously to strengthen and stabilize the society for political reasons, and at the same time to bring outsiders safely and productively into it: contradictory aims where they met in the home town. The characteristic Biedermeier way to avoid conflict was to maintain separate worlds; that was the social and political substance of the legislation of the early thirties. But in economics it did not work, and officials and hometownsmen were flatly opposed on questions of economic policy once they became questions of economic development. Attempts were made to hold the segments apart: the distinction between free and gilded trades, or a Bavarian distinction of the forties between a class of local trades licenses and a class of state trades licenses.[75] State patents for new processes were another way of

[75] BayReg 30 VII 1846.

distinguishing the dynamic economy of the general estate from the guild economy of the home town; but patents, which exempted their holders from guild rules, inevitably infringed upon the hometown economy and its social security. Significantly their volume followed the pattern of politics: hundreds were issued in Bavaria and Württemberg for example in the twenties, the volume dropped off in the early thirties, but then reached new heights by 1840.[76] They went hand in hand with occupational freedom. Occupational freedom, long the officials' aim for economic development, was their solution now for poverty, just as the hometownsman's customary communal exclusion was his solution.[77] But occupational freedom did not comport with communal stability.

State and community met head-on over economic policy because the very persons whose economic activity the states wished to encourage, outsiders both rich and poor, were the persons the communities wished to exclude, now by citing the threat of poverty (to which the rich by their economic practices contributed) and by using the communal powers over marriage and settlement, over the integrity of the home.[78] For that reason the Württemberg politician Carl von Varnbüler, back from a tour of France, called for a full separation of local economic rights from civil settlement, to deprive communal social and political powers of economic effect.[79] When Baden artisans kept petitioning for a real trades order to make real citizens, wherein local authorities would issue licenses rather than civil servants with their arbitrary disorderly bias for occupational freedom, the Interior Ministry told them to leave economic principles to those who understood them.[80]

[76] Regierungsblätter passim. For example the large number of Bavarian journeyman shoemakers given patents to make waterproof shoes in 1839; or "journeyman knitter Joseph Röckl of Auerbach for the making of so-called oriental hats" (BayReg 28 V 1839).

[77] Cf. Baden's collection of data from all over Germany, in the late thirties and early forties, on how to go about establishing Gewerbefreiheit: BGK 236/5819.

[78] Bavarian 1843 investigation of community Nährung proceedings in BHM, Geheime Raths Acta, Ministerium des Innern, Generalia, Gewerbswesen (1843–1848), MH 6142: 1–28; also the question (in 1847) of Realgewerbe as a basis for settlement in MH 6142: 45–56.

[79] Köhler, Das württembergische Gewerberecht, pp. 214–215.

[80] BGK 236/5819: 1–45; similar complaints from Würzburg artisans against Bavarian officials in BHM MH 6142:37.

The only novelty about hometown complaints against the states in the 1830's was the constant refrain of impoverization; not even that was really new in the Biedermeier period, but it was more persuasive now than in prerevolutionary times because of its broad political implications, and it was louder because of a widespread sense that technological changes and population growth, under way or impending, must have profound social and political effects. The irreconcilable conflict was economic. Communal plutocracy was one line of accommodation in the political realm; but the most striking crystallization out of the Biedermeier tension was social: the Home Law, *Heimatrecht*.

Home Law

Home Law can be a focal point and a summary of the Biedermeier division, and perhaps of this whole story: a body of law thrown up by the unresolved conflict between the aims of home town and of general estate. Its effect was to exempt the home towns from the concomitants of economic and social change, and that line of defense, oriented toward poverty, thereby became the stronghold of hometown autonomy and integrity. Technically Heimatrecht had to do with locating the community responsible for supporting a transient pauper; but the Biedermeier Heimatrecht built out from this to include the whole hometown cloverleaf, and its object was not the occasional pauper but the whole growing class of nineteenth-century outsiders. All the other communal rights—civic, economic, domestic—were made to depend upon the communities' acceptance of responsibility for poor support, and so all the other criteria for membership were brought to bear on that point. Heimatrecht replaced Bürgerrecht as the stem of the hometown cloverleaf. Rules for poor support became the keystone of the communal membership structure.[81]

[81] For digestibility's sake I shall not, in this summary, elaborate the legal and political detail that intertwined the areas of civic, economic, domestic, and poor rights into the body I am generally calling Home Law (and by which therefore I mean something broader than Heimatrecht strictly defined). The point at which all these areas intersected was the home town; without that point of intersection, none of these laws can be properly understood. Two articles by Herman Rehm, "Erwerb von Staats- und Gemeinde-Angehörigkeit" cited in Ch. IV, n. 62 above, and "Heimatrecht," *Handwörterbuch der Staats-*

This Biedermeier Home Law had its history between the 1820's and the 1860's. The poverty issue linked customary hometown defenses with the demographic and economic changes of those years. Because the officials, for fiscal and political reasons, could not assault them there with conviction and consistency, this was a strategic point from which the home towns could frustrate liberal and bureaucratic tendencies in the economic and in the domestic or moral lobes of the cloverleaf.

Home law had developed, wrote Vahlkampf in 1840, out of a conflict between two principles that had become flatly contradictory: first, that a man has a right to live and better himself, and must do it somewhere; but second, that the social community, lying between family and state collectivity, rightly has its own distinct group life, where human relations mature and cohere, and it has a right to defend itself against dissolution. "It is not a new struggle either," added Vahlkampf, "but an ancient and eternal one; only it is now more general than before." When guilds had mediated effectively between individuals and community, he thought, the problem had been less pressing; but by the forties guilds were no viable solution, because the problem's frame had changed.[82]

It might be better put that existing frames were unable to cope with present problems, and that Home Law emerged from that condition as a symbol of social crisis unresolved, an overgrowth to cover a steadily more serious lesion. Pressures on both communities and governments grew during the Biedermeier years, including the pressures they exerted on one another. Home Law was built out as the communities became not merely selective (the old frame) but unwilling on principle to accept any more members than they had to accept, and so grasped at any and all means to exclude them: a resistance on principle that grew proportionally with the numbers that sought entry, and with the growing incapacity of the guild structure to maintain selective social controls. Simultaneously offi-

wissenschaften, V (4th ed.; Jena, 1923), pp. 214–216 are explicit legal and logical treatments; Vahlkampf, Heimathgesetze, treats the Biedermeier Heimatrecht in its broad Biedermeier meaning; Shorter, "Social Change and Social Policy in Bavaria, 1800–1860," relates Heimatrecht with social, economic, and moral changes discerned by modern quantitative analytical techniques.

[82] Heimathgesetze, pp. 2–3.

cials were trying to channel hometown resistance into manageable legal forms, and to locate the communities within a changing German society. Both penetration by outsiders and the disarming of guilds had been goals actively pursued by state administrators before the actual changes in population and technology that came to aid them (and confound them too). On the other side, communal efforts to retain the whole of the old citizens' acceptance power had ranged from the formal rights of local self-government extracted from the states at opportune moments to such things as informal personal persecution or refusal to allow the rental of a dwelling. But by the 1830's, throughout the individualized country, they all came to focus on poverty; and that, as Vahlkampf concluded from his study of Home Law, had important consequences both for the meaning of poverty and the meaning of citizenship. Membership was thereby keyed to wealth, and poverty became thereby, he wrote, not a matter of social amelioration or of charity but of communal membership; poverty did not ask the question "Should this person receive help?" but rather "Is he or should he be allowed in this community?" [83]

Prussia did not know the expanded Heimatrecht of the individualized country, nor the volume of controversy and legislation that surrounded it. In Prussia communal powers of exclusion, particularly of economic exclusion, were far weaker; mobility was the rule; and the claim on poor support derived from state citizenship, not communal membership.[84] Consequently no communal membership complex became involved in the poverty question. When the cry of poverty arose (a significantly less strident cry in Prussia, except for a few cities), Prussia was able to move without difficulty toward a system of local political plutocracy combined with state police power which, while relieving the interests of the well-to-do and attracting them to the state, did not hinder social and economic movement and growth. Elsewhere the matter was more difficult; where hometown standards were alive, they were incorporated into the Heimatrecht.

The Home Law superstruction began with birthplace. That was the traditional way to tell home, and all the home laws said that

[83] Ibid., pp. 6–10 and passim.
[84] Rehm, "Erwerb von Staats- und Gemeinde-Angehörigkeit," pp. 249–261.

anyone legally born in a place, of parents legitimately at home there, had a claim on the minimum home right of poor support; but if he had that right, other rights to make his way in the community could hardly be denied him, not on grounds of poverty at any rate. For that reason the communities strove especially to see that nobody was legitimately born among them they might not wish as a full member, and marriage and settlement rights took on critical importance in the Biedermeier Home Law. But tying down home to birthplace had not been satisfactory to officials and theorists who wished to encourage free but still secure movement of individuals; and it had become more and more difficult to sustain as population grew and people moved about more in the nineteenth century, nor was it any solution to the problems that motion raised; and so the question of home became less a question of birthplace than acceptance. With that the original Heimatrecht reached from legal responsibility for poor support into the whole traditional *Bürgeraufnahme* complex and absorbed it. Legislative and "natural" economic and social changes had tended to facilitate movement and to lower the value of citizenship; the way to keep them from destroying community was to expand the content of Home Law. And its exercise necessarily engaged the whole question of communal government and local self-determination. The system of trades regulation was engaged because capacity for self-support was a criterion the communities insisted upon for rights to poor support.[85] It was relatively easy to tell whether somebody objectively did or did not have economic capability, resources, or even will. But the communities insisted, now through Home Law and the threat of poverty, that before they accepted a newcomer it should also be certain that he would have an opportunity to make a living. And that lay in their hands. They could make him a pauper if he wasn't one to begin with; and where the interests of communally settled tradesmen were threatened they were likely to do so, and lawmakers knew it.

Biedermeier preoccupation with domestic morality was familiar terrain to the hometownsmen, and favorable terrain because morality was hard to define otherwise than in social standards and religious belief, things really beyond the reach of general legislation:

[85] Vahlkampf lists prevailing rules in the several states in 1840 in *Heimathgesetze*, pp. 68–72.

witness the tenacity with which hometownsmen clung to "good reputation" criteria for communal membership, and the repeated elaborate efforts of states to define it in writing.[86] Reputation or some equivalent became thereby a usual element of Home Law, and there is no doubt of its close relation with what hometownsmen thought when they thought of paupers and outsiders. Prussia, by contrast again, not only forbade criteria of good reputation for entry into a community but actually ordered in 1835 that a community might not inform a released convict's new home of his criminal past.[87]

Hometownsmen could also argue with some force that the movement of strangers into a community created a particularly unhealthy kind of population growth inseparable from poverty: that people who moved around, and moved in, married (or cohabited) sooner; they had more children with less security than did those subject to the steady prudent family and community restraints of their native place. Besides, prosperous communities if undefended would attract more and more members until their prosperity was diluted out of meaning: corporate *Eigentum* could not coexist with free settlement (though here again there were elaborate legislative efforts to make them live side by side). Vahlkampf put a prediction in the mouth of a hometown mirror-Marx: "The cosmopolitan century makes everything equal, and will only be fully satisfied when there is nothing left to be greedy for; that is, when the principle of equality finds its only possible earthly realization in the misery of all." [88]

The counter-argument, that free movement and settlement would reduce poverty by allowing a man to move from a place where he had no chance of success to a place where he did have a chance, touched no part of hometown consciousness; it was in fact simply untrue of their society. So was the general estate's argument that "artificial" poverty created by exclusion would stimulate revolution instead of the useful individual endeavor of an open society. Uprisings of the excluded came in the cities, sometimes on the land, not in home towns.

The home towns feared poverty; but yet they did more to create it, I think, than any other human agency of Biedermeier Germany:

[86] Vahlkampf lists more than a score of such efforts, ibid., pp. 32–43.
[87] Ibid., p. 43.　　　　　　　　　　　[88] Ibid., p. 49.

poverty as a spectre, in their constant refrain, but also the real social poverty whose dimensions, concrete though it was, are harder to ascertain: unemployment, illegitimacy of birth, political exclusion. There is no way of telling how much the community reliance on Home Law and thus the threat of poverty did to inflate the figures on German pauperism during the early nineteenth century; all such figures were raised from local sources at times when some element of communal protection was at issue, so that they were surely exaggerated to inflate the spectre. It might be on the order of doubling them, with increasing exaggeration as time went on. Quite clearly the communities were concerned with something other than objective economic poverty; but they were able to cling to their right to exclude the *poor* through the heaviest storms of liberal bureaucratic administration, and so they attached to poverty all the hometown stigmata of exclusion. Poor, irresponsible, immoral, incompetent, wage laborer, promiscuous, homeless, groundrabbit: hometownsmen got laws and justification for excluding persons whom these labels fit, and they applied them to all those they wished to exclude. With the home-law galaxy, built like an inverted pyramid on the point of poverty, they succeeded in making hometown standards and qualities official; Home Law was a legal representation of the Biedermeier style. There the German idea of proletariat took shape in the late thirties, before the time of factories, as a figure of the disassociated, homeless, alien, uneasy; there the Biedermeier defined itself by its enemy and its opposite: a culture of still familiarity based on fear and rejection. Vahlkampf saw a "remarkable despondency" everywhere, of a kind that affected all parties to the question of Home in a similar way: "the endeavor to maintain the old ways loses heart in the instinctive feeling, or the clear awareness, that the tides of time will not stay dammed up in the end; and the believers in the system of free development are hard-put to ward away a prophetic melancholy that enters their thoughts with the spectre of poverty." [89] It is appropriate to the nature of the Biedermeier that hometown culture was carried to its apex there on a current bearing it to dissolution.

Home law came from the meeting of the communities with the changes in economy, population, and politics that were the most

[89] Ibid., p. 1.

serious enemies they had faced since the seventeenth century. The distinctive feature of the Biedermeier development was that the German community had got its defenses built, legally, politically, and culturally, under the relatively weak hostile stimulus of bureaucracy and its handful of commercial allies, before the much more powerful forces connected with industrialization were ready to dissolve it. It was innoculated with a mild related virus, so that instead of succumbing to the infection it developed antibodies, antibodies that became a permanent part of Germany's bloodstream.

But all the same it had been infected. The Biedermeier incursions to be sure did not break hometown walls but built them higher. But they were built higher out of materials not reliable for hometown defense, the criteria of wealth and poverty that the outside recognized and allowed to them. By adopting the enemy's weaponry the home towns were moving within his range, so that the two worlds of the Biedermeier were coming closer together even as the division sharpened into the pre-March and 1848.

CHAPTER XI

Eighteen Forty-Eight

THE "most miserable class that ever sneaked its way into history" (next to the peasantry) annoyed the young Friedrich Engels of 1847 most of all because it most perfectly represented the splintering tendency of German public life that frustrated historical progress. That gave hometownsmen their important place in his essay "The Status Quo in Germany." Engels thought that historically the *bourgeoisie* (here he used the French word) had sprouted out of the *Kleinbürgertum* (here the German word), but the two represented quite opposite principles: cosmopolitan trade, great industry, free competition, and the centralization of wealth were the realm of the bourgeoisie; local trade, artisanry, small and static capital, and restraint on competition the realm of the Kleinbürger; local affairs were all the Kleinbürger cared about, and they maintained as much distance between themselves and the state as they could; but the politics of the bourgeoisie were all-encompassing and strove for no less than mastery of the state and its relations within and without. In a fragmented Germany frozen on the status quo, political power was delivered over to the bureaucracy by default.[1] Thorstein Veblen, writing much later about the same second quarter of the nineteenth century that Engels was describing, noticed something quite different from Engels' fragmentation: growing uniformity. He compared the culturally unifying effects of the movement of ideas, the established basis of Germany's general estate, with the

[1] "Status Quo," pp. 235–245.

354

unifying effects of nineteenth-century technology. "The habitual consumption of print has much the same order of disciplinary effect as habituation to the wide-reaching standardization of the arts of life brought on by machine industry; but it goes without saying that the effect so wrought by the use of print will not extend much beyond the class of persons addicted to it . . . whereas the disciplinary value of life under the standardizing regime of the machine industry touches the illiterate perhaps more immediately and intimately, and almost as comprehensively, as it touches the classes who habitually read." [2]

The home towns had resisted standardization by print; industry was something else again. And with it came a third intruder, a third leg of the tripod upon which the politics of the forties rested: the crowd. Ferdinand Tönnies remarked that the deprecatory idea of "the crowd" united two divergent propositions (*Vorstellungen:* conceptions): first, great numbers of atomized and alienated people, disconnected and aimless; and second, a mob united in uniformity of purpose, a general, overriding, social will.[3] Common to both ends of Tönnies' antithesis is the strange hostile facelessness the crowd presents to the passive observer. His crowd, in the 1840's, was the outsiders, pressing massively across the fractural lines Engels identified. A historical resolution of Tönnies' paradox is that the alienated atomized crowd was conceived to be the product of a massive, internally consistent but uncrystallized, irreversible historic process of industrialization, population growth, and revolutionary social change: thus conceived by intellectuals, statesmen, and by hometownsmen.[4] Engels and Veblen seem to disagree because they emphasized respectively two contrasting aspects of the 1840's. What both of them missed, being preoccupied (like the German general estate of the time) with the prospective course of economics and technology, was the degree of identity the German communities had already reached in their struggle against outsiders, against the "es-

[2] *Imperial Germany and the Industrial Revolution* (Ann Arbor, 1966), pp. 74–75.

[3] "Die grosse Menge und das Volk," *SJ*, XLIV (1920), Heft 2, p. 1.

[4] Parliamentary debates, political literature, and hometown petitions all testify to this pre-March sense of historic process. I have developed the theme for Germany in *Germany and the Emigration*, and more generally in *Metternich's Europe*.

tateless" persons that a Prussian commentator described in 1845 as "the nonsettled, the capitalists, intellectuals, proletarians, and so on."[5] Tönnies was thinking more nearly out of that hometownsmen's identity.

Hometownsmen at the end of the forties actually directed their fire less against industry as such than against the traditional policies of state bureaucracy: against the legal undermining of the guild economy and against state incursions into communal self-determination. Their particularist-conservative side of the Revolution of 1848 joined together initially with the unifying-liberal side best represented in the Constituent Assembly at Frankfurt. The two main discontented elements of 1848, hometownsman and political liberal, really were discontented with one another; but both blamed existing German bureaucratic regimes for their discontents and so did not confront one another while the regimes stood. "In the end," wrote Veblen, "both parties to the misunderstanding were convicted of contumacy"; Wilhelm Heinrich Riehl's theme for a chapter on 1848 was "In vino veritas."[6]

Common hostility to bureaucracy joined the two together, or rather, joint hostility to the two faces of German bureaucracy respectively, its politically authoritarian face and its socially liberal face. Liberal intellectuals, including a great many civil servants, joined the revolt against bureaucratic regimes with respect to issues pertaining to their own spheres: censorship and political tutelage. But the antibureaucratic movement of the 1840's among movers and doers was directed not against the traditional policies of administrative bureaucracy but against a growing conservatism at upper governmental levels: against a takeover of administrative direction by the nobility in Prussia, against an entrenched body of high administrators in Bavaria.[7] Middle and lower bureaucracy could easily share in such a movement; it matched the long-standing difference between the upper (and local) levels of government

[5] K. F. Bauer, *Die ständische Gesetzgebung der preussischen Staaten*, II (Berlin, 1845), p. 2, quoted in Koselleck, *Preussen*, p. 341.

[6] Veblen, *Imperial Germany*, p. 76; Riehl, *Bürgerliche Gesellschaft*, p. 17. "Im Wein ist Wahrheit" was Riehl's actual phrase; Latin would not pass his lips.

[7] Koselleck, *Preussen*, especially pp. 352–354, 447, 486; Veit Valentin, *Geschichte der deutschen Revolution von 1848–49*, I (Berlin, 1930), 110.

I have called political in the individualized country, and the middle levels called administrative. But in the late forties all levels of government were uneasy and unsure, at a prospect of political and social upheaval; and deliberate conservatism was less important than a tendency to freeze into inactivity in an atmosphere where change seemed compelling, and to hold, uncertainly, to the status quo on all matters relating to the economic development and social change that seemed inevitable.

This confused pause of the forties on the status quo stimulated "bourgeois" hostility against the very bureaucracy that had always been the main political protagonist of free entrepreneurship, economic growth, and social mobility, against the static or circular communalism represented by the home towns; meanwhile home-townsmen still saw in bureaucracy their chief enemy. Engels in his analysis of the status quo tried to make bureaucracy and Klein-bürger political allies, so as to consolidate his enemies and concentrate his fire; but when he tried to work out the alliance theoretically he had to give it up because it was ill-founded, and the essay of March, 1847, remained an unpublished fragment.[8]

Inevitability and uncertainty

Almost everybody—certainly both intellectuals and hometowns-men—complained of bureaucratic arbitrariness in the 1840's, and with good reason. For administrators had no clear consistent direction to follow, and their decisions became unpredictable and incongruent. The Biedermeier contradiction was coming to a head in the pre-March. The "social problem" was basically a growth of population faster than Biedermeier social and economic institutions absorbed it. The two alternative attacks on the problem—to liberalize economy and society so as to absorb the outsiders, or to protect and strengthen existing institutions against penetration and dissolution—were contradictory; and as a consequence no effective policies were formed and there was little legislation to guide action. Legislative paralysis left individual decision in the hands of civil

---

[8] The events of 1848–1850 gave him more ammunition but did not solve all his systematic problems, both leading to even greater vituperation against the Kleinbürgertum: cf. *Revolution and Counter-Revolution, or Germany in 1848* (many editions, often under Marx's name).

servants and provincial courts; the bureaucratic bias for liberalization generally prevailed there, but in a piecemeal and unsystematic
way.

For intellectuals of the forties the key to the social problem was
industrialization, but there was a policy dilemma wrapped up in
that term; for while the factory might absorb the "proletariat," so
too it was conceived to be a creator of proletariat, by the precedents of England and France, Germany's two main windows into its
own anticipated future. Lorenz von Stein's *Socialism and Communism in Modern France,* published in 1842, connected the industrial
future with social revolution; Engels' 1845 *Condition of the Working Class in England,* although far less influential, was an altogether
credible reflection of what German Bürger and statesmen feared
might lie before them. Robert von Mohl determined from French
and British figures that crimes against property rose in proportion
with factories, and doubtfully proposed a kind of neo-guild system
that would accommodate industry but retain social cohesion by
slowing industrial development, keeping it decentralized, and putting a floor under prices to avoid economic desperation.[9]

The hard times that set in with the crop failures of 1845–1846 aggravated the dilemma but brought solution no closer, except insofar as they served to generalize conditions throughout the country.
Intensification of agriculture, notably the increased use of the potato, had probably helped to stave off social change much as communal legislation and communal resistance had done, by allowing
population growth without proportional population movement and
social change. Now with the potato failures of the later forties, the
dislocations that should have been spread out over the past thirty
years came all at once; peasants poured into the towns, where they
joined earlier outsiders as "overpopulation." [10] Or—with the encouragement of governments—they turned to the artisan trades
themselves or to peddling; or they stopped bringing produce to
hometown middlemen for trade. Nobody knew how to stop them
without the risk of making matters worse, and hostility between

[9] Angermann, *Mohl,* pp. 213ff., 239–240, 301–302.
[10] E.g. the description in Richard Kohl, "Herford, 1848," *JHVH,* XLIV
(1930), 10–12.

hometownsmen and countrymen grew more intense.[11] Journeymen unable to find accredited masters to employ them tramped from town to town, and their demands at each place for their traditional *Zehrpfenning* before moving on became hardly distinguishable, in hometown eyes, from a mass invasion of sturdy beggars bent on social blackmail.

A short-lived Hanoverian trades ordinance of 1847 opened the countryside to the crafts and forbade the ban mile; Bavaria renewed its effort in 1846 to define two economies, a hometown one to be protected and general one to be advanced.[12] Very many people, hometownsmen and liberal intellectuals and entrepreneurs alike, called for "trades orders to replace trades disorder," but by order they meant contradictory things: in Württemberg, for example, government and tradesmen both favored reform of the trades laws, but a government proposal of 1846 got nowhere because it contemplated just the systematic regulation and opening of opportunity that the tradesmen did not want.[13] At the beginning of 1848 the townsmen of Konstanz, aroused by a report that the Baden Diet was considering a trades ordinance based on "conditional freedom," sent a request that "the views of experienced tradesmen" be added to the "intellectual powers prevalent in the state ministry" before anything was done.[14]

Hessen-Darmstadt produced a new marriage law in 1847, though, patched together by a fearful and perplexed government to meet strong communal pressure coupled with opposition victories in the Diet election of that year; and Württemberg was on the verge of a similar law at the beginning of 1848. Hessen-Darmstadt marriage laws had been the most liberal in the individualized country; they dated back to the twenties and had withstood the counterswing of the early thirties. But since 1841 the Diet had been trying to in-

---

[11] Note the Hessen-Darmstadt *Hausiren* law of 1846, which—despite demands from the Diet for sharp restrictions on unlicensed retailing—left practically all trade in rural products free, or subject only to state approval: HDReg 28 XI 1846.

[12] Graf, "Stüve," p. 266, citing Oppermann, *Zur Geschichte des Königreichs Hannover*, I, 307–309; above, p. 345.

[13] Köhler, *Das württembergische Gewerberecht*, p. 158.

[14] BGK 236/5820: 1–2. Petition dated 25 II 1848.

crease community powers to control marriage, with much clamor about the better social protection communities got from the governments of other states. The government had claimed that severe marriage restriction would not only be unconstitutional civil discrimination, but would have the practical effect of legitimizing illict sexual activity and births out of wedlock and out of family, and cited in its turn Bavaria's notorious bastardy. Through the middle forties each side accused the other of immoral attacks upon the integrity of the home; the Diet repeatedly demanded a legislative draft from the government and the government regularly refused to provide one.[15] The Opposition thoroughly defeated civil servants in the Diet election of 1847 with a combination of smalltown mayors, small landowners, and liberal intellectuals of the post-Napoleonic generation, the Burschenschaft generation sympathetic in principle to self-government by the people and hostile to entrenched bureaucracy: Heinrich von Gagern may be taken as a representative of the latter.[16] At this the government, protesting its disapproval in principle, produced a draft for a law that would allow communities to forbid marriages directly, as well as indirectly through the citizens acceptance powers town councils held by virtue of the old Community Ordinance.[17]

The debate on this showed a signal division between communal and liberal Opposition to officialdom. Communitarians rallied the good Middle Ages against bureaucracy, the nineteenth century, and their joint works. To recognize the destruction of morality, living standards, and sound communal life in modern times "no serious study is needed"; just look around at the contrasts at hand. One communitarian argued that love, being blind, was no valid ground for a social decision like marriage, and that love as it was conceived by "effervescent youth" was the root cause of the proletarianization of all civilized countries, that and the breakdown of Eigentum through too-easy transfer of property. Another blamed modern social evils on a regular pattern of bureaucratic tyranny

[15] HDVerh 1841/42 (2), Beil. XXVIII, CXXII, and Protocols for 12 and 15 III 1842; HDReg 2 VII 1842; HDVerh 1844/47 (2), Beil. XLVII, CXXXVIII, and Protocols for 2 and 6 V 1845.

[16] Valentin, Revolution von 1848–49, I, 180. Compare opposition victories in Baden elections in 1846, and to the Prussian United Diet of 1847.

[17] HDVerh 1844/47 (2), Beil. CCLXXIII; HDReg 28 VI and 2 VII 1847.

that violated the people's social integrity. Gagern's contribution was impressive and important. He said that the restrictive law could not achieve its ostensible goals, and that it was politically and morally wrong. Not only would it discriminate against the poor: it would take effect against the industrious, the law-abiding and honorable poor, not against lazy irresponsible riffraff of the kind hometownsmen declared all outsiders to be. Such a law would in fact create an army of classless malcontents, the very proletariat everybody talked about. Nobody had a right, Gagern said, to seize property, but everybody had a right to enter civil society (thus he divided Eigentum into separate parts). He dismissed out of hand the notion that rising poor taxes oppressed the communities, or were the real causes of such symptoms of social discontent as the emigration; the sources of malaise lay deeper than that, and no false law like this one could reach them. When pressed to explain what ought to be done Gagern tried to distinguish between community rights of self-government and a Hessian subject's right to marry: the Paulskirche was not far away. By a large majority the Diet approved a law enabling town councils to prevent the marriage of anybody connected with the community, even a citizen, who *menschlichen Ansehen nach*—judging by appearances—was not possessed of a trade or property that would support a family independently and securely.[18]

The Hessian debates were closely watched from Stuttgart; the Württemberger were very uneasy about social and political unrest in 1846 and 1847. In 1846 the government felt obliged to forbid town councils and Citizens' Committees to hold their deliberations in public, on the grounds that a growing tendency to do so allowed too much "public influence" on their decisions, an increase of hometown pressure over state pressure at the intersecting point of local decision in Württemberg.[19] And the marriage question seemed to

[18] Technically, the community lodged a complaint against a prospective marriage, and the government (which issued Hessian marriage licenses) was to decide; but the marriage could not take place until the government positively dismissed the community position, with appeal going to the Ministry of Interior and Justice at Darmstadt, at that time headed by Du Thil. HDReg 20 VII 1847.

[19] WSL, Ministerium des Innern, Bürgerrecht betreffend, 1847–1864. E 146: 646/3, 4; WbgReg 20 III 1846. Note the contrast with the anti-oligarchy policies of eighteenth-century states.

lie close to the source of the dangerous communal unrest. Two commissioners were sent out in the spring of 1847 to feel the public's pulse and locate the causes of its discontent; and both reported that the communities all complained that the citizenship laws as they were enforced encouraged frivolous marriage and forced communities to accept the consequences, that the rules on reputation and self-support were not severe enough—and everybody wanted freedom of the press and public criminal trials.[20] Reports coming in through regular channels told the same story, though the language varied; most said the 1833 laws on marriage were not restrictive enough. Reutlingen said that property requirements could serve only as a rough guide, for state officials, and did not answer the problem; masters' licenses were no criterion either because townsmen who were jealous and officials who were permissive managed between them to license the least competent rather than the ablest. Rottenburg and Freudenstadt talked of overpopulation and machines; only tight social legislation could prevent the growth of a large rootless class with consequent damage to everybody's interests. Horb in the Black Forest said the trouble came from supposing, as the government seemed to suppose, that technical competence in a trade was enough to bring success at it; that misapprehension, which state law imposed upon town fathers who knew better, allowed young men just back from their wandering to marry, and settle and practice a trade to the detriment of "older and better community members," whose only peaceful way out was then to emigrate: "I will go while I still have something." [21]

The government tried to persuade communities and other corporate associations to set up loan funds for needy artisans so that they would not have to go on the public dole, a wistful effort to reinstitute the social services of guilds and endowments against whose social powers the government had fought long and rather successfully.[22] The United Charitable Society of North Württemberg petitioned for more restrictions on marriage.[23] In September of 1847 the government at Stuttgart asked the Department of Politi-

[20] WSL E 146: 646/1, 8.
[21] WSL E 146: 646/passim. Most of these reports were submitted by Oberamtmänner.
[22] WbgReg 15 VI 1847.
[23] Covering roughly the Jaxt-Kreis. WSL E 146: 646/35.

cal Economy of the University at Tübingen for an opinion on marriage rights. In December the political economists submitted their view that the state's duty was to uphold "with true liberality" individual rights to marry and settle, especially against arbitrary obstructions by communal officials, from whose treatment peasants, factory workers, and journeyman artisans suffered most. The professors used some contemptuous language about the arbitrariness, the Willkür, of community regimes, by which however they seemed to mean local oligarchies which they equated with bureaucracy, not with virtuous hometownsmen—perhaps the town councils and committees the government had been trying to shield from public influence. The state and its laws, they said emphatically but vaguely, ought to stay out of moral questions (where communal opinion had the advantage of them anyway) and ought to stand on clear economic criteria for social acceptability—although to be sure the question of whether a man would get acceptance and customers was an economic question, so come to think of it morals came in somewhere. Fear of competition from new members gave the communities no right to exclude them. But from there the political economists wandered into a dissertation on the community as a free association for the development of civic virtues, speaking of the unique personality (Persönlichkeit) whose formation was the particular genius of communal life. Finally they gave the opinion that a free community must have the right to choose its members (Genossen); but it should accept those whom it *ought* to accept.[24]

Nobody who has experienced academic deliberations on public policy can escape a shock of recognition from the Tübingen memorandum. By now the Paulskirche was even closer. On February 15, 1848, a week before the barricades went up in Paris, the King of Württemberg commanded his Privy Council and Interior Ministry to get to work on a modification of the marriage rules *now*, because "the voices of the public, whose views in this instance clearly have not been artificially evoked or proclaimed by persons with no right to speak," were unanimous that existing rules were inadequate.[25] But the changes set in motion in 1846 and 1847 were suspended through 1848 and 1849; the Württemberg hometownsmen had to wait for the beginning of the fifties for their new marriage law.

[24] WSL E 146: 646/21–22, 33.   [25] WSL E 146: 646/35.

Hometownsmen were nationalist along with nearly everybody else when the revolution of conflicting expectations broke out in the spring of 1848. The nation, the *Volk*, meant the people, in contrast with the states. Nobody was more sure of being the real people than hometownsmen, and nobody was more at odds than they were with the states they knew: the administrative caste that meddled in their affairs. Nobody was more devoted than they to self-government: the self-government they knew of the hometown community. Community was nationalist because both principles opposed the states in being; and hometown political convocations resolved for the creation of a new Reich to replace the states of the Confederation.[26] They anticipated, of course, no revolutionary social change from this relocation of high authority; quite the reverse; they expected the dismissal of state bureaucracies from the positions of power from which, in their repeated attacks upon the communities, officials had acted as agents of social revolution.[27]

The conservatism of German artisanry in 1848 has often been described,[28] but it is important to be discriminating here because we

[26] On hometown nationalism in the pre-March and in 1848 see, e.g., Ludwig Mayer, "Regensburg und die Revolution 1848," *VHVO*, CII (1962), 33–34; Helmut Renner, ed. "Der Bericht des Regierungspräsidenten von Zenetti über die politische Bewegung in der Pfalz 1848/49," *MHVP*, LIX (1961), 141; Friedrich Meisenburg, "Die Stadt Essen in den Revolutionsjahren 1848–1849," *BGE*, LIX (1940), 139–190.

[27] Probably the first serious indication hometownsmen had that this revolution was not following the course they wished was peasant violence, riotous peasant invasions of the towns, and quick peasant political victories—such achievements as freely alienable property, freedom of emigration, and the abolition of noble and town perquisites—in the March governments. Noisy demanding peasants within the walls had been a main source of growing hometown anxiety in the pre-March; and the peasantry were the first and perhaps the only victors of 1848 in the individualized country. Cf. Günther Franz, "Die agrarische Bewegung im Jahre 1848," *ZAA*, VII (1959), 176–193, and the sources cited there; August Sartorius von Waltershausen, *Deutsche Wirtschaftsgeschichte, 1815–1914* (2d ed.; Jena, 1923), p. 140; Heffter, *Selbstverwaltung*, pp. 284–285; Ernst Huhn, "Das Grossherzogtum Sachsen in der Bewegung der Jahre 1848–49," *ZVTG*, NF XXVII (1926), 248–261; Kohl, "Herford, 1848," pp. 10–12; Regierungsblätter 1848–1850 passim.

[28] Rudolf Stadelmann, *Soziale und politische Geschichte der Revolution von 1848* (Munich, 1948); Theodore S. Hamerow, *Restoration, Revolution, Reaction* (Princeton, 1958); Paul H. Noyes, *Organization and Revolution* (Princeton, 1966).

are coming to deal now with a comparison or transition between community and class. Artisanry as an economic idea overlaps largely with hometownsmen as a social and political idea; in the area of overlap stands the guild master with his location in local government and society. Economic petitions from the communities in 1848, again, did not so much denounce factories as demand restoration of community and guild controls over entry into the traditional local trades, which is not altogether the same thing. Hometown rejection of occupational freedom was not coupled with machine-breaking, which would in fact have made very little economic sense even for them, but rather with complaints against official liberality with trades licenses for unknown journeymen and with marriage and settlement rights.[29]

Journeymen pressed in the other direction: Saxon journeymen for easier entry into the trades and for abolition of the rule maintained in many localities that a journeyman who married gave up any right to become a master; Bavarian journeymen against the stinginess of communal authorities with settlement rights, and their inattention to the criteria of artisanal skill.[30] Journeymen were artisans too, but they were not hometownsmen—things had changed since the eighteenth-century days when journeymen had been the most ardent defenders of the guildsman's honor, keeping themselves pure for entry into the hometown trades. They were leaving the guild corporation for the outsider class, and calling for economic reentry on those terms. Hometownsmen wanted the revolution to strengthen local self-government of the social and economic rights that sepa-

[29] E.g. the complaint of the Community Deputies of Würzburg against the Kreis government "wegen mehrerer Ansässigmachungsbewilligungen," in BHM MH, Beschwerden über die ausgedehnten Ansaessigmachungsbewiligungen auf Gewerbe (1848–1855), 6133:2; the Regensburg *Gewerbeverein*'s demand that trades licenses be issued exclusively by the town, subject to guild approval, in Mayer, "Regensburg, 1848," pp. 77–78; the Nassau petitions against existing free settlement and occupational freedom, and for protective tariffs, in Wolfgang Klötzer, "Die nassauischen Petitionen an die Frankfurter Nationalversammlung, 1848/49," *NA*, LXX (1959), 145–147; Bavarian petitions in BHM MH 6142; and Ernst Schocke, "Die deutsche Einheits- und Freiheitsbewegung in Sachsen-Meiningen 1848–1850," *SVSM*, LXXXVI (1927), 43–45.

[30] Fritz Hauptmann, "Sachsens Wirtschaft und der soziale Gedanke, 1840–1850," *NASG*, LIX (1938), 179–184; BHM MH 6133:1.

rated them from outsiders. The governments listened, and waited to
see what would happen at the German Constituent National Assembly at Frankfurt am Main.

The view from the Paulskirche

The men elected to the Frankfurt Parliament were no political
dilettantes; they were highly experienced in German public life.
Total membership begins to break down this way:

Intellectual and free professions	277
Public officials	309
Soldiers	16
Economic pursuits	110
	712

Such an occupational composition might appear in any elected national parliamentary body. But that they were "experienced in German public life" in 1848 already confers a particular character upon
the assembly at the Paulskirche. Rearrange the figures more nearly
to match the long German encounter between state and community,
and the location of the Frankfurt Parliament in the pattern of
German politics is sharply defined:

Public officials:	
State civil service	289
Bürgermeister	20
	309
Economic pursuits:	
Large agriculturalists	60
Merchants (including	
industry and finance)	46
Crafts and small trades	4
	110

The fifty men from town economic life thus turn out to be forty-six
merchants, bankers, and manufacturers with spheres of activity and
interest outside local corporate life, and only four artisans; the body
of public officials that made up more than a third of the Parliament
turn out to be nearly three hundred state officials (305 counting the

army officers), with their center of gravity in the middle bureau-cratic and judicial ranks, and only twenty Bürgermeister. Most of the rest of the delegates were either academics or members of the university-trained free professions.[31] Hence these new totals:

State civil service, intellectuals and free professions, merchants	612
Soldiers	16
Bürgermeister and crafts	24
Large agriculturalists	60
	712

The general estate outnumbered hometownsmen by at least 612–24 at Germany's first national assembly. They were moreover the Bur-schenschaft generation of movers and doers, now in their prime of life, a generation that added to the traditional posture of that class a belief that historical progress was self-evident, and that economic development and social change were not merely advantageous to the whole society but inevitable aspects of the historic process.

The men who assumed the task of writing a legal constitution for Germany therefore occupied a distinctive and separate place in the political and social constitution of Germany, one that seriously affected their representative function. They came not just from the upper levels of political society, but rather from a traditionally and clearly defined segment of it. Legal training and background was their commonest educational characteristic; and the fathers of most members—the "vast majority," according to the most thorough analysis—had followed the same professions that dominated in the Paulskirche.[32] Their political caste tells far more about them than the Left-Right spectrum of western parliamentary politics they adopted, or divisions between rich and poor (most were neither), or even the regions they came from. No doubt indirect electoral procedures filtered out by stages more representative but less widely

---

[31] The lists are compiled from figures in Ernst R. Huber, ed., *Deutsche Verfassungsgeschichte seit 1789*, II (Stuttgart, 1960), 610. All men elected to the Parliament as delegates, not just those sitting at any one time, are included. Another set of figures, differing slightly from this one, is in Max Schwarz, *MdR; Biographisches Handbuch der Reichstage* (Hannover, 1965), p. 8.

[32] Frank Eyck, *The Frankfurt Parliament, 1848–1849* (London, 1968), p. 97; his occupational analyses, pp. 57–101.

known candidates, sending the general estate to Frankfurt in the end: artisan, town councilor, and Bürgermeister electors chose in turn business and civil service delegates to Frankfurt, few of their own number being well enough known outside their own communities to win election from whole districts.[33] There was a similar important difference between delegates to state diets and delegates to the national assembly. Bavaria for example sent 68 members of the general estate to Munich and 51 hometownsmen, but its delegation to Frankfurt was 83–3 in favor of the general estate. Not one of the 31 Franconian delegates to the Paulskirche was a communal officer or an artisan, most being state civil servants or free professionals; but 22 of 52 representatives at the Bavarian Diet were artisans or communal officers, and only 12 were civil servants or free professionals.[34]

The work of the Paulskirche that most directly affected the hometown communities was the Basic Rights of the German People, especially §§ 1–3 of the Basic Rights, on Reich citizenship and the rights that flowed from it, and § 43 on local self-government.[35] The Constitution Committee that drafted these provisions was surely the most distinguished of the Parliament; its roster was an honor roll of pre-March national liberalism, including among others Max von Gagern, Johann Gustav Droysen, Hermann von Beckerath, Paul Pfizer, Robert von Mohl, Friedrich Dahlmann, August Hergenhahn, Friedrich Römer, Robert Blum, Friedrich Bassermann, Johann Ludwig Tellkampf, and Georg Waitz. On the Basic Rights particularly

[33] Cf. Konrad Repgen, *Märzbewegung und Maiwahlen des Revolutionsjahres 1848 im Rheinland* (Bonn, 1955), pp. 224–235; Meisenburg, "Essen in 1848–1849," pp. 216–219. On "bourgeois" domination of elections to the Paulskirche, Theodore S. Hamerow, "The Elections to the Frankfurt Parliament," *JMH*, XXXIII (1961), 15–33.

[34] Zimmermann, *1848 in Franken*, pp. 435–455; Karl Mailer, *Die Wahlbewegung im Jahre 1848 in Bayern* (Ichenhausen, 1931), pp. 34, 47. It may be equally—or alternatively—significant that the Landtag elections took place considerably later than the Frankfurt elections. See also Norbert Matern, *Politische Wahlen in Hildesheim, 1848 bis 1867* (Bonn, 1959), pp. 28–64. In contrast with the Paulskirche but like the diets of the individualized country, a great many town officials were elected to the Prussian National Assembly at Berlin: Heffter, *Selbstverwaltung*, pp. 307–308.

[35] These became (roughly) §§ 132–133 and § 184 in the usual edition of the Constitution of March 28, 1849; but I shall use the numbers relevant provisions bore through most of the debates.

as they bore on the communities, it worked closely—but not so closely as to reach identical conclusions—with another powerful committee, the Economics Committee, similarly composed (almost half were university professors) but with a stronger dose of merchants and a smattering of industrialists.[36] The majorities of both committees believed that occupational freedom from the kinds of controls communities exercised was the only way out of the impasse created by economic and demographic changes within a rigid social and legal structure. Both knew that occupational freedom was illusory without freedom of movement and settlement, and vice versa. But both knew too that to call these freedoms irreducible rights of German citizenship would be to fly in the face of what a great many Germans meant by the Bürgerrecht; and the Constitution Committee was sensitive, both for doctrinal and for prudential political reasons, to the conflict between the civil rights it proposed for all Germans, and the rights of self-government it proposed for German communities.

These topics were never separate in debates on the Basic Rights. The draft clause on Reich citizenship submitted by the Constitution Committee in July, 1848 (after consultation with the Economics Committee) declared that any German might settle anywhere, carry on any trade and win (gewinnen) community citizenship, at present under existing state laws but ultimately under uniform Reich laws. Full freedom of movement and occupation was the goal. "But," the Committee hedged, "it must be taken into account that not only the welfare and ease of individuals is involved, but also the rights and interests of the communities; for to preserve and to elevate their independent existence and honorableness [selbstständige Haltung und Ehrenhaftigkeit] is one of the most important tasks of German political art [Staatskunst]." There would have to be general rules to determine "in what instances the commu-

---

[36] Franz Wigard, ed. Stenographischer Bericht über die Verhandlungen der deutschen constituirenden Nationalversammlung zu Frankfurt am Main (9 vols.; Frankfurt/Main, 1848–1849: hereafter SB), I, 682, 689; Eyck, Frankfurt Parliament, pp. 206–210; Walter Schneider, Wirtschafts- und Sozialpolitik im Frankfurter Parlament, 1848/9 (Frankfurt/Main, 1923), pp. 17–22 and passim, for the work of the Economics Committee; on the Constitution Committee, Johann G. Droysen, Die Verhandlungen des Verfassungsausschusses der deutschen Nationalversammlung (Leipzig, 1849), passim.

nity may have the right to reject those seeking to enter it"; but from the moment the Basic Rights took effect, subjects of any German state might enter any other state and be treated just as native subjects were—a temporary disadvantage (signs of anxiety here) for liberal states like Prussia, but a necessary stage on the way to full freedom.[37] And the Constitution Committee kept a saving phrase about "reputation" in its draft declaration of the rights of Germans in other than their native states. Political art, indeed.

The Economics Committee was ready to be more ruthless with local and state restraints on individual freedoms than the Constitution Committee. The plenum (at least by the time the important votes were taken) was more insistent simultaneously both on the rights of free individuals and on the rights of local self-government than either committee—generally speaking, the more radical the delegate the more emphatically he insisted on both; Frank Eyck remarks in his careful study of the Paulskirche how the Left-Right pattern broke down particularly over the "key paragraph," § 2 of the Basic Rights, on settlement, trades, and community entry.[38] The Economics Committee proposed that states be obliged in the Basic Rights to modify "state laws and local rights" to conform with the freedom of movement and occupation that flowed from German citizenship, and that the Reich (the Paulskirche) proceed immediately to draft laws on home rights and trades rather than relying "provisionally" on existing state laws. It argued that the German economy was a national economy; never again could economic issues be thought out in local terms. And "nothing does more to feed that disease, pauperism, whose cure is the most important task of our time, than bigotted confinement of movement." Reich law should "abolish all the conflicting guild privileges and government concessions in the several states," said the committee rapporteur, not remarking that to say this was to threaten every licensed tradesman and privileged merchant or manufacturer in Germany, not to mention the powers of the authorities who granted licenses and concessions. Yet, he continued, full economic freedom would be dangerous because the communities could not be trusted to see to proper training; that was why there had to be a Reich

[37] SB, I, 681–684 (July 3, 1848).
[38] Eyck, *Frankfurt Parliament*, pp. 216–221.

trades ordinance; "here legislation must come to the aid of conduct [*Sitte*]." [39]

The causes and consequences of poverty permeated economic debates at the Paulskirche, and despite reservations about the degree of economic freedom feasible, there was never any doubt which of the two conflicting solutions to poverty the Parliament would adopt: it would choose economic expansion, the solution of the larger and dynamic view, over the social restriction of hometown perspective. The two alternatives were economically so opposed as to allow no serious chance for compromise, and the experience of the foregoing decade and a half seemed to show that trying to pursue both at once meant deadlock and stagnation, deteriorating conditions, and constant political tension. During the spring and summer of 1848 the parliamentarians also feared, quite rightly, that continuing depression of the German economy would discredit and defeat their political revolution.[40] But they did not conceive this as a tactical or temporary choice, but rather as a stage in constitutional evolution (perhaps a final one) reflecting changes of historic magnitude in the society which demanded historic decisions from them.[41]

Bruno Hildebrand, professor of political economy at Marburg and member of the Economics Committee, declared it the function of the Basic Rights to provide all Germany with a basis "upon which the lasting welfare of the German people may be built," upon which "an intelligent solution to the great social problem of our time is possible." Inasmuch as the many petitions for a trades ordinance showed that "we have many different sets of economic circumstances in Germany, circumstances that really contradict each other," the Basic Rights had to be followed by a Reich trades law to resolve the contradictions; and its principles would have to include individual freedom of settlement, freedom to acquire property

[39] SB, I, 689–695, (July 3, 1848).

[40] Cf. Schneider, *Wirtschafts- und Sozialpolitik*, pp. 22–23; SB, I, 195 and passim.

[41] See the description by Georg Beseler, professor of law at Berlin and a vigorous Germanist, of the "great social movement that has seized all Germany," which the Paulskirche was obliged to meet with national unity, with measures to get out of the situation "to which the police state of the last centuries has brought us," and with the necessary adjustments in communal governance: SB, I, 700 (July 3, 1848).

anywhere, to carry on a trade, and to acquire communal citizenship rights.[42] Professor Wilhelm Stahl, political scientist at Erlangen, thought on the other hand that the many conflicting petitions showed exactly why the Paulskirche should write no trades ordinance at all, because if they tried to meet every need "we should have to write as many general German economic ordinances as there are places in the country." He too thought freedom was the way out, but with a different twist: in a free economy, he argued, each trade could develop its own rules naturally, by "associative right"; this would lead to over-all economic and social harmony without the hated intervention of state police power. Add freedom of movement to harmony among the trades, and German communities would "find it in their interest to arrive at unity in economic matters," spontaneously. This was really a restatement of Justi's theory of harmony among individual self-interests, updated and revised to include associations of individuals in a national frame. A great many members, particularly of the Left Center, held the faith that the rights of communities and trades to make their own rules did not conflict with individual freedom and national unity. It was an ambiguity on the substance of freedom easy enough to lay to their own intellectual distance from the communal life of German society, but it derived too from the actual nature of the German society which, inescapably, they faced, and which forced this ambiguity on freedom's meaning.[43]

Actually the debates leave little doubt that the Parliamentarians as a body knew quite well what the home town was all about and recognized the problem it posed them; or at least they were told often enough. Bavarian Ministerial Councilor Friedrich von Hermann put the hometown case, arguing that reverence for historical continuity and repugnance for social uniformity were the essential bases of German nationality, so that it was the Paulskirche's duty to sustain, not crush them. He began to give the game away, though,

---

[42] SB, I, 756–757 (July 7, 1848). The issue, an important one, was between the Constitution Committee's occupational freedom for every *Kunst und Gewerbe*, and Hildebrand's proposed phrase, *jeder Nahrungszweig*.

[43] SB, I, 775–776 (July 7, 1848). For the persistence of this ambiguity, Frank Eyck's summary of Stahl's speech, "Stahl pleaded for trades giving themselves their own rules. He wanted as much *laisser-faire* as possible." *Frankfurt Parliament*, p. 218.

with a dissertation on outsiders and insiders, complaining that the Parliament's majority seemed bent on unleashing a raid by "those who stand outside" on "those who actually are in possession" of social and economic rights. Finally he made the error of raising the famous comparison between Right-Rhine Bavaria and the Bavarian Palatinate. In Upper Bavaria, where communal and guild restrictions were operative, there were more journeymen than masters, proof (he said) of the prosperity of the trades there, whereas in the Palatinate there were only a quarter as many journeymen as masters. The Palatinate led Upper Bavaria only in its numbers of peddlers and wage laborers, which showed clearly enough what occupational freedom led to. "Let us leave it up to the people," he concluded, "to help themselves." [44] That stirred the physician and publicist Johann Eisenmann of Nürnberg to protest that he respected the mandate of the people as much as anybody did, but "not the instructions of a narrow *Spiessbürgertum*, not the mandate of any separate estate or caste, be it aristocracy, bureaucracy, or be it guildsmen: all the same to me." Still he thought there had to be rules that distinguished between the factory economy and the trades, so as to preserve skills; give me a hundred thousand gulden capital, he said, and I'll put up a bread factory that will ruin every baker in Frankfurt without my needing any skilled employees at all, and that would be too bad.[45] A thought that chilled: creamcakes and fruit torten were at stake.

The Palatinate comparison was one the general estate could not let by; the judge Adolf Lette of Berlin turned the figures against the speaker who had produced them, saying that for anybody who knew about Bavaria, such statistics argued precisely for free and uniform conditions. The Palatinate social economy of free and independent small craftsmen was exactly what Germany wanted, not the lackey journeymen and the swarms of illegitimate poor for which Old Bavaria was notorious. A Palatinate delegate joined the attack with an array of economic, moral, and criminal statistics.[46] Moritz von Mohl said that in modern circumstances community guilds, instead of preventing the overstaffing of trades, actually were the cause of their overstaffing: they required permanent occupa-

---

[44] SB, I, 757–759 (July 7, 1848).   [45] SB, I, 764–765 (July 7, 1848).
[46] SB, I, 777–778 (July 7, 1848); and II, 854–856 (July 13, 1848).

tional commitments from eleven-year-olds and forbade them to change their callings when the density and structure of the trades changed. There was the reason for the "overpopulation of the trades" in German small towns; communal guilds were like cages; once shut into one, you could do nothing but starve there.[47]

The younger Mohl's analysis reflected a general theory about Germany's economic and social malaise widely held at the Paulskirche: that capital and labor were out of harmony, and that free movement of both would restore balance. Professor Tellkampf of Breslau (sometime political scientist at Columbia College in New York) was sure that the "free development of individual powers," meaning of capital and labor, was the only cure to pauperism.[48] Debates on taxes early in 1849 turned inevitably to the relation between labor and capital; Commercial Councilor Carl Degenkolb from Eilenburg in Prussian Saxony (a prominent Economics Committeeman) thought that Germany's economic troubles came from erratic imbalance between them. Until 1840, capital had sought after labor; and now the more serious trouble was that labor could not find capital. The quest of labor for capital had brought economic necessity into conflict with Germany's social and demographic structure. Capital, and factories, had to be free to spread through the country to where the labor was; and labor had to be free to go and meet them.[49]

Probably that economic conviction more than any other determined the Paulskirche majority that there had to be freedom of movement, of settlement, and to acquire, accumulate, and invest property; and it was that conviction that brought them into conflict with the home towns and with those politicians receptive to hometown social standards or responsive to hometown demands. The summary effect was that the Paulskirche attacked communal and guild social institutions even though wishing to defend German communities as political institutions and even German artisanry as an economic class. It seems to have been clearly understood at Frankfurt that this was the most sensitive social feature of the Basic

[47] SB, II, 857–858 (July 13, 1848). Moritz was Robert's brother, a Württemberg economist and civil servant.

[48] SB, I, 762–763 (July 7, 1848). Cf. the Economics Committee's report, SB, I, 689–690.

[49] SB, VII, 5102–5103, and other debates of February 8 and 9, 1849, passim.

Rights, and in domestic politics perhaps the most treacherous element of the whole document. There were arguments that freedom of movement would drive German communities into a more restrictive posture "even than they have been observed to hold heretofore," and conversely that if such freedom were truly enforced it would destroy communal government by its "overwhelming pressure on existing communal relations." [50]

Almost nobody wanted, or admitted to wanting, unrestricted entry into full communal membership for any German anywhere in the Reich. They clung to a distinction between freedom to settle and pursue any trade, which the majority insisted upon, and a universal total citizenship enabling anybody to demand a share in existing communal property and poor funds, which it did not insist upon; and they hoped that reservation would satisfy the communities. After all the communities had laid their defenses along the lines of property and poor funds in recent years, and these were hard economic proprieties of a kind the Paulskirche was almost bound to accept, as private rights.[51] As private rights they could be defended consistently with the private rights to work, settle, and move, if the two kinds were kept separate, and their conjunction into something else in the home towns (and the home law) was ignored. The Saxon industrialist Bernhard Eisenstück, a member of the far-liberal fringe even of the liberal Economics Committee, was one who insisted that full communal citizenship could be kept separate from settlement and occupational rights. Still he thought that freedom of movement and settlement was "the single most important right of the people, both politically and socially. The right to choose freely one's place of dwelling and domestic establishment underlies the development and strength of the family; on this alone can the free state, the free community, and the free Reich be built." He attacked the home laws for having created a mass of people "who have been so regulated around the country [herumgemassregelt] that they have in effect been trying to find their homes for years and simply have no homes at all! [General applause]"; that condition had to be

[50] SB, I, 759 (July 7, 1848).

[51] Thus Hofgerichtsrat Christ of Bruchsal, SB, I, 744–745 (July 5, 1848); Appelationsgerichtsassessor Trütscher of Dresden, SB, I, 770 (July 6, 1848); Obergerichtsadvocat Cropp of Oldenburg, SB, II, 850–852 (July 13, 1848); and others.

ended.[52] Moritz von Mohl was one of the few who flatly rejected the distinction, trying to introduce a clause requiring every German to be a full citizen of some community; the alternative, he said, was to create a nation out of the homeless only, a nation from which the prosperous and the communities would hold themselves apart, a Germany made up of "Reich beggars." Franz Wigard of Dresden, Parliamentary Reporter, begged Mohl to be discreet and urged the assembly to remember that they were talking about basic rights, not obligations; it would be better to put off the obligations part for later legislation.[53]

The fact was, as Professor Karl Biedermann of Leipzig had pointed out early in the debate, that freedom of movement guaranteed by the Reich made Reich citizenship a source of essential communal citizenship, without the communities being consulted or empowered to stop it; and none of the distinctions thrown up in the debate really changed that. For the Parliament here faced the conflict between the Bürgerrecht of the state and the Bürgerrecht of the community, an old conflict that because of the changes of the preceding half-century was now more critical than ever before. One delegate, a lawyer and a scholar, suggested that the Basic Rights should avoid the term "Bürger" and especially "Staatsbürger" altogether. "Bürger" bore communal connotations, and the separate word "Staatsbürger" carried a red flag in much of Germany; it meant somebody without communal rights or standing.[54] Biedermann urged the Parliament to stay out of that political thicket if it could; but it could not. The opening speech of the Basic Rights debate had insisted that the idea of citizenship must distinguish between two different kinds of people: "the stranger, the temporary resident, the dishonorable, beggars and loafers, minors, single women (not counting widows)," on the one hand, and "those who as reciprocal warrantors [Burgen (sic)] mutually represent and protect one another's rights.[55] The term "reputation" ran jaggedly

[52] SB, II, 759–760 (July 7, 1848). For the kind of herummassregeln Eisenstück probably had in mind, Huhn, "Sachsen 1848–49," II (1929), p. 65, n. 1.

[53] SB, II, 1038 (July 19, 1848).

[54] Giskra of Mährisch-Trubau: SB, I, 739 (July 5, 1848).

[55] By the conservative Prussian Gerichtsrat Wilhelm Grävell: SB, I, 730–733 (July 5, 1848).

through the whole discussion. An Austrian delegate, a Town Syndic of Ried, thought that the communities, "to secure their honor and their positions of firm independence," should have the same rights "that every head of household has: not to take into his home any person of bad reputation or any person who cannot earn his way." This was a matter that only communities and juries could determine. "I have confidence in the people; the people is good; it will not let itself be abused." [56]

The Parliament heard repeated warnings, nearly all of them from the individualized country, of the real political perils that lay in proclaiming a German citizenship that would confer the essentials of community citizenship. "We'll be knocked dead if we go home with a law that gives any German the right to share directly in the perquisites of any community," predicted Privy Councillor Karl Mittermeier of Baden, a distinguished journalist and former president of the Baden Diet; if the country was to be brought behind the Paulskirche and its national constitution, some way must be found whereby "the German Reichsbürgerrecht, the Staatsbürgerrecht of the several states, and the Gemeindebürgerrecht can exist side by side and fit together smoothly." Another Badenser, Anton Christ of Bruchsal, said that "if we do not want to stir up a kind of insurrection in the communities, we must clearly separate the general Staatsbürgerrecht from the particular Gemeindebürgerrecht." [57] At the end of the long debate on § 2 Hermann Ritter von Beisler, a Bavarian statesman of long experience in provincial government and in the cabinet at Munich, gave the Assembly his sense of the political lay of the land. If the Parliament here declared a Reich freedom of movement and settlement, he said—and he was a nationalist and a loyal member of the Parliament; but even suppose the state governments were as powerless as the Paulskirche seemed to suppose—"on

[56] SB, I, 763–764 (July 7, 1848). Old Turnvater Jahn made merry over the idea of "reputation": the way Members slandered one another, he declared, not one of them had enough reputation left to get into any self-respecting community (General laughter). He made jocular remarks about the reputations of noble ladies he had known or heard about, and concluded seriously that home and economic rights were inseparable; no real nation could be made where people were shut out on grounds of reputation. SB, II, 955 (July 13, 1848). In the end the term was dropped from the Basic Rights, and the issue left in effect to the promised laws on Heimat and on trades.

[57] SB, I, 743–745 (July 5, 1848).

the day when we make a decision on Home Law and on the home question [*Heimathwesen*] which invades the rights of estates, which invades the real interests and perquisites of the communities, on that day we shall have given into the hands of those governments the power to reject all our decisions out of hand. For the communities will rise up against us, and turn to support the governments that defend their rights." [58] The prediction took little prescience: only a recollection of the constitutions of the teens and the hometown politics of the thirties.

The overwhelming majority of the Parliament, though, was set on finally reversing the old saw that town law goes before state law. It declared national membership preeminent, and tore off all three lobes of the hometown cloverleaf in the first article of the Basic Rights. The relevant clauses in their final form were these:

Every German has German Reich citizenship. He can exercise the rights thereby conferred upon him in any German land. . . .

Every German has the right to stay and take up residence in any locality within the Reich, to acquire real property of any kind and to dispose over it, to follow any gainful occupation, to win community citizenship.

Conditions for sojourn and fixed residence will be established in a home law, and for occupations in a trades ordinance, to be issued by Reich authority for all Germany.[59]

And then the Paulskirche held out to the communities the bare stump that was left, in its article on local government.

Self-government and German unity

The Frankfurt Parliament's treatment of the home towns combined almost total distrust of the actual communities with almost total acceptance in principle of the virtues of local self-government. Thus it first systematically nullified the social powers the communities cared about, and then went on to endorse their political rights in the same constitutional document. It is hard to say how much of the support for local self-government in the Basic Rights came from conviction (probably most of it), how much from po-

[58] SB, II, 871 (July 13, 1848).
[59] §§ 132–133 in Huber's edition of the constitution: *Dokumente*, I, 318.

litical calculation (surely some of it), or how much from reasoning that once communal misbehavior had been banned by the articles on individual rights, then rights of local self-government could not endanger national goals (combining conviction with calculation). It will not do to suppose the general estate at Frankfurt fell into a contradiction out of ignorance of the home towns' natures; rather they thought the communities could be converted—once abuses were forbidden—to the ways of the general estate, and that history was working with them in that transformation. In any case their faith in a politics emanating by right from the German people rather than the German regimes, a faith and a theoretical position necessary for the whole enterprise of the National Assembly at Frankfurt, obliged them to include local government together with national as the people's right. Not quite obliged them, perhaps: there was mention of the system of the new French Republic, which allowed a citizen's franchise in national representation and national politics but kept local administration and government, the *mairie*, in state hands; but it was a derogatory mention, for "we Germans"— thus the Westphalian priest Friedrich Evertsbusch—"have always had rather the impulse for individualization, and our constitution must carry out the principle of self-government from top to bottom." [60]

Many delegates felt misgivings, and talked of community arbitrariness—Willkür again. The provincial judge Anton von Nagel from Oberviechtach in the Bavarian Upper (not Rhenish) Palatinate, near Regensburg, described from personal experience the consequences of delivering local autonomy over to the home towns in 1818 and 1834, especially social controls. In great towns, he said, "where the enlightened [*die Intelligenz*] had got firm footing," the results had been satisfactory, but in small towns disgraceful. Communities combed through "every subtlety of the law" to find ways to exclude unwanted persons from membership; they twisted "every legal provision" for the advantage of those they favored. Able candidates for a trade were shut out to protect incompetents, while superfluous and even hopeless shops were permitted "in order, perhaps, to provide the daughter of a respected Bürger with a husband." By contrast poor care was perfunctory and formal—the compilation of

[60] SB, VII, 5161–5162 (February 12, 1849).

lists for higher authority—except where keyed to nepotism instead of need. So was participation in electoral politics; the communities were not really interested in the kind of self-government with which the Paulskirche wanted to endow them. All the same (reversing direction as he turned from social to political rights) self-government had to be given them. For "the longer you keep a child on the leading-string, the slower it learns to walk. Abolish guardianship entirely," and the communities would "ripen" politically.[61] Presumably as they ripened they would unlearn how to comb legal subleties.

Local self-government being accepted in political principle even by—perhaps especially by—delegates quite hostile to hometown society, most discussion concerned the limits of state oversight rights in local elections and especially over local exercise of the police power. A schoolteacher delegate from Rottweil (the place whose eighteenth-century constitution has contributed to Chapter II) called for a purge of the Roman-bureaucratic infection that had made state oversight a tyranny. Roman law had "been judged and condemned by scholarship, and banned from most recent community ordinances; still there is reason to fear . . . the bureaucratic crabbedness that only allows a community the kind of freedom that can be regulated by tables and wedged into a Spanish boot." The community should be "an asylum of freedom." [62] Indeed it was hard to see where state confirmation powers over elected communal officials fit into the Paulskirche's program of political self-government and individual freedom, and they moved in and out of the Basic Rights with successive readings and amendments until in the end, in March 1849, state confirmation of local officers was rejected: a promise of full electoral autonomy to the communities.

On the other hand a proposal explicitly to guarantee to communities absolute control over the Gemeindebürgerrecht was dropped quietly without a vote on grounds of insufficient support in the chamber.[63] And local self-government scraped audibly against individual freedom when it came to the police power. In

[61] SB, VII, 5160–5161 (February 12, 1849).

[62] The Schulrat Rheinwald: SB, VII, 5161 (February 12, 1849).

[63] SB, VII, 5156, 5166–5167 (February 12, 1849); VIII, 5617 (March 8, 1849).

its draft on local government (§ 43 of the Basic Rights) the Constitution Committee had gone out of its way to specify the "local police power" as a communal affair, to be administered locally and independently. There if anywhere it contradicted (unless by an uncommonly narrow conception of "Ortspolizei") the clauses on individual freedoms that opened the Basic Rights; for the police power had always included trades, marriage, poverty, and communal membership in some way and some degree. But the inconsistency between the clauses was never explicitly brought out (perhaps because the debate on local government came very late, in February of 1849). A number of speakers revived the relation of community size to proper exercise of the police power. An Oldenburg lawyer, for example, thought that local police could not be left in local hands in thinly populated areas, and that any provision that did so would give the states legitimate grounds to reject or evade the constitution.[64] A provincial councilor from Frankfurt on Oder developed the distinction: the police power should not be put in local hands in large cities, either, because they could not support the administrative structure that a growing population and economy demanded of them. That left only small and middle towns. He decided it would be better to leave local police powers out of the specified rights of communities altogether, so as to strengthen state supervision of the villages that were too primitive to run themselves and the cities that were too complex.[65]

An amendment to reserve oversight of local police administration to the state had failed at the first reading of the Constitution Committee's draft; then the Committee itself adopted the phrase for the second reading in March, 1849, and in this form the clause on communal police power was approved almost unanimously.[66] It seemed the best solution. It reflected too a growing anxiety, clearest to see in the Constitution Committee, over the revived confidence of the state governments and their growing independence of what went on at the Paulskirche. Thus for the March, 1849, second reading of the Basic Rights provision for free settlement, the Committee

[64] Max Rüder: SB, VII, 5162–5163 (February 12, 1849). Hanover was most distrustful of the doings in the Paulskirche.

[65] Oberregierungsrat August Naumann: SB, VII, 5163–5165 (February 12, 1849).

[66] SB, VII, 5167 (February 12, 1849); VIII, 5618 (March 8, 1849).

added a similar saving clause: that no state would be obliged to accept incomers under freer settlement terms than they had enjoyed in their native states. This was to persuade the states (notably Prussia) and the communities that Frankfurt was not threatening them with an inundation of migrant poor; but the amendment was rejected by the plenum. The Committee now also proposed stronger restrictions on the right of Germans to citizenship in other German states: "good reputation and sufficient resources for the applicant to support himself and his family." But that too was rejected and did not enter the constitution of March, 1849.[67]

The final form of the article on local government then read:

Every community has as the basic laws of its constitution:
    a) the election of its officers and representatives;
    b) the independent administration of its community affairs including local police, subject to legally defined oversight by the state [des Staates];
    c) publication of its budgetary accounts;
    d) normally public deliberations.[68]

Internal political rights are there, but so emptied of social and economic substance by the earlier provisions on civil rights as to be hardly more than administrative functions, to be exercised publicly and under the eye of "the state," whoever that was—an oversight which in the final language extended beyond local police to all "community affairs." The Paulskirche offered the home towns the burdens of self-government without any of the powers that made self-government worth their while. There was moreover a belligerent sound to "every community has as the basic laws [Grundrechte] of its constitution. . . ." Must every community have the same basic laws? If so, clearly they were to conform to the enumerated Basic Rights [also Grundrechte] of all Germans, which struck down the essential features of the hometown constitution. Did the general

---

[67] These tergiversations of the committee are best followed in Droysen, Verhandlungen des Verfassungsausschusses, especially pp. 190, 696–697. The extreme nervousness of the Assembly is apparent in the debates from February, 1849, onward.

[68] § 43 of the Grundrechte, § 184 of the March, 1849, constitution: Huber, ed., Dokumente, I, 322.

estate sitting at Frankfurt then have the right to say what the truly basic laws (or rights) of the communities should be?

But the question ultimately was not abstract right, nor even political wisdom, but rather political feasibility. That lawyers and professors may be knaves or fools needs no saying, and three rude and obvious facts make the Parliamentarians out to be fools: a conflict between their provisions on individual social rights and on communal political rights; the unrepresentative character of the assembly within the Paulskirche and its alienation from that political sentiment in the country which it needed to combat existing regimes; and then of course their failure. Yet it is hard to deny that their solution to Germany's social and political impasse was right on the merits. Neither social restrictions nor bureaucratic tutelage would serve. The conflicting elements of the Basic Rights put together did make a whole policy: an entry of the German people into a national political life where self-government must be consistent with individual freedom and equality. One uses phrases like these now with diffidence, but they are not empty rhetorical ones; they represent genuine and sound measures to ameliorate Biedermeier division, fear, and deadlock.

Any folly here came from the Parliamentarians' effort to present a positive program before their political power was secure. Their trouble was the Germany they were in. Here, though, the charge of isolation carries weight, in two forms: first, that political pragmatism required suppression of any program however valid that aroused hostility in the country and put weapons in the hands of the Paulskirche's enemies; and second, that the Parliamentarians did not sufficiently recognize, even as they did not represent, the actualities of German political and social life outside their own caste. But this line of criticism must take care lest it fall into its own presumptuous ignorance of "political realities." To call a national constitution a "program," as I have just done, points to one supreme political reality: that any effort to establish general principles for German political life was in itself a measure of legislative reform, not of government alone but of society, reform that attacked extant patterns of social and political rights. Theirs was no revolution to make the state conform to society, the revolution of western political theory, but rather, again, one to make society conform to the general estate. In the Germany of 1848–1849, no less than in the Germany that had met the contradiction of cameralism half a century before, positive law meant reform; the Frankfurt constitution of 1849 stood at odds with the true constitution of the country at that time: in a very real sense it was unconstitutional. No doubt the special place of its framers in German society had a great deal to do with that, but less because of any isolation from political reality than because they had a clearer sense of the social and economic changes in process, and where they were heading. The trouble was that the Parliamentarians saw these things too soon, before industrial capitalism and all that went with it had modified German society and redistributed power within it into a form that would support the constitution they wrote. They were ahead of their time, another phrase that is no banality here because it describes their supposition that a successful politics is one that perceives the course of history and builds upon where history is going, rather than one that acts as broker among interests in being.

This study of the home towns cannot of course by itself support the burden of explaining the Revolution of 1848, or the Paulskirche. Probably the Parliamentarians were encouraged to defy hometown sentiment by the thought that the small communities were too weak to matter, and so, by themselves, they were. The third proof of folly at Frankfurt, the revolution's ultimate failure, may be laid to international and dynastic politics alongside which parliamentary debates and constitutions were insignificant or at most tributary. Still the issues of local civic, economic, and social rights and of local government were the issues upon which the Parliament most directly engaged itself with the structure of German society and most vigorously debated it. It is possible to argue (though I am not quite ready to do so) that its positions on these issues were enough to assure its failure even without dynastic and foreign hostility, or to assure that at best (and this I do say) it could not have reached a better constitutional arrangement than Bismarck's Second Empire twenty years later, which was far from ideal—not without civil war, probably as a helpless ally of the Prussian bureaucracy. For only by going to Prussia early, on Prussia's terms, could the Paulskirche have achieved the force to overcome the states of the individualized country and the allies they found when the Frankfurt Parliament tried to break through the status quo in Germany.

Back in the states

Within the German states in 1848, community issues (as predicted) gave the Paulskirche's enemies important weapons, and steadily increased their number while disheartening its friends. Most state governments were markedly silent on the economic and social issues that affected the home towns during 1848. Such behavior by the March ministries is easy to justify on the grounds that these were acknowledged national problems that required national solution; they were Frankfurt's job. But it also shows the governments lying low and thus tacitly conceding hometown rule, as governments usually did in precarious times. The consequence was that hometown hostility was redirected from its traditional enemies in state government to Frankfurt, and secondarily to Berlin. The political publicist and theorist Friedrich Rohmer (Weissenburg-born, a clergyman's son) transferred his hatred of bureaucracy from Munich to Frankfurt that summer. In an essay on "Germany's Old and New Bureaucracy" he wrote that "a new formalism" at Frankfurt was replacing the old bureaucratic formalism, a new formalism of "lawyers, professors, and industrialists: that is, of the office, the study, the countinghouse." Germany had entrusted its revolution to the very people the revolution was against. "We wanted to clear out bureaucracy, and we gave the job, by agency of the industrialists, to the lawyers, who live from bureaucratism, and especially to the professors, who reared bureaucracy in the first place. . . . Bureaucracy remains bureaucracy, whether it starts from an abolutist position or a radical one." [69]

The March ministries did expand the local political and administrative powers of the communities. This in turn was in keeping with that half of Frankfurt's program; it could legitimately be done within each state, without affecting other German states as individual freedoms would—and it reaped popularity with the towns. Communal governments in Sachs-Meiningen were widely exempted

[69] "Deutschlands alte und neue Bureaukratie," in *Politische Schriften* (Nördlingen, 1885), pp. 572, 574.

from bureaucratic controls early in 1848; a Baden provisional law of June gave communities the right freely to elect officers to positions formerly filled by state appointment; Württemberg in 1849 modified its community ordinance to conform more nearly with the Baden law of 1831.[70] Nearly everywhere there were laws introducing jury courts and civil militias, both of them communally based and firmly in the hands of communal leadership.[71] The Württemberg law of April, 1848, for example, described the "citizens' militia of each community" as a "self-contained whole," organized by town councils and from which state officials and wage laborers were to be excluded.[72] Rules against open deliberations by town councils were relaxed or removed: a step described in Württemberg as a revocation of the bureaucratic 1846 decrees on the subject, and in Bavaria as an extension of the communal autonomies of 1818.[73] Hessen-Kassel communities were granted local police power in 1848. Hanover went a step further: its constitution of 1848 guaranteed communities the power to grant domicile, the "right to establish useful associations," and control over school, church, and poor affairs, and over local property and taxes. This was no innovation, although it generalized rights formerly held in particular. But Hanover also reversed the antiguild policy it had flirted with in 1847, when the ban mile had been forbidden and the countryside opened to the trades; its electoral law of 1848 rejected the Pre-Parliament's general suffrage in favor of a restrictive communally-based representative system; and Stüve by February of 1849 had flatly rejected the Paulskirche's Basic Rights because of their provisions of occupational

[70] Munzer, "Gemeindeverfassung in Sachsen-Meiningen," pp. 30–32; Schocke, "Sachsen-Meiningen, 1848–1850," pp. 27–28, 46–48. Baden law of 27 VI 1848; but on July 7, 1849 special state commissars were empowered to remove any of these elected officers, pending "restoration of constitutional conditions": BGK 236/13532. WbgReg 10 VII 1849: cf. Klein, *Entwicklung des Gemeindebürgerrechts*, pp. 42–43; and Dehlinger, *Württembergs Staatswesen*, I, 271.

[71] E.g., HDReg 17 XI 1848; BadReg 3 IV 1848; Huhn, "Sachsen 1848–49" I, pp. 275–278; BayGes 1848, pp. 193–214 (8 VIII 1848); Heffter, *Selbstverwaltung*, p. 296.

[72] WbgReg 2 IV 1848; see also the subsequent order, in 20 X 1849, instructing communities to refuse marriage and settlement rights to any *Bürgerwehr* conscript not fully equipped for service, and explicitly excluding from service *Gewerbegehülfer, Fabrikarbeiter, Lohnarbeiter und Dienstboten*

[73] WbgReg 27 VI 1848; BayReg 9 IX 1848.

freedom, free and compulsory education, and free divisibility of property.[74]

A pattern of state administrative reform quite general in 1848–1849 was a systematic weakening of the lower levels of state civil service, the layer of administration where friction with the communities was most severe: either by opening direct channels between communities and upper levels of government that bypassed bureaucratic stages, or by establishing elected officials and assemblies at the district level. The latter step, undertaken in Baden and both Hessens, seems a constructive effort to bridge the gap between state and community, but though it may have removed an obstacle to hometown influence on ministries, there is little sign the communities were seriously interested in it. Their aim after all was to stay clear of what went on outside their walls, not become involved in it.[75] In Sachs-Meiningen a reform ministry wrote an electoral law whereby members of its diet would be elected by district; the small towns asked to vote and sit separately from the industrial towns; the astonished government pointed out that this amounted to a reversion from popular representation to an estate system: just so.[76]

None of these political measures grappled with the economic problems that preoccupied the Paulskirche or the "social problem" everybody had been talking about for fifteen years.[77] The effect of adopting this half of Frankfurt's program and remaining silent on the more critical half, whether the March ministries intended it or not, was to slip back into the political patterns of the teens and

[74] Heffter, Selbstverwaltung, pp. 297–299; Graf, "Stüve," pp. 241–354, citing especially Oppermann, Zur Geschichte des Königreichs Hannover, I, 307–309, and II, appendix, 62–63, 80–83. The corporatist Bennigsen-Stüve March ministry in Hanover confronted a nationalist second chamber of the Diet, symptom of a partial inversion of alignments there.

[75] Heffter, describing these innovations in Selbstverwaltung, pp. 295–299, takes them more seriously than I because of his primary concern with this kind of linkage, and because of his different conception of the political relations between liberalism and self-government. See also WbgReg 7 XI 1848.

[76] Schocke, "Sachsen-Meiningen, 1848–1850," pp. 43–49.

[77] But Bavaria issued an income-tax law in 1848 that seems to have favored communities and the crafts, and at the same time—the two economic worlds—helped establish chambers of commerce in the larger Bavarian cities composed of merchants and factory owners. BayGes 1848, pp. 153–166 (June 15, 1848); BayOD 25 VII 1848; BayReg 5, 25 I (sic), 12 VIII 1848.

thirties; and that familiar pattern emerged clearly from the summer of 1848 onward (while the Paulskirche was debating the Basic Rights). What would have happened if the liberal governments had worked actively together with Frankfurt that summer and fall for the whole of its program instead of just the easiest part, for free citizenship, free trades, and free settlement as well as self-government, is an interesting speculation: quite possibly a real revolution and civil war. But they did not. Instead they moved in a divergent direction, almost an opposite direction on the sensitive points of the Paulskirche's program. A reason for the divergence was that state systems of administration, representation, and political intelligence made them quicker to feel and readier to respond to pressure from the communities and from hometownsmen in the diets than Frankfurt, possessing no such apparatus (or burdens), ever was. Frankfurt was trying to call a people into being, and the states worked with groups in being; Frankfurt was trying to erect a state to be, while governments were trying to manage existing states. In this simple sense the charge that the Paulskirche failed because it was doctrinaire, isolated, and alien to the German people is a serious one.

While Frankfurt was going one way in 1848, the communities were pressing their governments in the other, calling almost invariably for stronger restrictions on marriage, settlement, and the trades.[78] Local associations were formed and petitions drafted explicitly to protest the Paulskirche's tendencies in economic and social policy, especially the matter of free economic entry: the Bavarian town of Neuötting, for example, demanded of the government "strong resistance against all attempts, wherever they may come from, to free the trades, because this can only be considered an open attack upon our proprietary rights." [79] A liberal lawyer of Herford found in the summer of 1848 that all the artisans who had joined a nationalist Improvement Society he had founded were dropping out now, leaving only schoolteachers and booksellers; in a similar Constitutional Society nobody was left but pastors and civil servants. "Is it really incompetence that ruins everything and lets everything be ruined at Frankfurt and Berlin?" he asked his diary. "Another six weeks and everything will come to a stop; every

[78] E.g., the materials in WSL E 146:646; similarly BSM MH 6133.
[79] BSM MH 6142:52.

tradesman grows reactionary and wants the old ways back . . . people who voted at the beginning become now reactionary wailers."[80]

To be sure in a great many places, maybe most, nothing worth noticing happened at all in 1848. But governments heard of what did happen; they read provincial newspapers; they studied the petitions and annotated them. Württemberg called an economic congress to advise the government, made up neatly of eighteen artisans, eighteen manufacturers and merchants, and four teachers of trades: its report recommended strong guilds and social restrictions.[81] Civil servants had reason enough to fear for their own positions in a politically reconstituted Germany; and they found they shared other political interests with hometownsmen—fear of domestic upheaval. In December, 1848, the Economics Committee at Frankfurt produced and circulated a draft Reich Home Law that caused great stir, anxiety, and hostility from the North Sea to Lake Constance. The draft was in keeping with the liberal spirit and letter of the Basic Rights, but the trouble might have been avoided if the Committee had been willing to leave home law, as the constitution did, a vague promise for the future. Instead it wrote a draft that turned all that home law had meant since 1830 upside down—a draft that aimed to find people homes, not keep people out of them. The Baden government wrote excitedly around the individualized country describing its shock at this newest production from Frankfurt. The freedom of settlement spelled out here would bring swarms of apprentices and factory workers into the towns; they would "form workers' conspiracies" and make trouble for everybody. "One can hardly imagine the proletariat will either be reduced or be satisfied by such a measure." And the occupational freedom the home law draft imposed on the communities "would amount in many areas to total social revolution. It would arouse resistance of a most serious kind, and in the communities that have quieted down now would create frightful, perhaps unmanageable tumult." Another critic—Bürgermeister Smidt of Bremen, interest-

[80] Kohl, "Herford, 1848," p. 48. A mistranscription confusing *wählte* with *wühlte* is possible here.

[81] A later congress of 1853, composed of merchants and manufacturers, called essentially for occupational freedom: below, pp. 400–401.

ingly—wanted to know what the Economics Committee meant when it said the communities were obliged to allow anybody who was "competent" to settle among them: was a competent street musician "competent"? What if there was no call for the trade at which the applicant was "competent"? Outsiders were not subject to the same kinds of restraints and responsibilities as natives. Not even Bremen should be compelled to let in endless rootless merchants accountable to nobody.[82]

Meanwhile the Paulskirche itself, in the throes of its decision to offer Prussia leadership of the new Reich, received a petition from 146 Swabian communities begging it not to do so. State governments had bundles of similar ones, many of them linking the social protection of communities with withdrawal from the Zollverein, citing the "threat from the North." [83] The revival of state governments on the basis of community support or at least toleration seemed very like the pattern that had defended the Biedermeier princes against liberal national movements and against Prussia in the past. Still it is hard to believe many people really thought things would ever be the same. By the time governments had recovered from their fright it turned out that things were not.

Hometownsmen and Kleinbürger

From their passive acceptance of hometown support in 1848 the states moved by rapid stages to the strongest program of communal restoration that they had ever undertaken; the politics of 1848–1849 and of the early fifties showed the incubator described at the beginning of this book still operating as its end approaches. But then, at the end of the fifties, the states in unison turned around almost without a pause and annihilated those programs altogether, as the next and final chapter will show: an unmistakeable forerunner to the making of the Second Empire. Beginning with the Paulskirche's Basic Rights the pendulum of public policy swung

[82] WSL E 146:646/44, 45. The Home Law draft is in K. D. Hassler, ed., *Verhandlungen der deutschen verfassunggebenden Reichsversammlung zu Frankfurt am Main,* Beilagen II (Frankfurt/Main, 1848–49), pp. 693–710 (to the session of December 2, 1848). Guilds were very strong in Bremen, and the radical-democratic party there was proguild and anticapitalist. Cf. Böhmert, *Zunftwesen,* pp. 54ff.

[83] SB, VII, 5121 (February 8, 1849); Klötzer, "Nassauische Petitionen 1848/49," pp. 145–147; Mayer, "Regensburg, 1848," pp. 33–34.

more violently than ever before, so violently as to seem historically and politically improbable, and to demand description of another kind.

There was a uniformity of direction that underlay the radical swings of public policy, however these may have confused those who experienced them. One signal that this story is approaching its end is that the term "hometownsmen" is becoming uncomfortable. Kleinbürgertum is a better general word, and it comes nearer now to meaning petty bourgeoisie, or lower middle class. The growing prevalence of economic concerns beginning with the thirties has largely absorbed hometownsmen into artisanry, a name for an economic class. Uneasiness about the names of social categories is a sign that their essential substances are changing, and nowhere is it uneasier to talk of hometownsmen than when their social and moral qualities got the strongest state support, in the early fifties.[84] This means not that the hometownsman's own internal tissue had changed, but that the conditions of his existence had.

The hometown communities had been so to speak vertical units, with space around each of them; but class is horizontal, with layers above and below it; and that is why class definitions become more appropriate as national economic and political issues reached the home towns. Another component of class is awareness by its members that they are a class, and with respect to what. *In vino veritas:* hometownsmen in 1848–1849 found themselves clearly a class interest within the nation, not a collection of communal interests locally circumscribed; nor were they the only ones to make such a discovery in those years. Hometownsmen and Paulskirche had begun together in 1848 to make the nation and destroy state bureaucracy, but the communities learned that the main enemy now was not bureaucratic intrusion into local affairs but national unity on liberal individualist principles; and the men at the Paulskirche learned that the people did not want the nation: not insofar, at least, as the nation meant the general estate, and as the "people," the *Volk,* meant community, *Gemeinschaft.* The German general estate had forgathered for the first time at Frankfurt in 1848. The

---

[84] On the need to change the names of categories with time and circumstances—*pace* the ideal types of Max Weber—see Karl Bosl, "Kasten, Stände und Klassen im mittelalterlichen Deutschland," *ZBL,* XXXII (1969), 477–494.

defeat of its program was a general one, and not really like, for example, the piecemeal frustration of the Imperial Trades Ordinance of 1731. The incubator was not quite the same after all. Germany in 1850 was not the Holy Roman Empire. It had lost much of its essential quality of diffusion, and for this the general movements of population and economy were at bottom responsible.

Yet the events at mid-century reimpressed communal characteristics and communal prejudices upon the national class hometownsmen were becoming. Class fear of a free economy fell into the pattern of hometown safeguards against outsiders and groundrabbits; class repugnance for proletariat fell into the pattern of moralistic hometown revulsion toward irresponsible drifters; class distrust of political equality for everybody was quite in keeping with the hometownsman's sense of the Bürgerrecht. In one cultural sense all three lobes still hung together. But it was no longer a communalism that stopped at the hometown walls. Wilhelm Heinrich Riehl, writing in the aftermath of 1848, flatly rejected the common liberal excuse that the Revolution's failure proved that Germans were an "unpolitical people." Rather they were "a decidedly and almost exclusively sociopolitical people." That fact was what the Paulskirche, the "old school, that lives on constitutional questions on the one hand and conjectural politics on the other," never had got through its head. There were real sociopolitical parties in Germany, even, and not "artifically grafted on [eingeimpft], but natural growth [naturwüchsig]. Purely political party life by contrast has never taken hold," because the real sociopolitics of the communities simply was not oriented to the national partisan-political concerns of intellectuals, industry, and civil service. What was needed, Riehl thought, was to bring this dispersed sociopolitics into "an artistic whole [ein geschlossenes Kunstwerk]." Nor could the proletariat, that conglomeration some people called the fourth estate, have any communal place or even any social quality of its own: "It is inconceivable for the so-called fourth estate to have its own form of communal structure [Gemeindebildung], because it is a negation of a positive, only an abstraction of an estate" meaning precisely the opposite of community, "and because it will remain absurd for all eternity to speak of a community of vagabonds." [85]

[85] *Land und Leute,* (2d ed.; Stuttgart, 1855), pp. 21–23, 117. Compare Riehl's contemporary, the sociologist Johann Bluntschli: "Das Proletariat besteht

The wave of laws and orders that followed the Frankfurt Parliament's collapse and Prussia's failure to capitalize on the liberal national movement was a victory for the "sociopolitical party." Hessen-Darmstadt, after the revolutionary interval, resumed in 1852 the direction of 1847 with new rules on local citizenship and marriage. Henceforth the state rule was that nobody under twenty-five was eligible for either, but town councils might make exceptions for young men they were confident about. A bitter opponent in the Diet (where the debate was remarkably partisan and sharp) said that the law really meant that henceforth no *democrat* under twenty-five could marry, settle, or have local citizenship. That was a fair way of describing what this blend of community and politics did mean, for now hometown society was clearly ranged against democracy: *in vino veritas*.[86] But a law on local government decreed that Bürgermeister would be appointed by the state from among elected town councilors (the state's draft had added "or other eligible persons"). Social communitarianism seemed now not fully to imply hometown political self-government. To complete the picture there was a three-class electoral system of the local plutocratic kind, giving the payers of the highest third of local taxes a third of the votes, and so on. The law was almost defeated in the Diet by an oddly significant alliance between old-style communitarians and political radicals, who talked respectively of medieval freedoms and of the Rights of Man.[87]

Hanover proceeded majestically along the path initiated by Stüve's March ministry, which had hardly been diverted by the countervailing wind from Frankfurt and Berlin except to oppose it; Revolution to Reaction was one continuing process in Hanover. An 1851 Town Ordinance affirmed the corporate nature of the communities; citizenship flowed from communal membership, not from residence; and town authorities controlled citizenship, budget, and

---

zumeist aus den Abfällen (!) der andern Berufsklassen. Die vermögenslosen und vereinzelten (!) Teile der Bevölkerung, die sich deshalb auch der befestigten Ordnung sicher entziehen, heissen wir das Proletariat." Quoted (*sic*) without citation by Werner Sombart, *Die deutsche Volkswirtschaft im neunzehnten Jahrhundert*, (3d ed.; Berlin, 1913), p. 444.

[86] HDReg 25 V 1852; HDVerh 1851/55 (2), Beil. 545 and 609, protocols for 24 I and 22 III 1852.

[87] HDReg 16 I 1852; HDVerh 1851/55 (2), Beil. 396, 397, and 487, protocols for 21 and 24–28 XI 1851.

poor relief. The three-class system was rejected. But even in Hanover the new rules departed from the hometown tradition there: for one thing, this law replaced the wide variety of indigenous Hanoverian local constitutions with a uniform one provided by the state (there was another, later one for villages and countryside); secondly, the magistracies were protected by a series of devices from the citizenry below as well as from the state without; and thirdly, local police, while entrusted to the magistracies, was to be exercised by state authority (a shield against pressures within the community) and reverted to the state if officials found the local administration of it to be unsatisfactory.[88]

Baden's communities were not merely allowed to retain hometown social and citizenship practices; the government at Karlsruhe insisted that they must. It combined a purge of local government throughout the Grand Duchy with a new set of rules for community membership. The purge began with the suppression of the Baden republican risings of early 1849. It was entrusted to special commissars because regular district officials "had become unaccustomed to vigorous action," and it aimed at eliminating "democratic elements" as far down the governmental scale as the Citizens' Committees. In certain radical areas that amounted to very nearly a clean sweep, and state reorganization of hundreds of communal magistracies.[89] New electoral arrangements transferred the franchise of general community assemblies to Greater Citizens' Committees, which every town large or small was now obliged to have, and on which only solid townsmen were presumed to sit. Election to the Greater Committee was by the plutocratic three-class system, and election to the more serious town offices became semicooptive: a Smaller Committee and an administrative Town Council sat together with the Greater Committee to elect themselves and the Bürgermeister.[90] Communal elections, called when the government

---

[88] Heffter, *Selbstverwaltung*, pp. 299–304; Graf, "Stüve," pp. 363–371; Meier, *Hannoversche Verfassungs- und Verwaltungsgeschichte*, II, 556–576; Maurer, *Städteverfassung*, IV, 340–341; Gebauer, *Hildesheim*, II, 389–390. Interpretations of where the local police power lay are, unsurprisingly, various and ambiguous.

[89] BGK 236/3107, 3108 for full tabulated reports on the purge; also BadReg 14 IX 1849 and passim.

[90] BadReg 20 V 1851 for the Gemeindeordnung and Wahlordnung revisions

thought the time was right, were watched closely to see that nobody who might "obstruct community life" got elected; nobody was allowed to become Bürgermeister who did not have the confidence of the government; and the results were an almost total defeat for "trouble makers" even where, according to reports, they dominated numerically in the population.[91] Councils could forbid the marriage even of citizens and could accept or refuse new citizens, but had no discretion to admit paupers, criminals, bad householders, or—a new phrase—"such persons as follow an intemperate style of life [*ausschweifenden Lebenswandel*]"; and testimonials on householding and style of life were now to come not only from communities but also from state police officials.[92]

State enforcement of hometown society in Baden is one sign of what was happening to the relation between community and state as hometownsmen developed a class character. State pressure, now for local oligarchy, had become quite unlike the recurrent support of hometown internal integrity of the eighteenth century or even the Baden laws of 1831; and notice too that the officials here were not retreating from local politics as in the teens or thirties but rather were participating in them more intimately. The persistent refusal of the government to issue a new trades ordinance during these communitarian years is another signal; "the present time is not appropriate" was the official reply to petitions of 1853.[93] Württemberg, next door, combined a draconian marriage and settlement law with a trades policy whose meaning for hometownsmen was at best ambiguous. Local pressures, Diet, and government cooperated to produce the new rules on marriage and settlement, laws posed as a revision of the 1833 law on citizenship but which were needed, according to one high official, not merely to clarify citizenship but to preserve the individual economies of the communities and the whole order of the state. The government cited the royal order of February, 1848, when it began work on the new law late in 1850

---

of 25 IV 1851. The cooptive provisions are stronger and clearer in the government's Wahlordnung than in the Gemeindeordnung itself.

[91] BGK 236/3109, 13533 passim. [92] BadReg 26 II and 3 V 1851.

[93] An appeal from the Diet was filed away without comment in 1856; but in 1860 the government told the Baden Commercial Congress at Heidelberg that it was working on a new ordinance. BGK 236/5820:37, 46–116, 145, 153.

(apologizing for the delay), but the pattern of opinion within the lawmaking system had changed. Now Interior Ministry officials were ranged together with the communities and the Diet plenum against a more liberal Privy Council and Diet committee—though the latter two were very cautious, the committee allowing that "unlimited freedom of marriage was legally incompatible with communal relationships [*Genossenschaftsverhältnisse*]." The King, as usual in such times, threw his weight on the communities' side.[94]

The law of 1852 ("in response to many demands") required any applicant for community membership and marriage to "demonstrate" to community authorities his adequate means of family support; and permission could be refused "if his reputation . . . is defective in such a way that it may reasonably be believed that he will not be accorded sufficient confidence in his relations with others." The same qualities were to be demanded of his bride (tinsmith Flegel of Hildesheim would have found the terrain familiar, except with the bishop now on the other side). Council and Citizens' Committee were to decide on this; if appeal was made to the district Oberamtmann that official was obliged to consult with a committee of four local citizens of good reputation, chosen by community representatives, on the applicant's qualities, and not to overrule community judgment except in extreme cases. In actual administration of the law state officials did almost as much as communities to prevent marriages.[95]

This was a legal affirmation of a communal class. Probably the Württemberg government put the social measures of the fifties into the law of citizenship in order to hold ramifications for economic policy to a minimum. The law was not economically conceived; consider its nature. Riehl would have recognized it as a sociopolitical law. In that sphere hometownsmen had succeeded in getting their standards established in public policy, affronting the general estate's ancient goals of economic and population growth. The remarkable thing, looking at the nineteenth century in retrospect from the 1850's, is that even as the state grew, and the general economy grew, and both became more engaged in the affairs of the

[94] WHS E 146: 646/54, 57, 64, and 77–78; and E 33: G 112, II, 80.

[95] WbgReg 15 V 1852; Klein, *Entwicklung des Gemeindebürgerrechts*, pp. 44–45.

whole society, communal social exclusion got growing recognition and articulation in law. State recognition had a great deal to do with making a class out of the hometownsmen, starting with the wish to avoid the consequences of hometown hostility early in the century, but now discerning in hometownsmen's social practices a defense against an alien rootless class and against political radicalism.

By the 1850's the heart of hometown defense was the inhibition of marriage, and with this emphasis the web connecting social defense with local governmental and economic rights was dissolving. It was the aspect of communal society the states were readiest to accept, and here hometown standards probably had their strongest effect on public policy, and through it on the whole social structure, at the very time economic and political prerequisites for communal integrity were disappearing. I have already presented figures (page 333) to show how population growth in the individualized country kept pace with the centralized country until a change set in the 1830's, the time of socially restrictive legislation in the German South and West. Another set, ranking states by rate of growth from an 1840 base of 100, shows what happened then.

Relative population change in German states, 1840–1858

| | Year | | |
Place	1840	1855	1858
Kingdom of Saxony	100	120	124
Prussia		115	118
Thuringia		108	110
Nassau		108	109
Bavaria		104	106
Hessen-Darmstadt		103	104
Württemberg		101	103
Baden		101	103
Hessen-Kassel		101	decline

Slow population growth and hometown social defenses could hardly coincide more exactly; the bottom, slowest two-thirds of the list is hometown landscape.[96]

[96] Figures from Viebahn, *Statistik*, II, 204; compare figures for the density of towns, above, p. 32.

Moreover, population growth was slowest in just those areas where complaints of overpopulation were loudest, and these were the areas from which overseas emigration was greatest during the first two-thirds of the century.[97] What nineteenth-century Germany meant by overpopulation was the unabsorbed population it saw; and this was a kind of overpopulation that went together with slow population growth, socially inhibited. It is possible to think of other features of geography, economy, and history that could produce that effect, but most of them are just the incubative factors that created the native landscapes of the home towns themselves. The protective and exclusive social mechanisms of the home towns, held first against the states and then enforced by them as law, operated precisely to that effect of creating "overpopulation" while holding back population growth. Whether the laws themselves were responsible, or the community practices the laws affirmed, does not change the demographic correlation. It is almost certain too that one effect of blocking communal entries by prohibiting marriage was to increase the rate of illegitimacy, wherein the German individualized counry at the end of the fifties led western Europe:

Bavaria	22.6%
Baden	16.9
Württemberg	16.3
Hessen-Kassel	15.8
Kingdom of Saxony	15.8
Hessen-Darmstadt	14.4
Hanover	10.8
Prussia	8.3
France	7.5
Great Britain	6.5

The many illegitimate births show that marriage restraints were not altogether efficacious in holding back population growth; but the general population figures seem to say that high illegitimacy rates did not compensate for the demographic effects of inhibiting marriage.[98] That is, marriage inhibitions did not cause as many

[97] Walker, *Germany and the Emigration,* pp. 42–133.

[98] Figures for 1858–1862 in Hausner, *Statistik,* I, 209–210. On this question generally see Friedrich Thudichum, *Ueber unzulässige Beschränkungen des Rechts der Verehelichung* (Tübingen, 1866), pp. 121–130; John Knodel, "Law,

illegitimate births as they prevented legitimate ones, which seems reasonable enough (but by no means obvious, if for example unmarried outsiders were by definition as irresponsibly improvident as hometownsmen discerned them to be).

A Bavarian expert on community and home law estimated in the 1860's that communal restraints based on marriage and settlement laws had since 1834 cut Bavarian population growth in half, tripled the illegitimacy rate, and during the 1850's had reduced absolutely, not proportionally, the number of persons engaged overall in trade and manufacture.[99] In Württemberg there was a survey to find out what effects the marriage and membership laws actually had on the marriage rate. The figures showed that about one formal application for marriage in thirty was refused by the communities in 1847–1851, and that in 1852–1856, after the new law, about one in fifteen was refused by communities and state in combination. Neither figure takes into account the effects of informal community pressure, and neither takes into account the number of marriages delayed or prevented by the presence of the law without its formal invocation against the applicants.[100] Even though many of those rejected may have had later applications approved, there can be no doubt that the restrictions significantly depressed the rate of marriage and the growth of population in Württemberg, along with contributing to the increase of those visible outsiders called overpopulation; nor is there any reason to doubt that the same was true in other places where social and legal conditions were similar.[101]

Marriage, and Illegitimacy in Nineteenth-Century Germany," *PS*, XX (1966–1967), 279–294; Edward Shorter, "Middle-Class Anxiety"; and the sources Knodel and Shorter cite.

[99] Riedel, *Heimat*, p. 36, n. 1. Of course there is no way to prove such an assertion, and Riedel put it cautiously.

[100] WSL E 146: 646/78, 83, 90, 96, 116–122, and especially 123. I do not fully understand what procedures identified state as distinct from community prohibition: apparently sometimes state rejection of an appeal from community prohibition, and sometimes (especially later) official action in the first instance. Most rejections that reached state attention were grounded economically; reputation was almost impossible to appeal beyond community councils.

[101] Cf. Klein, *Entwicklung des Gemeindebürgerrechts*, pp. 45–46. But statistical analysis from detailed regional figures of just how this worked seems hopeless, because it cannot distinguish cause from effect, even if imponderable or

The Württemberg government retained its marriage laws into the 1860's, but—returning now to the narrative—although it was quite willing to support communal standards for domestic settlement and membership, it was not at all satisfied to see such standards applied to economic settlement and the trades. That presented too complicated a problem to be described here in detail, but it is important to know it was complicated and to note its stages. At first, a trades order of 1851 made trades licenses conditional on prior possession of community membership, but the restrictive law on citizenship and marriage made that unacceptable to many persons in government. The Oberamtmänner of the districts, who had the power to issue new licenses, then adopted (illegally) the practice of granting licenses without hearings from the communities affected and without public announcement; and the resulting uproar made a new law seem necessary.[102] By now it was 1853, and the government at Stuttgart asked the Center for Manufacture and Commerce, a congress of merchants and manufacturers it sponsored, to find a way for it out of the dilemma—to lay out principles for an ordinance on economic rights that would allow economic growth without weakening social cohesion or destroying the communal class. The congress decided it would not propose that guilds be abolished, only that they be forbidden to exclude new members: "guilds and economic freedom are not incompatible," which meant, if anything, that guild structures should be retained but should function on the government's and on the Center's terms. Nobody denied the corporate character and rights of communities, or their importance to the state's purposes; but there had to be freedom of movement for economic vitality

---

undiscoverable factors could be isolated. Suppose, for example, a high rate of marriage prohibitions coincides with a high marriage rate (as it often does): does that show prohibitions to have been ineffective, or were the prohibitions called forth by an even higher "natural" marriage rate resulting, say, from local prosperity or a young or immigrant population? Or suppose a low prohibition rate coincides with a low illegitimacy rate (as it tends to do): does that reflect emigration of young people from, perhaps, strong or quiet communities which feel no need to apply formal sanctions? If so, the demographic and moral effects cannot be observed. I am aided to this inconclusion by the detailed Württemberg figures in WSL E 146: 646/141. But still the gross effects are there.

102 WSL E 150: 600/2–11 and passim; WbgReg 9 IV 1851.

and to allow the excluded population to achieve economic security and become productive. The legal solution was the one proposed by Varnbüler ten years before: to split economic rights of settlement clearly away from marriage and citizenship rights. Let the communities be as tough as they like about their own membership, but leave the economy open. That in effect is what the Württemberg government said in 1854, when it ordered that a trades license, a master's right, could be issued before the applicant got settlement rights, if the prospective place of settlement was officially deemed an appropriate place for the exercise of his trade.[103] The communities were obliged to see newcomers settle among them to work and to sell, but they did not have to take them in; they had just been told they did not have to take them in. They confronted them as a class.

Württemberg had a long history of recognizing different rules of admission and practice for different trades and localities, and so had most states; but this rule replaced those vertical distinctions among trades and localities with a horizontal social and political distinction among tradesmen everywhere and of every calling, between those who were full members of the communities they lived in and those who were not, but who could no longer be physically or economically excluded. Bavaria's pursuit of its two economic worlds reached much the same point in the fifties. In 1850 the crown ordered that Chambers of Commerce and Industry be formed throughout the kingdom, gave them direct access to Munich over the heads of local authorities, and avidly followed their activities; meanwhile it forbade state officials to grant economic concessions that would "multiply tradesmen to the disadvantage of those already there."[104] In 1852 it gave the job of drafting a new trades law to a commission based on these chambers of merchants and manufacturers, supplemented by state officials; in the same year it produced a tax law whereby a tradesman might have one assistant with almost no added tax burden, but larger

[103] Above, p. 346; WSL E 146: 645/1–3, 10; other material from Baden, whose government watched these proceedings closely, BGK 236/5820: 46–116, 128–132; Köhler, *Das württembergische Gewerberecht*, pp. 158–159; Revised Instructions in WbgReg 27 IX 1854, and expansion thereof in WbgReg 23 XI 1854.

[104] BayReg 4 II 1850 and passim; BSM MH 6133 passim.

numbers of employees meant disproportionally higher taxes, and whereby a shop in Munich paid double the taxes the same shop would have paid in a town under 3,000 population. Wholesale commerce, banking, and transportation were taxed at the highest rate; factories and large retail trades in the middle; local traditional trades the least: Bavaria was reaping the revenues of the general economy while trying to preserve its small-town artisan class.[105] The new law on trades provided two sets of licenses, one ostensibly for big towns and one for small, on patterns already established in the thirties and forties, but with the division drawn more sharply along social lines. Commerce everywhere operated under big-town rules; and ordinarily no competence test was required of a person who wanted to set up a factory, wherever it was, and anybody could work there. In the traditional hometown trades, the well-being of existing masters "decided" the question of competence, of the applicant's capacity for self-support, and hence his claim on community membership. But the settlement condition for a trades license required the applicant only to have applied for, not to have acquired, a right of community settlement, apparently only to show his own will to locate, not that a community wanted him; and he chose his own testing commission (which however had to include two local masters along with a police official and an outside expert).[106]

A striking feature of the 1852 trades ordinance was that there was no talk of "community" in it, as there had been in the law of 1834, but only of "members of the same trade"; and a provision that all members of customarily guilded trades must enter trades associations revived 1825's administrative district organizations without any mention of 1834's intervening "historic" guild territories or "the organic life of these institutions." Nothing like that appeared in the trades law now. Bavarian home, citizenship, and marriage laws were still the most communal combination in Germany. But the trades law, though it had a place in it for the artisan class upon which the communities were based, had no place

[105] BayOB 13 II and 6 IX 1852; *Gesetzblatt für das Königreich Bayern* 8 VII 1852.

[106] BayGes 8 VII 1852; BayOB 6 IX 1852; BayReg 30 XII 1853.

now for 1834's "vital corporative principle that is the foundation of all social configurations." [107]

The similarity between the policies of the early fifties and the two constitutional hometown restorations earlier in the century is obvious, but the differences are more important. It was not really the violent pendular swing it appeared to be at first glance from the earlier perspective; rather, communal society and bureaucracy had reached another stage of accommodation in the individualized country. The terms of the accommodation reached back half a century, but it was only reached when communities and bureaucracy at the end of the forties were thrown on the defensive together and simultaneously, rather than successively and as political alternatives, as in the past. The change in the structure of politics was put most vividly by the Paulskirche's program of individual social freedom *and* of local self-government—not as alternatives but simultaneously. The 1848 attack on state authority and bureaucratic autocracy had been coupled with the basic rights not of social communities (as in the teens and thirties), but of free individuals; and that altered the position. The closer association of local leadership with state government was one symptom of the change.

Bureaucracy in the early fifties accepted hometown social standards and techniques as policy, not just political sops to the communities, while hometown political autonomy and hometown capacity to withstand general economic development lapsed. It appeared that Engel's political sense had been right in 1847 when he discerned an alliance between hometownsmen and bureaucracy. His trouble in finding a theoretical description for it, in finding a real commonality of interest between them, reflects an impurity that infected both parties in the mid-century crisis of national politics and the social question. For both parties—though there was by no means unanimity on either side—were seriously affected by the accommodation wrought in 1848. Bureaucracy surrendered its role as German champion of individual social and moral freedom.[108] Home-

[107] Cf. above, p. 339.
[108] Cf. Hauptmann, "Sachsens Wirtschaft und der soziale Gedanke, 1840–1850," p. 201, on the masked victory of Liberalism (a villain to him) through

townsmen paid for social protection from the general estate by becoming a client class, whose common principle was not communal
integrity or even communal defense, but only hometown prejudice
stripped naked to its rudest form, and fear of the inescapable. Both
sides had lost the constitutional foundations that have sustained
them in this history, but the consequences were more serious for
the home towns. Now they were Kleinbürger, sure enough. During
the years 1847–1854 communal institutions had become public
agencies for sustaining general stability. Never again could anybody seriously say "Stadtrecht geht vor Landrecht," at least not in
its constitutional meaning, for the legitimate constitutional source
of political right had moved clearly to state government: a perverse victory for the general estate after its failure at the Paulskirche.

Reaction (another); and from the opposing perspective Heffter, *Selbstverwaltung,* pp. 327–341, on the divorce between Prussian bureaucracy and liberalism
after 1848.

CHAPTER XII

Death and Transfiguration

THE political environment that had nourished the home town was destroyed between 1855 and 1870. Its destruction was part of the process that ended in the absorption of the individualized country into Bismarck's Second Empire. When Adolphe Thiers invoked the Treaty of Westphalia before the French Legislative Assembly in the spring of 1866, he testified to the principle that Germany and Europe had reiterated after every major political crisis of the intervening two centuries, the principle upon which European equilibrium and German diffusion was based.[1] For Germany, Prussia broke the equilibrium militarily by defeating Austria at Königgrätz that summer, and made the rupture definite by defeating the French at Sedan four years after that.

But by the time Thiers spoke it was already too late—if not for France, at least for the home towns. They had already felt the effects of changes not fulfilled on the international scene until 1871. Changing forms clear to see within the individualized country were intimations of the decisions that produced the Second Empire: beginning with the Crimean War's end, accelerating with the madness and death of Frederick William IV of Prussia, and reaching into the struggles of the 1860's—roughly the period Prussian history calls the New Era.

[1] Above, p. 15.

Destruction of the environment

This book's first four chapters set forth the environmental conditions and the internal essentials of hometown society: the political incubator of the Holy Roman Empire; the mutual dependence of hometown civic leadership and a stable citizenry; the guild economy of communal Bürger; and the hometownsman's awareness that his personal identity was found in the web and walls of familiar community. The first of these, the European balance and the German incubator, still seemed effective politically in 1848–1850. But it broke down when faulty French policy brought Russian defeat and alienation from Austria in the Crimean War, the meaning of which event for the political structure of Europe and of Germany was signaled by the absorption of Italy into the progressive, industrious, and militant kingdom of Piedmont, the "Italian Prussia," in 1859–1860. Similarly the way for state power was opened up in Germany as it had not been since the times of the first Napoleon; and this time it was Bismarck's Prussia, not Bonapartist France, that took and held the initiative.

Changes in the relation between hometown leadership and citizenry, affecting their combined integrity against outside intervention especially from the state, had been under way for longer, but they were especially apparent in the fifties. A synthesis of bureaucracy and oligarchy in town magistracies replaced the earlier tension between the two, in the form of state domination of local government together with insulation of the communal authorities from the communal governed. Communities had given up autonomy and integrity to the states under social pressure and out of social fear; and meanwhile governments had lost their hesitancy to interfere in the communities after the hostility between home towns and national liberal politics had been revealed in 1848. Local government became more professional, and more plutocratic: more like patrician than hometown government, except that now the local governors were associated directly with the state as well as the general estate; and an expanded community membership had become a separate and inferior class, largely excluded from government: citizenship had lost much of its political meaning. Johannes Miquel, past associate of Karl Marx and future Prussian Minister of Finance, became mayor of Möser's and Stüve's Osnabrück as Hanoverian government moved into pro-Prussian hands like his and Rudolph Bennigsen's, president of the German National Society. There were similar political shifts in Electoral Hessen, in Baden after the elections of 1860, and in Bavaria, whose king dismissed the conservative communalist Von der Pfordten in 1859.[2]

The governmental shifts of those years reflect an important shift in political expectations, or more accurately, reflected an expectation that changes long impending were about to be accomplished, but accomplished now not in the context of the German pre-March but in the context of the European and German interstate politics that succeeded the pre-March and the revelations of 1848–1850. A kind of embryonic Rhine Confederation looking to Prussia seemed to be developing in the individualized country during the New Era. It reached into the communities in rather different ways from a half-century before, but at least in comparable ways. The Bavarian government reversed a former rule by encouraging communities and local endowments to invest in railroads, instead of prohibiting this as in the past: the state would guarantee the stock. It increased the number of towns where—because their population was growing—general state testing commissions for the trades would take the place of local ones. It increased the social powers of town magistracies while restricting occasions on which citizenry might participate in local decisions, specifically forbidding communal debate of marriage and settlement questions: the professional governor's bias for freedom of commerce and settlement had entered communal councils.[3] Hessen-Darmstadt made a new rule that the highest-taxed person in any community automatically became a full member of the town council.[4] All these tendencies had their counterparts in Prussia. Prussia had moved still closer to the states of the individualized country by abolishing occupational freedom in 1849 and expanding local self-government in 1850; and then during the following decade, Prussia like the South and West German states increased both the scope of state oversight

[2] Meier, *Hannoversche Verfassungs- und Verwaltungsgeschichte*, II, pp. 576–583; Heffter, *Selbstverwaltung*, pp. 415–426.

[3] BayOB 26 II, 13 VI, and 4 VII 1856, 13 III 1857; BayOF 7 XI 1860.

[4] HDReg 11 V 1858.

and the local authority of town administrators, which thus might now fairly be called local bureaucracy.[5] The New Era in a way realized the cameralist aspiration of bringing local governance into state-supervised harmony, and of making Staatsbürger out of Gemeindebürger: state had replaced community as guardian of internal stability, taking on some hometown characteristics as it did so. Prussian local government was no longer a foil to that of the individualized country; the two were following the same rhythm now.

None of these political and administrative changes, though, compare in importance with the dramatic economic developments of the fifties and early sixties. Changes in the economy and in the regulation of the economy were mainly what brought political and administrative changes to bear on the communities. It would burst the bonds of this story to try to describe the growth of banking, credit, and investment in the fifties, of transportation and commerce, of factories and steam power.[6] All showed that the economy that mattered was no longer local but supra-local in its realm of interdependence; and it was by the destruction of that third condition of hometown community, the locally organized guild economy, that the general estate finally broke through the hometown walls, unrestrained now by the political anxieties of the teens, the thirties, or even 1848, and immeasurably strengthened by the general estate's economic components: commerce, industry, and finance.

In their bearing on the home towns, railroads and banking as economic phenomena offer close analogies to the territorial changes and the fiscal consolidations (respectively) directed by state administrators fifty years before; but they were much more powerful. Of thirty-three banks of issue operating when the Reich banking laws took effect in 1872, nineteen had been established in the 1850's under state license and law, seventeen of them—more than half the 1872 list—between 1853 and 1857. German railroad mileage tripled

[5] Cf. Heffter, *Selbstverwaltung*, pp. 214–219, 330–343, 407–414; Faber, "Rheinprovinz," pp. 144–148.

[6] All general economic histories treat the subject, but see the appropriate sections in Sartorius von Waltershausen, *Deutsche Wirtschaftsgeschichte;* or Sombart, *Deutsche Volkswirtschaft;* or David S. Landes, *The Unbound Prometheus* (Cambridge, England, 1969).

between 1850 and 1869, to make a net of about eleven thousand miles in a country some six or seven hundred miles in diameter.[7]

No set of industrial figures can accurately portray the effects of these changes on the communities, not even the near-quintupling of German coal and iron production between 1848 and 1864, nor the tripling of steam-engine capacity between 1850 and 1860 (to twenty-five times the capacity of 1840) and another tripling between 1860 and 1870.[8] Industrial statistics were not raised to describe community conditions, nor could they be. The nearest approach to hometown statistics are the figures for master artisans in relation to other segments of the population. During the first half of the nineteenth century, the proportion of master artisans in the population had generally risen; but their number declined, proportionally everywhere and in most places absolutely, from the fifties onward.[9] In Württemberg there were even fewer artisans, apprentices and journeymen included, in 1861 than there had been in 1835, this despite a tripling of the number of assistants per master; meanwhile the proportion of the population engaged in trade and manufacture as a whole was rising. That increase, plus the artisan decline, were both going into factories. In 1835, 58 per cent of Württemberg's trades-and-manufacturing [gewerbetreibend] population (and about 7 per cent of its total population) had been master artisans; in 1861, 29 per cent, just half that proportion, were master artisans (and less than 5 per cent of the whole population).[10] The number of master artisans in Baden declined by about 15 per cent between 1847 and 1861—about sixteen thousand Baden artisans emigrated in the fifties, mainly to America—but the number of

---

[7] The financial turmoil of 1857, following the chartering of all these banks, caused strong pressure for a uniform national banking system: "Banken in der Volkswirtschaft," *Handwörterbuch der Staatswissenschaften*, II (4th ed.; Jena, 1924), 190–194. Railroad figures from Landes, *Prometheus*, p. 194.

[8] Sartorius von Waltershausen, *Deutsche Wirtschaftsgeschichte*, pp. 166–168; Landes, *Prometheus*, p. 221.

[9] Schäffle, "Gewerbe," p. 328.

[10] Figures compiled from Köhler, *Das württembergische Gewerberecht*, p. 209. Much of this redistribution had taken place in the forties, and the decline of masters no doubt reflects deliberate restraints on admissions; but the number of *Gewerbetreibenden* rose despite that, and very much faster in the fifties than in the forties.

factory workers tripled. The patterns were the same in Bavaria and Saxony.[11]

Still Germany and especially the individualized country were remarkable in Europe for the high proportion of trained artisans in the population. In 1865, one European in 23.7 was an artisan, but consider the figures for western Europe and for Germany, ranked by density of artisans:

Bavaria, one in	13.1
Hessen-Kassel	13.4
Belgium	13.6
Hessen-Darmstadt	14.5
Baden	14.5
France	14.7
Württemberg	15.1
Great Britain	16
Prussia	16.1
Nassau	16.7
Kingdom of Saxony	17
Netherlands	17.7
Hanover	24.8

Apparently the individualized country (not counting agrarian Hanover in this connection) had an industrial cadre unmatched anywhere in Germany, and barely matched even in the far more advanced industrial countries of western Europe.[12] When German "factories" were counted (without reference to their relative size) in 1862 there turned out to be these many for every thousand population:

Württemberg	11
Bavaria	8
Baden	5
Hessen-Kassel	5
Kingdom of Saxony	5
Prussia	4
Hanover	4

And the number of factory workers per thousand population were: [13]

[11] Schmoller, *Kleingewerbe*, pp. 104–106, 126–127, 150–151; Zimmermann, *1848 in Franken*, p. 186.

[12] Hausner, *Statistik*, II, 255.

[13] Viebahn, *Statistik*, III, 1033, 1034. There was more steam horsepower

Kingdom of Saxony	96
Württemberg	49
Baden	46
Prussia	37
Bavaria	35
Hessen-Darmstadt	34
Hessen-Kassel	31
Hanover	24

The excursion into industrial statistics suggests a relation between the social economy of hometown Germany, with its notorious "overpopulated trades," and Germany's extraordinarily sudden industrial lunge that began in the third quarter of the nineteenth century. A very large number of potential industrial workers had been built up and stored in the preindustrial communities, guild-trained but skilled and disciplined, ready for the mechanized industry that came when there was enough financial and political support for it from the fifties onward. If it is true, as contemporaries believed, that the communal guild system "artificially" inhibited German industrialization, then conversely that system developed and preserved an artisan class that could pour immediately into large-scale industry as soon as its capacity to resist was broken.

Its resistance, which had seemed stronger than ever when the fifties began, was broken everywhere in the individualized country during a half-dozen years around 1860. State governments, however safely conservative they had seemed when they had absorbed communal powers and practices after 1848, were not to be trusted with them. At first, in the early fifties, they suppressed all questions of new trades laws, as Baden did; or they used the device of the two economies, as Bavaria did; or they did both. Saxony sat out guild reactions to its mildly liberal trades law of 1840 (allowing state-licensed factories in the countryside) through the forties and the early fifties, awaiting "quieter times," the government said in 1850, "so that," it was ready to explain in 1857, "positions could be clarified by developments and by experience." Figures available that year had shown the number of Saxon master artisans declining,

---

per thousand population in Prussia and in Saxony than in the south and west, but this probably reflects the extensive mining in those states, and the relative scarcity of water power: p. 1036.

and there was talk of the end of artisanry; and Saxony produced a law to ease entry into a declining number of trades still left guilded, and to encourage the establishment of factories in both town and country. It defined factories not by what they produced or what their markets were (which would have conflicted with the remaining rights of guilds) but by their use of natural power, division of labor, and large numbers of workers.[14] Then in 1860–1861 the two-economies system was dropped altogether. The requirement of communal membership for the guilded trades, retained in 1857, was now forbidden, along with tests of competence and the ban mile. The new trades law in fact established occupational freedom and freedom of movement for Saxon subjects. The other German states were headed in that direction, and "we may expect," the Saxon government told the Diet, "that the achievement of greater uniformity in economic legislation will be followed by a growing effort by the German nation for freer exchange among the elements of the population." With the support of Saxon industrial pressure groups and their newspapers the law passed the Diet easily.[15]

Württemberg followed. Through the later fifties the government had been building up Chambers of Commerce and Industry in the larger towns as alternatives to guild institutions; and it had steadily added to the list of things that any trades license entitled its owner to do—things like making goods and using processes other than those traditional to his trade, thus systematically breaking down the distinctions and barriers among trades.[16] Then in 1861 a law for occupational freedom was put through the Diet without difficulty by Carl von Varnbüler as Economics Committee rapporteur. It was probably the simplest trades ordinance ever issued in Germany: individual practice of all trades (except for special cases like pharmacy and inn-keeping) was freed of all proofs of competence and of social trades police; one might practice as many trades as he liked whenever and wherever he liked; one need not be a master to take on apprentices; and finally, flatly, "Guilds are abolished." [17]

[14] Paul Horster, *Die Entwicklung der sächsischen Gewerbeverfassung, 1790–1861* (Krefeld, 1908), pp. 77, 106, 111–122.

[15] Ibid., pp. 137–151.   [16] WbgReg, passim.

[17] WbgReg 22 II 1862; Köhler, *Das württembergische Gewerberecht*, pp. 218–237; report of Varnbüler's committee in WHS E 33: G 442, I, 148–1/2 [*sic*].

Baden established occupational freedom in 1862 also. All the governments raced for the band wagon, looking over their shoulders at one another and at Austria and Prussia. With the German question opening up, they were convinced that occupational freedom was economically and politically necessary, and so legislatively they were prepared for the free-trades laws that came with the North German Confederation and the Second Empire—indeed by 1862 they had laid the legal groundwork for those Imperial German policies throughout the individualized country.[18]

"Occupational freedom is no longer a question of taking an artisan's rights away from him," a master weaver told the new Congress of German Economists in 1859, "it is a question now of giving him the freedom he needs. . . . Great industry, allied with money and with learning [*Wissenschaft*] has undermined his whole legal foundation."[19] Rapidly changing technology, the application of processes developed in one trade to production in another, and mobile investment capital that pursued profit, were all incompatible with detailed regulation, be it by guild or by state. Guilds were incompatible with these economic circumstances for reasons of structure and of interest, but close state regulation was incompatible with them too because of its technical incapacity to keep up with changes and with variants. Consequently no state could merely abolish guild rights and put their regulative functions in state laws. To do so would have caused a flight of capital, production, and population to other states, something no government wanted in the New Era: hence the unanimity of the turn to occupational

---

[18] Sartorius von Waltershausen, *Deutsche Wirtschaftsgeschichte*, pp. 144–145; Erdmann, *Wirtschaftsverbände*, pp. 91–92. Bremen established occupational freedom in 1860 (after an effort of 1857 had been beaten back) "angesichts," said the liberal spokesman, "der in ganz Deutschland mächtig vorwärts schreitenden Bewegung für Gewerbefreiheit": Böhmert, *Zunftwesen*, p. 58. For the process in Hessen-Darmstadt, through its usual complex device of tax legislation (with overt occupational freedom delayed until 1866), HDReg 3 V 1856, 31 VII and 2 VIII 1858, 20 and 28 XII 1860; for Baden, Gall, *Liberalismus*, pp. 176–180. On the economic effects (which he thinks slight), Fischer, *Handwerksrecht und Handwerkswirtschaft*, pp. 69–70, similarly Schmoller, *Kleingewerbe*, passim.

[19] Johann K. Leuchs, *Realrechte und Gewerbs-Privilegien, beseitigt und versöhnt mit der Freiheit der Gewerbe und der Ansässigung* (2d ed.; Nürnberg, 1860), pp. 23–24; Erdmann, *Wirtschaftsverbände*, pp. 239–253. The greater proportion of the congress (if this was a typical session) was academics, then merchants, then civil servants.

freedom.[20] It was the obvious answer to economic conditions, now even for the many artisans who could not in their own trades, and in their own communities, withstand the power of the general economy.

But even though occupational freedom (and industrial growth and change) opened opportunity to Kleinbürger members of the "overpopulated trades," it broke up the whole structure of communal defense, based as that system had come to be on such criteria as competence, prospects of success, and inhibitions to movement and settlement. It meant the effective end of home law. No doubt the economic agencies described by the weaver at Frankfurt had undermined the legal defenses of artisanry, *de facto;* but the occupational freedom those agencies required undermined systems of communal integrity *de jure.* It "clearly meant the total annihilation of this kind of community," wrote Lorenz von Stein early in the 1850's; "where occupational freedom prevails, the community becomes only a quite accidental place where free individuals happen to find themselves engaged in their occupations. It is a complete atomization of economic life, in which the old community disappears completely." [21] Local controls over communal citizenship and settlement were incompatible with economic freedom and economic growth, Varnbüler told the Württemberg Diet; the local autonomies of the teens, the rights of social exclusion written into the laws of the thirties, and especially the very severe marriage and settlement rules of 1852 had moved in just the wrong direction and now had to be reversed and wiped out all at once.[22] The price paid for the Biedermeier split between hometown social defense and a growing free general economy and population was the shocking abruptness of its resolution; and the heritage was a highly dramatic contrast between two styles of life.

Only Bavaria, though it joined the procession to occupational freedom in the sixties, tried legislatively to temper its effect on the social communities. In 1861, the Diet, narrowly, rejected a Nürnberg deputy's plea that without immediate occupational freedom Bavaria would lose its ablest people and most productive enterprises to other states. But neither Diet nor government denied the

[20] Cf. Popp, *Gewerbefreiheit,* pp. 116–117. [21] "Gemeindewesen," p. 73.
[22] N. 17 above.

need to free the trades somehow (ministerial orders of 1862 resumed the policies of 1825); rather they were unwilling to throw the whole home law structure of communal government, settlement, marriage, and citizenship into chaos by suddenly jerking out its economic leg in the trades.[23] Therefore the government, at the Diet's request, began in 1865 to work out a complex of four elaborate laws treating all these together: the so-called "Social Laws" of 1868–1869. But they turned out to be a detailed elimination of home law's effects, in each part of the legislative complex, retaining only home law forms. The law on trades was the first to appear, under Prince Hohenlohe's ministry early in 1868, and it passed a Diet that paid no attention to hometown complaints about it. All Bavarians—and foreigners too—were to have free exercise of any trade, or several trades at once, wherever they liked, or in many places at once. The existing trades associations were abolished, though voluntary societies without restrictive powers could be formed.[24] This was, despite clouds of communitarian rhetoric, a quite blunt and unequivocal statement. Marriage and home rights were effectively freed of communal intervention later that spring: marriage became free and everybody, even if he (or she) was poor, was to have a legal home, the state would see to it that everybody did, and the communities were to take care of their own whether they wished to acknowledge them or not.[25] The whole system was capped off with a new community ordinance in the spring of 1869 that gave every resident (the state could assign residence) a right to community citizenship after five years if he paid taxes to the state, and after ten if he paid none.[26] Councils had no acceptance powers; Bürgermeister had to be approved and sworn by the state; and the communities were administratively

[23] Note the 1862 Instruction that revoked the instructions of 1834 and 1853, freeing more trades and abolishing the two-class system of tests, and allowing an artisan like a factory to produce by any method and sell anywhere he chose, but not entering upon settlement rights: BayReg 19 V 1862.

[24] BayGes 6 II 1868 for the Trades Ordinance.

[25] Home, Marriage, and Sojourn Law in BayGes 25 IV 1868; the follow-up Poor and Sick Care Law in 22 V 1869.

[26] The time and tax provisions were stated in the home law, but home rights conferred citizenship by terms of the Community Ordinance: BayGes 14 V 1869.

"subordinated" to district administrators, respecting all community affairs and, especially, local police.

The Bavarian Social Laws required a great deal of verbiage because they tried to uphold home law and abolish it at the same time. By special arrangement Bavaria kept its own system of home laws (but not its trades law) into the Second Empire, the only state to do so.[27] Most states did not bother to revise or revoke the several components of home law after they had been emptied of content by the occupational freedom of the early sixties.[28] They left the subject hanging in a legislative limbo until Prussia's expansion into the individualized country administered the quietus.

Prussia had never known home law;[29] and the constitution of the North German Confederation, and then of the Second Empire, gave to the Confederation and the Imperial government—both directly dominated by Prussia—legal competence over movement, home, settlement, and the trades. Communities were promptly forbidden to interfere in any of these matters, and individual Germans declared free of hometown restraints. The 1867 Confederation law on free movement abolished "all special laws and privileges of particular places and districts which permit restrictions on residence"; only a trace of the old community powers, for extreme cases, remained. Marriage was declared free in 1868: "Members [Angehörige] of the Confederation need, in order to marry or set up domestic households of their own, neither membership in a community, nor a right of residence, nor the approval of a community,

[27] In 1884 Bavaria briefly and apparently ineffectively revived the rights of communities to forbid marriage on account of bad reputation. For the Social Laws generally Popp, Gewerbefreiheit, pp. 128–137; Riedel, Heimat (6th ed.; Munich, 1892), pp. 53–67; Hermann Rehm, "Eheschliessung," Handwörterbuch der Staatswissenschaften, III (2d ed.; Jena, 1900), 287–289.

[28] E.g. Rehm's article, "Heimatrecht," after showing the progressive enrichment of home law from a poor law to the whole panoply of communal defense, simply adds that it ended (except in Bavaria) in the sixties and cites Reich legislation. But royal Saxony followed occupational freedom with a change of 1834 rules to allow settlement by "notification" to the community that one wished to pursue a trade there, and Bürgerrecht was automatic after five years' residence; and Sachs-Meiningen forbade communities to deny Heimatrecht in 1867: Horster, Gewerbeverfassung, p. 162; Munzer, "Gemeindeverfassung in Sachsen-Meiningen," pp. 35–36.

[29] See above, p. 349; but Prussia had briefly introduced the settlement principle in an 1860 law on local taxes: Rehm, "Erwerb," p. 272.

or of the poor district, nor any official permission"; and specifically, marriage could not be blocked on economic grounds nor for reasons of "reputation." The Trades Law of 1869 guaranteed free choice of occupation, though leaving powers to regulate the exercise of the trades to the states.[30]

At the beginning of the century hometownsmen had rejected state citizenship in favor of local Bürgerrecht; in the thirties they had turned from civic Bürgerrecht to the social Heimatrecht. The Frankfurt Parliament, trying to reverse this process of political abdiction for the sake of social and economic defense, had instead only forged a contrary alliance between local oligarchy and bureaucracy. Now in the fifties, economic change had destroyed trades localism and with it the Heimatrecht, and the politically stunted communities were helpless. Political incubator, communal citizenship, and guilds were gone, leaving communal consciousness to find its way without them.

Community and society

The fourth quality of hometown society did not die so readily; it was less immediately tied to the political and economic forms that had nurtured it, so that it survived them into a false environment. Belief in the primacy of communal membership, mistrust of floating individuals, and righteous hostility toward the outside were the hometown legacy to the Germany of the later nineteenth century and at least the first half of the twentieth. Hometownsmen themselves were submerged in the Second Empire, or at least had become harder to locate, because the society had changed its apparent shape. That is not to say they were gone. "Even in the new Germany the classes of precapitalist times have by no means vanished," warned Werner Sombart just after 1900. "Above all, the Kleinbürgertum of the old breed still are an important part even of

---

[30] Rehm, "Erwerb," pp. 268–269; Sartorius von Waltershausen, *Deutsche Wirtschaftsgeschichte*, pp. 226–227; texts in Max Proebst, *Das bayerische Gesetz über Heimat, Verehelichung und Aufenthalt vom 16. April 1868, mit . . . Novellen* (Munich, 1892), pp. 117–119, 132–133, and in Huber, *Dokumente*, II, 227–247; Klein, *Entwicklung des Gemeindebürgerrechts*, pp. 48–54. For a liberal polemic citing the moral rightness of the policies Prussia would bring to Germany, Karl Braun, "Das Zwangs-Zölibat für Mittellose in Deutschland," VVK, XX (1867), 78–79.

the new society, seriously to be reckoned with and not to be under-estimated." [31] Special epithets for intruders (*Hereingeschmeckte* is a telling example) and contempt for the inhabitants of newer settlements outside some visible or tacit traditional communal limits have remained noticeably strong in German small-town life even until now; and the shops of incoming artisans have been wrecked by native members of the trade within present memory. In itself this is not remarkable, and we cannot here trace out what part of it should be explained historically, as a cultural residue, and what part explained otherwise, by contemporary circumstances. That is the "lower middle class" problem that has bedeviled German politi-cal observers from Engels to the electoral sociologists and party campaign planners of the 1970's; and nearly all this study has to say about it has already been said. At any rate, though, these were not "perversions" of hometown culture by modern times, as apolo-gists like Möser and Riehl had been claiming for a century and a half; the hometownsman remained hardly more or less "philistine" than he always had been. Not his own tissue but his environment had changed, and his national aspiration, when he had one, was to make the national environment fit him.

A more distinctive, clearer, and more important path along which to trace the legacy of the home towns from the 1850's and 1860's into subsequent German history is not through the actual com-munities as social entities, but through the transfiguration of their kind of social consciousness into national politics and thought. It is a path bounded by a rejection of the workings of the national state and economy in the name of community on one side, and by a wish to shape them to the style of community on the other, so that there are parallel paths, one traveled by Kleinbürger and one by intellectuals and politicians of the general estate; and without the latter, the actual social residue of hometownsmen would have mat-tered very little. The second path out of the 1850's is the acceptance into orthodox German political and social thinking of an ideal of community that was different and in some way—in many ways—antecedent to and truer than existing society and state: a distinction analogous to the older one between Roman and German law but now, appropriately to the times, described socially rather than

[31] *Deutsche Volkswirtschaft*, p. 459.

legally. The two paths, hometown prejudices and the sociology of intellectuals, have converged at critical points in German history.

The German sociology that developed after 1848 found state and society in very different respective positions from the ones western political theorists like John Locke had been able to bridge by the social contract; and it built new layers on the historical pathology of Karl Friedrich Eichhorn.[32] Lorenz von Stein, characteristically of the difference, wrote in 1849–1850 that the principle of the state was "the elevation of all individuals to the fullest freedom, to the fullest possible development," whereas the principle of society (*Gesellschaft*) was "the subjection of individuals to other individuals, the fulfillment of the one through the dependence of the other." Human social life (*menschliche Gemeinschaft*) was made up of a constant tension between those polar opposites. The Revolulution of 1848, he thought, showed the unresolved mutual hostility between German society and the national state.[33] Other writers of the fifties considered the same problem in their own ways: Victor Aimé Huber, for example, in his efforts to reconcile communalism —*Genossenschaft*—with an industrial economy; and Riehl with his multi-volume "Natural History of the People as a Foundation for a German Sociopolitics," which was meant to bring German national politics and "social ethnography" into harmony at "a turning point between an old time and a new." [34]

The American Albion Small, who opened his 1924 book on *The Origins of Sociology* with Savigny and Eichhorn, found the German sociology of the 1850's to be perverse. "Certain political scientists began to be impressed by the perception that there are considerable ranges of human activity which are not primarily political." Small did not undertake to describe what might have wrought that im-

[32] Cf. Julius Weiske's introduction to his 1848 collection of *Gemeindegesetze*, pp. v–vi, where he determinedly distinguishes the Roman meaning of corporation (*societas*), a convenient legal fiction, from the German corporation, an actual group of people.

[33] *Geschichte der sozialen Bewegung in Frankreich*, I (Leipzig, 1850), xxxi, xliii–xliv, cxxxiii–cxxxv. For these citations to the 1850 edition I am indebted to Andrew Lees, "The German Intellectuals in the Aftermath of Revolution" (unpubl. diss., Harvard, 1969), Ch. VII.

[34] Huber, *Ausgewählte Schriften über Socialreform und Genossenschaftswesen* (Berlin, 1894); Riehl, *Bürgerliche Gesellschaft*, p. 1, and *Land und Leute*, preface to the 1st ed. (Stuttgart, 1853).

pression upon them, but proceeded: "thereupon these activities were conceived as constituting an entity, to be called society, presumably occupying its preserve in space, with relations similar to those of the state toward people, and presenting subject matter for a science to balance the science of the state." Small represented this "interesting blend of mysticism and objectivity" graphically as "two intersecting circles, one labeled 'the State,' the other 'Society,' the contents of each presenting the material to be controlled by a distinct 'Science.'" It was, he thought, "a dualism as difficult as that of the supreme church and the supreme state in the era of Henry and Hildebrand." [35]

These taunts were addressed mainly to the shades of Robert von Mohl; they were careless and not altogether just. But it remains true, to quote Mohl's biographer, that German sociologists of that time were not engaged in empirical studies of men's interactions with one another; rather, "they thought they saw in society a form of human life clearly distinguishable both from the lives of individuals and from the sphere of politics and the state," and they were trying to isolate and identify that form.[36] They were trying again to solve the contradiction of cameralism, as it had been revived and modified by the 1848 experience. The almost inevitable consequence of separating "society" from both state politics and from individual life was to conceive "society" in the image of the home town; and that was not so mystical and abstract a notion as Small supposed. Mohl himself wrote a long theoretical essay in 1851 to set the boundaries separating the science of society from political science: to distinguish the study of social forms and their behavior from that study of individuals and of the state whose limitations seemed now apparent to him. Individual life and the study of it always came down to the single ego (*das eigene Ich*), he wrote, and the state represented and enforced from above the total collectivity of such interests; but society consisted in groups of persons mutually dependent upon each other—not upon their individual selves or upon the whole, the state. Although the groups themselves were brought together by specific interest, they developed a general interest in maintaining themselves; and although they had individuals in them, and the same individuals were in the

[35] P. 318.   [36] Angermann, *Mohl*, pp. 330–331.

state too, still they had the special quality of being "fellowships naturally rooted [*naturwüchsige Genossenschaften*]," "natural associations [*natürliche Gemeinschaften*]" which as a rule possessed no clear formal organization.[37] Mohl listed a series of these. The first, vaguely but traditionally, he called estates, *Stände*: groups made up respectively of persons engaged in one of the main areas of human activity. Estates overlapped the individual and state spheres, but their essence was social: "a shared sphere of [*genossenschaftliches*] life, common interests, the same customs, moral standards, and sentiments. . . . It is a clinging together, and a seclusion against nonmembers, quite outside political organization, although reinforced by the latter insofar as it sustains the external conditions that produced the estate." [38] The next kind of social group was the community, to be distinguished from the estate by its circumscription within a locality. "The continuous living together of many people in the same place, and their constant pressure upon one another, creates needs and interests which on the one hand do not arise in individual and temporary situations, or at least cannot be satisfied there, and which on the other hand have nothing to do with the state's conception of unity and its organization [*Organismus*]." Again Mohl acknowledged that the state had a place in the governance of communities, and that individuals lived in them; yet a community was "a fellowship of a unique kind, that follows its own laws, with its own often very important implications for members and outsiders, and which is by no means absorbed into the state." To these categories Mohl added race (biologically defined), economic groupings based on work and possession, and groupings by religion or education.[39]

Mohl's fiercest critic was the young historian Heinrich von Treitschke, whose inaugural essay at Leipzig [40] was an attack on all

[37] Mohl, "Gesellschafts-Wissenschaft und Staats-Wissenschaft," *ZGS,* VII (1851), 46–48. Angermann's description of Mohl's analysis and the subsequent controversy with Treitschke (*Mohl,* pp. 330–387) is excellent, and I have drawn from it extensively; but I shall cite Mohl and Treitschke directly when I quote them.

[38] Mohl, "Gesellschafts-Wissenschaft," pp. 35–36. It is hard to tell just what Mohl meant by "estate," apparently something to do with birth; in later writings he dropped the term altogether: Angermann, *Mohl,* p. 348.

[39] "Gesellschafts-Wissenschaft," pp. 38–41.

[40] *Die Gesellschaftswissenschaft: Ein kritischer Versuch* (Leipzig, 1859).

those—Stein and Riehl along with Mohl—who thought sociology should be developed as a separate discipline. He attacked them on two main grounds: first for their emphasis on the discreteness of the community in actual life, and second for their analytical distinction between state and society, between political and social science. On the latter point Treitschke exhibited a curious ambiguity that betrayed his polemical purpose. For although he tacitly acknowledged that state and society categorically were different and even conflicting things, he simply would not allow it to be so, and that determination got him into contradictions that he could only overpower, not resolve. "The state *is* society in society's unitary organization; therefore it stands in contrast to the particularism of the separate social circles. The state encompasses the whole life of the people, in that it orders all these special group relations by law, civilizes [*versittlicht*] them, and defends their independence with its power." [41] Again: "The activity of the highly developed state encompasses the whole life of the people, but it is manifest only in moderate measures, in the removal of certain obstructions." He insisted that political science must "take its content and life from the concrete life of the people" or lose all meaning, for "people and state may not be separated even in thought; if they could, there would be an absolutely rational state, an error . . . if they could, political science would be a mere formal doctrine." [42] Justi, then Möser, then back, and forth; now the state as creator and high trustee of rational harmony, now the state as an admittedly irrational embodiment of a real society. Only an act of will could hold them together; it was a description of what Treitschke thought ought to be, not anything that ever was. The issue between him and Mohl might be put as between two ethical conclusions from the events of 1848, two alternative correctives to the general estate's failure of leadership then. Mohl and those like him were prepared to call the state a structural instrument of social interests, but could not suppose it society itself; Treitschke insisted that the

[41] Ibid., p. 81 (my italics).
[42] Ibid., pp. 73, 90, 95. The similarity to present (1970) demands for academic "relevance" needs no pressing; Treitschke's contempt for pedantry and abstraction permeates his essay.

state must be—surely he meant it must become—not an instrument of society's interest, but society's actual fulfillment.[43]

The other prong of Treitschke's attack, the one against Mohl's description of local communities, makes the meaning of all this a little clearer. He denied the communities any right to purposes separate from the whole people's and from the state's. But he did not reply to Mohl, as the older state orthodoxy might have done, that the communities should be considered mere agents of the state, or as administrative intermediaries between the whole people (or state) and individuals. Instead he showed a remarkable deference toward the communities together with his insistence that they could not be thought of separately from the state. Indeed of all social institutions, he said, only the local community could be considered on a par with the state and thought about in the same ways; only the community could itself function the way a state did, alone, if all other connections were severed. "This may not be said of other social bodies; they have nothing about them comparable to the state, just as the community has little or none of that hostility to the state characteristic of all particularist associations, the hostility of special interest [πλεονεξία]." [44] The community was intimately akin to the state because it was a totality and not an interest; of all associations then only the community was (like the state) truly political in its governing processes.

"A nation made up of dozens of clans, small towns, and social groupings, and at the same time a nation of scholars!" lamented Riehl. "In this antithesis lies the tragic in the German national character." [45] Treitschke used the analogy of local community with state as the opening sally of his declaration against separating society and state intellectually (I have reversed the order of his argument because he put his solution first). He can hardly have supposed that existing communities and existing states were so alike. Mohl in 1851 had managed the home town theoretically by separating it from politics and from the state; Treitschke in 1859 instead absorbed and incorporated the home town into his theory of politics and into his ideal concrete state. The state *would* be

---

[43] Angermann, *Mohl*, p. 377.   [44] *Gesellschaftswissenschaft*, p. 5.
[45] *Bürgerliche Gesellschaft*, p. 26.

society; and to attain that, both were the community writ large.

A whole parade of German scholars after the 1850's struggled along the way that has led (in this history) from Möser and Justi through Eichhorn to Mohl and Treitschke. Otto von Gierke, legal historian and theorist of the *Genossenschaft*, was, according to recent judgment, "a genuine champion of corporate autonomy as well as a good German patriot of the Second Reich, and his theory is an unsuccessful attempt to reconcile . . . irreconcileables: to have it both ways."[46] Gierke seems to have supposed that unfettered communities would flow spontaneously together into national community: a kind of national home town made up of free corporate wills, an *"allgemeine Genossenschaft."*[47] He used historical projection as a synthetic device; so did a great many others. The trick was to assume that a communal true Germany of the past unfolded naturally into a national true Germany of the present and future. The historical school of economics proceeded on the course its mentor Wilhelm Roscher had set for it in the 1840's: "to accomplish for the public economy what the Savigny-Eichhorn method did for jurisprudence."[48] The Socialists of the Chair, historians all, still tried to overcome the contradictions of cameralism by uniting particular group realities with a collective national aim through a dimension of historical evolution from one into the other, distending communal qualities into quite different kinds of associations and circumstances.[49] Ferdinand Tönnies tried to sort out Trietschke's (if not the Second Empire's) monstrous assimilation by elaborating the

[46] Wolfgang Friedmann, *Legal Theory* (4th ed. London, 1960), p. 189, quoted (but inaccurately cited) in Georg G. Iggers, *The German Conception of History* (Middletown, 1968), p. 133.

[47] Heffter, *Selbstverwaltung*, pp. 525–530; Rupert Emerson, *State and Sovereignty in Modern Germany* (New Haven, 1928), pp. 126–154, though he seems to think Gierke was born *sui generis*, carries this "begged question" through Hugo Preuss and the Weimar constitution.

[48] Small, *Origins of Sociology*, p. 155, quoting Roscher, *Grundriss zu Vorlesungen über die Staatswirthschaft nach geschichtlicher Methode* (Göttingen, 1843), without page citation.

[49] Thus their spokesman Gustav Schmoller on their controversy with neoclassical theorists of modern economy: "Statistics and history may be contrasted with those procedures which aim to set forth the general nature of economic phenomena. But this contrast must not be treated as an unbridgeable gulf." *SJ*, VII (1883), 977.

distinction, social and historical at once, between familiar community on the one hand and fluid society on the other, between *Gemeinschaft* and *Gesellschaft;* but he spoiled the effect, much as Riehl and so many others had done, by displaying a marked preference for the former even in the 1880's.[50] The German past and present posed to scholars a critically difficult and hence a perilous intellectual task. For a community (as they understood the word) of a whole nation (as they understood the word) was truly impossible in theory, history notwithstanding. Then how about politics?

Community and politics

Hometownsmen were most notable in the politics of the Second Empire for their absence. This implies neither disloyalty to the Empire nor enthusiasm for it; rather, national politics after the decisions of the fifties and sixties had very little to do with communal affairs, and local politics, such as they were, bore little relation to doings in Berlin. National questions that exercised comparable people in the United States, such as slavery and the disposal of western lands, had no real counterpart in Germany. The issue of social legislation at the end of the seventies and the early eighties, though it touched a chord in the hometown tradition, addressed mainly urban problems; and tariff questions, though hometownsmen were by reflex protectionist, affected them far less than they affected cities and agriculture. Emigration and colonialism (probably the nearest analogy to American slavery and land questions) did catch their interest, as channels for diverting things that troubled them to the outside; and certainly it is no fortuity that the one occasion when Bismarck developed an interest in local self-government was in the early eighties, around the time when he developed his social program, his tariff protectionism, and his colonialism: the time of his break with the liberal parties that had sup-

---

50 Cf. Fritz F. K. Ringer, *The Decline of the German Mandarins* (Cambridge, 1969), pp. 170–171, arguing that Tönnies "and others of his persuasion" fought against vulgar state-oriented communitarianism associated with "cameralist bureaucracy"; they "saw the state as the chief enemy, not the potential source, of community." For subsequent developments on the theme, Ringer's *Mandarins* and René König, *Soziologische Orientierungen* (Cologne, 1965), passim.

ported the formation of the Reich, when he tried (successfully) to divide and discredit them.[51]

The separation of hometownsmen from national political life here takes on a very serious negative importance, though: it was a source of the weakness of the national parties, particularly the liberal ones heir to the Paulskirche. Like the content of national politics, the organization of national parties had only tenuous relations with local political groupings; party discipline hardly extended outside the Reichstag, and its weakness within it resulted partly from the unreliability of political constituencies, together with the absence of ministerial responsibility and of patronage powers. Without these unifying features familiar to western parliamentary politics, local town-hall parties—Rathausparteien—were built almost entirely on local issues; they had their own local names, and the national parties had almost no means of stabilizing electoral coalitions in the districts.[52] The same was true of the parties of the Republic that followed the collapse of imperial government in 1917–1919, but in more aggravated circumstances, for now the parties had assumed responsibility as the main bearers of national politics. The epithet "interest politics" to describe parliamentary representation and compromise was a malevolent contrast with the real or fancied nature of communal decision; and amidst the extraordinary strains of the twenties and early thirties, it was a lethal one.

The ubiquitous yearning for organic wholeness seems the most important legacy of hometown history to twentieth-century Germany.[53] This is not to say the hometownsman was himself the only

[51] Paul Dehn, Bismarck als Erzieher (Munich, 1903), pp. 284–285; Walker, Germany and the Emigration, pp. 195–246. At that time too there were feeble efforts in Bavaria and Württemberg to revive communal social powers: Klein, Entwicklung des Gemeindebürgerrechts, pp. 54–61; Riedel, Heimat (1892), pp. 62–63.

[52] The study of German party organization by historians is only beginning; the older tradition of Ludwig Bergsträsser, Geschichte der politischen Parteien in Deutschland (many editions) treated ideology and national policy with almost no mention of organization; of the organizational studies that began after World War II, probably the most important is Thomas Nipperdey, Die Organisation der deutschen Parteien vor 1918 (Düsseldorf, 1961).

[53] This quality has been discussed generally by Peter Gay, Weimar Culture: the Outsider as Insider (New York, 1968); and as a study in the sociology of intellectuals by Ringer, Mandarins.

or even the main repository of it. It is to say that the sharp juxta-position between the kind of organic integrity attributed to com-munity (which smothers conflict) and the "fragmentation" of na-tional parliamentary politics and a liberal economy (both based on conflict) was the proximate cause of German preoccupation with moral and social wholeness and with total integrity. Turning it around: the totality of community exemplified in the home town was what made the newer and larger entities appear as disintegra-tion and contradiction. "Atomization" is another epithet Germans applied to modern society, a term born of the contrast with the power of community over individual in hometown society; "mechan-ism" is yet another, and it means that nobody had been able to set forth in material and rational terms just how the community, in contrast, really worked—only in sentimental and mystical terms.

In the Third Reich the two paths, the longings of intellectuals for national community and hometownsmen's parochial values, came closest together; or at least National Socialist rhetoric undertook to combine them, a rhetoric with real and wide powers of political attraction. Surely that is part of what so many serious and informed participants meant when they said Hitler had solved the German question. The National Socialist revolution was—among other things—a movement of communal sentiments from a negative place (as in the Second Empire and especially the Republic) to a positive place in the national state. The lines connecting the home town with National Socialism must remain here general, and hypothetical in proportion. To explore the social continuity fully, for example, would be a complex exercise in history and political sociology, for which the usual analytical categories will hardly serve (that has been a reason for offering this one). Continuity through the educa-tional system and through the popular arts of journalism, fiction, and the film is easier to trace, at least superficially. But whatever the lines of continuity, similarities between the home town and the theory and practice of National Socialism are obvious, and they often serve to distinguish the latter from the other modern political movements to which it is readily compared.[54] The pogroms and political persecutions of the Third Reich are quite on the pattern

[54] Cf. Ernst Nolte, *Three Faces of Fascism* (New York, 1965); and George L. Mosse, *The Crisis of German Ideology* (New York, 1964).

of hometown drives after groundrabbits and outsiders, now elevated into national state policy. The enemies National Socialism proclaimed to be German enemies were hometown enemies; it chose them for its guise as defender and restorer of the true Germany. It justified its use of illegal techniques and its contempt for the legal state, the *Rechtsstaat,* by its claim to defend the intuitive values of German community against pedantry and materialism.[55]

Again it will not do to equate hometownsmen with National Socialism, one to one, nor to equate either with the formulae of classic elite conservatism. In the communities as in the state, party prominents seem at least as commonly to have been outsiders to established society and government, who achieved place and power through the national movement at the cost of older leadership. At any rate the National Socialist seizure of power was not accompanied locally by the home town's traditional retraction in crisis to its traditional social leadership; old mayors and councilmen were more likely to be expelled or forcibly converted, as philistine and provincial obstructions to the national community being born, the *Volksgemeinschaft.*[56]

National Socialism was, more nearly, a political expression of a tortured synthesis between hometownsmen and general estate. It was no restoration, but rather a revolutionary effort to accommodate community with modernity on a national scale. Its political success came from the conversion of hometown bigotries into national virtues, and from providing a way for the movers and doers of the general estate to unite finally with the German people, with the people as German history, sociology, law, and literature had described them for a century and more. Political disaster came from

[55] There was a major revival of Riehl under National Socialist auspices: Viktor v. Geramb, *Wilhelm Heinrich Riehl: Leben und Wirken, 1823–1897* (Salzburg, 1954), pp. 562–593.

[56] Cf. William S. Allen, *The Nazi Seizure of Power: The Experience of a Single German Town, 1930–1935* (Chicago, 1965); Irma and Mack Walker, "Weissenburg II," a companion piece to the essay that appears as Chapter VII above, straddling the Third Reich as that chapter does the Napoleonic period, and prepared from sources that still must be regarded as confidential. I suspect there may have been a reversion to old local leadership during the postwar period of political reconstruction, particularly in the American zone.

the falsity, the vulgarity of the synthesis: from making the hometown negatives into national positives, from making hometown withdrawal, resentment, and fear into a triumphant program of massive
general action.

In a narrow political sense it really was a solution to the German
problem: resolving the conflicting themes of national unity and
community by translating hometown values into national organization. But of course the two could not be truly reconciled by pretending a modern state was a home town, and only a deliberate or
despairing suppression of consequential logic could make it possible
to suppose they could be reconciled that way. David Schoenbaum
has described in detail the conflict within National Socialist doctrine
and politics that reflected the aspiration for galvanic power and
unity without change, the claim that power and unity would come
through a reversion to earlier social and economic forms. He puts
it that the social revision backwards to the small business, the small
town, and the small farm was incompatible with revision of
Versailles; and that Hitler, when he had to choose, picked the latter,
and with it big banks, big industry, big cities, big labor organizations—all enemies of the home town—and so brought social revolution rather than restoration.[57] Of the internal incompatibility of
Hitler's program there can be little doubt, nor of Hitler's choice; but
whether he did effect a social revolution through economic and
military mobilization is less certain. The postwar shuffling of population (especially the pouring of millions of refugees into small
towns) and the industrial explosion of the 1950's were far more
revolutionary for small-town society at least. Placing dates along a
slope of decline seems arbitrary but is not meaningless; 1960 might
be a good date for the final demise of the home town in German
society and politics—even though one of Germany's most promising
young politicians, an Interior Minister of the Bonn Republic, concludes a book on industrial politics by discussing the industrial enterprise as the new Heimat, and the application of home law to it;
and even though one of Germany's most admired political scientists,
a historian of the Weimar Republic, has condemned efforts by

[57] David Schoenbaum, *Hitler's Social Revolution* (New York, 1966), passim,
especially pp. 287–291.

national parties to absorb local *Rathausparteien* as undemocratic; [58] and even though uncritical local historical societies flourish; and though new community leadership—refugees, civil servants, and all —seem to have developed an interest in local social traditions, the structure of club membership, and other such artifacts that have little to do with the tourist trade. But agreed: the failure of the Third Reich effectively destroyed the idea of national community, *Volksgemeinschaft,* that was its watchword; and by the 1960's the home town seemed shattered beyond recovery, in body or spirit. Supose it was; what then?

Richard Hughes, in his remarkable 1961 novel about Europe in the 1920's, *The Fox in the Attic,* offered two metaphorical explanations of what went wrong in Germany then, and why the Republic failed. One was historical, one social and psychological; and both come very close to what I have undertaken to say about the hometown community. In one place he ascribed the Republic's failure to its effort to build a new structure out of old, secondhand lumber, the prewar society that would not fit or support liberal republican institutions. That was the historical explanation. The other is more difficult and even more metaphorical: that human personalities by their nature require a limited, finite extension and reflection of themselves into their immediate surroundings. Hughes writes of a penumbra, a part-shadow that an individual casts upon his environment and where he can see his own presence. The shadows tell people they are neither totally isolated nor totally exposed. This description implies (as the first does to a lesser degree) that in modern life that condition of identity and protection has been lost. The hometown community seems rather like that system of finite shadows, with its capacity to affirm individuality through partial reflection and subjection by others, and with its protection of the area of the self's extension to others.[59]

If the first explanation is the important one, the explanation from old lumber, then the destruction of the home town means the end of its story. Its place in modern history is over, and Germany can

---

[58] Ernst Benda, *Industrielle Herrschaft und sozialer Staat* (Göttingen, 1966); Theodor Eschenburg, "Rathausparteien: Das Zunftmonopol der 'Politiker,'" in *Zur politischen Praxis in der Bundesrepublik* (Munich, 1961), pp. 136–141.

[59] (New York, 1961), pp. 101–104, 120–121, 349–350.

go on to build with new lumber: a liberal industrial society that has come to terms with civic equality, change, unfamiliarity, and calculated conflict.[60]

But if and where the second explanation seems more important, then the story of the home towns takes on the character of a historical allegory disturbingly like Justus Möser's, about conditions and aspirations of social existence that are chained to no historical circumstance and that by no means have passed away with the communities. The anarcho-communalism that developed among academic youth in the 1960's, to take an example that comes readily to mind at the writing,[61] has been nothing new in human history, but may have taken its special vehemence from what Hughes called an absence of the penumbra that gives individuals identity and protection in society even as it subjects them to society. And it seems significant that the unusual vehemence, and confusion, has occurred among this most unhistorical generation of modern times, an antihistorical generation with no use for old lumber save as an object of damnation; German youth movements of the 1810's, the 1890's, and the 1920's by contrast not only delighted in old lumber but made up and aged some of their own.

This phenomenon touches that perennial problem of modern German history, most recently described as "overcoming the past," *Bewältigung der Vergangenheit.* If it was only a matter of getting rid of old lumber, it was probably solved in the liberal years after World War II, so that the passing of the home town is part of the history of a transition now accomplished. But if it was a matter of penumbra, then the passing of the home town is an opening to what is only just beginning.

[60] A good general discussion of this question is Dahrendorf, *Society and Democracy in Germany.*

[61] When I began this study in about 1964 the obvious analogy seemed the small town of the American South: perhaps a significant evolution of issues from lumber to penumbra.

Appendix

THE IMPERIAL TRADES
EDICT OF 1731

PATENT

TO REMEDY ABUSES
AMONG THE GUILDS

Dated Vienna, August 16, 1731

WE CHARLES THE SIXTH, by the Grace of GOD, chosen
Roman Emperor, for all times increaser of the Reich, King in Germany
[here follow seventy-three further titles, concluding] Lord upon the
Windisch Mark, of Portenau, of Biscay and Molins, of Salins, of Tripoli
and of Mechlin. Present to each and every Elector, Prince, Spiritual and
Secular, Prelate, Count, Baron, Lord, Knight, Bondsman, and all other
loyal subjects of Us and the Reich, and also to the Reich's Generals,
Higher and Lower Officers and ordinary Soldiers of horse and of foot,
whatever they are called, and whatever their rank, station, or condition,
who shall read or see this Our Imperial public document or an attested
copy of it: Our friendship, grace, and good wishes, and herewith we
give you to know: Since it has happened that, although in various
Imperial Edicts, but especially the organized Reformation of good
Order [*Polizey*] of the year 1530, Tit. 39, and 1548, Tit. 36 & 37,
and also 1577, Tit. 37 & 38, respecting the removal of abuses spreading
among artisans generally but especially with regard to menials, sons,
journeymen, and apprentices many very salutary provisions have already been made, still these have not altogether been lived up to, and
even other abuses have gradually crept in among the said artisans: So
that it is held necessary, with regard to the said provisions and the
section on artisans in the Last Imperial Conclusion of the year 1654, as
is ordained by the *Causis mandatorum & simplicis querelae* etc. 106,
not only to renew, but in the following ways to improve and extend
them.

1. In the Holy Roman Empire the artisans shall have no power to hold meetings without the prior knowledge of those properly in authority over them, or of someone deputized by their will and in their name; and in no place shall any guild articles, practices, or customs be sustained unless they have been confirmed and ratified after prior and sufficient consideration and adjustment, according to the existing state of things, by the appropriate authorities of the land, or at least of each place (just as in any case all sovereign power, and accordingly the power to alter and improve guild articles within their territories, is in all ways reserved to each Imperial Estate if this is opportune to the time, events, or circumstances, by virtue of their occupying sovereign prerogative). Conversely all those which have been established by the artisans, masters and journeymen, on their own account, without the aforesaid permission, approval, and confirmation, or which in the future may be established or introduced, are null, void, invalid, and without force. And should such persons, anywhere in the Holy Roman Empire, set willfully about establishing their own practices in defiance of this, and not cease to do so upon official admonishment, then they shall, by properly enacted official judgment, be excluded from the practice of their crafts in any place in the Holy Roman Empire because of this trespass and disobedience, and shall be regarded by all persons as unsound and incompetent in their trades; and if they go elsewhere their names shall be posted on public buildings and they shall be everywhere ostracized [*aufgetriben* *], for so much and so long, until they have paid to the authorities the penalty for their crime and disorder, and are readmitted to the craft by public authority. And the same punishment shall be inflicted also upon any masters and journeymen who disregard such official notification, and accept such transgressors as sound and competent, and encourage them to practice their trades.

2. So that henceforth, along with these abuses and the damage they do to the trades, an end may be put to the practice of ostracism by journeymen that has become almost universal and customary, and to their senseless rebellion and refusal to work; and so that the roots of all the disorders that have afflicted the trades may be pulled from the

---

* *Auftreibung*, a characteristic expedient in the jurisdictional circumstances of the Empire, usually meant pursuit of a disgraced artisan who moved to another place, by word of mouth or with letters announcing his disgrace, so that the new place could not accept and employ him without itself incurring dishonor and ostracism and risking rebellion on the part of its own journeymen. Guilds were the main users of this procedure (cf. §§ 2 and 10).

ground: so the latter with the former is herewith totally forbidden and abolished on pain of the punishments specified in this renewed and improved regulation. But to the masters is reserved a wise and healthy power of such a character that in each and every trade and guild, whatever it is called, every single apprentice when he is indentured shall place his birth certificate or other valid documentation of his antecedents in the guild chest of the place where he is apprenticed; and the certificate of training as well, when he is released; so that he shall give both originals to the said guild chest for safekeeping, until he deposits them in the single place where he genuinely wishes to settle and become a master, from which place he must bring attested notice of his intention bearing the seals of the authorities and of the guild there. But the guild must provide him with an attested copy of his birth certificate, or a valid copy of his equivalent as aforesaid, and of his training certificate, for the purpose of his travels when he begins them, and wishes to seek work in other places; but once and for all, and not more than one, on pain of inevitable punishment (unless he sufficiently prove that he really and innocently lost the first, and so properly asks for a new one), with the guild seal and the signatures of the overmasters, with a clerical fee of about 30 to a maximum of 45 kreuzer, according to the length of the thing; and it shall furnish him without further charge a printed attestation of his behavior according to this formula:

> We the sworn over- and other masters of the (N) guild in the . . . town of (N) certify herewith, that this journeyman, named (N), born in (N), . . . years old, and . . . in height, and with . . . hair, has worked with us here for . . . years and . . . weeks, and throughout this time has shown himself loyal, industrious, quiet, peaceable, and honest, as such an apprentice ought to be, which then we attest, and therefore request as is fitting that all our fellowmasters everywhere support this journeyman in accordance with guild custom.
>
> (Place, date)
>
> (Signed) (N) Overmaster
>   (N) Overmaster
>   (N) As master, where the above
>   journeyman was in service

With this then the journeyman goes upon his travels, and presents himself to the guild in the town where he seeks work, and when he displays it all masters who need journeymen are bound and obliged to assist him without objection. Now when work is promised him in a place he has come to, as soon as he commences he must deposit for safe-keeping in the guild chest there the guild-certified copies of his birth and apprenticeship certificates, or documentation, which he has brought with him, along with the guild certificate he received; and he must leave them there until he decides to leave that place and continue his travels. When then such a journeyman decides to leave this place where he has been working and move on, he must notify his master of his planned departure at least a week in advance (except where a longer period is the custom, up to three to six months, as for example barbers and printers); thus all claims of any kind which the authorities or any-one else may have against him may be satisfied and carried out. And the masters are to make sure that the motive for departure is not some crime committed but not yet discovered, and are obliged to give the authorities notice, if it is, failing which they are to expect proper pun-ishment in accordance with the degree of their connivance. But in such a case the credentials and the testimonial shall not be delivered to the journeyman; he shall remain deprived of both until he has satisfied the debt or the claim, and thus be obliged to stay on the spot until the mat-ter has been settled.

Now it often happens too that those guilds, whose confirmed charters for sufficient reason have allowed them some punitive powers over people accused in this way, have too strong a tendency to go to ex-tremes: therefore hereafter neither the masters, nor much less the journeymen, may deprive an accused person of his credentials and certificate by themselves alone, nor to punish him; rather they should always report the claim to the Overmasters and officers and to the deputy of the authorities for handwork affairs as well; and these to-gether should investigate the matter, and then settle it promptly without unnecessary expense, the Overmasters and officers or the deputies for handwork affairs being obliged to decide such things without compensation, or at most, if the affair is of greater difficulty and importance, then to be compensated with about one or two gulden Rhenish in the form a minor trade fine, or if there is a likelihood of some further serious litigation, not to adjudcate it themselves, but to take recourse to the judgment of the proper authorities of the place. But if the journeyman has behaved in all respects well and irreproach-ably, and if the definite notice has been given in the manner described, and things have been managed properly, and he wishes then to start his travels, then not only are his deposited birth or antecedent and training documents to be returned to him, along with the testimonial he has brought, but also he is to be furnished without fail by the guild of this last place with a new testimonial to his good behavior, in the form described above, at the cost of about and no more than 15 kreuzer; but on the immediately preceding older one it shall be briefly noted that at (N), on . . . day he received a new one (as the older one by virtue of the resumed travel is in any case to be considered invalid, without force, and extinguished, and is only left in the hands of the journeyman insofar as he wishes to keep it for his own edification and satisfaction). Moreover should it happen that a journeyman is given no work in the place where he has arrived, then the Overmasters of his guild there shall note without charge upon the testimonial he has brought and exhibited that inquiries were made but that there had been no master in need of a journeyman, so that he has had to travel further. But whenever a journeyman does not possess such a copy of birth and training credentials under guild seal, and the guild testimonial described above (with respect to the latter, if he really has had one but accidentally lost it, and it is satisfactorily proven or confirmed by oath that this is the case, then the authorities, and they alone, of the place where he first reports this loss and where he is staying at the time, after writing to the authorities of the place where the last certificate was made, especially if the journeyman lacks the means to travel back personally, may replace the old one) then he shall be given work by no master, under any pretext whatever, on pain of a fine of Twenty Reichsthaler, nor shall he receive training, nor the gift,* nor any other guild benefit. And if after this and the above prohibition have been received and published some journeyman or other, who because of evil behavior has had or should hereafter have his documents held back in the described way, should nevertheless spread slander, ostracism, and abuse in order to avenge himself against the guild which has withheld his credentials: then upon the notice which the masters are especially obliged to give promptly on pain of punishment, or upon complaint of the authorities of the place where he has committed the slander, he shall immediately be brought to punishment by any authority in the whole Holy Roman Empire as a wanton and a rebel, and obliged publicly to take back his insults and abuse in the place where he made them, though saving his honor if there are signs of genuine reform; and beyond that if need be he may be punished with jail, penitentiary, or forced labor. But if he should take flight to a foreign country, and the foreign powers cannot be brought to deliver him over, then the magistracy of the place where he committed the slander is

* See below, § 7.

to write to his birthplace and through the courts there attach the property he has already acquired and what he may hope to inherit; also, if he is now foreign and has nothing of which to be deprived, he may, after report has been made to the territorial sovereign, be declared infamous, and his name posted on the gallows.

3. When a journeyman has learned his trade in one place, according to the usual and officially approved craft ordinances, statutes, and customs of that place, and particularly from an honorable master, approved by the people in authority there, then no distinction is to be made between this and other journeymen of the same trade from any other places, though there be other customs and craft regulations there, or even though fewer or more apprentice years be required; and there will be no imposition of any special further requirements whatever before they are accepted as decent and qualified, which presumptuous practice heretofore has appeared again and again.

4. And accordingly as the Regulations for Good Order of 1548, Tit. 37, and 1577, Tit. 38, provide that the children of certain persons be not excluded from guilds, corporations, brotherhoods, and associations, so this is emphatically confirmed, and those basic rules shall in the future be fully and exactly followed, understanding this to mean the children of the servants of the state courts and the towns no less than those of the guards of the courts, guards over forced labor, over the jails, or the fields, or of gravediggers, watchmen, beadles, street sweepers, ditch clearers, shepherds, and the like, in sum no profession and occupation is to be excepted but hangmen to the second generation only, provided always that the first choose a different and honorable occupation, and pursue it with his own family for at least 30 years—all must be admitted to the trades without obstruction.

5. Should it indeed happen that a master or a journeyman be accused of having done something improper and detrimental to the craft, then shall neither one master another, nor one journeyman another, nor a master a journeyman, nor a journeyman a master, let alone several of either, or against several, on that account either orally or in writing undertake to reproach, slander, or insult, much less ostracize them or harry them (since all ostracizing and harrying, apart from that coming from the authorities, has already been sharply forbidden in § 2 above, and is here once more forbidden without the smallest exception), but rather shall be fully content with the path of justice and

judicial advice or opinion; therefore let them bring the matter to the attention of the authorities, and patiently and peaceably await their investigation, knowledge, and judgment, in such fashion that until a legally binding decision is made no master and no journeyman be held as censured, disreputable, and incapable of his craft; but rather the other masters and journeymen are and remain obliged willingly to work with and beside him, respectively. Any masters or journeymen however who themselves undertake to obstruct an accused person in the pursuit of his trade are to be considered dishonorable, and by temporary summary edict of the authorities to be provisionally suspended from carrying on their trades, so that what they in their headstrong and shameless proceedings thought to do to others come back upon them, for so long, until the claimed injury or else the crime of the first-accused be legally considered, or the affair amicably settled.

Moreover should one or more masters or journeymen refuse to admit such-and-such a boy for such-and-such reasons to the craft, or to prevent him from continuing training he has already begun, and complaint is made to the authorities about it, then in this case too they must speak and give reply and accept the judgment and the decision of the authorities most obediently. Surely one cannot suppose that the masters in any case would presume to raise resistance and rebellion against the authorities in contravention of their duties as citizens or subjects, but besides no authorities would lack adequate means for compulsion and punishment. But if as in past experience the journeymen still indulge themselves a taste for staging walkouts on some pretext or other, and so for collecting into crowds, either to stay stubbornly on the spot and do no more work until some pretended claim or complaint be satisfied, or else even to swarm out in crowds, to do whatever other destructive and rebellious mischief they set upon: such great wantons or misdoers shall not only be subject to the punishments of jail, penitentiary, forced labor, and the galleys mentioned in § 2 above, but also, where circumstances warrant and there is high defiance, and they have been responsible for real evils, to the penalty of death. And when an authority of that place, or some state authority, is unable to suppress them alone, he will know enough to call upon neighboring authorities, also the imperial district administrative or military officers, for help in such a situation, whereupon such neighbors and imperial administrative and military officers are obliged to give sufficient help, and above all to bring these striking journeymen into captivity, and either deliver them over to the offended authority, or at least punish them appropriately themselves.

Moreover in no place in the Empire, to which such arrogantly rebellious sorties of youngsters from the trades might go seeking refuge, shall they be admitted to inns or any kind of shelter, far less allowed to remain, or be supplied with food and drink; and not only the wanton handwork youngsters themselves, but also their concealers, as accessories of the insurrectionists, shall be strictly visited with the above penalties.

6. And inasmuch as the frequent distinction between high and low guilds causes great confusion and divisions, so that a trade is considered worthier in one place than it is in another, and attracts the journeymen, and anyone who does not enroll in that guild is deemed unworthy in his training and his mastership, and therefore is sometimes prevented from working in one place or another: so each and every such high guild or so-called high lodge is herewith and by force of this abolished, removed, and put away; and so too the challenges, wrongly raised in some places, against handwork credentials from other territories, are forbidden; rather it is reserved to state authorities to erect guilds and headquarters in their lands, exclusively to establish laws regulating them, to punish the unruly at discretion, and to settle and remove all handwork differences without communicating with other estates or towns (unless they themselves find it necessary to do so); and masters or journeymen who rebel against them shall not be received, supported, or protected by any other estate, but rather henceforth shall be held unworthy and unsound for handwork, throughout the whole Roman Empire. Pursuant to this it is ordained that in the future the guild of one land and place shall be considered as good and valid as the others are, and accordingly no guild, as these former high guilds have done, nor by any pretext, shall pass judgment on the guild of another place, especially that of another territory, for example, even though some recognition or other be voluntarily accorded it; nor shall it usurpatiously accept this status and impose fines; yet this may not bring any disadvantage to those Electors, Princes, and Estates in the privileges here upheld or legitimately descended.

From this it is nearly impossible to see what grounds the guilds of different places or even territories have for corresponding with one another; rather the correspondence among artisans could cease entirely. When nevertheless cases do arise which seem to make correspondence necessary, let the letters not be sent except through the place's authorities, with their knowledge and consideration of the contents attested by signature, so that except at the pain of 20 Reichsthaler penalty no guild may write to another, nor any guild receive, open, or answer any letter from another. But in no manner whatever may masters or above all journeymen, in trade matters, matters therefore pertaining to the whole guild of their locality, correspond with one another, to which end also the abuse of the fraternal seal by journeymen should by all means cease; and as they cannot establish any brotherhood without a seal, they should not be allowed to have one, but rather where they have in the past presumed to have one it should be demanded from them and put in the guild chest for safekeeping. So too all deputations of masters and journeymen to the guilds of other places, which may be attempted without specific and individual written and certified permission from the authorities, are in the same way forbidden and will be punished severely.

7. Moreover and whereas it has been found that often at the indenturing and at the signing out of the apprentices, as also at the gifting of the handwork journeymen, where some handworkers are not satisfied with the gift freely given but expect to be furnished by the masters with costly and special foods; and also with regard to fees and fines and in other ways, great and burdensome excesses are committed by masters and journeymen: so excesses of this kind shall be totally abolished; the necessary indenturing, learning, and signing-out fees and also the mastership fees of all places shall be made as fixed as possible by the authorities, and published for the information of everyone, and transgressors punished with all severity when complaints are received. And the frequent distinction between gift and nongift trades, especially insofar as it has heretofore implied a greater honor and dignity, is by virtue of this erased; also each traveling journeyman will receive as a gift, where this is the custom, not more than at most 4 to 5 good groschen or 15 to 20 kreuzer Rhenish, be it in hard cash or in food and drink from the hostel; and begging on doorsteps is to be strictly avoided. But when a journeyman, running as many do from one place to another just for the sake of the gifts, refuses to accept a place offered him, then he is not to get the gift.

8. Also certain penalties of gift and nongift trade masters, sons, and journeymen shall no longer be imposed, held, or used until they are given force by guild charters and craft ordinances revised and issued by the authorities, after the publication of this Imperial Law, the sooner

the better, which will specify the instances and the degree of punishment, and provide that in every case the deputy of the authorities for craft affairs shall be informed.

9. Moreover the artisans often reckon so exactly that they prevent apprentices who may not have fulfilled their apprentice years by some few days or hours from entering the journeyman rank; or at the signing-out they are subjected to all sorts of peculiar customs, some ridiculous, some offensive and humiliating, such as planing, polishing, preaching, christening, as they call it, putting on unusual clothing, leading them around the streets, or sending them around, and such things; likewise they hold so stubbornly to their guild greeting, silly turns of speech and other such senseless things that anyone who for example in an oath or a statement leaves out a word or a dot must submit to a given money fine, or travel further, or often indeed travel a long way back to the place he came from to bring the greeting in another form. Also the artisans work out certain forms for birth certificates and other documents in which there appear clauses which are foolish or superfluous, and clauses which contradict the laws and the Imperial constitutions: as for example that the parents of the person presenting the certificate were brought publicly on the street to the church at the time of their marriage; * and further and similarly, they use and even demand birth and apprenticeship certificates from the authorities. Moreover it also happens that journeymen commonly and willfully absent themselves from work on Mondays and other days which are not properly holidays: the which and all similar unreasonable abuses and improprieties named in this ordinance, or not named, shall be abolished by the authorities; and the wearing of the dagger by artisans, which is especially forbidden to apprentices at pain of confiscation or other penalty, is forbidden in the towns. Especially fully to disappear henceforth is the so-called guild greeting, which by virtue of the certification described in § 2 becomes all the more superfluous and unnecessary to demand of every traveling journeyman; and accordingly herewith also for example the derived distinction in the masons' trade between greeters and paper carriers. Also when a journeyman who has once properly learned his trade seeks his bread and fortune outside that trade for a period short or long, and goes into the service of this or that sovereign [*Herrschaft*] of grand or lesser estate, but subsequently either goes back to his learned trade as a journeyman or attempts to become a master; when in the latter instance he has in all other respects learned his trade properly, pre-

* A shotgun wedding.

pared the master piece, and presented valid evidence of good behavior from the sovereign whom he served, then his acknowledged service outside the trade shall not bring him the slightest disadvantage or hindrance, provided that during his service he does no injury to local masters by taking on outside work for unprivileged persons. As, moreover, sometimes the youngest or last-accepted masters are hindered and kept from their work when the older ones cause them to run errands, pay attendance, and such services, to their substantial injury and soon their impending ruin: so hereafter let young masters not be too severely burdened in this way, nor in this other way: that when a properly guilded master is called temporarily to another sovereignty, he is required beyond the dues for enrollment in the trade to go through the guilding process anew in the place to which he has been called; where need be all authorities should watch this and see that it be not burdensome.

10. But this abuse especially breaks into certain trades, contrary to all sense: that the journeymen, by means of a court usurpatiously established among themselves, summon the masters before them, give them orders, impose all kinds of absurd rules upon them, and when these are rejected then scold, punish, and even rebel against the masters, and also ostracize the journeymen who work for them and hold them to be unworthy. These disorders and insolences definitely are herewith totally and irrevocably abolished; for together with the guild statutes and customs established or introduced by the artisans, masters and journeymen, without official permission, forbidden in § 1 of this ordinance, shall be included the so-called journeymen's customs especially, whether they have been put on paper or not; either way they are abolished and shall remain so. Rather let the authorities who have heretofore themselves issued or confirmed these so-called journeymen's charters promptly revoke them and cancel them, or at least set themselves to revise them in accordance with present conditions. And as in some guilds and corporations the evil custom has crept in, and incoming masters are sworn to it, that they shall keep the guild's secrets and reveal them to no one, herewith they are fully freed of any such oath, and they are not to escape severe official punishment in the event of any such secret commitment in the future.

11. As it also happens that in the guilds, especially the so-called gift guilds, discrimination is exercised against children illegitimately conceived and born before or after priestly legitimation, also against those

legitimized by Us the Roman Emperor or otherwise by the Imperial Power, so that some artisans will not accept even those legitimized in such fashion, or by the marriage of a female person made pregnant while unmarried by still another person, or by a forced marriage between those who broke chastity together: so shall the aforesaid discrimination be abolished, and the female or male person legitimized in one or the other ways here mentioned shall be considered equal with respect to admission to the guilds, and nothing more placed in their way.

12. Similarly too it is well known that damage and ruin are incurred by journeymen in many trades in this way: by the making of various peculiar, expensive, and worthless master pieces, as well as by excessive and unnecessary assessments for food and drink, and by the finishing and displaying of pieces demanded by masters, leaders, and sometimes the authorities themselves: so shall it be left to the authorities of each place to abolish these as they find proper, and wherever there are such useless master pieces, in the future to order more useful ones, and to grant mastership for these and not the favorite special pieces of the guildsmen. So too the aforementioned unnecessary fees and excesses shall by the said authorities be modified, changed, and reduced through prompt and healthy penal legislation; and should the guild wish to reject a master piece made in accordance with this on the grounds that it is not the equivalent of their customary but useless one, then there should be official intervention, and he who made it should still be admitted as a master provided he has been found acceptable in other respects. But when other disputes and confusion break out between the masters and the maker of the master piece, the decision as to whether it has been rightly and well made is in the discretion of the authorities, which may if that be appropriate lay it before a disinterested craft tribunal from another place, but with the greatest possible restraint on costs and duration, or settle the question of this piece of work by some shorter and easier way using sufficiently expert persons. Moreover any person who has already made the master piece in one place and become a master, and has a credible deposition of this, shall when he wishes to settle in another place be accepted there without making a new master piece (though the authorities of the place may with sufficient grounds find another necessary).

13. In addition to the above, it happens now and again that other disorders and abuses have crept in, such as:

1st. That the tanners and the tawers * in some places brawl with one another over the processing of dog skins, and over other useless disagreements among themselves, and those who will not process them call the others dishonorable, and also will have it that apprentices who have worked in places like that should be punished by the others. Similarly if an artisan stones a dog or cat to death, or beats it, or drowns it, or even just touches a carcass, an impropriety is wrung out of that, to the point that the skinners take it upon themselves to pester such handworkers by sticking them with their knives and in other ways, and in such fashion as to oblige them to buy their way out of it with a sum of money. Or further the wholly groundless and absurd impropriety consequently held against even those who have, even though quite unconsciously or unintentionally, drunk, traveled, or walked with skinners, help to bear one of them, or their wives and children to the grave, or accompany them there; or who cut down, pick up, and bear to the grave persons who took their own lives as a result of a known melancholy which has been recognized as such by the courts; likewise those who in times of war and pestilence, for want of a skinner, or else in great cattle plagues, have taken cattle out of their sheds and buried them; likewise cloth workers who work with [unfinished] wool, often indeed the very children of such people, are subjected by the artisans to great trouble and annoyance.

2d. The handworkers have this practice among them, that what one master begins another may not finish; and especially the bathers and wound healers make difficulties about the removal of a bandage, or the final cure of an injured person, even at the injured person's request, when another has begun it; or that accusations are made against barbers and bathers if they undertake to treat malefactors, such as those who have been tortured; also some guilds seek to make a crime of the parents a hindrance to the practice of a trade by the son; similarly if someone leaves one master and goes to another, even when the first has been paid off, the latter refuses to accept the services; and also what a locksmith or a blacksmith or a like master makes, or sells if it is otherwise made, others will not offer for sale or in any other way put work of their own into it.

3d. The aforesaid artisans at times, independently and among themselves, set and agree to a certain price for their work, so that none among them shall sell it at a lower, or work for a lower daily wage, or at least with this intent one lets the other know the price at which he

* *Rothgerber* and *Weissgerber:* two tanning trades using different materials and techniques.

offers his wares, so that the buyer, or he who hires work at a daily rate, must pay whatever the artisans please.

4th. An artisan is sometimes not tolerated if he has been subjected to prison or inquisition because of an accusation of some crime against him, even after he has proven his innocence by withstanding torture, or in some other legal way, and has been officially acquitted.

5th. Say a master commits a serious offense, and afterwards gets it erased; or the wife of a master commits such offense, and is received back by him after undergoing official punishment, and full restitution of good name; or for one reason or another is simply held suspect: in such cases persons never disqualified, or at least rehabilitated, or what is worse, whole guilds are held dishonorable, and the young artisans go out and brawl and beat one another.

6th. In some places no one is allowed to attain mastership if he is already in married estate, but in other places an unmarried journeyman, when he is accepted as master, may not practice the trade or open his shop unless and until he marries, and into the guild besides.

7th. In a good many places there is the false custom that a young master, even though he has spent many years at the trade, still may not commence to practice it until he has spent a certain number of years in the place, and attended the so-called Brotherhood so and so many years, or buys his way into the guild with a certain amount of money; while on the other hand the son of a local master, and also young men who marry the widows or daughters of masters, are accepted and given various advantages in the way of shorter wanderyears and also in the master piece, which considerably damages the whole community by burdening it with bad craftsmen; moreover in some places no more than a formerly established and traditional number of masters is allowed; and no master, however excellent, industrious, and skillful, so that he gets more work to do and does it cheap, may have more journeymen than his fellow masters.

8th. In various parts of the Empire this abuse and insolence appears in the papermaking trade: that when the high authorities for sufficient reason give the papermakers a privilege, by excluding outside paper-makers from collecting rags in certain districts of their lands and terri-tories, then the others treat as dishonorable a master who has held this privilege, or who has leased a paper mill and overbids when his lease has run out, and the journeymen will not work there and the boys who have learned their trade there are not accepted; and the said journeymen apply different rates to the masters, for their living expenses or however else it is arranged; moreover they will accept no official certification or attestation, only from their guild; nor will journeymen work with masters who use hammer blows rather than polishing with the stone, but hold them dishonorable.

Now as experience attests what great inconveniences and difficulties are caused throughout the entire Holy Roman Empire through these, and many other abuses, disorders, and mischievous practices not mentioned here: so shall these, and others which may appear to the rulers and the authorities of all places, be corrected, and genuine measures be taken against the transgressors, with earnest intent, in accordance with this new ordinance; also to this end let the authorities willingly and promptly offer one another aid, and not protect the refractory in cases of this kind, let alone encourage them, but rather truly punish them in accordance with the nature of the mischief and transgression; and along with that see to it especially that the good artisans and craftsmen, as well as the younger masters in general, are not buried under dues and costs, acceptance fees, and the like, and thus handicapped to the detriment of their welfare and their good intention of settling in this or that place, even as such places themselves are handicapped in their supply of artful and skillful people, to the notable damage and destruction of their commerce. Moreover every Estate [*Stand*] preserves the right to make special appropriate dispensation in the case of one or another good worker and craftsman on the merits of the case, and to admit him and let him attain mastership against the will of the guild, but especially too in places where there may not be enough masters to form a guild.

14. From this and what was advisedly ordained above against the mischievously absconding artisan youth and their foolish rioting, vandalism, and slander, as the true source of the profoundly destructive disorders among the artisans, one might indeed reasonably expect that masters and assistants would hereafter, for their own good, strive for a more proper and peaceful life, and show a seemly obedience to the civic authorities set over them; yet nevertheless it will be necessary and inescapable to put away the patience of the past and show earnest intent to masters and journeymen, so and in such a way that where, ignoring all this and notwithstanding it, they persist in their previous mischief, evil, and obstinacy, and continue unchecked so to behave: then We and the Empire may take the first opportunity, after the example of other realms, and thus too so that the public may not be further hindered and burdened by such wanton private bickering, to fully remove and abolish all guilds together and entirely.

And in order that each and every statute and article of previous as well as this revised Imperial Ordinance, or additional ones at the disposal of the sovereign and the authorities of every place, may be obediently lived up to, true to its clear content, and so that there can in no way or fashion be defensible excuse for ignorance or misunderstanding: so shall this revised and improved Imperial Ordinance not only be published and read annually to the guild masters and journeymen, but also it will be publicly posted in each guild hall or so-called hostel, so that every one of them can read it; but especially it is to be put clearly before the apprentices at the signing-out, and they shall take an oath to abide by it thenceforth.

15. Finally, and for the greater uniformity and stricter maintenance of all the maturely considered points and articles in this revised and improved Ordinance, let there be good correspondence with neighbors, and let them be requested by the adjoining Circles or Estates to join in such an essential and renewed regulation and healthy ordering of things, and also to see if they may wish to observe it as well.

And as commonly other various complaints are made, according to which the high wages of menials and wage laborers heavily burden not only the artisans who do not work at a wage rate but quote a price for the whole job, and people make comparisons and hire as they choose, but also [heavily burden] everybody else: therefore let not only the Estates of each Circle correspond with one another, but every Circle with every neighboring Circle, and work out a reasonable and permanent regulation of wages and labor.

Now as each and every foregoing point and article of this revised and improved Ordinance, designed, amended, and established for the increase and spread of the common advantage with the advice, knowledge, and consent of the Electors, Princes, and Estates of the Holy Roman Empire, and We too have given them Our gracious approval: So henceforth the same is to be sustained and promulgated by every Estate of the Empire, whatever its quality or nature, in its territory through its chief administrator, deputies, officials, guardians, and all its servants and subjects with all attention and severity, especially against violators of this Our Imperial command and prohibition. To which sound purpose this Our Imperial Ordinance is to be announced without delay to all places in the usual ways and made universally known. That is Our will and Our earnest opinion, in attestation of this rescript, sealed with Our Imperial Seal, given in Our city of Vienna, the Sixteenth of August, in the Year Seventeen Hundred and Thirty One; of Our Roman Crown the

Twentieth, Our Spanish the Twenty-Eighth, but of the Hungarian and Bohemian the Twenty-First.

CARL

(L.S.)

Vt. J. A. Count von Metsch.

Ad Mandatum Sacrae Caes. Majest.
proprium
E. Baron v. Glandorff.

Abbreviations and Citations

WHAT follows is not a true bibliography, nor even a balanced representation of the materials used, but a reference guide for footnotes to the text.

I. Abbreviations

A. *Unpublished materials,* listing archival rubrics for all such materials cited, to aid in their retrieval and to indicate their general nature.

BGK Badisches General-Landesarchiv, Karlsruhe

236 Ministerium des Innern

3107 Generalia. Gemeinden(dienste). Die Reorganisation der Gemeindebehörde nach Unterdrückung der revolutionaeren Gewalt im Grossherzogthum.

3108 [Tables of local officers suspended.]

3109 Generalia. Gemeinde(Dienste). Die Gemeindewahlen im Jahr 1851, die bei denselben sich kund gegebenen Stimmung der Wähler und der Einfluss der Umsturz-Parthei auf solche (1851-1852).

5818 Generalia. Gewerbe. Die Beschränkung der Landleute auf die Erlernung bestimmter Gewerbe, nun die Aufhebung dieser Einschränkung.

5819 Generalia. Gewerbe. Die Einführung der Gewerbefreiheit und einer Gewerbeordnung, auch Ertheilung von Gewerbe-Privilegien (1832–1847).

5820 [Same] (1848–1860).

13530 Generalia. Normalia. Gemeinden. Die Ortsvorgesetzte/ Vögte- Bürgermeister/ und Gericht/: Stadt- und Ortsgerichte- Gemeinderäthe:/ deren Wahl und Entlassung & im Allgemeinen, Wahlordnung (1807–1833).

13531 Generalia. Normalia. Gemeinden. Die Bürgermeister und Gemeinde-Räthe, deren Wahl, Entlassung & im Allgemeinen, Wahlordnung (1834–1837).

13532 [Same] (1838–1851).

13533 Normalia. Gemeinde-Dienste. Die Gemeindewahlen im Allgemeinen; Wahlordnung; Entlassung von Gemeindebeamten.

BHM Bayerisches Hauptstaatsarchiv, Munich

MH Ministerium des Handels

6133 Acten des Koeniglichen Staats-Ministerium des Königl. Hauses und des Aeussern. Beschwerden über die ausgedehnten Ansaessigmachungsbewilligungen auf Gewerbe (1848–1855).

6142 Geheime Raths Acta. Ministerium des Innern. Generalia. Gewerbswesen. Conv. IX (1843–1848).

6145 Acta des Ministerial-Bureau des Innern. Den Vollzug des Gewerbs Gesetzes von 1825, nach aufgehobener Instruction. 1834.

Staatsrat

2340 Act. des Königlichen Staats-Raths. Das Stiftungs und Communal Vermögen betr.

2613 Act. des Königlichen Staats-Raths. Die Ansässigmachungen und Verehelichungen betreffend, 1825.

2616 Act. des Königlichen Staats-Raths. Antrag der Stände auf Abänderung des Gesetzes vom Jahre 1834 über Ansässigmachung und Verehelichung, specialiter die Güter-Zertrummerungen betrff. (1843–1852).

StAW Stadtarchiv, Weissenburg / Bayern

Because references are concentrated in Chapter VII and the rubrics appear there, I shall not here duplicate them.

WHS Württembergisches Haupt-Staatsarchiv, Stuttgart

E 31–32 (Verzeichniss, Geheimrats-Akten II)

G 584 Communalangelegenheiten 1817–1818.

G 585 Gemeinde-Deputirten.

E 33 (Registraturplan, Geheimer Rat III)

G 112, I Akten des K. Geheimen Rats. Gemeindebürgerrecht (1820–1829).

G 112, II [Same] (1830–1875).

G 442, I Gewerbeordnung 1821–1830.

G 442, II Gewerbeordnung, 1833–1851.

G 442, III Gewerbeordnung, 1854–1862.

WSL Württembergisches Staatsarchiv, Ludwigsburg
Ministerium des Innern
E 146:

642 Bürger- und Beisitzrecht. Generalia. 1807–1847.

643 [Same] 1848–1866.

644 Bürgerrecht. Gemeinde-Bürgerrecht. Acta betr. das Gesetz über das Gemeinde- Bürger- und Beisitzrecht v. 15 April 1828.

645 Generalia. Bürgerrecht. Entwurf eines Gesetzes betr. die Niederlassung und die Erwerbung des Bürgerrechts in den Gemeinden, 1852/53 etc.

646 Bürgerrecht Betreffend (1847–1864).

705 Canzleien. Generalia. Die Vereinfachung des Geschäftsganges im Departement des Innern.

E 150:

600 Gewerbe und Handel. Das bei neuen Gewerbe Concessionen einzuhaltende Verfahren, etc.

B. *Official publications,* listing all diet protocols and administrative serials cited. The latter changed their titles very often, and I have adopted for citation in each case an abbreviation that most nearly shows the area where the serial circulated, giving here also the title under which it seem most commonly to be catalogued or indexed. Many laws and directives though general in application might (especially in Bavaria) be published in one province but not in another, nor even in the serial issued by the central government.

BadReg	Grossherzoglich badisches (Staats- und) Regierungsblatt
BayGes	Gesetzblatt für das Königreich Bayern
BayMF	Intelligenzblatt des Rezatkreises [Mittelfranken]
BayNB	Intelligenzblatt der Königl. Bayer. Regierung für Niederbayern
BayOB	Königlich Bayerisches Kreis-Amtsblatt von Oberbayern
BayOD	Amtsblatt der Königl. Bair. Regierung des Oberdonau Kreises
BayOF	Königl. Baier. privilegirtes Intelligenzblatt für den Ober-Main Kreis [Oberfranken]
BayReg	Regierungsblatt für das Königreich Baiern
BayUM	Intelligenzblatt für den Unter-Mainkreis des Königreichs Baiern

HDReg Grossherzoglich Hessisches Regierungsblatt
HDVerh Hessen-Darmstadt: Verhandlung in der zweiten Kammer der
    Landstände
SB   Franz Wigard, ed. *Stenographischer Bericht über die Ver-
    handlungen der deutschen constituirenden Nationalver-
    sammlung zu Frankfurt am Main.* 9 vols. Frankfurt/Main,
    1848–1849.
WbgReg Staats- und Regierungsblatt für das Königreich Württemberg
WbgVerh Verhandlungen der Kammer der Abgeordneten des König-
    reiches Württemberg

C. *Journals,* listing all scholarly and/or unofficial journals cited, and
those official journals concerned not with laws or directives but analysis
or general information.

ADRG *Annalen des Deutschen Reichs für Gesetzgebung, Verwaltung
    und Statistik*
AHR *American Historical Review*
AK *Archiv für Kulturgeschichte*
BGD *Beiträge zur Geschichte Dortmunds*
BGE *Beiträge zur Geschichte von Stadt und Stift Essen*
DJ *Düsseldorfer Jahrbuch*
DV *Deutsche Vierteljahrsschrift*
EKB *Einzelarbeiten aus der Kirchengeschichte Bayerns*
ES *Esslinger Studien*
FBPG *Forschungen zur Brandenburgischen und Preussischen Ge-
    schichte*
FHS *French Historical Studies*
HG *Hannoversche Geschichtsblätter*
HGB *Hansische Geschichtsblätter*
HJH *Hohenzollerische Jahreshefte*
HPZ *Historisch-politische Zeitschrift*
HZ *Historische Zeitschrift*
JF *Journal von und für Franken*
JHVH *Jahresbericht des Historischen Vereins für die Grafschaft
    Herford*
JHVM *Jahresbericht des historischen Vereins für Mittelfranken*
JHVR *Jahresbericht des Historischen Vereins für die Grafschaft
    Ravensberg*
JM *Juristisches Magazin für die deutschen Reichsstädte*
JMH *Journal of Modern History*

JNS	*Jahrbücher für Nationalökonomik und Statistik*
JSH	*Journal of Social History*
MGKS	*Mitteilungen der Gesellschaft für Kieler Stadtgeschichte*
MHVP	*Mitteilungen des Historischen Vereins der Pfalz*
MOGV	*Mitteilungen des Oberhessischen Geschichtsvereins*
NA	*Nassauische Annalen*
NASG	*Neues Archiv für Sächsische Geschichte*
OJ	*Oldenburger Jahrbuch*
OM	*Osnabrücker Mitteilungen*
PS	*Population Studies*
RA	*Rheinisches Archiv*
RB	*Der Rheinische Bund*
RVB	*Rheinische Vierteljahrsblätter*
SA	*Sachsen und Anhalt*
SBHV	*Schwäbische Blätter für Heimatpflege und Volksbildung*
SGFS	*Schriften der Gesellschaft für Flensburger Stadtgeschichte*
SJ	*Schmollers Jahrbuch für Gesetzgebung, Verwaltung und Volkswirtschaft im Deutschen Reich*
STLV	*Schriftenreihe zur Trierer Landesgeschichte und Volkskunde*
SVSM	*Schriften des Vereins für Sachs-Meiningische Geschichte und Landeskunde*
VHVN	*Verhandlungen des Historischen Vereins für Niederbayern*
VHVO	*Verhandlungen des Historischen Vereins für Oberpfalz und Regensburg*
VSDR	*Vierteljahrshefte zur Statistik des deutschen Reichs*
VSWG	*Vierteljahrschrift für Sozial- und Wirtschaftsgeschichte*
VVK	*Vierteljahrschrift für Volkswirthschaft und Kulturgeschichte*
WJ	*Württembergische Jahrbücher für Statistik und Landeskunde*
WVL	*Württembergische Vierteljahrshefte für Landesgeschichte*
WZ	*Westfälische Zeitschrift*
ZAA	*Zeitschrift für Agrargeschichte und Agrarsoziologie*
ZAGV	*Zeitschrift des Aachener Geschichtsvereins*
ZBG	*Zeitschrift des Bergischen Geschichtsvereins*
ZBL	*Zeitschrift für Bayerische Landesgeschichte*
ZGAE	*Zeitschrift für die Geschichte und Altertumskunde Ermlands*
ZGR	*Zeitschrift für geschichtliche Rechtswissenschaft*
ZGS	*Zeitschrift für die gesamte Staatswissenschaft*
ZPGL	*Zeitschrift für Preussische Geschichte und Landeskunde*
ZPSL	*Zeitschrift des Preussischen Statistischen Landesamts*
ZSSG	*Zeitschrift der Savigny-Stiftung für Rechtsgeschichte, Germanische Abteilung*

ZVTG   *Zeitschrift des Vereins für Thüringische Geschichte und Altertumskunde*

II. *Works cited*, listing those studies and collections, keyed when appropriate to the abbreviations above, that are cited in more than one *chapter* of the text (about a quarter of the total). In a handful of instances I have inserted works cited in only one chapter, because their general importance seems to justify special mention.

Angermann, Erich. *Robert von Mohl, 1799–1875.* Neuwied, 1962.

Becher, Johann J. *Politischer discurs, von den eigentlichen ursachen des auff- und abnehmens der städt, länder und republicken.* Ed. of Frankfurt/Main, 1759, annotated by Georg H. Zincken.

Bevölkerungs-Ploetz: Raum und Bevölkerung in der Weltgeschichte. Ed. Ernst Kirsten, Ernst W. Buchholz, and Wolfgang Köllman. 2 vols. Würzburg, 1956.

Böckenförde, Ernst-Wolfgang. *Die deutsche verfassungsgeschichtliche Forschung im 19. Jahrhundert.* Berlin, 1961.

Böhmert, Victor. *Beiträge zur Geschichte des Zunftwesens.* Leipzig, 1862.

Clauss, Wilhelm. *Der Staatsbeamte als Abgeordneter in der Verfassungsentwicklung der deutschen Staaten.* Karlsruhe, 1906.

Clément, Horst. *Das bayerische Gemeindeedikt vom 17. Mai 1818.* Kassel, 1934.

Dahrendorf, Ralf. *Society and Democracy in Germany,* New York, 1967.

Dehlinger, Alfred. *Württembergs Staatswesen in seiner geschichtlichen Entwicklung bis heute.* 2 vols. Stuttgart, 1951–1953.

Dickmann, Fritz. *Der Westfälische Frieden.* Münster, 1959.

Ebel, Wilhelm. *Geschichte der Gesetzgebung in Deutschland.* 2d ed. Göttingen, 1958.

——, ed. *Quellen zur Geschichte des deutschen Arbeitsrechts (bis 1849).* Göttingen, 1964.

Eichhorn, Karl F. *Deutsche Staats- und Rechtsgeschichte.* 4th ed., 4 vols. Göttingen, 1834–1836.

——. "Ueber den Ursprung der städtischen Verfassung in Deutschland," *ZGR,* I (1815), 147–247; II (1816), 165–237.

Engels, Friedrich. "Der Status Quo in Deutschland." *Marx/Engels Gesamtausgabe,* Erste Abt. Bd. VI, pp. 229–249. Berlin, 1932.

Ennen, Edith. "Die Organisation der Selbstverwaltung in den Saarstädten vom ausgehenden Mittelalter bis zur französischen Revolution," *RA,* XXV (1933), 1–257.

Erdmann, Manfred. *Die verfassungspolitische Funktion der Wirtschafts-verbände in Deutschland, 1815–1871.* Berlin, 1968.

Faber, Karl-Georg. "Die kommunale Selbstverwaltung in der Rhein-provinz im 19. Jahrhundert," *RVB,* XXX (1965), 132–151.

Fischer, Wolfram. *Handwerksrecht und Handwerkswirtschaft um 1800: Studien zur Sozial- und Wirtschaftsverfassung vor der industriellen Revolution.* Berlin, [1955].

Forberger, Rudolf. *Die Manufaktur in Sachsen.* Berlin, 1958.

Franke, Wilhelm. "Die Volkszahl deutscher Städte am Ende des 18. und Anfang des 19. Jahrhunderts," *ZPSL,* LXII (1922), 102–121.

Frensdorff, Ferdinand. "Das Zunftrecht insbesondere Norddeutschlands und die Handwerkerehre," *HGB,* XIII (1907), 1–89.

Fries, Peter. *Das Nürnberger Stiftungswesen vom Ende der reichs-städtischen Zeit . . . etwa 1795 bis 1820.* Nürnberg, 1963.

Gall, Lothar. *Der Liberalismus als regierende Partei: Das Grossherzogtum Baden zwischen Restauration und Reichsgründung.* Wiesbaden, 1968.

Gebauer, Johannes H. *Geschichte der Stadt Hildesheim.* 2 vols. Hildes-heim, 1922–1924.

Gerstlacher, Carl F., ed. *Sammlung aller Baden-Durlachischen . . . Anstalten und Verordnungen.* 3 vols. Frankfurt/Main, 1773–1774.

Gerth, Hans. *Die sozialgeschichtliche Lage der bürgerlichen Intelligenz um die Wende des 18. Jahrhunderts.* Frankfurt/Main, 1935.

Gierke, Otto F. v. *Das deutsche Genossenschaftsrecht.* 3 vols. Berlin, 1868–1881.

——. *Deutsches Privatrecht.* 2 vols. Leipzig, 1895–1905.

Goltz, Theodor v. d. *Geschichte der deutschen Landwirtschaft.* 2 vols. Stuttgart, 1902–1903.

Graf, Christa. "The Hanoverian Reformer, Johann Carl Bertram Stüve, 1798–1872." Unpublished dissertation, Cornell University, 1970.

Grönhoff, Johann. "Kieler Bürgerbuch: Verzeichnis der Neubürger vom Anfang des 17. Jahrhunderts bis 1869," *MGKS,* XLIX (1958), 1–518.

Hartlieb von Wallthor, Alfred. *Die landschaftliche Selbstverwaltung Westfalens in ihrer Entwicklung seit dem 18. Jahrhundert. 1. Teil. Bis zur Berufung des Vereinigten Landtags (1847).* Münster, 1965.

Hausner, Otto. *Vergleichende Statistik von Europa.* 2 vols. Lemberg, 1865.

Haussherr, Hans. *Verwaltungseinheit und Ressorttrennung vom Ende des 17. bis zum Beginn des 19. Jahrhunderts.* Berlin, 1953.

Havemann, Wilhelm. *Geschichte der Lande Braunschweig und Lüne-burg.* 3 vols. Göttingen, 1853–1857.

Heffter, Heinrich. *Die deutsche Selbstverwaltung im 19. Jahrhundert.* Stuttgart, 1950.

Hegel, Georg W. F. *Grundlinien der Philosophie des Rechts,* in *Sämtliche Werke,* vol. VII. Stuttgart, 1952.

Hiereth, Sebastian. "Zur Geschichte des Landkreises Landshut. I. Teil. Das Landgericht alter Ordnung, 1803–1862," *VHVN,* LXXXVIII (1962), 1–66.

Hölzle, Erwin. *Württemberg im Zeitalter Napoleons und der deutschen Erhebung.* Stuttgart, 1937.

Huber, Ernst R., ed. *Dokumente zur deutschen Verfassungsgeschichte.* 3 vols. Stuttgart, 1961–1963.

Juhr, Hannelore. *Die Verwaltung des Hauptamtes Brandenburg/ Ostpreussen von 1713 bis 1751.* Berlin, 1967.

Justi, Johann H. G. v. *Die Grundfeste zu der Macht und Glückseligkeit der Staaten, oder ausführliche Vorstellung der gesamten Polizeiwissenschaft.* 2 vols. Königsberg, 1760–1761.

———. *Grundsätze der Polizeywissenschaft, in einem vernünftigen, auf den Endzweck der Polizey gegründeten, Zusammenhange und zum Gebrauch Academischer Vorlesungen abgefasset.* 3d rev. ed. Göttingen, 1782.

———. *Staatswirthschaft, oder Systematische Abhandlung aller Oekonomischen und Cameral-Wissenschaften, die zur Regierung eines Landes erfodert werden.* 2d ed., 2 vols. Leipzig, 1758.

Klein, Ludwig. *Die geschichtliche Entwicklung des Gemeindebürgerrechts in Württemberg.* Tübingen, 1933.

Knipschildt, Philipp. *Tractatus politico-historico-juridicus, de juribus et privilegiis civitatum Imperialum . . .* Ulm, 1687.

Koch, Diether. *Das Göttinger Honoratiorentum vom 17. bis zur Mitte des 19. Jahrhunderts.* Göttingen, 1958.

Koch, Joseph. "Geschichte der Aachener Nähnadelzunft und Nähnadelindustrie bis zur Aufhebung der Zünfte in der französischen Zeit (1798)," *ZAGV,* XLI (1920), 16–122.

Köhler, Ludwig. *Das württembergische Gewerberecht von 1805–1870.* Tübingen, 1891.

Koselleck, Reinhart. *Preussen zwischen Reform und Revolution: Allgemeines Landrecht, Verwaltung und soziale Bewegung von 1791 bis 1848.* Stuttgart, 1967.

Kreittmayr, Wiguläus X. A., ed. *Sammlung der neuest- und merkwürdigsten Churbaierischen Generalien und Landesverordnungen . . .* Munich, 1771.

Krieger, Leonard. *The German Idea of Freedom.* Boston, 1957.

Laufs, Adolf. *Die Verfassung und Verwaltung der Stadt Rottweil, 1650–1806.* Stuttgart, 1963.

Lomberg, Joseph V. *Historisch-politische Staatsrechtsabhandlung von Abstellung der Missbräuche bey den Zünften und Handwerkern in den Landen teutscher Reichsfürsten.* Bonn, 1779.

Loss, Carol R. "*Status in Statu:* The Concept of Estate in the Organization of German Political Life, 1750–1825." Unpublished dissertation, Cornell University, 1970.

Lotheissen, Hans. *Der ständisch-korporative Gedanke . . . in den Schriften Hegels und Lists zur württembergischen Verfassungsreform.* Giessen, 1928.

Lünig, Johann C. *Das Teutsche Reichs-Archiv . . . ein vollkommenes Corpus Juris Publici des Heiligen Römischen Reichs Teutscher Nation.* 24 vols. Leipzig, 1713–1722.

Maurer, Georg L. v. *Geschichte der Städteverfassung in Deutschland.* 4 vols. Erlangen, 1869–1871.

Meier, Ernst v. *Hannoversche Verfassungs- und Verwaltungsgeschichte, 1680–1866.* 2 vols. Leipzig, 1898–1899.

Meyer, Christian. *Preussens innere Politik in Ansbach und Bayreuth in den Jahren 1792–1797: Enthaltend die Denkschrift des Staatsministers Karl August v. Hardenberg.* Berlin, 1904.

Meyer, Moritz. *Geschichte der preussischen Handwerkerpolitik.* 2 vols. Minden, 1884–1888.

Meyr, Georg K., ed. *Sammlung der Kurpfalz-Bairischen allgemeinen und besonderen Landesverordnungen,* 6 vols. Munich, 1784–1799.

Möser, Justus. *Sämtliche Werke.* 14 vols. Oldenburg, 1944– .

Mohnhaupt, Heinz. *Die Göttinger Ratsverfassung vom 16. bis 19. Jahrhundert.* Göttingen, 1965.

Montgelas, Maximilian J. Garnerin de. *Denkwürdigkeiten . . . über die innere Staatsverwaltung Bayerns (1799–1817).* Munich, 1908.

Moser, Johann J. *Teutsches Staats-Recht.* 27 vols. Nürnberg etc., 1737–1754.

——. *Von der Landeshoheit im Weltlichen.* 3 vols. Frankfurt/Main, 1772–1773.

——. *Von der Reichs-Stättischen Regiments-Verfassung.* Frankfurt/Main, 1772.

Munzer, Egbert. "Die Entwicklung der Gemeindeverfassung im ehemaligen Herzogtum Sachsen-Meiningen," *SVSM,* LXXXV (1927), 1–45.

Oppermann, Heinrich A. *Zur Geschichte des Königreichs Hannover von 1832 bis 1860.* 2 vols. Leipzig, 1860–1862.

Ortloff, Johann A. *Das Recht der Handwerker, nach den allgemeinen in den deutschen Staaten geltenden Gesetzen und Zunft- und Innungsverordnungen.* 2d ed. Erlangen, 1818.

———, ed. *Corpus juris Opificiarii.* 2d ed. Erlangen, 1820.

Popp, August. *Die Entstehung der Gewerbefreiheit in Bayern.* Leipzig, 1928.

Preuss, Hugo. *Die Entwicklung des deutschen Städtewesens. I. Entwicklungsgeschichte der deutschen Städteverfassung.* Leipzig, 1906.

Pütter, Johann. *An Historical Developement of the Present Political Constitution of the Germanic Empire.* Tr. Josiah Dornford. 3 vols. London, 1790.

Rehm, Hermann. "Der Erwerb von Staats- und Gemeinde-Angehörigkeit in geschichtlicher Entwicklung nach römischen und deutschen Staatsrecht," *ADRG,* XXV (1892), 137–282.

Reichard, Heinrich G. *Historisch-politische Ansichten . . . betreffend die Frage von der praktischen Ausbildung der städtischen Verfassungen in Deutschland.* Leipzig, 1830.

———. *Statistik und Vergleichung der jetzt geltenden städtischen Verfassungen in den monarchischen Staaten Deutschlands.* Altenburg, 1844.

Reuter, Ortulf. *Die Manufaktur im fränkischen Raum.* Stuttgart, 1961.

Riccius, Christian G. *Entwurf von Stadt-Gesetzen oder Statutis vornehmlich der Land-Städte.* Frankfurt/Main, 1740.

Riedel, Emil. *Commentar zum bayerischen Gesetze über Heimat, Verehelichung und Aufenthalt vom 16. April 1868.* 1st ed. Nördlingen, 1868; 6th ed. Munich, 1892.

Riehl, Wilhelm H. *Die bürgerliche Gesellschaft.* 3d ed. Stuttgart, 1855.

———. *Land und Leute.* 1st ed. Stuttgart, 1853; 2d ed. Stuttgart, 1855.

Roscher, Wilhelm. *Geschichte der National-Oekonomik in Deutschland.* Munich, 1874.

Rosenzweig, Franz. *Hegel und der Staat.* 2 vols. Munich, 1920.

Runge, Joachim. *Justus Mösers Gewerbetheorie und Gewerbepolitik im Fürstbistum Osnabrück in der zweiten Hälfte des 18. Jahrhunderts.* Berlin, 1966.

Sartorius von Waltershausen, August. *Deutsche Wirtschaftsgeschichte, 1815–1914.* 2d ed. Jena, 1923.

Savigny, Friedrich K. v. "Die Preussische Städteordnung," *HPZ,* I (1832), 389–414.

Schäffle, Albert. "Gewerbe," in J. C. Bluntschli and K. Brater, eds., *Deutsches Staats-Wörterbuch,* V (1859), 318–336.

Schell, Erwin. *Die Reichsstädte beim Übergang an Baden.* Heidelberg, 1929.

Schlözer, August L. *Briefwechsel, meist historischen und politischen Inhalts.* 10 vols. Göttingen, 1777–1782.

Schmoller, Gustav. *Zur Geschichte der deutschen Kleingewerbe im 19. Jahrhundert.* Halle, 1870.

Schönfeld, Roland. "Studien zur Wirtschaftsgeschichte der Reichstadt Regensburg im achtzehnten Jahrhundert," *VHVO,* C (1959), 5–147.

Schott, D. August F., ed. *Sammlungen zu den Deutschen Land- und Stadtrechten.* 2 vols. Leipzig, 1772–1773.

Scotti, J. J., ed. *Sammlung der Gesetze und Verordnungen, welche in dem vormaligen Kurfürstenthum Cöln . . . ergangen sind.* 3 vols. Düsseldorf, 1830–1831.

Shorter, Edward. "Middle-Class Anxiety in the German Revolution of 1848," *JSH,* II (1969), 189–215.

——. "Social Change and Social Policy in Bavaria, 1800–1860." Unpublished dissertation, Harvard University, 1967.

Sieber, Jacob G. *Abhandlung von den Schwierigkeiten in den Reichsstädten das Reichsgesetz vom 16. Aug. 1731 wegen der Missbräuche bey den Zünften zu vollziehen.* Goslar, 1771.

Slawinger, Gerhard. *Die Manufaktur in Kurbayern.* Stuttgart, 1966.

Small, Albion W. *Origins of Sociology.* Chicago, 1924.

Soliday, Gerald L. "The Social Structure of Frankfurt am Main in the Seventeenth and Early Eighteenth Century." Unpublished dissertation, Harvard University, 1968.

Sombart, Werner. *Die deutsche Volkswirtschaft im neunzehnten Jahrhundert.* 3d ed. Berlin, 1913.

Stadelmann, Rudolf, and Wolfram Fischer. *Die Bildungswelt des deutschen Handwerkers um 1800: Studien zur Soziologie des Kleinbürgers im Zeitalter Goethes.* Berlin, 1955.

Stein, Lorenz v. "Das Gemeindewesen der neueren Zeit," *DV,* 1853, I, 22–84.

Süssmilch, Johann P. *Die göttliche Ordnung in den Veränderungen des menschlichen Geschlechts.* 2d ed. Berlin, 1761.

Vahlkampf, A. *Ueber Heimathgesetze: Der Streit der Interressen und Ansichten in Beziehung auf das Heimathwesen.* Frankfurt/Main, 1848.

Viebahn, Georg v. *Statistik des Zollvereinten und nördlichen Deutschlands.* 3 vols. Berlin, 1858–1868.

Walker, Mack. *Germany and the Emigration, 1816–1885.* Cambridge, 1964.

——, ed. *Metternich's Europe.* New York, 1968.

Weiske, Julius. *Sammlung der neueren teutschen Gemeindegesetze. Nebst einer Einleitung: Die Gemeinde als Corporation.* Leipzig, 1848.

Wintterlin, Friedrich. *Geschichte der Behördenorganisation in Würtemberg.* 2 vols. Stuttgart, 1902–1906.

Wolff, Christian. *Vernünfftige Gedancken von dem Gesellschafftlichen Leben der Menschen, und insonderheit dem gemeinen Wesen.* Edition of Frankfurt/?, 1747.

Ziekursch, Johannes. *Das Ergebnis der friderizianischen Städteverwaltung und die Städteordnung Steins: Am Beispiel der Schlesischen Städte dargestellt.* Jena, 1908.

Zimmermann, Ludwig. *Die Einheits- und Freiheitsbewegung und die Revolution von 1848 in Franken.* Würzburg, 1951.

Zorn, Wolfgang. "Die Reichsstädte Bayerisch-Schwabens, 1648–1806," *SBHV,* X (1959), 113–122.

Index

(Cont. p. 472)

GERMAN HOME TOWNS

Designed by R. E. Rosenbaum.
Composed by Vail-Ballou Press, Inc.,
in 10 point linotype Caledonia, 3 points leaded,
with display lines in Weiss Series III and Weiss Roman.
Printed letterpress from type by Vail-Ballou Press
on Warren's 1854 text, 60 pound basis,
with the Cornell University Press watermark.
Bound by Vail-Ballou Press
in Interlaken AL1 book cloth
and stamped in All Purpose foil.